HOW TO BUILD
GLUED-LAPSTRAKE
WOODEN BOATS

John Brooks & Ruth Ann Hill

A WoodenBoat Book

Dedications

To John and Annette Orr and Bernard Brooks
To Betty and Raymond Hill

For Leigh.

Published by WoodenBoat Publications, Inc.
Naskeag Road, PO Box 78
Brooklin, Maine 04616 USA
www.woodenboat.com

ISBN: 0-937822-58-2

First Printing 2004

Book design: Lindy Gifford
Cover design: Olga Lange

Front cover and large backcover photograph: Peter Travers
Peregrine photo page 14: Mike O'Brien
All other photos and drawings by John Brooks and Ruth Ann Hill

Printed in the USA

Library of Congress Catloging-in-Publication Data

Brooks, John, 1957-
How to build glued-lapstrake wooden boats / by John Brooks and Ruth
Ann Hill.
        p. cm.
    Includes bibliographical references and index.
    ISBN 0-937822-58-2 (alk. paper)
        1. Boatbuilding. 2 Wooden boats-Design and construction. 3.
Gluing. I. Hill, Ruth Ann, 1958- II. Title.

VM351 .B755 2002
623.8'44-dc21

        2002028856

ACKNOWLEDGMENTS

There is no shortage of people who helped this book become real, all those who had faith in us to get done what we promised (eventually) and all those who encouraged us to keep going when we thought we couldn't. We'd like to thank the following who helped with all aspects of research, writing and book production: Trevor Allen, Walter Ansel, Scot Bell, Carl Cramer, Jane Crosen, Jerry Cumbo, Lindy Gifford, John Hanson, John Harris, Rich Hilsinger, Annette Najjar and Chris Kulczycki, Mac McCarthy, Jim Miller, Ted Moores, Matt P. Murphy, Mike O'Brien, Bernice Palumbo, Greg Rössel, Kim Sexton, Peter Spectre, and Peter Travers.

We'd also like to offer a special thank you to the following customers who were a tremendous help in the creation of boats and boat designs: Greg Askins, Ellen and Harry Brawley, Paul Brinkman and Jane Beezer, David Gordon, Nora Gordon, Pat, Keith, Christine, and Mark Gummerson, Bill and Ellen Howell, Trig and Roxanne Ignatius, Peter and Paula Lamoreaux, Derek Marsh, Andy Oldman, Phil and Teresa Patterson, Mike and Marty Powers, Lorna and Carl Russell, Conrad and Patty Shisler, David and Elaine Smith, and Elizabeth Spicer.

A very large offering of immense gratitude goes to John's WoodenBoat School students, from whom we have learned so much. Thanks for special efforts go to Bruce and Edie Beglin, Emilie Lengel, Paul Kessinger, Bob Milledge, and John Thistle. Abundant thanks also go to course assistant and former student Dennis Costello.

At this point, the author normally thanks his or her long-suffering spouse. Instead, we'd like to thank our good friends Jean Hoekwater, John Gordon, and Ian Gordon; Reggie and Joan Hudson; Beth, Wythe, Lucas, and Nathan Ingebritson; Amy, Rob, and Jacob Pollien; and Michele Corbeil, Hans Vierthaler, and Mia Vierthaler for their advice, patience, and support. Time to get back out on the water!

A FEW NOTES ABOUT THIS BOOK

We wrote this book to describe our method of glued-lapstrake construction in general. It is not meant to be a manual for the construction of any particular boat. You will notice, however, that we have chosen to follow one particular design, our 12' Ellen sailing dinghy, through the building process, with excursions into other designs when appropriate. We took this approach to make the process clearer. The Ellen encompasses many of the challenges of glued-lapstrake construction and requires most of the necessary techniques: spiling, scribing, fitting, laying out, beveling, and more. However, no one boat can be all things, so we have included examples from other boats, showing different techniques as well as how to build and install particular parts.

We also focus primarily on small open boats, which are deceptively simple. Nothing is hidden in an open boat. You can't bury sloppy joints and fits behind bulkheads and decks; everything is exposed for all to see. It is also right out there for us to show you, step by step, how to do things properly. We haven't neglected those of you with boats featuring bulkheads and decks but have included helpful techniques for installing these as well.

Once you've learned the techniques in this book, you will have the groundwork that you need to build just about any boat in the glued-lapstrake method, including larger boats. Certainly heavier, larger pieces will require appropriate adaptations of jigs and techniques. But big-boat methods are all variations on the ways things are done on a small boat.

CONTENTS

The Beauty of Glued-Lapstrake

Early in life, I decided that lapstraked boats are the loveliest there are. They never failed to please my eyes. From Viking longships to elegant Thames skiffs, I liked them all. Whenever I thumbed through a book on maritime history featuring ships, schooners, or ferries, I always peered at the smaller boats in the photos—the lapstrake boats: tenders and lifeboats stowed on decks, daysailers and rowboats tied up near the big boats, and fishing boats and yachts moored in the inner harbors.

I started out learning to be a modern boatbuilder, working in a West Coast boatyard 'glassing up hulls in molds and building the boats' interiors with plywood and modern adhesives. Solid wood entered the picture largely only for trim. Although I loved the way fine lapstrake boats looked, I thought lapstraking would be too complicated for a beginning boatbuilder like me.

A few years later, I came across a British book, *Dinghy Building*, by Richard Creagh-Osborne. (The book, originally published in 1978, is out of print, alas.) This little volume covered various methods for building British "dinghies": smallish to medium-sized racing sailboats, not tiny yacht tenders. One chapter covered lapstraking, which the British call clinker planking. Creagh-Osborne described something I'd never seen, a thoroughly modern

method of building lightweight lapstrake hulls with thin, high-quality plywood planks that were glued together along the laps. Although these were boats built for speed and therefore able to withstand the considerable forces exerted on the hull by a large, tall, modern sail rig, they needed very few internal frames, vastly simplifying their construction. To quote Creagh-Osborne: "The glued clinker type of construction is very strong and quite easy for the amateur, as well as having the advantage of need-

John's 15' rowing gig ROZINANTE.

Ellen Brawley in the original ELLEN on launching day.

ing only a skeleton jig." At this time, I was especially interested in designing and building light, fast rowing and sailing craft, so not long after acquiring *Dinghy Building*, I picked up a book titled *Ultralight Boatbuilding*, by Thomas Hill (no relation) and was pleased to find that it was wholly devoted to glued-lapstrake small boats.

The glued-lapstrake boats I had seen looked gorgeous, and the method of glued-lapstraking was fascinating. I was completely hooked. It was only a matter of time before I built one. A year or two later, I drew up a design for my first glued-lapstrake boat, a 9' tender based on Captain Nathanael Herreshoff's famous *Columbia* tender, but never got a chance to build it. It was a couple more years before I did build my next glued-lapstrake design, *Rozinante*, a 15' rowing gig. This boat was just as fun to build as I thought it would be and came out looking rather nice. But she was far from perfect. I learned a number of valuable lessons, and there were things I definitely did differently on the next boat. And

Who We Are

We wrote this book together as we run Brooks Boats, our design and boatbuilding business, together. We do have different experience and skills, and we have tried to reflect this in the text. John is the designer, builder, and teacher; it is his method and techniques that you will learn within these pages. He is also the fount of jigs. The joke around the shop is that a problem is simply an excuse to create another jig. Ruth is the writer, graphic artist, and boat naturalist; she contributes to the design work and helps with a few building operations, mainly planking. We both finish the boats, though Ruth is the color and finishing guru. John is the sailor, Ruth the paddler, and we both row and have been known to operate boats with outboards and engines. When we are not working with boats or using them for fun, we are keeping up with our young daughter, Leigh.

every boat since then has offered a chance to try new techniques and improve the method. One of the joys of glued-lapstrake for the professional builder is not being locked into building the same boat, or small group of boats, over and over again. Every boat that has come out of our shop has been an individual, even the Ellens, our most popular design.

For me, glued-lapstraking has turned into an enduring love affair and a livelihood. Here are some of the advantages that I find in glued-lapstrake construction:

Elegant and strong

Few can resist the elegant look of the sweeping curves of the lapped planks; these same laps form stringers that run from stem to stern, adding stiffness to the shell of the hull.

Lightweight and watertight

With planks made of high-quality plywood and the laps glued with epoxy, the planking can be thinner, and there is little need for all the frames found in a traditional boat. Glued-lapstrake construction effectively creates a single-piece hull that can't "work" (move back and forth) and that stays completely watertight. This quality makes glued-lapstrake ideal for smaller, lighter boats that spend a good part of their time out of the water, such as dinghies, canoes, rowboats, outboard skiffs, and daysailers.

Seaworthy

As with a traditional lapstrake boat, glued-lapstrake lends itself to seaworthy designs, plus the laps form little spray rails that help to keep the boat (and her crew) dry.

The easiest way to build a good-looking, truly round-bilged boat

Do we see some raised eyebrows out there? Consider this:

Take the 12' Ellen sailing dinghy, which we use as our primary exhibit throughout the book. She has seven planks on each side, for a total of fourteen planks to be fitted and installed. (And you make the planks in pairs, so you only have to measure and cut the seven different shapes.) If you were to strip plank the same hull, it would take more than a hundred 3/4" strips. If you decided to cold mold the hull using three layers (two diagonal, one horizontal), you would need about 150 veneers, 4" wide.

Easy to set up

Don't underestimate the value of a jig system, as it allows you to build a wide range of boat shapes, old and new, and it gives you something to work against instead of having to armwrestle with long, floppy panels in empty space. With our system of glued-lapstraking, the molds (the forms over which the hull is planked) usually are spaced 2' apart with no battens in the molds. Some methods require a batten under each lap; we use a temporary batten on top of the lap where it is much easier to attach, serves as a full-length clamp, and can be reused for other planks. For a strip-built hull, you would need twice as many molds. For a cold-molded hull, you almost have to build another hull first, installing many closely spaced battens on the molds to support the thin veneers.

Building different designs is simple and efficient

Our jig is easy and inexpensive to build and can take the molds from a wide variety of boats. Setup for each new design is efficient and requires a minimal investment of money and time.

No sheathing, no fairing

Most strip-built and cold-molded boats are designed to be covered with fiberglass or other cloth and epoxy. This is a messy job that adds expense, weight, and expletives—and means another round of sanding, this time on epoxy, which isn't fun. We have heard of people sheathing glued-lapstrake boats with 'glass cloth and epoxy, but we're not sure how they managed it. We have sheathed the bottoms and/or garboards on a couple of boats that were beached daily, but the idea of doing a whole boat gives us the horrors. And it is completely unnecessary.

Then there's one of the finer advantages for glued-lapstrake: fairing the hull. The glued-lapstrake hull needs only a relatively light sanding of the bare wood before finishing…if you heed our admonitions about removing epoxy putty before it cures. Strip-built and cold-molded hulls must have all the strip edges and other irregularities in the planking smoothed out, a laborious and tedious job finished up by hand with a long sanding block known for good reason as a "misery board."

Easy to maintain

High-quality sapele (African mahogany) marine plywood provides a very stable base for finishes—some of our boats have gone three or four years before needing to be repainted. (Varnish must be recoated every year, but that is because of sunlight not the wood.) When the time comes to sand and repaint, you'll find the almost total absence of frames on the inside a delight.

A good method for beginners

Glued-lapstrake designs benefit from and reward skilled, patient work, yet the method is forgiving enough of first-time efforts to make the boats enjoyable and satisfying projects for builders with less experience. The planks overlap, not butt, each other, so there is a certain latitude in the fit of the planks. Yes, you have to bevel the laps for the next plank, but the gap-filling qualities of epoxy give you plenty of margin for error as you learn how. If the plank ends up a little narrow or a little wide, everything will fit just fine, the width of the lap will be a wider or narrower, and only you and God will know. Your boat will be fine.

Ruth tries the first Salicornia double-paddle canoe.

BUILDING THIS BOOK AND BUILDING YOUR BOAT

Back in my late twenties, I entertained the idea of becoming an instrument maker. It turned out that my grandfather had also considered instrument making in his younger days and had bought all the wood for a violin along with a thin volume on violin making. They had all sat in a box for forty years, and, one day, the box arrived in the mail. I was touched. I opened up the little book and quickly saw why the neat blocks of wood in the box had never seen a saw, chisel, or plane. The book covered the whole ocean of knowledge on violin construction in about ten gigantic steps. I stopped in the section about assembling the violin and read, "Put the back on the violin." That was it on attaching the largest piece of wood in the whole instrument; there were no little hints, no discussions of pitfalls to watch out for, no indication of how much glue to use, no "what if's" that you and I are sure to encounter.

Writing down all the details is hard work. Countless times, Ruth would interject into my (I thought) eloquent prose, "Can't see this," "Need more here," or simply "HELP?!" Writing down all the details also makes things look complicated. But we've done our best to cover everything you'll want to know—including how to avoid or deal with plenty of "interesting" situations that we've experienced (often with epoxy kicking).

We hope that you'll use this book in the shop. Launch her proper, and put her to work. Just as a boat doesn't come alive until she floats, a boatbuilding book isn't really living a full existence until she has sawdust in the binding, epoxy putty on the cover, coffee stains on the pages, and wooden bookmarks distributed liberally within.

Ready? Let's go build a boat.

Chapter 1

Plans and Lofting

IRIS, an Ellen 12' sailing dinghy design.

CHOOSING A BOAT DESIGN

First, there are the dreams: The gray walls of the cubicle billow and fill with a fresh breeze, the kids' backseat squabbling settles into the rhythmic splash of waves along lapstrake planks, the din of rush-hour traffic subsides into a steady thrum as you head out past the breakwater....

There are countless boat dreams, but no boat can fill any one perfectly. Your goal, then, is to find a design that fits your most persistent dream as closely as possible. For this, you need to climb right into your vision and look hard at the details. Bring a pencil and paper, and begin a working list. For starters:

How many people are with you? How much stuff? Check again; can your dream boat really hold all that stuff?

How does the boat work? Sail, row, paddle, motor—or some combination? Be specific: Which rig? Where do the sheets run? How many rowing stations? What size engine? Gas, diesel, or electric? Can you handle the boat alone? or with passengers with little or no experience? What sort of conditions do you expect to encounter? The

best? The worst? Worse than worst?

How do you transport the boat? If she is carried, how many people does it take? Does the dream include buying a new truck to haul her? Where does the boat live during the active season? Where and how will you store her?

And so on. Once you have a good list, you can start shopping.

Buying your plans

If a design piques your interest, most designers will send you a brochure or catalog giving descriptions, specifications, and small, simple overview drawings. These can give you enough information to know whether or not you want to proceed, but in many cases you'll want more before making up your mind completely. You will want to see a study plan, which gives you a more detailed overview. Most designers will supply one for nominal cost and may apply the cost of a study plan to the price of a full set. If the design passes the study plan review, you should order the full set of plans and take a good look at her lines as well as her construction details. If there are

5

Fig 1.1 The study plan shows an overview of a design's shape, layout, and construction.

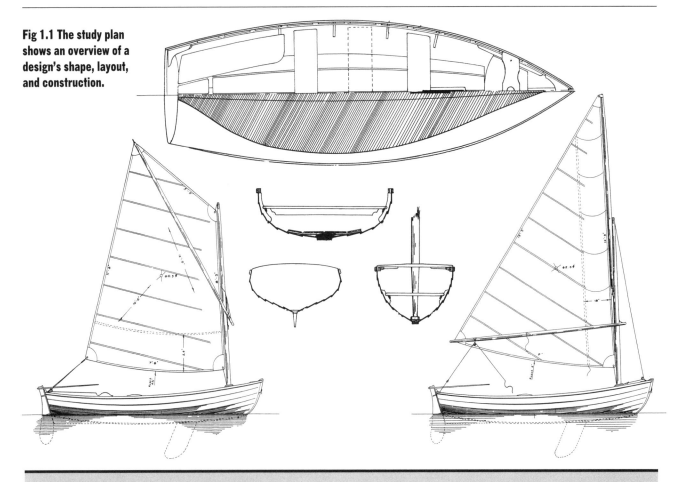

Some Frequently Asked Questions

Is this a good first project? *The answer to this depends entirely on your skills, patience, desire to learn, ability to handle frustration, and availability of expert advice when the going gets sticky. Only you can decide if you would be better off building a simpler boat first or whether you won't be able to stay inspired to keep going unless you build the boat of your dreams, no matter how challenging that might be.*

How long will it take me to build her? *This one's a poser. It is impossible for us to offer an accurate answer, because it's impossible to know your skill level, how your shop is set up, and the way you work. We recommend taking estimated building times with the proverbial grain of salt, especially if you will be working on the project on weekends and such. It nearly always takes longer that way, because you must set up anew each time you recommence work. Instead of trying to gauge total hours, consider whether you feel good about taking on the project and seeing it through to the end, even if it takes twice as long as you thought.*

How much will she cost? *The plans or designer may give you a rough estimate, but your choices can make a* tremendous difference. You'll have to sit down with the plans and list of materials, make your choices, and call around for prices.

How much does she weigh? *Your plans should give you an estimated weight, but keep in mind that your choices can affect the weight of your boat as built. For example, choosing mahogany over pine thwarts and seats and adding full-length cedar floorboards and gunwale guard adds about 20 pounds to a 12' Ellen sailboat, a sizable gain to a boat that normally weighs 120 pounds. Though you might not think about it, surface coatings also can add significant weight to a small boat. Start covering surfaces with epoxy (with or without cloth) or fancy two-part finishes, and watch the scale climb. (We don't recommend these two operations for other excellent reasons; please see Chapter 2, "Materials and Tools," and Chapter 12, "Painting and Varnishing.")*

By the way, don't confuse displacement with hull weight. Displacement includes the weight of the boat, plus people, critters, and cargo. The displacement given in the plans is usually for an average loaded condition.

several close contenders, order the plans for all of them. It's the only way to adequately compare and consider the different designs and is a small investment in helping to choose the right boat for you.

WORKING WITH PLANS

Boat plans must depict a complex, curvaceous, three-dimensional object on two-dimensional paper. To do this, the boat must be broken apart into different views. You often have to look at two or three views to get an idea of what a part or shape will look like in the finished boat. Combining these in your mind to see the true shape can be a real trick if you're not used to it. And, some shapes cannot be accurately reproduced on flat paper. The only way to be certain of these is to build a model or build the boat.

An experienced musician can hear the music while reading sheet music; an experienced boatbuilder or designer can see the boat while looking through a set of plans. Don't get discouraged if your set of plans seems confusing at first. Plans are put together with a language and logic all their own. As you work with them, things will become much clearer.

What's in a set of plans?

The plans for the 12′ Ellen sailing dinghy (for example) include the following twelve drawings:

1. Study plan
2. Lines
3. Construction plan
4. Construction sections
5. General construction details
6. Sail plan
7. Spar plan
8. Sections and transom; full-sized patterns
9. Stem and transom profile; full-sized patterns
10. Daggerboard trunk; full-sized patterns
11. Rudder, daggerboard, tiller; full-sized patterns
12. Alternate sections and transom, for wineglass transom; full-sized patterns

The Ellen plans also include written specifications for the construction drawings, spar plan, rigging, and materials

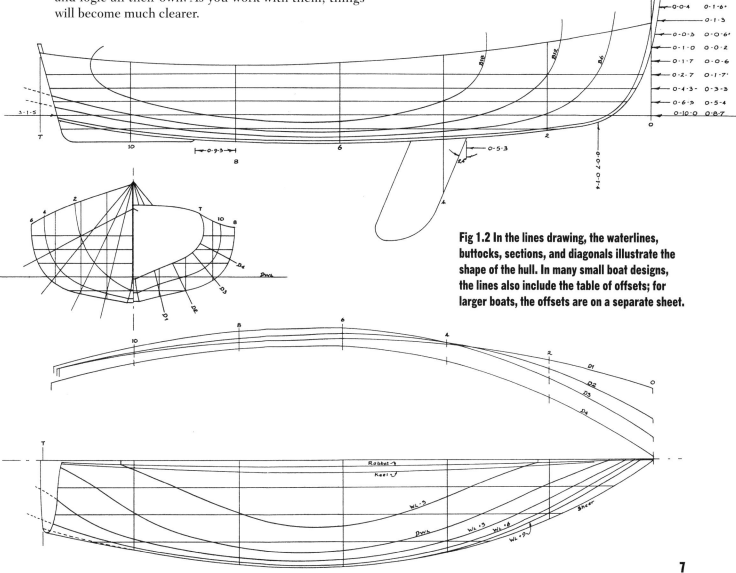

Fig 1.2 In the lines drawing, the waterlines, buttocks, sections, and diagonals illustrate the shape of the hull. In many small boat designs, the lines also include the table of offsets; for larger boats, the offsets are on a separate sheet.

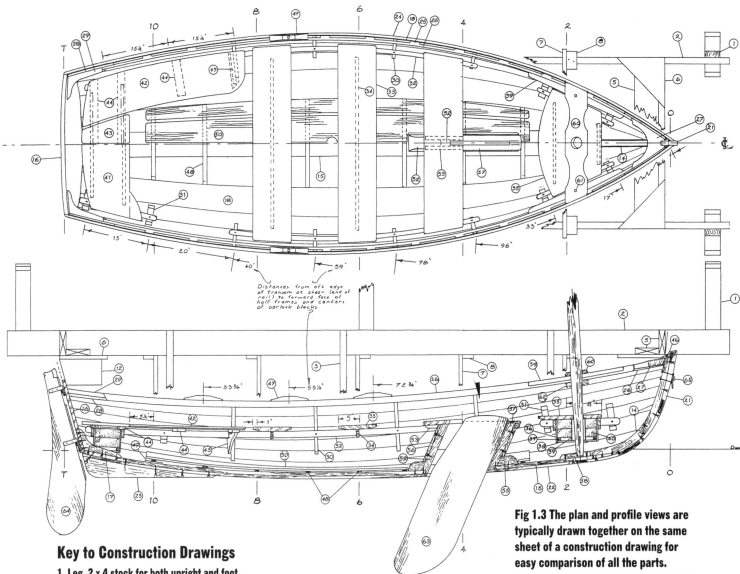

Fig 1.3 The plan and profile views are typically drawn together on the same sheet of a construction drawing for easy comparison of all the parts.

Key to Construction Drawings

1. Leg, 2 x 4 stock for both upright and foot.

2. Side beam, 2 x 6 or 2 x 8 stock, 14' long. Two required.

3. Diagonal braces, 2 x 4 stock. Lay out length and angle from sections of full-sized patterns.

4. Center beam, 2 x 6 stock, 8' 6" long.

5. End beams, 2 x 6 stock.

6. Gusset, ¾" plywood or mold stock

7. Mold, made from 1" x 10" #3 softwood boards. Bolt two yardsticks together to use as a large bevel gauge to help determine the miter angle.

8. Mold stop blocks, 1 x 3 stock or mold stock scraps. At each mold, one on each side beam and two on the center beam; 20 required.

9. Miter block, mold stock 4 ½" x 10"; 13 required.

10. Filler, scraps of mold stock. Some molds may need this filler to reach the center beam. Note: Actual contact with the center beam is not required; the molds only need to be close enough that the two mold stop blocks can hold the mold vertical. The side beams carry the weight of the molds and hull.

11. Hole for centerline string, about ¾" diameter. All holes are drilled at the same height above the center beam. This is usually easily done once the molds are set up on the jig.

12. Transom support blocks, 2 x 6 stock with transom angle (from full-sized patterns). Two required.

13. Sleepers for concrete floor, 2 x 10 stock.

14. Inner stem is of mahogany and is 1½" thick. After the inner stem has been shaped and beveled, drive two screws through the glue joint. Glue the inner stem to the keelson and fasten with three or four #8 screws.

15. Keelson is of mahogany, ¾" x 5 ½", and the rough length is 11'. The taper at the forward end can be roughed in with measurements from the full-sized stations and finished up when the keelson is beveled for the garboard plank.

16. Transom is ¾" and made of two 10" boards or three 8" boards 34" long and joined with glued butt joint, spline joint, or biscuits. Mark the aft side (outboard face) with both the aft face and forward face lines, saw the transom out along the forward face line, then bevel the transom with hand tools to the aft face line.

17. Transom knee, made of white oak, ⅞" thick. Fastened to keelson and to the transom with three screws. All screws #8.

18. Planking, 6mm sapele or khaya (African mahogany) plywood. Use a high-quality marine-grade plywood. We scarf plywood at a 6:1 ratio. With 6mm plywood the joint is 1½" wide. Fasten ends of planks with #8 x ¾" screws. Along the keelson, fasten the planking with #6 x ⅝" screws.

19. Plank batten, Douglas-fir, ½" x ¾", 14' long. See Details sheet for screw sizes and spacing. Make enough so that the epoxy can harden for 24 hours before the batten is removed.

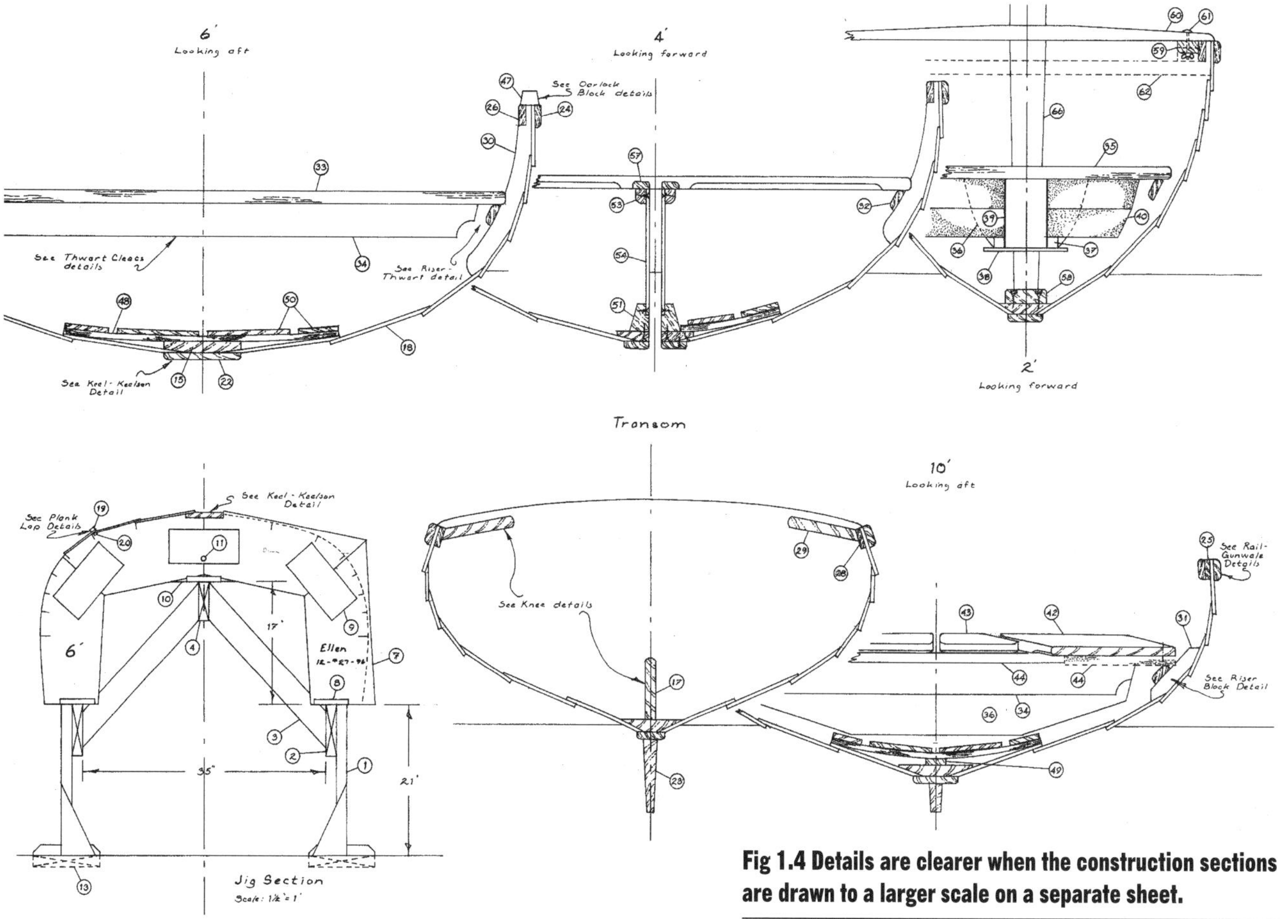

Fig 1.4 Details are clearer when the construction sections are drawn to a larger scale on a separate sheet.

20. Plank block, hardwood such as oak (see Details sheet for dimensions); 12 per batten required. Wax these blocks and the battens to keep errant epoxy from gluing them to the planking.

21. Outer stem, white oak, glued up out of ⅛" x 1⅛" strips. Plane to 1" thick after gluing. Outer stem beveled to ½" face below the second plank. Fasten to inner stem with #8 screws and bedding compound.

22. Keel, made of white oak, ½" thick. Widths taken from full-sized patterns. Prime both faces and edges of the keel before fastening with bedding compound and #8 screws.

23. Skeg, made of white oak, ⅞" thick. Can be either straight-sided or tapered as shown in the sections drawings to ½" at the greatest width of the skeg.

24. Rails, ½" x 1½" x 13' hardwood of your choosing such as oak, ash, or mahogany. Fasten on before hull is removed from building jig. The Details sheet shows how the rail is fastened on. Attach with bedding compound. If you are not able to attach the gunwales within a week or two, we suggest driving ⅝" screws where the gunwale blocks are to go and removing them just before the gunwale goes in.

25. Gunwale filler blocks, same as rail and gunwale stock, 1" x 1½" x 2". At least 11 are required, more if you want to space them closer than shown in the drawing. Lay out spacing of blocks on gunwales and clamp both gunwales to the blocks. When dry, clean up the top and bottom faces either with a hand plane or by running the assembly through a planer; with a router, round-over the lower outside edges, and all the inside edges, including the forward and after edges of the blocks; then saw the gunwales and blocks apart at ⅞" (½" gunwale, ⅜" spacer).

26. Gunwales, ½" x 1½" x 11' hardwood (same as rails). Forward end mitered to fit angle of breasthook. Clamp gunwale in place, determine length to quarter knee, cut end a little long, and trim to fit quarter knee. Leave a little proud, then plane and sand flush with sheer.

27. Breasthook, made from 6/4 stock (same wood as gunwales and rails), glued up in halves with a spline or biscuits in the joint running along the centerline. Finished thickness, 1¼". When installing, raise after corners ¼" to ⅜" above the sheer, and camber the top after all the sheer parts are installed. Bed and fasten with #8 x 1¾" or 2" screws driven through rails and plugged.

28. Breasthook and quarter knee spacers (same stock as gunwales etc.), ⅜" x finished width of gunwales x 11". Four required. After the hull is pulled off the molds, these are the first pieces to be fitted and fastened in place, followed by the quarter knees and breasthook.

29. Quarter knees, same wood as gunwales, ⅞" thick. See Details sheet for the shape. The angle at the forward end is 35 degrees. Bed and fasten with #8 x 1½" screws through the transom and #8 x 2" or 1¾" screws through the rails, all screw holes plugged.

30. Half frames are best made of oak or ash, ¾" thick. The half frames are laid out to be perpendicular to the sheer and the planking. This makes the fitting, attaching, and fastening of other pieces much easier. Fit them before the gunwales are installed, drill for fastenings, rabbet the tops for the gunwales, and permanently attach. Put a clear sealer on the mating surfaces.

31. Riser blocks, oak or ash, 1" x 1¼" x 6". Scribe to fit perpendicular to sheer and planking; attach with epoxy and screws.

32. Risers, oak or ash; 6/4 stock makes two, ½" x 1¼". See Details sheet for variations.

33. Thwart, pine or cedar, ⅞" or ¾" and 8" to 9" wide. See Details sheet for variations.

34. Thwart cleat, pine or cedar, ⅝" or ½" x 1¾". See Details sheet for variations.

35. Bow thwart, pine or cedar, ¾" or ⅝" x 15" x 24". Usually glued out of two 8" planks, butt, spline, or biscuit jointed.

36. Foam cover, made from the planking plywood, 5" wide.

Key to Construction Drawings (continued)

37. Cleat, ¾" square mahogany.

38. Bottom panels, planking plywood, 3" wide.

39. Thin-walled plastic drain pipe, 3" to 4" diameter. (Not required; it just keeps one from seeing the foam.)

40. Closed-cell foam, 2". We usually use insulating foam in either pink or blue.

41. Stern thwart, pine or cedar, ¾" or ⅝" x 11".

42. Helm seat wing, pine or cedar, ⅝" x 12" stock.

43. Helm seat fillers, pine or cedar, ⅝".

44. Horizontal cleats, pine or cedar, ⅝" x 1¾". The ends on the risers may be treated in the same way as the thwarts as shown in the Details drawing.

45. Helm seat knee, mahogany, ¾".

46. Stemhead filler, oak.

47. Oarlock block, oak or same as rail and gunwale stock.

48. Floorboard frames, oak, ⅜" x ⅞". Make sure the end-grain is flat in these pieces. Soak kiln-dried frames overnight. Steam frames for about 30 minutes. They should easily bend into place. Once they have cooled a minute or two; hold the shape, drill and fasten the frame with a screw to the keelson.

49. Floorboard frame spacer, mahogany, 1¼" wide by 4" long. Used where the curve of the sections is too sharp. It makes the bending of the frames easier and prevents the floorboards from splitting. To test for the need of a block, use a ⅛" softwood batten. If the batten bends hard into the curve or breaks, you need a block.

50. Floorboard planking, cedar, ⅜" thick. Make the plank shapes from 5/4 stock, resaw on the bandsaw and plane to final thickness. Fasten to frames with #8 x ⅝" screws.

51. Trunk logs, mahogany; 1⅞" x 2⅝" block makes a pair when split at the angle shown in the full-sized pattern. You'll note that these logs project past the trunk posts. These projections have filler blocks in them. It's best to build the whole trunk dry, take it apart, reassemble the logs and fillers, then scribe them to the curve of the keelson. When they fit nicely on the keelson, reassemble the whole trunk (including the logs) with epoxy. When the epoxy is hard and the trunk cleaned up, install the trunk, using Thiokol or some other rubbery type of nonadhesive sealant under the logs and 2" screws from the keelson.

52. Trunk posts, mahogany, ⅞" x 1½".

53. Trunk cleats, mahogany, ¾" x 1". Filler piece in forward projecting end.

54. Trunk panels, planking plywood, fastened to various other parts with #8 x ¾" screws and epoxy.

55. Trunk log filler, mahogany, 1¾" x 1¼".

56. End cap, mahogany, ⅝" x 1½". These are purely decorative pieces and can be left out if desired.

57. Top cap, mahogany, ½". These pieces are installed after the trunk and thwarts have been installed. Make these pieces overlong, glue them to a filler piece at the forward end, trim the forward end, rout the edges, then trim the aft end to fit the length of the exposed top edge of the trunk.

58. Mast step, oak, 1" x 3" x 8". See #21 in the Spar Plan for details.

59. Rail reinforcing, oak or gunwale stock, 1" x 1½". Scribe to fit curve of gunwale.

60. Partner, oak, 1" x 5¼".

61. Carriage bolt, 5/16" x 2½", with washer and wingnut.

62. Alternative position for rail reinforcing and partner. This position requires more fitting work to make the ends of the partner fit nicely against the planking, but looks cleaner.

63. Daggerboard, mahogany, ¾". See full-sized patterns for width, length, and shape of tip and section. One nice feature of this design is that with the angled trunk, the daggerboard wedges itself in the trunk instead of floating up.

64. Rudder, mahogany, ¾". See full-sized pattern for shape of outline and section.

65. Painter hardware, 2½" strap-eye, two #10 x 3" machine screws with nuts and washers, and a 2" ring. Open up a thimble and put it over the ring, close the thimble again, then splice the painter around the thimble.

66. Mast.

and fastenings, as well as instructions for building the jig and a step-by-step list for building the boat.

Plans for larger boats have many more drawings, including a general arrangement plan, deck plan, machinery arrangement, diagrams for wiring and plumbing, and many more detail drawings.

The lines

Find the sheet containing the boat's lines. Four groups of lines describe a hull's shape; they represent slices of the boat through different planes. Because you probably don't want to take a chain saw to some poor boat to see what her lines look like in three dimensions, we suggest the following exercise to help you see what the different types of lines represent:

- Get a cutting board, sharp knife, and nicely symmetrical, firm pear.
- Slice the pear from stem to blossom end, making two "hulls" with a flat sheer.
- Now split each pear hull vertically from stem to blossom end, along the hull's centerline, making four half models.
- Waterlines: Take one half-model and cut it into several slices that run parallel to the sheer.
- Sections: Cut the next half model perpendicular to the centerline at even intervals.
- Buttocks: With the third, make your cuts parallel to the centerline and perpendicular to the waterlines.
- Diagonals: Finally, place the last half model face down on its centerline from sheer to keel. Cut along the length of the "hull" in two or three places by angling the knife to cut perpendicular to the skin.

Considering the Scale of Drawings: When Smaller Is Larger

More than a few people find the conventional manner of referring to a drawing's scale confusing. Here's how it works: A small-scale drawing shows a larger area; a large-scale drawing shows a smaller area. Try thinking of it this way: A small-scale drawing has room to show several whole-body views of your dream boat. The large-scale view can show a detailed view of, say, just the very stern of the boat, but you will be able to see exactly how the rudder should be attached.

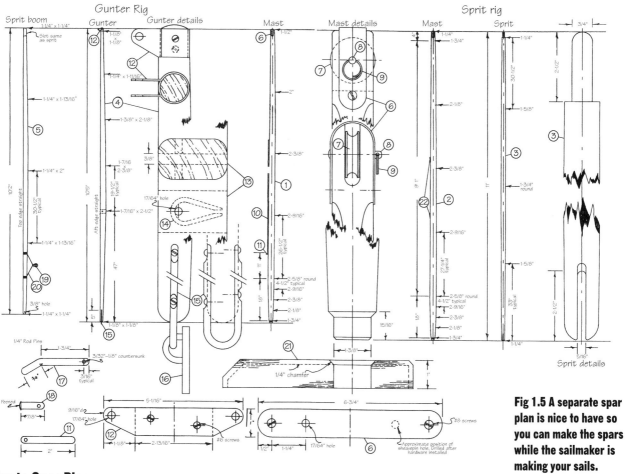

Fig 1.5 A separate spar plan is nice to have so you can make the spars while the sailmaker is making your sails.

Key to Spar Plan

1. **Gunter mast:** For both masts, glue together two pieces of 2x stock. Eastern spruce can warp a bit, so gluing also helps to prevent this. Both spars are round; diameters are shown in the drawings.

2. **Sprit mast:** Same diameter as gunter mast but a little longer, and the taper is a little different.

3. **Sprit:** Round to dimensions shown.

4. **Gunter yard:** Rectangular; dimensions show thickness and width. Corners can be either bullnosed with a router or rounded by hand.

5. **Sprit boom:** Rectangular; corner treatment same as gunter.

6. **Masthead plate:** 1/16" x 1" bronze plate.

7. **Sheave:** nylon.

8. **Sheave pin:** 1/4" bronze rod, 2" long, one end peened, other end drilled for cotter pin.

9. **Cotter pin.**

10. **Track:** 5/8" x 48".

11. **Car stop pin:** 1/4" bronze rod

12. **Gunter head band:** 1/16" x 1" bronze plate. (See alternative in photo No. 29.)

13. **Halyard slot.**

14. **Halyard thimble.**

15. **Bail:** 1/4" x 12", bronze rod.

16. **Track car:** 5/8".

17. **Halyard pin:** 1/4" bronze rod.

18. **Sail peak pin for #12,** 1/4" bronze rod.

19. **Block for 3/8" line** such as Harken Big Bullet Block 125.

20. **Rope bridle:** 1/4" with an eyesplice at each end and lashed to sprit boom.

21. **Mast step:** Same as No. 58 in construction and sections drawings.

22. **Wedges for snotter tackle.**

Before you eat your demonstration pear hulls, take a look at the Ellen lines shown. Stack your pear pieces to match the drawings. (Pare a thin slice off each diagonal wedge and stack these.) Notice that the sections are divided amidships, with the forward sections to the left, aft section to the right of the centerline. The waterlines and diagonals are paired along the centerline also. The buttocks stand alone. This arrangement of lines is traditional.

Offsets

The table of offsets gives the locations of points on the hull surface. Plotting these points on a full-sized grid and connecting the dots with fair curves is the heart of the process called lofting. There should be a note on the plans telling you how to decipher the offsets. For example, the Ellen plan offsets are given in feet, inches, and eighths, which is typical for boats of roughly her size. Thus, 4-10-3 means 4' 10 3/8".

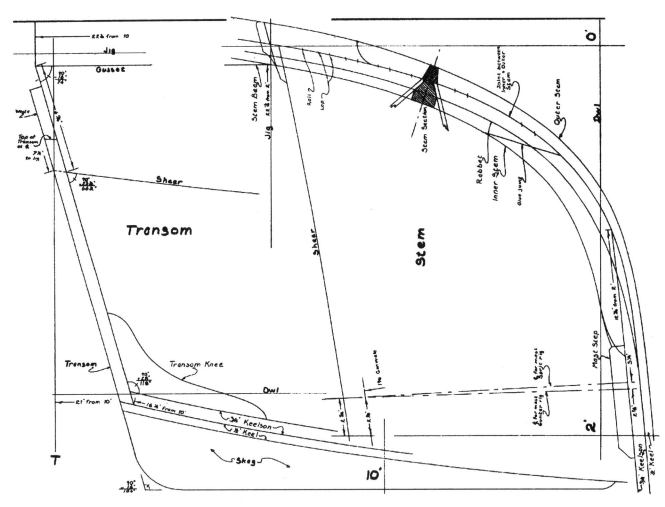

Construction drawings

These show profile (sideways, lengthwise) and plan (overhead) views of all of a boat's various parts. Some plans also include the sections, showing the view of the various parts from that perspective, drawn on the same sheet to the same scale. However, section details drawn to a larger scale on a separate sheet are easier to read, so we include them in our plans, as do many others.

Sail plan, spar plan

The sail plan shows the general arrangement of the sail rig and gives all the dimensions of the sail(s) that a sailmaker needs. Some sail plans also show the spar dimensions. Complicated and larger boats usually will have separate sheet(s) for spars and other rig details, including hardware to be fabricated.

Full-sized patterns

In recent years, small-boat plans that include full-sized patterns have become increasingly common. Full-sized patterns eliminate the need to loft the boat. Typically, the patterns will include at least the sections, transom, and stem. Some plans will include more, particularly for parts of the boat where a pat-

Fig 1.6 Full-sized patterns save you the job of lofting and are commonly included in many modern plans. These are patterns for the inner and outer stem, transom knee, and skeg, and show precisely where the transom and inner stem are attached to the building jig.

tern makes the job simpler.

Full-sized patterns for the planks are less common. These can work for simple designs with just a few planks per side, so long as they are printed on a stable base such as Mylar. Full-sized paper patterns for planks are worse than useless. Paper shrinks and swells, and the difference over the length of the boat is enough to make the patterns completely inaccurate. For most round-bilged glued-lapstrake boats such as the boats we design, you're much better off learning how to spile (see Chapter 7, "Planking," for a look ahead). No boat turns out exactly like her sisters. Measuring and fitting each pair of planks as you go allows you to make mid-course corrections and build a boat with planks that are right from garboard to sheerstrake.

Plans for larger boats rarely have full-sized patterns, as the costs of lofting and producing these drawings are prohibitive. Lofting is the builder's job.

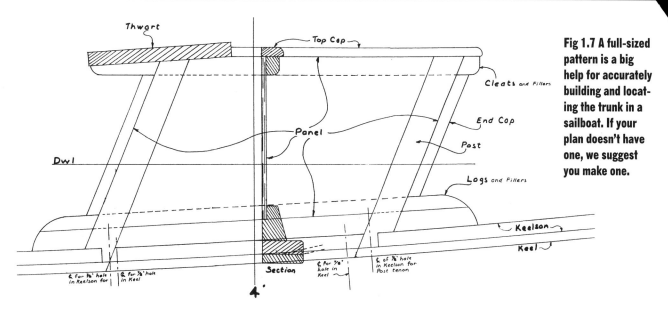

Scale plank patterns

Some plans include drawings that show the plank shapes, drawn to scale. You scale these up to full size using the measurements given. This approach allows the designer to give you plank patterns without having to pass along the high cost of printing full-length patterns on Mylar.

Specifications

Written specifications that accompany the plan drawings range from notes set down right on the drawings to a multi-page booklet. At the very least, they will contain brief notes keyed to the drawings listing the materials for each part. Some plans include a detailed, illustrated booklet that gives step-by-step instructions on how to build the boat.

ADAPTING THE PLANS

First, a couple of cautionary tales:

A few years ago a fellow knocked on the shop door, introduced himself, and said a colleague had sent him our way, thinking that John might be able to offer some advice on his boat project. Pulling out a worn copy of John Gardner's *The Dory Book*, he turned to one of the first boats, the 32′ Penobscot River bateau. These tough and graceful craft were used on hard-running Maine rivers, especially during log drives, and were designed for that job with a narrow bottom, extremely flaring sides, and correspondingly raked ends. Next, the fellow pulled out a pile of snapshots featuring a banana-shaped object made of wood. The high ends swept down to an extremely low waist that looked like it would swamp when you put your lunch and sneakers in the boat.

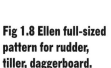

Fig 1.8 Ellen full-sized pattern for rudder, tiller, daggerboard.

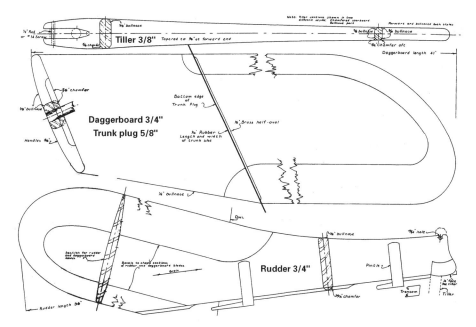

...ned it to 24 feet!" he exclaimed proudly.

...t have showed his horror, because this in-...uer quickly told John that he planned to put on ...another plank to raise the sheer in the middle. Oh, dear.

But this wasn't why he'd come seeking advice. No, he wanted John to tell him how to install a sail rig with a centerboard. Why did he want to do that? Well, he and some friends planned to take this object down the McKenzie River into Hudson Bay.

How do you tell a person that he is describing the closest thing to suicide that you care to hear about?

John should have told him the story about his first boatbuilding job, working on fiberglass commercial salmon trollers on the West Coast. The yard had a mold for a 35' semi-planing hull, but none of the boats it turned out were that long. They laid up a hull without a transom, then a few feet of the aft section. They then married the two together to make a 40-footer. This lengthened the boat by about 14 percent, within the realm of reason for the type of hull. For comparison, the fellow with the abbreviated dory had shortened his boat by 25 percent, way too much.

Shortly after John arrived, the yard was sold to a couple of guys whose previous experience was in the construction of fiberglass septic tanks. Freed of all picky constraints of functional boat design, they built a 45' boat by lengthening *and widening* the original 35' hull. They split the hull in two directions, scabbed in pieces, and grafted a keel somewhere near the middle. The owner had the yard install a cabin for a 55' heavy-displacement boat on this creation.

That was it for John; he quit working for the yard. That summer, the 45' boat rolled over and sank in a moderate swell; fortunately, another troller nearby rescued the crew.

Doing it right

The preceding tales don't feature glued-lapstrake boats, they just happen to be the most dramatic ones in our experience. But they apply. After years of talking to people about their boat dreams, we are convinced that the powerful urge to Change the Plans is universal. Doing this is not necessarily a bad idea; but it is something that should be approached very, very carefully. Changing your plans means redesigning the boat to a greater or lesser degree. You should expect to put in the same amount of work and thought that the original designer did. You can't instantly make yourself a bigger, smaller, wider, or narrower version that will work. Other changes, even apparently minor ones, require careful checking. Put a sail rig for a bigger boat on your Ellen hull, and you're in for a wet surprise. Load down a 18' Peregrine rowboat with fancy seats and cabinetry if you will, but don't be shocked if she doesn't row or handle as well as you expected.

"Can't I just stretch (or shorten) the molds to make a longer (or shorter) version?" is a very popular question. You can for many designs, but only within a limited range. Roughly 10 percent of the original length is considered a reasonable benchmark, but this can vary a good deal depending upon the type of design. Very interesting and often very unpleasant things happen if you go beyond the design's "reasonable range." Weird shapes are likely, and important handling characteristics, particularly stability, suffer greatly. It doesn't take much to change a good design into an unusable, possibly dangerous, one.

For example, our 15'8" Merlin fast rowboat is only about 2' shorter than her big sister, the 18' Peregrine. John took the idea of the Peregrine, including her semi-circular midsection, good stability, general look, and excellent rowing abilities, but made the Merlin a completely new design by shortening the overhangs, widening the midsection, and fining up the transom. If he had just shortened up the station spacing, she would have been tippier and much slower. Not exactly dangerous, perhaps, but definitely not elegant and not as much fun to row.

When you build a boat, you are making a long-term investment. The few hours you save in haste now could mean a future of unhappiness with your boat, until you give her up as a bad job or she meets an early demise. We strongly urge you to consult experts, work the necessary calculations, do all of the required drawings—then sit on things for a while to reassess your changes for a few days or weeks. You might want to make a half model, which is certainly pleasurable work and results in an inspiring decoration for your wall.

Take the time to figure out how all of the parts of your boat will work together, now, on paper. Leaving this until "later" is sure to lead to problems, some of which may be serious. Nothing in a boat is totally independent of the rest. Check everything over before you make a single cut.

It is easy to overbuild or make things more complicated than they need to be. It usually takes a great deal more thought, more drawings, and perhaps a couple of prototypes before the simplest, most elegant, and best de-

1.1 Adding a lot of weight to a light rowboat like this 18' Peregrine will make her a ballerina in lead dancing shoes.

1.2 GEM, an Iain Oughtred Grebe design extended to 15'.

sign emerges. Approach your design challenges from different angles, starting over from scratch if need be. Figure out how to jar your mind out of an unproductive rut. When you're absolutely certain that you're happy with what you've done, go ahead and build the boat.

The story of Gem

A customer came to us with Iain Oughtred's plans for a 13½' yawl called the Grebe. The customer liked the boat a great deal. He particularly liked its classic British rig and appearance. But, he wanted a boat that was a little bit bigger, about 15'. He also was concerned about how well the boat would maneuver in tight anchorages packed with boats and in channels winding through shoal areas.

Changing the boat's length to 15' meant an acceptable eleven percent increase. John handled this by increasing the spacing evenly between stations. He decided not to make the boat any wider, partly to keep her reasonably easy to row. The new boat, to be called *Gem*, would gain stability from her greater length. The winds in southern New England summers tend to be fairly light, so it wasn't necessary to be terribly conservative on the new, bigger rig. John did give her a generous reef for afternoon squalls and fall days on the bay. To make sure that *Gem* could worm her way through boats and banks on the way out to the bay, he put more rocker in keel, which shoaled up the forefoot.

After the customer approved the redesign, which included drawing a new set of lines and sail plan, John lofted the hull to make sure that the stretched stations and other changes would fair out at full-size. Everything worked perfectly. The finished boat turned out to be everything that we, and her owner, hoped she would be. She even won a WoodenBoat Show Concours d'Élégance award.

Adapting traditional lapstrake designs to glued-lapstrake

Because lapstrake boats have been built for thousands of years, it is very possible that there are old designs out there that you would like to consider for building in the glued-lapstrake method.

Keep in mind that glued-lapstrake boats are often much lighter than traditional boats. (Adirondack guideboats, double-paddle canoes, and similar boats are notable exceptions; these boats should weigh about the same when built in glued-lapstrake.) If your boat floats too high, it will affect her performance and stability adversely: she will be more affected by wind and chop, especially as she has more windage, and will have less mass to help carry her forward through the waves; and she will likely be distinctly tippy due to the fact that you have effectively raised her center of gravity by making her lighter. It is a good idea to ballast the boat down to her designed waterline. If you truly need a lighter boat, you need a new design that takes this into account and that captures the looks of the older boat that is the apple of your eye.

Also, resist the urge to take out all of the frames. Though it is true that glued-lapstrake boats do not need the frames as structural members in the same way that a traditional lapstrake boat does, your boat will likely require some full or partial frames in strategic places. She's likely to need at least half-frames to stiffen and strengthen the hull against the stresses from rowing and sailing, and she may need a full frame or several to keep her from flexing unduly. If she's a powerboat, consider carefully the forces that she will endure while underway, especially if she has a planing hull, and build her with enough frames for adequate support under the worst conditions.

If you're unsure about how to redesign the boat, seek professional advice.

What Size Should the Lap Joint Be?

If you're redesigning a traditional lapstrake boat, the lap given in your plans may not be right for glued-lapstrake. We use a ¾" lap on our small boats up to 18'. If your planking is more than ¼" thick, consider increasing the lap width, using three times the thickness of the planking as a rule of thumb.

CONSIDERING LOFTING

Many plans for glued-lapstrake boats, including ours, come with full-sized patterns, eliminating the need for lofting. If yours are among them, you may want to scan through the next section and pick up again with the suggestions for organizing the project that follow.

Full-sized patterns are convenient, but don't let the fear of lofting stop you from considering a design that requires you to loft. At first, lofting may seem hopelessly confusing (especially when reading about it), but it really is a straightforward step-by-step process that will make increasing sense as you do it.

Lofting a boat for glued-lapstrake construction is no different than lofting any other. There are several excellent books that describe lofting in detail. We particu-

1.3 Lofting on plywood panels.

larly like Greg Rössel's *Building Small Boats* and Alan Vaitses's *Lofting* (see Appendix B, "References").

I truly enjoy lofting. Here's a few thoughts and suggestions that I have found helpful:

Lofting is the process of drawing your boat in two dimensions on a grid by plotting given points on the grid, then drawing curves through (or almost through) those points. Lofting is an essential, important, and, frankly, fun part of boatbuilding. For one thing, it is the first time you will get to see your boat full size, albeit somewhat flat. You will be a step closer to being in the boat. The lofted boat begins to feel real: how many steps does it take to walk her length; how far it is to reach across the beam; and, wow, that's how much she'll really draw. You start to get a sense of what it will be like to sit in the boat and tug on the tiller or pull at the oars. As a designer, it is hard for me to express just how exciting it is to plot points and bend long battens around the shape of a boat that started as a tiny sketch on graph paper. Although I use lines drawings and half models to design my boats, I make small but important final decisions about shape on the lofting boards. Lofting is crucial because it allows you to find and fix inaccuracies.

Even if your plan has full-sized patterns, lofting portions of the boat can prove worthwhile. By drawing the boat full-sized (perhaps the profile, a buttock or two, the deck view, and a couple of waterlines), you will have a much clearer understanding of the boat and have a handy full-sized reference guide for making patterns and checking the shapes of parts. You will feel especially virtuous if an error crops up, which can happen in the most carefully drawn set of plans. Changing things on the lofting with pencil and eraser will save you materials, time, and expletives when building the boat.

Where to loft?

Unless you can kick everyone out of the living room for a week and you feel good about pounding small nails into the polished maple floor, you're probably going to wind up lofting on a cement garage floor or an irregular planked wooden floor. Though it would be nice if I had a perfectly flat, smooth wooden floor I could devote entirely to lofting, working floor space is at a premium around our shop, so I built a set of movable lofting boards consisting of 4'-square, ½" lauan plywood panels screwed to 2x2 and 2x4 frames. Offset the panels on the frames in the lengthwise direction by a couple of inches, so that you can screw the lofting boards tightly together with no break in the surface. Painting the boards with white paint makes the lines easier to see. I use clean new sheets of ¼" birch plywood for each new design, and I store them in the plywood rack, pulling them out for reference throughout the building process and when making changes to a new design.

Tools and equipment

You'll need an assortment of perfect battens for lofting. Please see Chapter 2, "Materials and Tools," for details on making battens. Your lofting book will outline the rest of the necessary tools. A good set of lead ducks (spline weights) will be a treasured asset. If you should see a flock in an auction at a fair price, grab them. You can make your own ducks; see Chapter 11, "If Your Boat Has a Sail," for general instructions on casting lead. You can certainly loft without ducks; full cans of paint or pennies can serve as heavy weights to hold battens.

Enlarging Your Plans

As enticing as the idea may appear, you can't eliminate lofting by enlarging your plans to full size on a large-format copier. We are asked about this more often than you might suppose. The copier will produce drawings of apparently the right size, more or less, but that's about it. Each line will blow up to ⅛" or more thick, rendering accuracy impossible. Errors are magnified many times over. Please loft your boat.

A few hints

When you're ready to loft, knee pads securely in place and sharpened pencils and erasers at the ready, here are some suggestions that may prove useful:

• Pay close attention to the diagonals: If you bend a lovely fair batten over a half model, the line that it traces most closely will be a diagonal. This line will also be the path the water takes around your hull. Because the diagonals are very important in determining hull shape, I rely primarily on them when fairing the hull in the lofting.

• Lofting staffs: Make a lofting staff for each station. You can put both the heights and the half-breadths on one staff, which is very convenient when marking and laying out (see Figure 1.9).

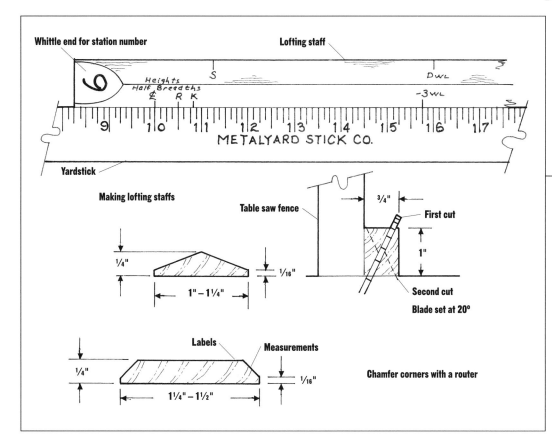

Fig 1.9 Marking the dimensions from a table of offsets onto lofting staffs helps reduce measuring errors.

- Marking the lofting staffs: Mark all the measurements on all staffs from the offsets at the same time. Lay a yardstick next to each edge of each staff to accurately mark the correct distances. Rather than work from the end of the yardstick, which might be off, I usually work from the 10″ mark, as it is easy to add 10″ to all your measurements from the offsets.
- Drawing the grid: Use a large beam compass to draw precise perpendicular station lines, after you have drawn all of the waterlines, buttock lines, and centerlines of the grid.
- Drawing curves: When you draw a curve, mark any deviations from the points with an arrow. When you make the change on the appropriate lofting staff, erase the arrow.
- Drawing multiple curves: Lay out the points of several curves on the same view at the same time, then drive nails into all the points. Bend a batten around the outermost set of nails and mark the curve. Pull this line of nails, and the batten will spring to the next set of nails.
- Recording information on parts: In a short while we'll talk about using 5″ x 8″ index cards to help you make parts and build the boat. It is worthwhile taking the time to draw some parts (such as a centerboard trunk) on the lofting and record the various dimensions and angles on these reference cards, particularly the setup and layout cards.
- Determining bevels: For the transom, use the diagonals. For the stem, use the waterlines.

- Fitting our jig to your boat: If you are using a boat from another designer, you need to work out some details on the lofting if you would like to use our building jig (see Chapter 5, "Building Jig and Molds").
- Parts that should be drawn on the lofting:
  Stem profile and bevel
  Developed transom and profile
  Thickness of keelson
  Keelson and keel, on the sections
  Trunk and all of its parts, in profile
  Height of the seats and thwarts
  Mast centerline, in profile
  Skeg
  Breasthook, in plan
  Deck openings
  Crown of the deck
- Making patterns for parts: I draw many parts full-sized on graph paper or on ¼″ plywood, and it is very helpful to refer to the shape of the hull on the lofting when making these patterns.
- Making corrections and changes: Keep your eraser handy; it's more efficient to change things now than later.
- When I've finished the lofting, I record the shapes of stem and transom profiles; the section and transom shapes; and the centerboard or daggerboard trunk on easily stored Mylar sheets. This allows me to put away the lofting boards, freeing up shop space.

LINING OFF

If you are lofting your boat, you must determine its plank widths by lining off. You'll need to work on this when making the transom, then finish the bulk of the process on the molds and backbone after they are set up on the building jig. For a look ahead, see Chapter 6, "The Backbone, and Lining Off."

Chapter 2

Materials and Tools

SETTING UP SHOP

Having too much shop space is rarely a problem. Certainly not for us. Our shop building is 24' x 30'; one floor for building, with storage for parts and paint (and household overflow) on the second floor. This may seem like a lot if you are thinking about building your boat in a garage, but take away floor space for stairs and a woodstove, and add in a rack of plywood, an exceedingly stationary planer, and a couple of posts to hold up the second floor, and the space available for boats shrinks very quickly.

Think movable, break-apart, or compact

Though there are times when John lusts for a heavy-duty saw with a dedicated outfeed table, the shop would not work at all if we added any more immovable objects. Our table saw is a contractor's model, set on a shopmade wheeled base. The workbench is light enough (barely) to be pushed around. The 14" bandsaw can be waddled into the best position. The drill press tends to stay put in an out-of-the-way corner but can be moved if necessary. The plywood router table and table saw outfeed table are es-

sentially flat pieces of plywood and easy to store away. They rest on tall sawhorses when in use. All of our sawhorses stack or nest together.

Because building the hull is only one step in the process, we can't afford to devote permanent floor space to hull assembly. Both the hull-building jig and plank-cutting table come apart completely and are stored in the lumber rack. Each boat's stack of molds hibernates in the attic.

Think vertical and look up

Clear flat areas are usually at a premium in a small shop and must be kept clear for working. That leaves the walls and ceiling for storage.

Store solid lumber and long thin pieces on a wall rack. Ours is above and below a bench that runs along the prime building space.

We like tools out where we can reach them, not stored away in tool chests. Hand tools and measuring tools live on a section of shop wall covered with tongue-and-groove pine boards. Each tool has its own shaped

19

wooden rest or dowel pegs, which encourages us to put the tool back exactly where it belongs, making it possible to find tools quickly. Power tools and their accessories live on narrow shelves under the shop windows. Infrequently used patterns and such hang along the wall near the ceiling. Getting out the stepladder once in a while beats digging through piles.

We built the shop with an 11'-plus ceiling, leaving enough room to store a couple of hulls suspended upside down.

Get stuff off the floor

This is the biggest battle in the shop. If we don't know where else to put new things, they wind up on the floor, and usable floor space shrinks. Small parts end up in boxes on the floor, and pretty soon walking near a hull under construction becomes an exercise in tap-dancing through drills, hand saws, clamps, lights, and little boxes of screws. Machines that reduce wood to smaller pieces collect the detritus of their activities at their feet.

This leads to the next suggestion:

Clean up and put things away, regularly

We'd all rather work on the boat than clean up the shop, but attending to this task will make the boatbuilding go much better. Tripping over things, looking for missing tools, and waving boat parts and tools around in a futile search for someplace to set them down slows progress and makes for frustrated and grumpy boatbuilders.

Keep dust under control

Trap as much dust as you can before it enters the air or hits the floor. The ideal is a complete dust collection system. This is hard to set up in a small shop full of movable tools, and John is still figuring out the best way to set one up for our shop. Meanwhile, we invested in an air filtration unit that hangs from the ceiling and catches dust down to one micron. It runs quietly and is surprisingly effective at capturing very fine airborne dust. We also aim to catch as much dust as it is made, using sanders with collection bags whenever possible. The table saw is one of the worst offenders. John catches much of the sawdust in a box, but the rest ends up in the air. The table saw, router table, and planer will be the first tools hooked up to the dust collection system.

Keep after the dust with a good shop vacuum. If you need to buy one, we've found that the louder the vac, the more useless it is. Also look for one designed to be hooked up to tools and operated in that manner for extended periods.

PROJECT MANAGEMENT

A few axiomatic suggestions for improving the boatbuilding process:

• *To gain perspective, you have to walk away.* When you've had it up to here with the boat or a particularly difficult part thereof, give yourself a break before you start pitching tools or doing things with epoxy that you'll regret later. Taking a little time away from the problem and returning to it with fresh brain and eyes can make all the difference.

• *Remember the law of diminishing returns.* You can push yourself only so far before you are in danger of reversing progress. Quit and get some rest before you're so tired that you start making avoidable mistakes.

• *It's easy to give advice when you're not the one with the tool in your hand.* Keep the advice and comments of all volunteer superintendents in perspective: if they're truly helpful, great; if not, smile and nod. Try this all-purpose answer for the hard cases: "You could be right." It is not necessary to elaborate on the concurrent arrival of freezing temperatures in the lower regions of the Devil's abode required for this to happen.

• *People using loud machines, especially those featuring quickly moving dangerous blades, are interrupted less frequently.* If your well-meaning guests are keeping you from building the boat, try picking up a router if they overstay their welcome. Of course, you should always stop all work requiring concentration while talking, for safety and error-prevention, but an announcement that it's time to rout those edges will dampen the efforts of the most ardent "helper." If you'd like a quieter solution and you're at the appropriate stage, the appearance of a sanding block with an invitation to use it is often highly effective as a conversation-stopper…or will get some sanding done.

• *Keep the whole project in mind for inspiration, but concentrate on getting the next thing done.* Building a whole boat can be overwhelming, but making the molds is not, nor is setting up the jig, making a transom, etc. Break it down. Do the next measurement, make the next cut. Pretty soon you'll have a boat.

Selecting Woods
CHOOSING PLYWOOD

Plywood is a marvelous material: consistent, stable, strong, and conveniently sized. High-quality marine plywood is extremely strong, can be glued easily, and provides a stable base for finishes. Plywood allows you to build a boat that won't dry out and leak and that is strong and lightweight.

Use only marine plywood of the best quality. This means that nothing from the lumberyard will do. If someone tells you that the exterior-grade house plywood is good enough, let us save you a great deal of heartache by conveying the lessons learned by John with a couple of boats he worked on early in his boatbuilding life: It isn't.

What to look for

Species. We use plywood made from sapele, an African species in the mahogany family. It looks like a mahogany, albeit with a wilder grain pattern. Sapele works and finishes well, and is quite resistant to rot. We almost exclusively use sapele marine plywood made by Shelman Marine to the British standard WBP 1088. Each sheet carries a Lloyd's of London registry label. It satisfies all our requirements well and has consistently been a high-quality material. We have never refused a sheet.

We also have used khaya for a special bright-finished boat. This is the species commonly referred to as "African mahogany." It is rather dear and scarce, but equals sapele for rot resistance.

Quite a few people use okoume, another African species (not a mahogany). Okoume's advantages of lighter weight and slightly lower initial cost are more than offset by its low rot resistance, in our opinion—especially after you add in the hassle, expense, and weight added by the fiberglass and epoxy coating required to protect the wood.

It is possible to buy marine-grade "Philippine mahogany" plywood. This catch-all term includes the lauans, which have moderate to low rot resistance, and the meranti species, which are highly rot-resistant. It is worth looking for high-grade marine meranti from a reputable supplier (see Appendix B: "Resources"). Carefully inspect all marine "Philippine mahoganies;" manufacturing controls and grading standards seem to vary from pretty good to nonexistent. Species and veneer thickness vary considerably. The Philippine mahoganies do finish well.

We get lots of questions about Douglas-fir plywood, and we don't recommend it. You'll need cans of putty to fill the grain, and your beautiful paint job won't last long. Douglas-fir has the nasty habit of checking, and we've never heard of a way to stop it. This includes epoxy coating, with or without fiberglass.

Number of veneers. In general, the more veneers, the better. For a guide, the plywoods we use have the following: 3mm and 4mm, three veneers; 5mm and 6mm, five veneers; 9mm and 12mm, seven veneers.

Waterproof glue. The plywood should be manufactured with a glue rated to be water- and boil-proof (the "WBP"). Though you may not plan to boil your boat, a dark hull in strong sunshine on a hot day will get pretty darn warm. (We know, we know; it should be white.)

Quality. You need plywood made with consistently high-quality wood for all veneers. Plywood cannot be judged by its faces alone. The inner veneers must be a durable, rot-resistant specie, and completely free of all voids. Voids are where the rot starts.

If you walk into a sizable lumberyard and ask for mahogany plywood, they are likely to have something to sell you. It probably will be designed for the interiors of houses and have two paper-thin layers of mahogany glued to a middle of some kind of wooden "mystery meat." Presuming that you can get past the problem of unknown wood with probable voids, those two thin layers of mahogany will be a big problem for your boat sooner than you might imagine. It is extremely easy to scrape or sand through them down to the unknown, which looks awful, opens the interior to rot, and significantly weakens the plywood.

Suppliers of good-quality marine plywood usually will have a similar product, made with better glue and better insides, but still with a thin, decorative surface veneer. These panels normally wind up in yacht interiors, where refinishing is reasonably rare. It's one way to get a quartersawn (read, straight-grained) face for a deck or other area where you don't want the wild rotary-cut pattern of the regular plywood. But, it's really not designed for hulls. Think about looks versus durability and check out the thickness of the outside veneer and the weatherproofness and longevity of the inside material.

The very best marine plywood has nice, thick outer veneers and even inner layers, with absolutely no voids. Check a sample if you're ordering sight unseen. We have found that suppliers are happy to send them.

Other sheet materials

There are a couple of other strong, lightweight sheet materials that may be of use.

Baltec's Durakore. This has a balsa core sandwiched between two thin layers of fiberglass. It is also available with lauan or meranti glued to the fiberglass. Yes, it contains "that stuff," but it works well for very light bulkheads and air tanks. The catch is that you must keep all water from reaching the balsa, which rots at the thought of moisture. Seal all exposed edges with epoxy, including the insides of holes drilled for screws.

Rigid Plus. Shelman Marine makes this lightweight sandwich of closed-cell foam between layers of marine-grade lauan plywood. The thinnest available is ½". Though this material is not as light as Durakore, it's stronger, more durable, and still weighs about half as much as solid plywood.

CHOOSING SOLID WOOD

Picking out the solid woods for a boat is a little bit of a challenge and a lot of fun.

If your boat will stay in the water and live a pretty rough existence in the marine environment, choose from among the resilient, durable, and rot-resistant traditional boatbuilding woods such as northern or Atlantic white cedars, Eastern white pine, white oak, cypress, mahogany, or Douglas-fir.

If your boat will be dry-sailed and have a pretty easy life, including protected storage, your range of options is a little wider. Woods that might be used on the interior of a large boat, such as cherry, spruce, ash, and black walnut, can be used successfully. Just don't get carried away and overdo the decorative woods; you are still building a boat, and a reasonable degree of rot-resistance and durability is important.

Shop carefully for your wood, but don't concentrate wholly on price. Buying the cheapest available is nearly always false economy. Usually, the wood is of poor enough quality that you end up throwing so much away that the final price winds up being as much or more than you would have paid for the pricier stuff. And, you don't get paid for the time wasted and swearing effort involved in trying to get your pieces out of lousy stock.

Local woods milled by a reputable sawmill can be a good choice, and often a good deal, if you know what you're looking for.

It is definitely worth looking for woods that have been harvested responsibly from sustainably managed forests. Unfortunately, it not always possible to be certain that the wood you've bought was indeed managed and harvested in a manner worthy of its "green" label. Especially in places where large valuable trees are found in isolated areas, it's all too easy for some folks to increase their profits by labeling any and all logs as green-certified. As certification programs around the world become more common and more mature, this problem should lessen.

How dry?

Most of the wood we buy is kiln-dried. Air-dried wood is not common and can be very dear when offered by suppliers to the makers of fine furniture. You may be able to find a small local mill that air-dries some of its wood.

Kiln-dried wood does not bend well when steamed. Soaking the pieces for at least twenty-four hours makes a tremendous difference. If your project calls for lots of steam-bent wood, which is not typical for a glued-lapstrake boat, use air-dried wood, or buy green (undried) wood if you can, as it will steam and bend the easiest of all. Air-dried wood is the next best choice, as it will steam and bend easier than kiln-dried.

If you buy newly sawn wood from a local sawmill to air-dry yourself, separate the boards with small, evenly sized flat sticks (stickers) and cover the top of the stack with a tarp, or roof. Plan on air-drying for softwoods about 1″ thick taking about six months; for hardwoods about 1″ thick, about a year.

A short list of woods we like

The following notes some woods we like and use. Other woods with similar qualities will work as well. It's particularly worth asking around about woods traditionally used in your area.

White oak. Fair rot resistance; heavy; open grain; works well with sharp tools; does not always glue well with epoxy; steambends well. We use this for rails and gunwales, breasthooks, risers, mast partners, keels, skegs, and occasionally seat and thwart frames. The grain opens and moves a fair amount throughout the life of the wood, making the maintenance of finishes a continuing challenge.

Ash. There are several ash species, and these are usually lumped together. Fair rot resistance; heavy; reasonably tight grain; works well with exertion; glues well. Ash is tough and resilient and steambends well. It can be used instead of white oak if you keep in mind ash's lesser rot-resistance. We often use it for caned seat and rowing thwart frames. We have done one ash transom with a carved name. Not easy, but possible.

Cherry. Good rot resistance; medium weight; fine grain; works well; glues well. Cherry makes an attractive, warm reddish trim for lightweight canoes and similar boats.

Black walnut. Good rot resistance; heavy; fine but pronounced grain; works well with effort; glues well. A traditional wood for yacht interiors and very nice when strategically used on a dry-sailed boat.

Northern white cedar. Excellent rot resistance; light; decent grain but typically with frequent knots; works easily; very soft; glues well. Here in Maine, we can buy Northern white cedar directly from a local sawyer. Because the trees are relatively small, knots are a fact of life. Pick your wood carefully, then glue or plug knots as appropriate. We use cedar for floorboards and occasionally for seats and thwarts when weight is a prime consideration.

Atlantic white cedar. Prime, highly rot-resistant wood; light. A classic boatbuilding wood. In demand; of environmental concern throughout most of its much-diminished range along the Atlantic coastal plain. We don't use it normally, but strategic use—especially of salvaged boards—in a light canoe, guideboat, or similar craft would be lovely.

Eastern white pine. Medium rot resistance; light; soft, fine grain; works well and carves okay; glues very well. We often use white pine for seats and thwarts as well as for contoured carved rowing seats. It paints well and doesn't look half bad varnished. Seal resinous pockets and knots before finishing.

Douglas-fir. Moderate rot resistance; medium weight; pronounced annual grain pattern; works well; glues well. This West Coast tree is not a true fir. The wood is very different, an attractive banded warm wood with yellow to red tones. We use Douglas-fir for spars and quite often for varnished seats and thwarts.

Spruce. Lousy rot resistance; light weight; minimal grain; works easily, glues well. We occasionally use spruce for masts and other spars. Advantages: light weight, resilient toughness, availability, and low cost. Disadvantages:

warping; "unwinding" of spiral grain; low rot resistance (keep up the varnish; bed and regularly check under fittings). If you have a choice, black spruce lives a difficult, patient life in swampy land, and therefore is tough, with a tighter grain. Lumberyard "spruce-fir" 2×s can work; pick them over carefully, and avoid the fir. Finding perfectly clear Eastern spruce is difficult, as the trees do not grow especially large. Seal new spars right after you set down the sandpaper.

Sitka spruce. Low rot resistance; very light weight; minimal grain; works easily; glues well. Sitka is very dear both in terms of price and diminished numbers. We use it only for very lightweight hand-carved performance oars and every once in a great while for spars.

Cypress. Moderate to high rot resistance, works well, looks great. Recycled cypress offers interesting possibilities for seats, thwarts, etc.

Honduras mahogany. Medium rot resistance; medium density; fairly fine grain; works easily; glues well. Beautiful stuff, in demand—and threatened in large part due to its value and desirability. Use it wisely and well. Plan carefully to get your varnished pieces from the best parts of the boards, and use the rest for parts in which weight, workability, and gluing matters but looks don't, such as the inner stem and keelson. You shouldn't have enough scraps left over to boil a tea kettle.

Khaya, "African mahogany." Medium rot resistance; medium density, fairly fine but confused and obstreperous grain; glues well. We've tried this for transoms and internal parts. It varnishes beautifully, with a positive sparkle to the grain. (The rowboat on davits shown on the back cover has a khaya transom.) Getting to this point is the challenge; khaya is not easy to work. Like most members of the mahogany family, khaya is greatly desired, valuable, and therefore of concern.

Spanish cedar. A fairly soft, lighter weight alternative to mahogany from Central and South Americas. Good rot resistance; glues okay; coarser grain than the mahoganies; pronounced odor when sawn that is mildly unpleasant. Was less expensive than mahoganies until cigar humidor makers drove up demand; prices have been falling as cigar craze has abated.

Holding It All Together
WORKING WITH EPOXY

In the old days when life was simple, there was one kind of epoxy commonly available: the Gougeon Brothers' WEST System.

Now you can find epoxy in nearly every marine supply and hardware store, much of it WEST System but also excellent epoxies manufactured by other companies. Different companies make different formulas, some of which are suited to specific jobs. Now the problem is how to choose the right one(s) for your project.

What is epoxy?

If you slept through chemistry class, you might want a quick cup of coffee now.

To quote epoxy manufacturer System Three's *Epoxy Book* (a useful little volume):

"The resin that is the basis for all boatbuilding epoxies is the diglycidol ether of bisphenyl A (DGBEGA). Bisphenyl A is produced by reacting phenol with acetone under suitable conditions. The 'A' stands for acetone, phenyl means phenol groups, and bis means two. Thus, bisphenyl A is the chemical product made from chemically combining two phenols with one acetone. Unreacted acetone and phenol are stripped from the bisphenyl A which is then reacted with a material called epicholorohydrin. This reaction sticks the two (di) glycidol groups on the ends of the bisphenyl A molecule. The resultant product is the diglycidol ether of bisphenyl A, or the basic epoxy resin. It is these glycidol groups that react with the amine hydrogen atoms in hardeners to produce the cured epoxy resin."

We couldn't have said it better ourselves.

Epoxy manufacturers take this thick basic resin and modify it for specific uses according to their own proprietary formulas.

Ready for more?

"Hardeners used with room-temperature-cured epoxy resins are most commonly polyamines. That is, they are organic molecules containing two or more amine groups. Amine groups are not unlike ammonia in structure except that they are attached to organic molecules. Like ammonia, amines are strongly alkaline. Because of this similarity, epoxy resin hardeners often have an ammonia-like odor, most notable in the dead air space in containers right after they are opened. Once in the open this odor is difficult to detect because of the high vapor pressure of the polyamines.

"Reactive amine groups are nitrogen atoms with one or two hydrogen atoms attached to the nitrogen. These hydrogen atoms react with oxygen atoms from glycidol groups on the epoxy to form the cured resin—a highly crosslinked thermoset plastic. Heat will soften, but not melt, a cured epoxy. The three-dimensional structure gives the cured resin excellent physical properties.

"The ratio of glycidol oxygens to the amine hydrogens, taking into account the various molecular weights and densities involved, determines the final resin to hardener ratio. Varying the recommended ratio will leave either unreacted oxygen or hydrogen atoms depending on which side is in excess. The resultant cured resin will have lower strength as it is not completely crosslinked.

"Epoxy hardeners are not catalysts. Catalysts promote reactions but do not chemically become a part of the finished product. Epoxy hardeners mate with the epoxy resin, greatly contributing to the ultimate properties of the cured system."

Epoxy passes through recognizable stages as it cures. It may thin slightly at first, but as the reaction progresses it eventually begins to gel—commonly referred to as "go off" or "kick." It thickens and soon becomes sticky. At this point, the epoxy will be very hard to spread and should be discarded unless you can use it up quickly. Once the epoxy reaches the sticky goo stage, it slowly becomes harder and tack-free, but this takes longer than the transition from clear workable to unworkably sticky. As the epoxy cures and hardens, over the course of several days to a week, it becomes stronger.

So, what we have here is a chemical reaction that proceeds according to its own innate rules. Learn the rules, and working with epoxy will involve much less anxiety and cursing.

Keep the reaction under control

Working with epoxy requires that you forget what you know about working with substances that "dry." Fill a quart container with paint, and it will sit there placidly for a good while, then begin to thicken and skim over. Do the same thing with a batch of epoxy, and you will have a quart of dramatically and rapidly reacting chemicals.

The epoxy curing reaction is an exothermic one, which means that it gives off heat. Keep the following in mind:

- *Warmer equals faster.* Try to work with epoxy when the temperatures are in the 70s (°F) or below. If you are cursed with a life on a tropical island, several epoxy manufacturers offer a very slow hardener that will give you more time. Check with the supplier for specific details. You can cool a container of epoxy to slow it down some, which can be a useful thing to know in a pinch.

- *Big batches get hot, fast.* Fill an old soup can with a batch of epoxy, and in minutes you'll be running for the door with a hot can. The can, or any similarly shaped container, traps the epoxy's own heat very effectively. Whenever possible, work with small batches of epoxy. We use one-cup yogurt containers (filled about half full) to mix epoxy and epoxy putty and rarely need anything larger. Many builders like the glued-lapstrake method because we typically work only with very small batches of epoxy, making it possible to work neatly, cleanly, and sanely.

- *Increased surface area means cooler, slower-reacting epoxy.* If you must coat a large area (not that we're suggesting you do a lot of that), mix successive small batches unless you absolutely must use a larger batch. If you've got a potful that has to go on, pour or spread it in a thin puddle on the receiving surface or in a disposable paint tray, then spread it where you want it. The epoxy's heat will dissipate quickly, and the reaction will proceed more slowly. Remember this property of epoxy and use it whenever you're working with the

stuff. For example, if you're buttering up a plank lap joint and you need all time you can get before the epoxy kicks, take the putty out of the cup you mixed it in, spread it out over a small scrap of plywood, and work from that. If you're not that desperate, it also helps to simply spread the putty around on the inside of the container.

Measure carefully and mix well

Most of the failures we've had with epoxy have stemmed from not measuring or mixing properly. Using the calibrated pumps supplied by the epoxy's manufacturer will go a long way toward eliminating faulty measuring. Watch out that the level of resin and hardener doesn't drop close to the bottom of the pump tubes, because the pumps may not draw the full amount, and you may not realize that this has happened until it's too late. (See Appendix A, "Oh, @#!".)

Over time, typically several months or more, the resin will crystallize, especially if it is cold. The crystals often form in the pump mechanisms first. This doesn't seem to hurt the resin, but it will make your pumps inaccurate if it doesn't block them completely. Completely dissolve the crystals by soaking the jug in hot water.

When you pump epoxy, methodically pump in "sets": one pump resin, one pump hardener; repeat as needed for larger batches. Do not try to pump all the resin, then all the hardener: "Let's see, is this number three or four for the hardener?" Uh, oh.

Mix and stir the resin and hardener well until it goes from hazy to clear. Don't worry about small air bubbles. This often takes a minute or a little more, so be patient.

Check on the epoxy's progress

The vast majority of the time, you'll have nothing to worry about. The epoxy will go off right on schedule. But to ease your mind, and to catch that rare time when your measuring is faulty, keep the emptied mixing container with a little leftover epoxy still in it to check on the progress of epoxy otherwise hidden in joints.

The "amine blush"

A surface film of amine carbamate forms when most epoxy cures. More will form if your shop is cool and damp rather than warm and dry. We have not had any problems with amine residue on our boats, largely because we religiously scrape off and otherwise remove epoxy squeeze-out and do not coat our boats. If you have residual epoxy that worries you, remove the water-soluble amine film by washing (sponging).

Why should you be worried about the dreaded amine blush? The metallic driers in some alkyd paints (most boat paints are alkyds) can react with the unreacted surface amines in the epoxy, and the paint will skim over but not dry underneath. Epoxy specifically designed for clear-coating boats does not form an amine blush, so if you feel obliged to cover all or part of your boat with epoxy, get the right stuff from your supplier. Also check that the paints you choose are compatible with the epoxy coating, by asking and by doing a test patch first.

Clean up all excess epoxy immediately

We'll be mentioning this again (and again), but the time to remove excess epoxy is before it hardens. Uncured epoxy can be removed relatively easily; cured epoxy will come off but not without plenty of effort and time that could be better spent actually building the boat.

Choosing your epoxy

There are several excellent marine epoxies that work very well at their intended task of gluing wood together. The formulas differ slightly, and you may find that one company's offering works better for you and your boat than the others. For example, System Three's standard combination takes a little longer to reach the rock-hard stage than does WEST System. This can be a help, because it allows you to do things like go to bed and wake up to epoxy squeeze-out that is still a little rubbery and therefore much easier to scrape clean. Several companies make epoxies that can be used at low temperatures, down to 35°F. We haven't tested these, but if your shop is hard to heat, you might want to check them out. There also are epoxies designed for clear-coating (if you must) and other special jobs.

Work clean and smart

Epoxy is not good for you. It may not be as bad as some things, but it's not completely benign, either. One of the great advantages of glued-lapstrake construction is that it allows you to limit your exposure to epoxy, which is all to the good. It is possible to become sensitized to epoxy after prolonged exposure, to the point where your skin will break out whenever you come near the stuff. We've both worked in enough boatyards where the macho "I don't wear no crummy protection" attitude prevails. If you don't care now about how much epoxy you get on your skin, you may well live to regret your, er, rash decision.

- *Keep the epoxy off your skin.* Wear disposable gloves, or try a barrier cream for jobs where gloves are a hassle. Spread epoxy with disposable brushes. We clean the business ends of brushes and putty knives in a tiny amount of acetone when we're putting on several planks a day. If you do this, keep the acetone off your skin as well. It's better to scrape off the worst of the epoxy from tools, then chisel off the remainder after it cures overnight. You can remove uncured epoxy from tools with vinegar, while wearing gloves, of course. Denatured alcohol also works.

Protect your body with clothing—no shorts, no bare chests, no bikinis—and change if epoxy soaks into the cloth.

Don't use solvents on your skin for any epoxy that manages to land there. Use shop hand cleaner or wait and peel the cured epoxy off.

- *Limit your exposure to epoxy fumes.* The fumes tend to linger near the boat's surface, but your lungs, brain, liver, and assorted other vital parts don't care how tough you think you are. If you're working with epoxy in close quarters, especially if you're working with a large surface area, wear a respirator. If you're not sure whether you need it, wear it anyway. We generally find that the amount of epoxy used on the plank laps is small enough that good shop ventilation is adequate.

Limit your exposure and save yourself time and money by working neatly. Put the epoxy only where it's

Epoxy-Coating: Yea or Nay?

Ask around about coating boats with epoxy, and you're likely to find yourself thoroughly confused. We've heard all of the available opinions, from those who maintain that epoxy-coated boats last forever and hardly ever need refinishing to those who swear equally vehemently that boats so treated rot from the inside out. Rot happens when decay fungi find a conducive environment—one that offers adequate moisture, oxygen, and proper temperature as well as an organic material for a food supply, in this case, your boat's wood. Deprive the fungi of one or all of life's necessities, and they cannot do their damage. This is the goal of any rot-prevention method, including epoxy-coating. However, unless the coating is maintained perfectly intact, water enters through tiny cracks and scrapes, then works its way out very slowly after staying in the wood long enough to promote rot.

In the early 1980s, John built a prototype rowboat, of Honduras mahogany plywood, that provides a blistered, unhappy example of what happens to an epoxy-covered small boat when it is used among rocks and barnacle-covered pilings on the coast of Maine. She began blistering within a few years and quickly developed pockets of rot. The epoxy coating, thorough as it was, utterly failed to protect the wood underneath because it scratched through quickly under normal, careful use. The coating then made the situation worse by acting as a "plastic bag" to trap the water.

We do not epoxy-coat any boat we build nor do we recommend that you do so. We will re-emphasize the importance of building the boat with the highest quality marine plywood, however.

needed, and thoroughly remove all excess.

- *Need an alternative?* If you should become sensitized, John Guzzwell shares your pain, and itch. He has written several articles for *WoodenBoat* on building modern wooden boats using epoxy alternatives, so you could check out his suggestions. One possibility is Aerolite glue, a two-part, gap-filling glue that should work. It was used to build airplanes in World War II.

GLUING WITH EPOXY

Epoxy works as an adhesive by soaking into the wood, then hardening around the fibers to make a joint that is stronger than the wood. Keep the following points in mind when gluing up:

- Epoxy for gluing must be thickened. Straight epoxy soaks well into the wood, but it can also run right out of the joint, resulting in a starved joint.
- Epoxy soaks into the wood so well that you must brush a coat of straight epoxy onto both of the joint's mating surfaces before applying the epoxy putty; otherwise the wood will draw the epoxy out of the putty, leaving mostly filler behind—and creating a starved joint.
- An epoxy joint requires a small gap. Most glues require heavy clamping pressure to bond properly, but the same amount of pressure will force the epoxy putty out of the joint. Yup, another starved joint.
- Epoxy is one adhesive that can save you if your joints are not perfect, because it not only needs a small gap to work properly, but can fill significantly larger gaps. Still, there's no reason not to try for gorgeous joints. But if yours aren't…

Standard gluing procedure

1. Brush on enough straight epoxy to dampen, but not drown, both surfaces of the joint.
2. Mix thickened epoxy and apply to one surface. Don't be shy about putting it on; plenty of squeeze-out is good, and gaps will be difficult or impossible to fill later.
3. Screw, clamp, and/or tape the joint together, using just enough pressure to close up the joint and achieve healthy squeeze-out. Heavy weights can also be used to hold the pieces together until the epoxy kicks.
4. Clean up the excess epoxy with a putty knife.

Fillers and thickeners

We rely primarily on two fillers: silica thickener and wood flour. Of the other fillers available, your plans might call for microballoons or microspheres. Adding fillers to epoxy makes it a thixotropic fluid. This is definitely desirable; it's why the epoxy putty hangs together until you apply pressure to spread it with a putty knife, and it keeps the putty attached to the lap joint while you attach the plank as well as firmly settled in other joints. Ketchup is also thixotropic, which is why it lurks in the bottle until you whack it a good one, whereupon it flows out all over the plate.

Always thoroughly stir the resin and hardener mix before adding any thickener.

Silica thickener. Also called Cab-O-Sil or colloidal silica. A very fine white powder that makes a lovely smooth putty. Airborne silica is not good for your lungs, so mix it carefully. We go heavy on the silica for filling holes and other jobs where a lumpy putty would make a mess. It takes a surprisingly large amount to make a proper putty. Its two disadvantages are that it is very light-colored, which looks awful on a bright-finished mahogany boat, and it is hard to sand (try scraping or filing first).

Wood flour. We harvest all the wood flour we can use from the belt sanders' dust-collection bags and store different wood species in marked containers. Wood flour makes a putty that matches for varnished parts, thickens the epoxy with less material, and sands easier (though the epoxy itself is largely what makes sanding epoxy putty a ball of fun). You can buy wood dust if you haven't made enough, though we've never seen mahogany dust for sale. Commercially available dust tends to be light-colored and coarse.

Mix your own. Even very fine wood flour makes a putty lumpier than we like. For most jobs, we mix about equal parts silica to wood flour. Add more silica for a lighter, smoother putty; less for a better match with your wood. Add the silica, then the wood flour to reduce flying silica.

Microballoons. We get lots of questions about using microballoons. As we said, we rarely use this filler. We have tried it in a couple of applications: to make large fillets on bulkheads and to fill the weave of Xynole cloth on one of the few occasions that we sheathed a boat's garboards. Microballoons make a thick and lightweight putty that is fairly easy to sand. However, putty made with a high percentage of microballoons is difficult to spread evenly, leading to an ugly job that requires excessive sanding. Add silica to microballoon putty for a smooth-spreading putty that won't sag. Experiment before attacking the boat.

Boatbuilders Love Squeeze-Out

The beautiful sight of glue or caulking squeezing out from a joint or around the edges of a fitting brings joy to a boatbuilder. Sure, you have to clean it up, but healthy squeeze-out means that there are no gaps that will let in water or cause the joint to fail.

If you hang around with furniture builders, be prepared to be scorned and ridiculed for your barbaric practices. Pay them no heed; they don't have to launch their Queen Anne highboy, never mind asking her to beat against the tide in an afternoon chop all the way up the bay.

If you're heading for lots of squeeze out, mask off the adjacent wood with painter's masking tape. Be sure to pull the tape before the epoxy cures hard.

Five-minute epoxy

Forget to patch that ugly screw tear-out? Reach for the five-minute epoxy. Mixing blobs of appropriate size on a scrap of plywood works fine. Color it with sawdust for a perfect match. Most five-minute epoxies are not completely waterproof, so use only above the waterline for boats kept in the water. Thoroughly waterproof five-minute epoxy is available from some manufacturers.

OTHER GLUES AND GOOS
Resin glue

Resin glue, such as Weldwood, is a single powder that you mix with water. It won't fill gaps, but it doesn't soak into the wood like epoxy does. A tight joint (such as in the transom) will be nearly invisible. Under most conditions, it glues oak better than epoxy, provided that the joint is really tight. This glue is classified as water-resistant, but it holds up very well in our boats, protected by paint or varnish.

Waterproof carpenter's glue

Carpenter's "yellow glue" is very handy for all sorts of gluing jobs, such as putting together seats and gluing in bungs over screw holes. It's convenient, doesn't make a big mess, cleans up easily (let it turn rubbery), and dries quickly. It also seems to hold up well. Like resin glue, it needs tight joints.

Bedding compound

Bedding compound is a flexible goo that keeps water out of joints and remains flexible to move with the wood. If you need to remove a bedded part, pull the fastenings and gently pry off the part. No chiseling or swearing necessary.

Some brands, such as Woolsey's Dolfinite, seem to stay pliable longer than others. Bedding compound is the original tar baby and seems to magically appear on tools that weren't even nearby. Clean up with turpentine or paint thinner or wait until it hardens and scrape it off.

3M 5200

If you need to stick two things together with a rubbery stuff that will *never* come apart, 5200 is your goo. Wood and fiberglass will shred before the joint lets go. If you try to get a fitting off or two pieces of wood apart, you will discover two things: (1) when you pry on the parts, the 5200 just stretches, (2) if you try to cut into the joint with a chisel and mallet, the chisel just bounces. Usually 5200 takes several days to cure. Clean up with paint thinner.

3M 101

This is a much less aggressive adhesive, though it still sticks. We use it for attaching daggerboard and centerboard trunks. Once dry, 101 cuts and scrapes off easily. Down the road, the parts can be separated with a little effort. This adhesive also takes several days to cure.

Sikaflex

This falls somewhere between 3M's 5200 and 101 in adhesive quality. It dries harder than 5200, making it easier to cut. It cures quickly.

Silicone

We don't have any reason to use silicone in our boats. If your project has a place for it, use the marine varieties.

Silicone doesn't have much of a desire to stick to things. This can be an advantage, but we have seen fittings that moved a little, allowing water to work its way past the silicone to the wood and fitting. If you use silicone, put plenty on the fitting and tighten up the fastenings until they are only snug and there is a nice bead of silicone. Let the silicone harden, then tighten the fastenings and cut off the excess bead. Silicone dries quickly. Be advised that it may cause fisheyes in finishes.

BoatLIFE Life Caulk

This is a one-part Thiokol polysulfide that bonds well (but not too aggressively), is waterproof, and holds up very well to weather. It dries fairly hard but stays rubbery and can be cut and sanded. It can be used for bedding trunks, and it works great for deck seams.

FASTENINGS

A healthy supply of fastenings warms a boatbuilder's heart. In our shop, there is a good-sized cabinet with a set of drawers. The top drawer is full of a large selection of bronze screws. The second drawer is a similar selection of stainless screws. The third drawer holds bronze bolts and machine screws, plus a variety of nuts and washers.

Boat plans often will specify the types and sizes of fastenings required. In general, the length of the screw should be about twice the thickness of the part being fastened. Spacing screws about 8″ apart—a typical hand span—is a useful rule of thumb. Another good guide is: "That looks about right."

The common sizes of smaller fastenings usually come in boxes of one hundred. Larger screws and bolts come in boxes of fifty or twenty-five. You can buy smaller amounts, but you'll pay extra for handling.

Always buy extra fastenings, particularly screws. They get dropped or lost, heads break off, or it turns out that you need more than you, or the boat's designer, thought. The goal is to never run out of relevant fastenings. Being forced to stop work on a boat for the lack of a few quarters' worth of screws is beyond irritating.

Bronze screws and bolts

Be sure to buy your bronze fastenings from a reputable marine supplier. Inexpensive brass or "bronze" fastenings from the local hardware superbox store disappear in the marine environment with astonishing speed.

Flat-head Reed & Prince screws. The crossed slot in the top of a Reed and Prince (or locking recess) screw looks a lot like that of a Phillips-head screw, but it's not. This design works much better in the softer bronze. You will need a matching screwdriver and bit for these screws. Don't try to drive them with a regular Phillips screwdriver; you'll quickly strip out the heads.

Oval-head screws. These come with a straight slot and look nice and finished wherever you need to leave screws exposed and don't mind a small rounded protruding screw head. We use flat-head screws on thwarts, seats, and other spots where bare legs or feet might encounter them.

Bolts and machine screws. We use these mainly for fittings as well as for parts of the boat that need to be easily removed by hand, such as a mast partner. In general, if you need a large and long fastener, use a machine screw or bolt. If your fitting will encounter shearing (sideways) stress, you can use wood screws. If the fittings should be removed for refinishing, using machine screws or bolts with nuts and washers wherever you can so that you don't have to worry about worn and stripped-out holes.

Stainless screws

You can use high-quality stainless fastenings as well as, or instead of, bronze. If your boat will be kept in the water, don't mix metals in vulnerable places where galvanic action will cause corrosion, especially below the waterline. The harder stainless screws have some advantages, notably the fact that they drive more easily, and their slots are less prone to stripping out, particularly when driven with power.

Self-tapping screws. These screws can be purchased with a Phillips head, for driving with a screwgun. Although it is easier to spin off the head of a self-tapping screw than that of a wood screw (with threads that start about a third of the length below the head), the self-tapping screw's long, deep threads work very well with plywood and softer woods such as mahogany.

Bronze and stainless nails

Nails don't make an appearance in our boats. They require pounding on the thin, light, bouncy boat parts. Ring nails or Anchorfast nails, favorites for some types of boat construction, are nearly impossible to pull out when necessary. If your design calls for nails, don't let us stop you, but do consider whether screws would make your life easier and build a better boat.

Fasteners for temporary use and jigs

Drywall screws. How civilization managed to ad-

vance as far as it did before the invention of drywall screws, we have no idea. We reach for them all the time, for everything from building jigs to clamping the plank laps together.

We like the coarse-threaded ones, because they work well in softwoods. Get a full range of sizes: 1 ″, 1 ¼ ″, 1 ⅝ ″, 2 ″, 2½ ″, and 3 ″ will do. You don't need the more expensive galvanized screws.

Not that you ever would, but don't even think of using these in your boat. You soon will be left with screw-shaped objects made of rust, a material not known for its strength or holding power.

Finish nails. Bright 3d or 4d finish nails work for all sorts of temporary holding jobs: battens, straightedges, patterns. They almost completely replace any sort of lap clamp for holding the planks while they are fitted and fastened in place. Buy the thinnest and smoothest ones you can find.

Brads, small finish nails offered in increments of ⅛ ″ from ½ ″ up to 1½ ″, are perfect for holding the battens when cutting out planks and holding patterns for pattern-routing.

Drilling for screws

Before you reach for that screw gun, back up a minute and find your drill index. With only a few exceptions, you must drill for screws before driving them.

Tapping hole. The tapping drill needs to be smaller than the size of screw, the exact size depending on the hardness of the wood. The harder the wood, the bigger the tapping drill should be.

The tapping hole is the first hole you drill for a screw and needs to be as long as the screw plus any extra

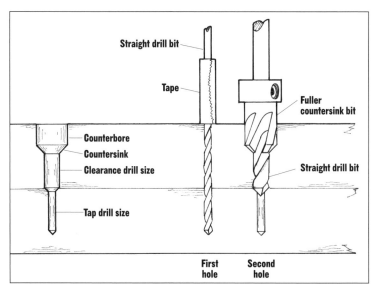

Fig 2.1 Drilling for screws with two drill bits and a Fuller brand countersink allows you to use different-sized drill bits for the tapping hole, bigger for harder woods and smaller for softer woods.

for plug and/or countersink depth (see Figure 2.1). If your screw is short, wrap masking tape around the drill for a soft stop-collar.

Clearance hole, countersink, counterbore. This set of operations can be accomplished with a combination bit. Countersink refers to the beveled hole that receives a screw head to make it flush with the surface; counterbore, to the straight hole made for a bung.

Fuller type C countersinks are best. You can buy the countersinks separately or in a set. If you get the set, throw the tapered drills away. They either make a hole too small in diameter for short screws, resulting in split wood, or too big for longer screws, resulting in a screw that often spins uselessly in its hole. Replace the tapered bits with a regular straight bit of the same diameter as the shank of the tapered bit. (The straight bit will be used to bore just for the shank of the screw.)

Set the depth of the clearance drill for the distance through the first piece of wood to be fastened by adjusting the Fuller countersink bit with an Allen wrench. The Fuller bits also can be fitted with a stop collar to control the depth of the countersink. This is often crucial in plywood and thin pieces.

Fuller also makes a counterbore that cuts a flat-bottomed hole to receive a washer and bolt head. These are worth searching for, because the counterbore can be used *after* you have drilled for the bolt, unlike paddle or Forstner bits. Try companies that sell wooden boatbuilding supplies and tools. The Fuller company also makes cutters for producing bungs that fit snugly into the holes made by their countersink bits.

Driving screws

Finally, it's time to drive the blessed screw. Stay the irresistible urge to drive that puppy home so hard that it goes through the bottom of the countersunk hole. Set the clutch on your drill so the screw stops neatly in its countersunk home. Driving the screw farther in won't make it hold any better.

If you overdrive a screw that you want to remove someday, when that day comes you will discover that the wood fibers have swollen over the screw head, making for an ugly bunch of torn-out wood when you back out the screw. Driving a screw can help pull two pieces together, but generally speaking you should apply a clamp or otherwise help the pieces together first.

Err on the side of caution until you get the feel for how much force is needed before a screw will bury its head. Drive the last bit by hand if you are unsure. A word of warning: If you think you can wind screws into nice hard oak with abandon, be advised that oak often will split at the instant that the head starts to bury, especially if the screw is located near the end of a part such as a keel or rail. (See Appendix A, "Oh, @#!".)

The Tools for the Job

What tools do you need to build a glued-lapstrake boat? The following are recommendations; don't feel that you have to run out and buy everything on the list. Most jobs on a boat—or any woodworking project—can be accomplished in several different ways with any of half-dozen different tools. It all depends on your skills, the way you like to work, and the tools you have available.

When it comes to tools, there is no replacement for developing skills. Acquisition of a new tool unfortunately does not confer instant acquisition of the skills required to use it well. On the other hand, when you are well-versed in the use of a basic tool, you will find that you can often use it in a variety of ways that will get you by when you lack a more specialized tool.

Don't wait until you have all the "right" tools. Get started with what you have, borrow or rent the majority of the rest, and buy only what you absolutely must have (or desire greatly).

Good-quality tools are cheaper in the long run. Not only will they last longer, but you will not blame yourself for terminal ineptitude and get discouraged because a tool won't do what it is supposed to. Better to buy a few good tools and spend time working with them.

A LIST OF USEFUL TOOLS
Hand tools

When you need a new hand tool, take your time and shop around. Don't run down to the local hardware store and buy the first bubble-packed one that you see. Many mass-market tools are pretty much ornamental and will simply never work right.

How do you find acceptable hand tools? Talk to knowledgeable friends, read the reviews—and reconcile yourself to the fact that most of the time you get what you pay for.

Chisels. A selection of about a half-dozen chisels from $1/4''$ to $1 1/4''$ or $1 1/2''$ wide will do. These should have long blades—$5''$ or $6''$ long—so that you can hold on with both hands when paring a bevel or such like. I also have a patternmaker's chisel with an $8''$-long blade that is very handy at times. The widest chisel is particularly useful for paring: it's wide and heavy enough to allow you to remove a lot of material. These attributes also allow you to cut with a surprising amount of control. A cheap or old "beater" chisel is handy for chipping hardened glue and epoxy off tools.

Planes. The workhorse is a $7''$- to $8''$-long smooth plane. It will get nearly constant use from the moment you start making parts until nearly the last piece is fitted. Block planes are also busy tools. These are about $6''$ long. I prefer the low-angle versions. Record makes one with a $1 5/8''$ blade that I find a little too wide to operate comfortably one-handed. I much prefer the Stanley and Lie-Nielson versions with $1 3/8''$-wide blades. Lie-Nielson also makes a $5''$-long block plane with a 1¼"-wide blade. This tool fits extremely nicely in my hand for making precise trimming cuts.

Rabbet plane. A 7"-long rabbet plane is nearly essential for cutting the half-lap gains in the planks (see Chapter 7, "Planking"), though it rarely sees work on the rest of the boat. You can get by with a 4"-long rabbet plane. It will be harder to use on the plywood, but will be more useful for trimming things in tight spots.

Spokeshave. Spokeshaves come in a variety of shapes, and all of them are useful at one time or another, but you really need only one plain-vanilla flat-face spokeshave. One with double depth-adjustment knobs will save you a lot of frustration.

Handsaw. I have Western-style rip, crosscut, backsaw, and dovetail saws. A few years ago I was given a Japanese Ryoba saw, and now I almost never reach for the other saws. The thin blade and pull-stroke cutting of the Japanese saw takes a little getting used to, but it stays sharp for a very long time and makes an extremely smooth, precise cut. You can also bend the blade to cut around curves.

Hammers and mallets. You can certainly manage with just a 16-ounce regular carpenter's hammer, but you may want to eventually expand your collection to include a 5-pound sledge, a ball-peen hammer, and a 10-ounce tack hammer.

My mallets are homemade, with oak handles. One has a 2"-square dense tropical hardwood head for working with chisels and encouraging large pieces to fit tightly. My smaller 1⅛" bubinga-headed mallet is indispensable for fine adjustments to parts and jigs, and for driving bungs into countersunk holes.

Scrapers. We're talking about the hook-bladed scrapers with handles typically used for removing paint. I've seen all kinds of commercially available scrapers, and few of them work well. The fancy ones often have very hard blades that can't be sharpened with a file. The reasonably inexpensive ones range from the totally useless to those that sharpen and cut well but clog after a stroke or two due to the design of their handles. Scrapers are such useful, versatile tools, especially around cured epoxy, that it's worth making some good ones using good commercially available blades (see Photo 2.1).

Files. You will want woodworker's files in various sizes and cuts for shaping wood and removing cured epoxy and finer metalworking files for sharpening scrapers and shaping metal parts. One flat file that I like has one side fine enough for sharpening a scraper and the other side coarse enough to efficiently remove cured epoxy. A handle on the end of the file is convenient. Triangular and half-round files are useful along plank edges; bend the handle 90 degrees if it gets in the way. Get a file cleaner (file card) when you buy your files.

Rasp. A four-sided hand rasp is useful for shaping wood.

Putty knife. Look for a 1¼" putty knife with a comfortable handle and a blade that flexes nicely. The blade shouldn't be so thin that it bends at the slightest pressure nor so stiff that you can barely bend it. You will be using the putty knife a lot for the epoxy work, so shop for a decent one. Slightly round all the sharp edges and corners of your new putty knife with a file so that the knife won't dig in and mar the wood.

Screwdrivers. Most screws will be driven with the cordless drill-drivers, but you'll need a standard set of flat- and Phillips-head screwdrivers. You'll also need a Reed and Prince screwdriver for bronze screws with this head.

Pliers, Vise-Grips, adjustable wrenches, socket wrench set. You'll use these mostly for making and attaching hardware, but you'll want them around for other jobs on occasion.

Hacksaw. Essential for cutting metal and the occasional wayward screw.

Clamps. It is true that "you can never own too many clamps," but you probably won't need as many for a glued-lapstrake boat as you may fear. For starters, you'll be clamping the plank laps together with battens, drywall screws, and small blocks while the epoxy cures.

Laminating parts is one job that is a clamp hog. You can modify your clamping form or block setup with cleats, dowels, and wedges to work around a paucity of clamps.

Here is a list of clamps, with the most useful given first:

Adjustable bar clamps. Several sizes from 2½" × 12" to 6" × 18" will be handy. My 4" × 12" and 4" × 18" clamps see the most use. Avoid the spring-loaded locking kind, as they are usually too heavy or too light.

Wooden hand-screws. These are extremely versatile. Get at least two.

Pipe clamps. Useful mainly for gluing up large panels such as the transom—and for pulling a slightly warped building jig into alignment.

C-clamps. Capable of very positive clamping, but slow to ad-

2.1 Shop-made scrapers using commercially available, hooked, single-edge scraper blades.

just. There are times when a set of tiny ones is very useful.

Lap clamps. I made a set of 20 lap clamps for my first glued-lapstrake boat, but they have spent most of the last decade sitting under a bench, collecting dust. The batten-and-block lap-clamping system eliminates the need to make these specialized clamps.

Handheld power tools

In general, I prefer to use handheld machines on large and long pieces of wood and plywood rather than trying to arm-wrestle them through my rather small stationary tools. For this reason, a circular saw, jigsaw, and router get plenty of use in my shop.

Circular saw. I use a 6½″ worm-drive saw for heavy-duty work, such as ripping and cross-cutting planks to rough size. I also have a 6″ sidewinder saw, and it has turned out to be ideal for trimming planks to rough size and other lighter weight jobs.

Jigsaw. My high-quality variable-speed jigsaw is one of my favorite small power tools. It is the tool of choice for many jobs. If you don't have easy access to a bandsaw, you will find yourself using a jigsaw even more than I do.

Router. A router comes in handy for cutting out planks, trimming parts, and shaping edges, though this work can be accomplished with other tools. If you're in the market, look for at least a 1½ horsepower model. Routers rated at 2 horsepower and above often offer desirable features such as soft-start and variable speed.

Cordless driver-drills. As you will see, these tools get a workout in our shop. Try different models until you find one you like. It is nice to not have to constantly exchange pilot drill, countersink, and screwdriver bits, especially when planking, so you might ask around for a loaner or two. A 9.6-volt drill has plenty of power for most of our work. For bigger holes and bigger boats, either investigate heftier battery drills, or reach for a….

Corded drill. Once you've switched to cordless drills, you'll hate to go back to the electrical umbilical. A ½″ heavy-duty drill is good to have around, however.

Belt sander. A 4 x 24 belt sander is marvelous for shaping and finish sanding: hold it in your hands on large pieces or flip it over and clamp it to the workbench for small pieces. Invest in a good solid tool, and buy one with variable speed if you can.

Random-orbit sander. We don't use small power sanders much, but a good 6″ random-orbit sander is useful for finish-sanding transoms, daggerboards, and other sizable parts. The lighter 5″ orbitals are nice to have around if you will be doing a lot of sanding on the hull.

Palm sander. We rarely pull the jitterbug off the shelf, but it is useful for boats with flat bottoms and/or wide planks.

Grinder/polisher. There's really no reason to use one of these on the boats we'll cover in this book. If your boat is substantially larger, this tool will be of greater utility.

Power plane. I occasionally use one for making spars but find it quicker and better to make scarfs in plywood and do other similar jobs with a hand plane.

Stationary power tools

It may be possible for you to mill your boat's rough lumber in a community shop or adult ed class, or you could pay a woodworking shop to do some or all of the work. If you are thinking about adding stationary tools to your shop, here's a list in descending order of desirability:

Bandsaw. Life will be much easier with a bandsaw. I have an older 14″ model that works wonders. This machine has substantial castings, good guides, and will cut up to 6″ thick for resawing. You could get by with a smaller bandsaw, say 12″.

Table saw. A standard home shop table saw will handle most of ripping and cross-cutting required for these boats, though you might find a professional shop with a larger saw to do some of the larger hardwood planks. I have a 10″ contractor's saw, and though I sometimes long for something bigger, sturdier, and more powerful, it serves well and stays accurate. If you're in the market for a new saw, consider at least a heavier duty contractor's model with an excellent table and fence.

Drill press. You can get by without a drill press, but you'll be particularly thankful for one when drilling lots of perfectly straight, aligned holes in wood and when drilling bronze for hardware. A drill press makes it easier to drill all of the many holes required when making parts for any boat. It can also serve, in a pinch, as a sort of vertical lathe for making small parts.

Planer. I have an old 12″ planer that has prompted many jokes about buying tools by the pound, especially from the four people who helped us move the top and bottom halves—separately. Heft in a planer is a good thing. If you're in the market for a new planer, talk to people, read the reviews, and try a test run if you can.

Jointer. A 6″ or larger jointer is nice to have but can be replaced by the table saw and/or a router and a straight-edge. A hand plane will serve for flattening twisted boards.

Buying used stationary tools

I wouldn't have a shop and we wouldn't be in business if we hadn't bought good used stationary tools. Maine is blessed with a weekly swap-and-sell publication that is a state institution; if you want something or want to get rid of it, that's where you turn first. Older used tools can be an excellent way to stretch your shop dollars as far as they will go, but check the tools over very carefully. Take a knowledgeable friend along with you to help you vet candidates for soundness if you're unsure.

Older tools usually feature heavier castings than today's lightweight wonders. These heavier tools often run smoothly without annoying vibration. Their fences and tables stay where you set them.

MEASURING AND MARKING TOOLS

In a pinch I could live, reluctantly, without many of my cutting tools. I could make do with one saw instead of five or six, two or three chisels instead of a dozen. But I would be seriously hampered without nearly all the measuring tools in the shop. In many ways, the real work of boatbuilding is figuring out *where* to cut; *how* you cut is a detail and matter of personal choice.

Most measuring tools are readily available and they don't have to be break-the-bank expensive, though the more costly tools will be more accurate.

Marking tools

Pencils. Very handy, but rather crude tools where accuracy is concerned. Many folks try to compensate for the relatively fat lines a pencil draws by making tiny, light marks and labels. This may work fine for furniture where the work is small and close at hand, but on a boat, marks that aren't intelligible from several feet away are useless. Use a #1 pencil to make big, dark labels, and a #2 for finer lines of reasonable accuracy.

Utility knife. This is useful for marking accurate score lines. You'll be using it for countless other things, so get a comfortable one and a packet of extra blades.

Permanent markers. You'll want big, fat ones and little, fine ones. Markers are great for making big, clear labels and marks on anything you don't mind having permanently labeled. The smaller markers also work well for marking out bronze plate and rod when making hardware.

Awl. The awl is essential for marking wood blanks by pricking through paper or Mylar full-sized patterns. Although it makes a fattish score line on wood, the awl marks good, sharp lines on metal.

Centerpunch. The awl is too fine for marking the centers of holes and such. The blunter tip of a centerpunch works much better.

Measuring tools

You'll need an assortment of squares, in order of usefulness:

Try-square. (Also known as a combination square.) This is a vital tool. It functions as a try-square, miter square, marking gauge, and depth gauge. The blade alone can be used as a ruler and straightedge. A 12″ blade is typical, but you can buy an 18″ blade for the better squares for those times when you need just a few more inches.

Framing squares. A 24″ square is good for lofting and cutting rough lumber into smaller blanks. It's a little big for small-boat work, so I often use a 12″ square instead.

Engineer's square. A 4″ engineer's square is handy for marking small parts and is particularly useful for setting up tools. You might not see much reason for this square at first, but you'll find yourself reaching for it more and more.

Adjustable square. This is the same size as the small engi-

On Measuring

You will need a good tape measure or two, along with assorted ruled measuring devices. But you will not be using them as much as you might expect. Measuring everything is not the most accurate approach to transferring marks and distances and is prone to error. We'll be talking about various methods for working without use of tapes and rulers throughout the book. So keep these measuring tools handy for the jobs where they do well, but plan on giving them a good rest for considerable periods.

neer's square, with the added advantage of serving as a depth and marking gauge, like the combination square. I used one of these when making harpsichord keyboards, and I find it nice to have around when building boats as well.

Small wooden blocks. If you have an accurate table saw with a smooth blade, you can make small square blocks of solid wood and plywood that come in very handy when the official squares are too big.

Tape measures. My in-the-pocket tape is a ½″ × 12′. You'll need a tape several feet longer than your boat for setting up the jig and measuring the longer parts.

Aluminum yard stick. Not the most precise measuring device, but certainly handy, and a serviceable straightedge.

Flexible steel ruler. These are the thin steel 18″ rulers with the cork backing that you can acquire from suppliers of office and graphic arts supplies. A 6″ model is handy to keep in a shirt pocket for quick checks.

Steel straightedge. Very precise, heavy, wide—and pricey. Great for lofting, nice but not essential otherwise.

Plywood straightedges. Make these up of ½″ lauan or birch plywood in a variety of sizes up to about 8′, as needed.

String. Smooth string is the best way to mark out a long, straight line; just make sure that the string isn't hung up anywhere. For very accurate work, support the string on small blocks at each end so that the whole string is suspended above the surface. Place a square block so that it just touches the string, then draw along the block's

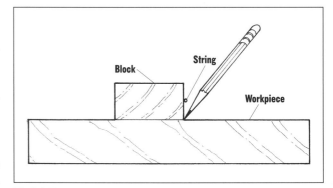

Fig 2.2 Marking along a square block just touching a suspended string is the first step in making an accurate straight line.

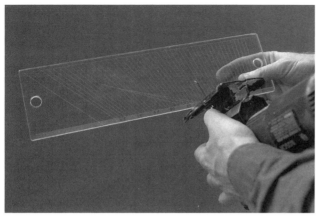

2.2 A bevel board made out of clear Plexiglass.

bottom edge to accurately mark the location of the string above.

Compass. Shop around for a good 8″ pencil compass that will hold its setting firmly with an adjustment knob. Avoid the cheap grade-school kind; they're worthless.

Dividers. A pair of 8″ dividers is the handiest for precise layout work.

Bevel gauges (or sliding bevel). Because a boat is full of angles other than 45 and 90 degrees, you will need a couple of decent bevel gauges. A garden-variety one with an 8″ blade will work fine, although the wing nut often gets in the way. Replace the nut with a teardrop-shaped "knob" made of ⅛″ metal drilled and tapped for the gauge's carriage bolt. If you can, spend a little more and buy a bevel gauge with an adjustment knob on the end of the handle.

A 3″ or 4″ bevel gauge is indispensible for small-boat work. You can order one, or make your own. Instructor and boatbuilder Greg Rössel likes making them

from two pieces of old hacksaw blade. A 12″ bevel gauge is nice to have but not essential.

Bevel board. You'll need to make a bevel board (see box) for determining angles with the bevel gauge.

Levels. An 8″ bullet level gives me level or plumb while working on the boat. (If your boat is sizable, you will also want a 2′ level.) To level the whole jig or boat, I use a 2′ level and a water level. (See Chapter 5, "Building Jig and Molds.")

Making a Bevel Board

If you don't have a bevel board for measuring angles, now is the time to make one. Take a little time and make a decent one; it will be getting plenty of use. Stiff, transparent sheet plastic makes an ideal bevel board, because being able to see through the board makes easy work of setting precise bevels on the table saw miter gauge and the jigsaw.

Saw out a 4″ by 10″ blank with perfectly straight and parallel sides. For a plastic board, you'll need an awl to score the lines. For a plywood board, varnish or lacquer the wood, sand with 220-grit, and mark with a ballpoint pen (permanent markers bleed when finished).

Draw a line parallel to one long edge about ⅜″ away. On a plastic board, sand this border with 220-grit; you'll use it for labeling.

Draw the first angle line across the width of the board with a square. Mark this "0." Draw the rest of the angle lines up to 45 degrees using the bevel gauge, set with a protractor. Draw the lines for angles divisible by 5 all the way across (as you did for 0 degrees); stop all of the rest short at the labeling line. Space the angled lines about ¼″, and label every 5-degree increment.

If your board is plastic, you're done. If plywood, finish with a couple more coats of varnish or lacquer.

Some Useful Sawhorses

You can never have too many sawhorses. The typical sawhorse is sturdy, stackable—and takes up a lot of floor space. They trip us up all the time in our small shop. Pictured here are some simplified European horses. Traditional European horses are a wonder of mortise-and-tenon joinery. Ours are a testament to the handiness of drywall screws and glue.

These designs involve a basic pair of legs, a couple of posts, and several cross members, including the top, that join the posts together. All the parts can be made with 90-degree crosscuts. These horses are plenty strong enough, relatively light, and much kinder to the shins. They nest together when not in use.

2.3 Modified European-style sawhorses nest compactly together and are less likely to bite your shins.

MAKING BATTENS

The time to make battens depends upon whether or not you need to loft the hull. If you do, you might as well cut all the other battens you'll need eventually at the same time. If you have full-sized-patterns and thus do not need to loft, the battens can wait, but you will need some early in the building process for cutting long curves, such as the keelson.

Take care of your battens. It takes a bit of work to find and make good ones, and no effort at all to lose them in the shop shuffle.

For lofting. *You'll need a wide variety of sizes, to accommodate the curves to be drawn: thin, short ones for the sections and stem; longer, thicker ones for waterlines and buttocks; and the thickest ones for the diagonals and sheer. Make them from the best clear, straight, tightest-grained stock you can find.*

Immutable Laws of Lofting Battens: Never pound nails, drive screws, or drill holes into your lofting battens. Never use the edges as guides for cutting. Store them flat and well-supported. Check them every time you use them, and mercilessly eliminate any that develop unfair characteristics.

For parts-making. *These are used for making and cutting long curves, notably the planking but also keelson, plank keel, and floorboards. These battens are also useful for shaping spars.*

Parts battens will have nails driven through them to hold them firmly in place. The edges serve as guides for saws and routers and therefore must be smooth.

My parts-making battens are all ½" thick. Most are ¾" wide, particularly the battens used for cutting out planks. It's also nice to have some thinner, shorter battens around for drawing the curves on parts. Pairs come in handy when cutting out parts with curves on both sides.

For building the hull. *You'll need battens to clamp the laps together and hold the planking fair while the epoxy cures (see Chapter 7, "Planking"). The number you will need depends upon how many planks you can put on in 24 hours. You'll need at least two, because you'll be making and attaching the planks in pairs. If you're planning on doing more than that, especially if you're working with a group using the phantom-plank method, you'll want at least three or four pairs.*

The clamping battens are made the same width as the boat's laps, ¾" for most of our boats, and of a thickness appropriate to the amount of curve in the hull. For example, ½"-thick battens work well for the 12' Ellen. Conveniently, this is the same size as the parts-making battens.

Choosing batten stock

For long battens, I much prefer clear, vertical-grain Douglas-fir, which is often sold as molding or decking.

Marking gauge. Vital for marking the width of the plank lap joints and running centerlines down the edges of parts. Commercial marking gauges score a line with a metal pin. When you need a pencil line, such as when marking the backs of the plank lap joints for epoxy, take a compass set to the proper width and run its metal point along the edges.

Marking gauges aren't hard to make out of hardwood (for a good explanation, see the book *Woodworker's Essential Shop Aids & Jigs* by Robert Waring). One that holds a pencil would be handy.

Circle template. Get decent ones from a graphic arts or drafting supply house, with holes up to 3½". Your shop and house are also full of circle templates: cans, tape rolls, empty yogurt containers, and whatever other perfectly round objects are lying about close to hand.

Battens. Good curves require good battens, and you will have to make them, preferably of wood (see box).

Lead drafting ducks (spline weights). Very handy for lofting and drafting your own patterns, as well as for holding marking battens and Mylar patterns in place on parts. You can make your own, buy them new (gulp$!), or luck into a set at an auction. Lead ducks are an investment worth considering if you are planning to build more than one boat.

Story sticks and tick strips. Transferring measurements from one part of the boat to another is best done with these. They can be made of plywood, thin battens, card stock, or even paper. A distance marked on one of these is precise and clear and much, much less likely to cause confusion and error than trying to remember which 32nd it was and squinting at a ruler.

When Curved Is Better

Furniture makers work very hard to keep their sharpened edges dead straight. Because most books and magazines are written for these folks, the grinding methods you'll commonly read about will instruct you to grind the blade until no ray of light gleams between a square and your blade's edge.

We boatbuilders are doing a different sort of work. John grinds a shallow curve into nearly all of his plane and spokeshave blades, and chisels over ¾". Why? When you cut a bevel with a perfectly straight blade, you will end up with a convex shape unless you cut it absolutely perfectly. A curved blade cuts a slight hollow, which makes the joining piece seat very nicely. This hollow is especially good where gap-loving epoxy

Search for stock with the tightest, straightest grain. White pine works better for thin battens, as Douglas-fir ones tend to break. Eastern spruce tends to have many knots and windy grain and therefore usually doesn't make good battens. Sitka spruce is better, but might be a pricey choice. Some folks like to use maple for very thin battens.

Always make your battens several feet longer than the curves they will define, so you can "spring" them in position. If you need battens longer than your stock, scarf them as you would rails and gunwales (see Chapter 8, "'Outbone' and Rails, Then Off the Jig").

Cutting and finishing

Generally, you want the grain to run parallel to the batten's widest side. With the thin edge up, these battens will bend in the tighter curves. Battens that will be used flat for cutting guides should have the grain oriented the same way, as the nails will be much less likely to split the wood.

Battens must be cut to the same thickness and width so they bend consistently. Cut a batten off each edge of the board a little too wide, set the fence for finish width, and trim off the factory edges. Cut the rest of the battens by flipping the stock to make cuts from alternate sides. This helps keep the moisture content the same on the edges, which helps keep the stock from warping as you saw.

Cut the battens for lofting and parts-making a little oversize, as you'll be planing them smooth.

Finishing lofting and parts-making battens. The faces of battens destined for lofting and parts-making must be smooth and free of machine marks. If yours don't qualify, clean them up. If your planer has sharp blades and cuts very smoothly, take a light cut off each face. Otherwise, remove the machine marks with a sharp hand plane or a belt sander outfitted with a fine belt, sanding several at a time to keep the sander flat.

Parts-making battens can have small, shallow saw marks, but lofting battens must be planed perfectly smooth.

Finishing plank-clamping battens. The clamping battens can be used straight from the table saw as long as all the faces are reasonably smooth and the thickness consistent. Make spares. They occasionally break under pressure when asked to hold difficult curves, livening up the shop and alarming innocent passersby. Label them with a pyramid pointing forward. When you re-use the battens, knowing which end was at the bow will be helpful, as the batten will be familiar with the greater curve at that end of the boat.

Wax the bottom and sides of the battens with paste wax. Do it now before you forget. Everyone who sees our jig system for the first time worries a little bit about gluing the battens to the boat. Wax now and worry no more.

KEEPING AN EDGE ON YOUR TOOLS

When it comes to tools for sharpening, there is a staggering and baffling array of choices. One quality tool company devotes ten pages of precious catalog real estate to devices for sharpening, from stones of all kinds to various "sharpening systems." When John teaches sharpening to

is involved. The amount of curve is typically between $\frac{1}{32}$" and $\frac{1}{16}$", depending on the width of the blade.

You will often need to plane to a precise angle. Epoxy doesn't mind a gap, but your boat will go together much better if your angles are as close as possible. With a curved blade in the plane, the middle of the plane will remove more wood than the edges. Center the blade over the area of a high spot on a bevel you want to trim, and the edge of the plane blade will ride on the wood and not cut anything. This is much easier than trying to hold the plane at a precise, and often changing, angle.

John does not grind a curve in the blades of the following tools: chisels narrower than ¾", rabbet planes, curved spokeshaves, gouges.

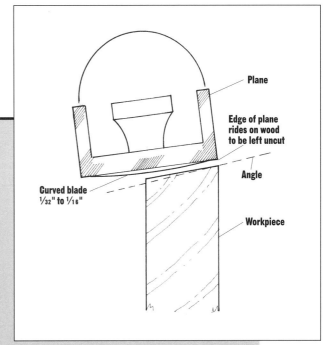

Fig 2.3 A curved blade aids precision when cutting a bevel.

Labels in figure: Plane; Edge of plane rides on wood to be left uncut; Angle; Workpiece; Curved blade $\frac{1}{32}$" to $\frac{1}{16}$"

his classes, he invariably hears a chorus of "Have you tried...?", "Have you used...?". The answer is no; John has been sharpening tools in about the same way since he was ten, using a method his grandfather taught him. There are probably about as many good sharpening methods out there as there are decent materials and tools with which to sharpen—and an abundance of fine instruction manuals devoted to both. John's approach is very simple, inexpensive, and effective. No matter what sharpening method you choose, take the time to keep your tools sharp. It will make all the difference in the enjoyment and quality of your work.

There are two steps to sharpening. You must grind the blade to the proper angle (typically 23 degrees), then hone it to actually sharpen it until it cuts as you wish. For grinding, you will need a slowspeed grinding wheel. John has used a simple hand-cranked bench grinder for years. It takes a certain knack to turn the handle with one hand while holding the blade properly with the other, but it never burns a blade and doesn't demand much bench space.

If your blade has a nick in it or you have honed it out of square, grind the edge back until the nick disappears or the edge is square—you will often need to do both at the same time. John also likes to grind a shallow curve in nearly all of his plane blades and chisels (see box pp. 34–35). Hold the blade square to the wheel while shaping it, then grind the bevel until sharp.

For honing, John has two stones, a commonly available carborundum with medium grit and coarse (which is rarely of use); and an Arkansas stone with medium and fine sides. Light oil or kerosene on the stones helps them cut quicker. He hand-holds the blade at the proper angle (typically 30 degrees). The metal filings become suspended in the oil, which can be cleaned up with a paper towel to keep the stone from clogging. Strop the blade when done; the best strop in the world is your flat palm (be careful).

Protecting Thyself

The equipment necessary to protect the body while building a boat is a necessary, if not always fun, part of the shop. Glued-lapstrake boatbuilding is a much less noxious enterprise than some forms of boatbuilding, but it still requires care and a little investment in good safety gear and practices.

MASKS AND RESPIRATORS

Wearing a respirator isn't especially fun, but it has to be done, so it's worth testing a few different designs to find the ones that fit well.

Disposable masks, for dust

Forget the cheap, single-elastic, disposable, "nuisance" masks that you can find in any hardware store. They are

useless. Better disposable masks have two substantial elastics to hold the mask tightly against the face and a bendable metal noseclip that allows you to seal the mask around your nose. If you get too hot and damp under the mask or keep fogging your glasses, several companies make good disposable masks with exhaust valves. Most marine suppliers carry at least a basic two-strap mask.

Light respirator, for dust

If you have a face smaller or larger than the generic "American male," you may get a better fit by buying a lightweight rubber or silicone face piece and fitting it with simple dust filters. Ruth finally gave up trying to make the disposables fit her "American female" face and bought one of these respirators, size small.

Although it seems like the rubber faceplate would be hotter than the disposable material, it's not, because these masks are true respirators with inhale and exhale ports that allow ample air exchange. A good deal of moisture in your breath is exhausted, keeping your face cooler and your eyeglasses clear. The disposable particle filters also last much longer, as they don't become soaked with your clammy breath.

Cartridge respirators, for fumes

Shop carefully for one of these. Your respirator comes between your brain cells and whatever noxious material you must use, and if it doesn't fit tightly, forbidding unauthorized entry by the ambient air, it's worthless. If it's not comfortable, you won't wear it. The faceplate should be soft and seal on the face well. The cartridge filters must be placed so that they're reasonably unobtrusive and out of the way.

We use this type of respirator only for the vapors emitted by epoxy, paints, and varnishes. We should probably wear ours more often for epoxy work, but we strive to keep the amount of epoxy in use at any time to the bare minimum and keep the shop well-ventilated. We definitely wear a respirator on those extremely rare occasions when we coat a large surface, such as a bottom or bulkheads, with epoxy.

Check with your supplier to be sure that you're getting the proper cartridge for the material you plan to use.

Follow the manufacturer's instructions about proper wearing technique, but these general rules should help:
1. Put the facepiece on and tighten the straps. Exhale and inhale energetically, checking to see if air is leaking anywhere around the edges of the facepiece. Adjust the straps and facepiece until the leaking stops. Alternately, check the mask by placing your hand over the exhaust valve—to keep air from exhausting—and exhaling to pressurize the mask. Any leaks will be obvious immediately.

2. If you can smell or otherwise sense anything but the inside of the respirator, it's not working. Check for leaks. If there are none, it's time to replace the cartridges.

3. Store the respirator and spare opened cartridges in a sealed plastic bag. The cartridges keep working even if you're not wearing them.

Full-face respirators

If you have abundant facial hair, a half-face mask respirator probably will not seal well enough. You are a candidate for a full-face, positive-flow respirator. We've also seen a minimalist respirator rig, apparently designed by a bearded scuba enthusiast and woodworker. It consists of a mouthpiece and nose clamp, which might take some getting used to.

HAND PROTECTION

Working clean is the best hand protection. The less noxious stuff you slop around, the smaller the problem altogether. However, there are times when it's smarter to wear some kind of gloves or employ other hand protection.

Latex surgical gloves

We use these for messy jobs involving epoxy, other glues, varnish, and paint. Though not solvent-proof, these gloves will keep your hands free of most goos. Make sure you remove all the talc before wearing them for painting or varnishing.

Vinyl gloves

These reasonably inexpensive, thin, green gloves available from epoxy suppliers fit well and are tougher than the surgical gloves. We use them often.

Chemical-resistant gloves

These are essential for cleaning brushes in paint thinner or dealing in any way with evil chemicals like acetone. Read the gloves' label carefully; make sure that the ones you choose are made of material resistant to the chemicals you plan to use.

Barrier cream

This hand lotion-like material is simple to use and very effective. It is better than gloves for many delicate but epoxy-rich jobs. Wash and dry your hands, then carefully apply the cream to all of the nooks and crannies of your hands. Remove with shop hand-cleaner. Wash and dry your hands, then re-apply the cream if necessary.

Green mesh tape for fingers

You can tell when it's spring varnishing season in the local boatyards, because a bunch of people suddenly sprout green or blue fingertips. They're wearing ¾″ self-adhesive mesh tape carefully wrapped around their tender digits to keep from sanding their fingerprints off.

This tape has appeared in woodworking catalogs as "high-friction guard tape."

EYE AND EAR PROTECTION
Safety glasses

A pair of good, comfortable safety glasses with clear lenses and side shields should be worn whenever you're around things that you do not ever want to find in your eyes. Because we both wear eyeglasses, we are more lax about this than we should be. Safety glasses that go over prescription glasses are available. We should wear them, and so should you.

Hearing protectors

What's that you say? If there's anything people seem to hate wearing as much as a respirator, it's ear protectors. We prefer the earmuff type, because we are constantly taking them on and off. Buy good ones that are comfortable and fit well.

Wear them. You'll not only protect your hearing, but you won't be as distracted while you're working with loud, potentially dangerous machinery, and you'll be a lot less tired at the end of the day. (Loud nasty noise is not good for the human system, and it always feels as if your body spent the whole day trying to escape from the obvious threat posed by these helpful tools.) Good hearing protection makes the work bearable.

Avoiding bodily injury

Many of the following suggestions will be things you've heard before. Oh, we knew this stuff too. So did all of the other people we know who also have spent some quality time in the emergency room.

(What has happened to us? John managed to feed a table saw a fingertip by ignoring a little inner voice that said, "I don't like doing this the way he asked me to…" Ruth has stayed away from all power tools with whirring, sharp blades, but managed to drive a 2″-long sapele splinter into the ball of her thumb by hurrying too much with the tack rag.)

• Pay attention, eliminate distractions, and don't zone out on standard safety procedures. (We won't ruin your lunch with dozens of horror stories but will point out that a woodworker of our acquaintance achieved a hand with considerably shorter fingers by ignoring the basics: While working in a noisy commercial shop, he absentmindedly reached into a large planer to clear some chips, thinking it wasn't running; it was.)

• Learn how to use your tools.

• Use the right tool for the job.

• Take the time to set up the tool properly, make jigs, or do whatever it takes to do the job safely. It's going to take a lot longer to build the boat "singlehanded."

• Don't work when you're tired, angry, or just plain sick of the project.

- Don't rush. This includes spending time thinking out your moves in advance.
- Clean up, often, and don't forget the floor.
- Be humble. We can all learn how to work more safely and better with tools. Carefully watch others with more experience. (And critically, for they likely have some bad habits as well.) Take a class, not just in boatbuilding but in the woodworking skills you would like to gain.

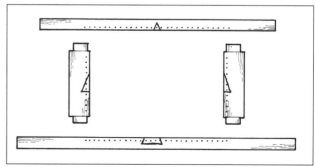
Locating the center with a compass.

Chapter 3

Some Very Useful Techniques

MEASURING AND MARKING
The builder's pyramid

Throughout a boatbuilding project, you will need to label the orientation of the pieces and parts: what's up, which way is forward, how do two, three, or four pieces go next to each other, which face is the good one. The most powerful tool for the job is a simple triangle borrowed from furniture makers, who call it a builder's pyramid.

You will recognize and understand a triangle much more quickly than numbers or letters. Try a little experiment: Take four pieces of wood. On one side of each piece, label it with a consecutive number or letter (A,B,C,D or 1,2,3,4). On the other side, draw the portions of a triangle as shown in the figure. Now orient the pieces to each other, first using the numbers or letters, then flipping them over and using the triangle. You'll find the triangle is not only faster, you also can't switch pieces on opposite sides, or flip the pieces end for end, as you can with the numbers and letters.

Our brains want to aim the pointed end in definite directions: up or forward. Early on, John tried using the

pyramid on the planks by drawing them with the point toward the sheer. On an upside-down hull this meant it was also pointing toward the floor. The resulting confusion and urge to turn the plank over was almost overwhelming. He quickly changed to drawing the triangles pointing toward the ceiling.

Fig 3.1 Drawing portions of a triangle, the builder's pyramid, on the pieces of a seat frame makes assembling them in the wrong orientation impossible.

Staying centered

There will be many, many times that you will need to mark the middle of a part. If you try to measure the width or length or thickness of the piece, then work the math to divide it in half, you will find the mental gymnastics time consuming, and the mark will usually be a little off center.

A quicker and more accurate method is to measure an equal distance from each side or end to find the middle.

To locate the middle of a length or width of a part, say a thwart, use a tape measure or try-square to lay out an equal distance from each end. Work to the nearest quarter- or half-inch increment, making it an easy job to find the precise center between the two closely spaced marks.

To accurately mark the middle of the thickness of a part, use a try-square or a marking gauge. Set the tool a little shy of the middle and then make two parallel pencil lines or score lines. Aligning another part's center mark or resawing between two closely spaced (about $1/16''$ is good) lines is easier than trying to accurately position or cut on one fat centerline.

A quick way to mark the center of the thickness or narrow width of a part is with a pencil compass set to roughly halfway. Drag the pointer along the edge of the part as the pencil draws a line, then flip the compass and mark a second line from the opposite edge.

Occasionally, you need to mark a centerline on a part with no straight edges. Set a compass *larger* than half the distance of the dimension you are bisecting. Draw the arcs drawn from each end or side. Line up a ruler at the points where the arcs cross to draw a square centerline.

Parallel body parts

There are many times when you need to draw a quick line parallel to an edge or an end. A compass works well for this, but there's no need to go digging for a tool; grasp a pencil in the usual writing position with your thumb, pointer finger, and middle finger, then use your ring finger (for small distances) or your pinky finger (for larger distances) as a guide along the edge of the part as you draw the line. Lock your hand and mark from both sides to mark a surprisingly accurate centerline on the edge or narrow width of a part.

For very small distances, about $1/4''$, use your middle finger as the guide as it holds the pencil. Move the pencil up or down in your fingers to change the distance from the edge you are gauging from.

USING BATTENS TO DEFINE CURVES

The fact that boats are made of curves frightens many away from ever building one, but once you've practiced using a batten a few times, you will find that drawing a curve is nearly as easy as drawing a long straight line.

The keys to drawing curves are good battens (see "Making Battens," in Chapter 2) and learning to see a fair curve. Seeing a fair curve is an acquired skill, but it isn't particularly magical—John's hull-building students are proficient at it by the second day of planking.

Drawing a fair curve

1. Lay out the points of the curve on your material. Your points may be spiled or scribed from the boat or laid out on a grid from measurements such as the offsets from your plans.
2. Drive a 3d or 4d smooth finish nail (for small boats) at each point along the curve.
3. Select a batten that is longer than your curve. Battens are usually rectangular in section; the thickness and width of the batten will vary depending on the amount of curve. You want a batten that comfortably goes around the nails. One that is too limber will be difficult to fair, one that is too stiff puts undo strain on the nails and can even break. Most often, battens are used on edge, but they can also be used flat if you need the batten to be stiffer.
4. Place the batten alongside a nail on the outside of the curve near the middle of the curve. Drive a nail to hold the batten against the first nail.
5. Bend the batten around the rest of the nails on the points of the curve, holding the batten in place with a nail opposite the last point on each end of the curve. (For the moment, ignore whether the batten is touching all the nails or not.)
6. Between the last two nails at each end of the curve, the batten straightens out because there is no point—and no nail—to hold it in a curve. Correct this by springing the end of the batten:
   - Pull on the batten near the end until there is enough curve to cause the batten to start moving away from the second nail from the end.
   - Relax the curve enough so that the batten goes back to just touching the second nail again.
   - Drive a nail where you are pulling on the batten to hold the curve.
   - Repeat on the other end of the curve.
7. Check to see that the batten is touching all the other nails along the curve. If it is and the batten looks fair from each end of the curve (see box), mark along the batten between the nails. Hold the batten down firmly as you draw so the pencil won't push it away from the nails.

Of course, oftentimes the batten doesn't touch all the nails. Pulling one or two nails will frequently let the batten pop against the rest of the nails. If the error at any one point is more than $1/4''$, it is a good idea to fair the error over several points. Before drawing the curve, make sure the entire batten is fair.

The batten often won't touch all the nails where the curve changes from a hard bend to a gentler curve. Drive a few nails to hold the batten to the nails on the

What Is a Fair Curve?

A fair curve is one that is smooth, without hard or flat spots. After you have worked with a batten a few times and find the delight in seeing a fair line, you'll understand why these curves are also called "sweet."

However, a curve that is fair is not necessarily a constant curve, as if it were a portion of a circle. Not only can a curve vary from gentle to sharp, it can also reverse and still be fair. The load waterline of many boats is a typical example; there will be a little hollow at the bow that becomes a gentle convex curve for most of the length of the boat, then it will become a sharper curve at the stern.

A waterline is a good example for understanding a fair curve: it looks good to a boatbuilder because water flows over it best. A flat or hard spot will create eddies that mean extra resistance and a slow boat.

How do you see a fair curve? The time-honored method is to stand or kneel at one end of the batten and lower your head until your eye is just a little above the level of the batten. Looking at the batten this way foreshortens the curve and makes unfair portions more obvious.

Walk to the other end of the batten and look again. Now go to the middle of a batten and peer toward one end, then the other.

But don't limit yourself, especially if you are lofting. Walk around to look at the batten from a variety of angles. Climb up on a stepladder or the workbench to look at the curve from above. If you are lining off a set of molds and backbone for planks (see Chapter 6, "The Backbone, and Lining Off"), you will have a better time seeing fair curves if you stand bent over at the waist so you can look at the run of the battens with your head upside down, just like the hull.

As you look at a batten, you may see where it appears to kink at a nail. This is a hard spot. Pull the nail to see the batten relax back to fair. At other times you will see where a nail appears to squash a portion of the curve, forming a section that looks straighter than the rest of the curve. This is a flat spot. Pull the nail to see the batten pop out to a fair curve.

points, then look carefully to see that the curve is fair.

If you are having a great deal of trouble getting a fair curve, double-check the measurements: it is easy to misread a ruler or make a mistake transferring points. (If you are lofting and took the time to make lofting staffs, this is one place where you will be overjoyed you did.)

Holding thin battens

Battens that are less than ¼″ thick are difficult to use with nails. The ideal tool to use with thin battens are lead drafting ducks (spline weights). But purchasing these or making your own can be a sizable investment in time and money, especially if you don't plan to loft. Handy "ducks" around the shop include quart cans of paint, jars full of coins or screws, a helper's fingers.

Using parts-making battens

Battens function as guides for tools cutting out the curved shapes of the planks, keels, floorboard planks, spars, and tapered rails as well as for making patterns.

Nails are driven through a parts-making batten to leave the batten's edges clear for the smooth running of a tool guide and to hold the batten firmly in place;

Battens ½″ × ¾″ serve most purposes. They are used flat, the nails spaced no more than 12″ apart. For sharper curves, a ½″ square batten works well. The type and size of nails or brads you use will depend on the tools you will be using.

Start in the middle of the curve and nail the batten at the points you measured or laid out on the lumber or plywood blank for the part. Keep in mind, the batten wants to be nailed to the wood that will become your part, not on the waste. If you are using brads, leave the heads exposed when you first nail the batten in place. You will be pulling some of them to fair the batten.

To spring the ends:
- Pull the second nail from the end just far enough to release the batten.
- Start a nail halfway between the last two nails.
- Pull on the end of the batten until it bends back to the point at the nail you pulled. Drive both nails to hold the curve. If the curve is sharp, you may need another nail driven between the new nail you just drove and the end of the curve.

A parts-making batten is held firmly in place so it can't naturally find a fair curve. As you peer at the batten to look for unfair portions, you also need to determine which nail (or nails) to pull that will allow the batten to find the fair curve.

SAWING OUT PARTS
Trim right on the edge, but no closer

Whatever you do, whether sawing or trimming, don't cut off the punch marks or pencil line that defines the desired edge! Stop before you do.

If you must deviate from the marks, cut outside them. You can always trim off the excess later. Once the marks are gone, you have no idea where in space you are. Are you ¹⁄₃₂″ past the mark—or ½″? It is especially important that crucial parts like the inner stem keep to the original shape as drawn in your plans or lofting. But please remember this admonition when cutting out, trimming, or beveling all parts.

Curvaceous parts

We suggest marking out many curved parts from full-sized patterns with a series of closely spaced punch marks made with an awl, not a continuous line. (For an example, see Photo 6.2 showing an inner stem being bandsawed out, page 81.) When sawing out curved parts like the stem, look at the punch marks coming up, not the blade. Keep sweeping the piece in a curve rather than trying to connect the dots in a series of straight cuts. Doing it this way takes a little practice, but the cut comes out very accurately. Glance at the blade every once in a while to make sure you're cutting just right. Try this technique on a scrap first.

USING PATTERNS

We know. Making patterns when you could be cutting out actual pieces seems like useless extra work, especially if you're planning to build only one boat. But stay with us for a minute.

Many boat parts come in pairs. Making one pattern means that you can produce a couple of identical parts without a second thought. Many other parts, like the mast partner and under-thwart support cleats, exhibit bilateral symmetry. Make your pattern for one half, mark out or shape that side, then flip the pattern over for the other end. But even parts that require a single pattern, such as the rudder and daggerboard, prove easier to make with a pattern.

Patterns give you a chance to experiment, to settle on exactly the right shape or detail before you attack that pricey piece of hardwood. If you don't like your first effort, toss it in the woodstove and cut out another. You don't have to start all over with milling another piece of valuable solid stock (that you may or may not have).

Then there is always the possibility that you or one of your friends might decide to build another boat. Besides, think how spiffy your shop will look with all those boat patterns hanging around.

Making patterns

Three-ply ¼" lauan or birch plywood from the lumberyard is fine for most patterns. It is easy to mark, cut out,

---

Two Sample Patterns

Breasthook. *If you make a single pattern for the entire breasthook, it is easier to get the critical curve on the aft side just right.*

If you aren't sure of your hull's shape, lay out a couple of stations and the stem from the offsets on a piece of scrap plywood. Lay out both sides of the hull and the centerline. Draw in the shape of the breasthook's aft edge.

If you laid out the breasthook on your lofting, you'll need to transfer its shape to a piece of pattern plywood. Lay small-headed (not finish) nails on their sides about ¼" apart along the lines of the breasthook, hull, stem, and centerline, tapping the heads lightly to set them in position. Transfer the "points" by firmly pressing a piece of ¼" plywood on the nail heads. Connect the dots on the straight lines with a ruler. Cut out the shape and clean it up. This method works well for transferring the shapes of other parts, including the molds and stem, from the lofting.

To see if your pattern is perfectly symmetrical:
1. *Bring the centerline down over the edges; flip the pattern and mark the centerline on the back.*
2. *Trace the aft curve on a scrap of plywood and mark the centerline at both ends.*
3. *Flip the pattern. Line up its centerline marks with those on the plywood. In an instant, you'll see where the drawn line and the pattern differ. Trim wherever*

the line disappears under the pattern. As you trim and match, inspect the whole curve. If a hump starts to form at the center, trim it sweet and fair.

If you decided to make a half-pattern, test it by drawing a straight line on the scrap plywood. Line up the centerline edge of the pattern on the line. Trace the pattern, then flip it over and trace again. Does the whole look good? If not, trim until it does.

The flipping method is a good way to check any pattern that must be symmetrical. Tillers and hiking sticks come to mind.

The breasthook pattern normally serves only for tracing. Breasthooks are usually too thick for pattern routing (on our equipment, anyway). But, once you've tried to trim the end-grain of a hardwood like oak or ash, you'll appreciate the fact that you made your decisions about the breasthook's shape on a thin piece of plywood.

Under-thwart support cleat. *Many of our boats' thwarts have cleats underneath for support. These are symmetrical, and therefore you need to make only a half-pattern. These parts don't have to be fancy, but they do offer a nice place to include a nice curve or two.*

This pattern can be used to shape the cleats by pattern-routing. Mark the desired grain direction and router directions on the pattern. (See text.)

---

shape, and clean up. Also, save any sizable scraps from cutting out planks. The marine plywood makes great, durable patterns.

Lay out your patterns on the plywood. Locate the centers of holes to be drilled with a punch mark and label their diameters. For parts that have one or two edges requiring final fitting in the boat, extend the pattern on those edges to provide plenty of extra for trimming later.

Bandsaw the patterns just outside the line. A jigsaw is useful for separating patterns into manageable pieces before bandsawing and can be used to rough out the patterns.

Trim the patterns with a belt sander set on its back. (see "Shape-sanding curved parts," later in this chapter). Sand the edge until about half of the line remains. Finish up by hand with a few strokes of sandpaper over the whole curve. For tight curves, cut a cloth-backed sanding belt into manageable pieces and sand away. The belts are somewhat stiff, which will help you fair out sharp curves. For shallower curves, fold a piece in half. You also can use hand tools to trim and shape the patterns. A spokeshave is particularly handy. Your tools must be sharp or they will chatter.

If your part has holes in it, drill a small hole at each location just big enough for the tip of a centerpunch.

Label the pattern with permanent markers.

PATTERN-ROUTING

If you want to use a router to cut curvaceous pieces, we recommend using ¼" plywood patterns as guides. Doing it this way makes using the router quicker, easier, and safer—and gives results that are accurate and predictable.

It also allows you to make your design decisions ahead of time so that you can concentrate completely on running the router and not be wondering with some small part of your mind about whether that curve would look better if you adjusted that one section a quarter-inch.

Use the pattern to mark out the parts on the machined stock. Saw the part out on the bandsaw, cutting between ¹⁄₁₆" and ⅛" wide of the line.

Attaching the patterns

Attach the plywood pattern to the piece with small brads or heavy-duty double-sided tape. Clearly mark the grain direction on the pattern (see Photo 3.2). Note: During the course of writing this book, John has gone from using only tape, to tape and a brad or two, to only brads. We'll describe both options: you can choose.

With brads. Although small brads leave small holes behind, they can't come unstuck at an inopportune moment. Brads also let you use thicker plywood for the patterns, which provides more bearing surface for the guides on the router blades. Use two brads for small patterns, three or four for larger ones. Use enough brads to hold the pattern reasonably tight to the wood blank.

With double-sided tape. If you use tape, its adhesive needs to be sticky enough to hold the pattern and blank together firmly, but not so tenacious that pulling the pieces apart and cleaning up any remaining adhesive becomes a problem. We use 1" fabric tape procured from a local sailmaker. Woodworking catalogs sell double-sided tape, mainly for lathe work. To ensure that the tape sticks, give the mating surfaces of pattern and part a thorough swipe with an alcohol-dampened rag and let dry. Use plenty of tape: two or three 6" to 8" pieces is about right for most small-boat parts. Stick the tape on the pattern, and pull off the backing just before you're ready to apply it to the part. Positioning the pattern on the part can be tricky. Try tipping the pattern so you can line up its edge with a line on the part, then slowly ease the pattern

3.1 For the first step of pattern-routing, the pattern faces up. The router, in a router table, is fitted with a flush-trimming bit.

3.2 As the part moves against the router bit, the arrows on the pattern show where the bit should start and stop and in which direction the bit should travel to cut with the grain.

down. Give the pattern a good rub to make sure all is well stuck.

Setting up

A simple router table top made of plywood and 2×4s set on a pair of tall sawhorses will suffice. Two routers can be mounted in this top: one with a flush-trimming bit, the other with a pattern bit. With these two bits, you can trim curvy pieces in which the grain changes direction several times. Group the pieces by thickness, as the flush-trimming bit must be adjusted for each.

Always use sharp bits. Life will be safer and a great deal more pleasant if you do. Always wear a dust mask and hearing protection.

First cut: Flush-trimming bit

The first cuts you will make will be on the flush-trimming bit. Because the bearing is above the cutter, the pattern faces up, keeping your direction marks visible.

Make your cuts from left to right, always cutting with the grain. They should start from the top of a "hill" and go to the bottom on the "valley" or off the end. Place the part on the table with the hill near the spinning bit. With your right hand firmly holding the part and acting as a pivot, gently move the part toward the cutter. There will often be a brief moment when the bit will cut and grab the part. Keep a firm grip. Once the a pattern rides against the bearing, all will be reasonably placid. Move the part-pattern sandwich smoothly toward the bottom of the valley. You shouldn't have to push much, but don't go so slowly that you get burn marks. Run each section over the bit twice to make sure the cut perfectly matches the pattern. When you've finished the first cuts, turn off the router.

Second cut: Pattern-cutting bit

The remaining sections will be trimmed with the pattern-cutting bit. We would like to call your attention to the fact that the exposed cutters will be sticking up above your pattern-part sandwich as you trim it with the pattern bit—and to how easy it would be to slip a finger into those hungry knives. It is an excellent idea to make a simple guard to maintain a desirable separation of fingers and cutters (see Photo 3.3).

Flip the pattern-part sandwich over. Trim the uncut sections, cutting from left to right. Make two passes.

Finishing up

Locate any holes to be drilled in the part before you remove the pattern by sticking the centerpunch in each hole in the pattern and tapping with a hammer.

To separate the pattern and part, slip a long pocketknife blade between the two as far as you can, then gently twist the knife, levering the two apart. You'll likely find that the tape holds quite well.

Quick! Somebody stop me before I rout again

The possibilities of what you can cut with this arrangement are endless. With typical home or small shop routers—1½ or 1¾ horsepower—cutting stock over 1″ thick isn't easy, but very few parts are that thick on a small boat. Trimming pieces this way is so versatile that it is remarkably easy to be seized by an idea for a shape of a part, cut out a pattern, and make the part.

LAMINATING

Laminated parts are fascinating and strong: the modern equivalent of natural crooks. There are many parts in a curvy boat that can be laminated. The only limits are your free time and imagination. But remember that a nice touch here and there is much more elegant—in our opinion—than laminating nearly everything just because you can. Also, we suggest reining in any impulses to laminate everything in sight out of contrasting woods. A touch of contrast, perhaps a single edge band carried throughout the boat, can be very attractive. For another interesting and strong effect, make a part mostly of solid wood, then glue several veneers to its curved edge. Knees and breasthooks can both benefit from this treatment. Inner stems also are sometimes done this way. But too many stripes, everywhere, translates to what we call the Breadboard Look and takes attention away from the boat itself.

In the Ellen, only the outer stem is laminated. Our light rowboat designs, the 18′ Peregrine and 16′ Merlin, also have a laminated full-frame amidships and sometimes laminated quarter knees. Your boat's design may specify a laminated inner as well as outer stem, more frames, quarter knees and/or other parts—perhaps a laminated passenger seat frame….

Before you begin

Laminating is one of those jobs that can't be stopped once you've started. Before you start, make sure you're

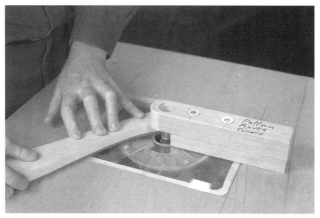

3.3 For the second step of pattern routing turn the part over to put the pattern on the router table and trim the remainder of waste with a pattern bit in the router. The guard keeps slipped or dangling fingers out of the hungry blade.

prepared: Collect all the materials you'll need; attend to essential matters regarding input and output of the digestive tract; and plan on ignoring the phone and the dogs. Don't forget the gloves, and wear clothes that you don't care about or an apron.

Do a dry run first. Better to "waste time" on a dry run than have to redo the whole job, beginning with re-cutting the veneers.

Cutting out the veneers

Cut the veneers long; you'll trim the part to fit later. Make sure that both edges of your blank are straight, so that you can cut veneers from both edges, flipping the blank after each cut. Use a brand-new push stick. Be absolutely certain to push each veneer clear of the saw blade. Making these thin pieces is a little nerve-wracking, but goes well given proper attention and care, especially if the pieces are ⅛" or thicker.

Check to make sure that the grain of all veneers runs in the same direction so you won't get chip-out when you plane the glued-up part.

General gluing procedure

If your part is made of white oak, a resin glue such as Weldwood is best. If it is made of mahogany or ash, epoxy works fine and is easier to use. Resin glue dries surprisingly quickly when rolled out thin. But, it only needs to be applied to one surface. Epoxy must be applied to both mating surfaces.

Using resin glue. Lay five or six veneers flat on a strip of waxed paper on the bench. With a 3″ roller, apply plenty of glue to one side of each veneer and stack them together dry face to wet face. Lay out some more, apply glue, stack, and so on until you have a slithery oozing pile. Don't put glue on the last veneer, or you'll glue the feet of your clamps to the pile. Resin glue requires more clamping pressure than epoxy.

Using epoxy. Take an even number of veneers (say eight), coat one face with epoxy and stack them wet face to wet face in pairs. Apply epoxy to one dry face of each pair. Join one pair's wet face with another for a stack of four. Spread epoxy on one dry face of each quadruplet, and join wet faces for an octuplet. Continue in this manner with the rest of the veneers until you achieve the aforementioned slithery oozing pile.

Goo control. Resin glue doesn't squeeze out a tremendous amount. Given its short open time, it's wise to get all the clamps on (or screws driven) then clean up the excess. Epoxy, on the other hand, squeezes out a surprising amount. If the squeeze-out is allowed to run, it makes an unholy mess, so it's best to deploy a clamp (or screw) or two, clean up the majority of squeeze-out, and so on. Go

Tactical Maneuvers for Laminating

First secure your stack of veneers at whichever end has the sharpest curve so you can use the longer, straighter part as a lever when bending. Trying to force the short end of a stack of veneers over a sharp bend is sheer frustration.

If you're laminating over a form or the adjustable jig, secure one end with a clamp, then bend the veneers generally into place and hold them with a clamp at every third hole or block, applying only light pressure, then put the rest of the clamps on. This approach lets you put most of the clamps on with two hands, which is a lot easier. Tighten the clamps when all are in place.

On the form, you can keep the veneers aligned with your fingers. On the adjustable jig, tap the veneers down with a mallet and wood scrap as you clamp. The screws align the veneers when laminating on the boat.

back and clean up the whole thing again when you've got it firmly clamped.

Clamping to a form

A laminated piece must be clamped over a form while it sets up. You can use a plywood form made to the shape of the part. If your boat needs several laminated parts, or you plan to build several different boats, the adjustable jig will reward the extra effort required to make it. For some parts, such as an outer stem or quarter knees, you may want to use the boat itself as the form. We also have used the jig with attached battens, much as you would the boat itself, to laminate floor frames for a larger boat, such as our Somes Sound 12½.

Springback

When you release your newly cured laminated part from its form, the veneers will do their best to straighten out. The glue will do its job to try and prevent this, but the part will still relax, or spring back, to some extent. Just how much a given part will spring back depends in large part on the number and thickness of the veneers: a piece with a few thick veneers will spring back more than one with many thinner veneers. The stiffness of the wood and the amount of curve in the part also influence the amount of springback. You need to consider the possibilities and make any necessary adjustments for the inevitable when making or setting up your laminating form.

Laminated parts typically spring back only a fraction of an inch. For parts that will be fastened to other parts, like the outer stem, you can pretty much ignore springback because the fastenings will pull the part back into the proper shape. However, for parts such as laminated full frames that will stand alone, you should

3.4 This clamping form for an outer stem is made of two layers of ½" plywood.

arrange the blocks in the adjustable jig or make your form with springback in mind. At the ends of the part, set the blocks or cut the form ¹⁄₁₆" to ¼" inside the line indicated by your plans. Set the blocks or form incrementally closer to the part's designed line as you approach its middle. Experience is the only way to know for sure how much a part will spring back. For an initial guide, the full frames for our Peregrine and Merlin rowboats (with a beam of about 46") come out right when overbent ⅛".

Method 1: Plywood form

(See Photo 3.4 above.) The plywood form needs to be beefy and provide plenty of bearing surface for the veneers to be clamped against so they don't become twisted. For example, a form made from two pieces of ½" or ¾" plywood works well for the Ellen's 1⅛" wide veneers for the outer stem.

Mark the part's curve on one piece of plywood. Also mark key lines, such as the sheer. Glue the two pieces of plywood together.

After the glue dries, bandsaw the curve and clean it up. Cut notches and drill holes for the clamps. Coat the working edge and down the sides a couple of inches with paste wax, or use 2" clear packing tape. Let the wax dry.

Use your dry run to see how many clamps you need and how things will go. Now's the time to find out if you need another clamping notch or hole, or more clamps, or more fingers.

Glue up and clamp. Keep the part centered on the form as you put on clamps so you don't put a twist in it.

Method 2: Adjustable laminating jig

(See Photo 3.5 and Figure 3.2.) John created this clamping jig with adjustable blocks when he needed to make a set of laminated frames for a boat a thousand miles away. He laid the boat's hull molds on a sheet of plywood and positioned blocks around one side of each one, then laminated the frames with veneers that were wide enough for two frames. After the glue dried, John sawed the frames in two and cleaned them up with a planer, then packed

them up for an airplane journey. The frames required minimal fitting, and he came home determined to refine the jig so it could be used for all curved laminated parts.

This jig could also be used for steam-bent parts (see below for instructions on steambending).

The blocks are made of 6" sections of 2×4 with ¾" × 1½" × 10" pieces of pine or spruce glued and nailed to the bottom.

Rip the 2×4s to 3" wide to take the bullnoses off, creating a better gluing surface for the joints on the bases.

Glue and screw or nail the blocks and bases together, noting that one end of the base projects farther than the other. The short end should be just long enough to take a drywall screw, about 1½" long. Trimming the corners of this end will allow closer spacing of the blocks in tight curves.

Drill the long base projection for a screw. Draw a line down on each side of the base, flush with the end of the block. These lines will be used to align the blocks properly.

For parts that are relatively narrow, like the Ellen's outer stem, you will need spacer blocks to raise the part high enough to center the clamps on the strips. The spacers go between the regular blocks, so you'll need as many spacers as you have blocks.

Rub paste wax on the working areas of the blocks and all faces of the spacers. Let dry.

Transfer the curve for the part to be laminated from your plans or lofting to a sheet of plywood with an awl or nails. We use a ¼" piece that stores easily and can be set on a bench, the floor, or other flat surface that doesn't mind having screws driven into it. Connect the punched transfer marks, using a batten and a dark pen.

Lay a sheet of clear plastic over the panel. Line up the lines on the blocks with the curve, setting them about 2" to 3" apart. It's very helpful to locate the edge of a block next to key lines, such as the sheer in the case of the outer stem. Work your way around, lining up the lines

3.5 With a few clamps holding the stack of veneers to the adjustable laminating blocks, a scrap of wood and a hammer are used to align the edges of the veneers.

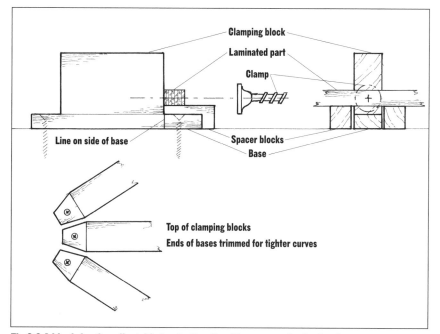

Fig 3.2 A block for the adjustable laminating jig with a spacer for laminating narrow veneers.

on each block with the curved line and driving one screw to hold it in place. Do all of the blocks. Drive the second screw in each block after making sure that each is still lined up with the curve.

Stack the part's veneers for a dry test clamping. Check especially to see whether the clamps' pads are centered in the middle (vertically) of the veneers. If they are not, the wetted-out veneers will be pulled up by the pressure, and the part will wind up twisted and cockeyed. To fix this problem, insert the spacer blocks to raise the veneers.

Now that you've worked out the bugs, glue-up the stack and clamp away.

Method 3: The hull

(See Photo 3.6.) Using the hull as a form has the advantage of eliminating a jig. It's certainly the least work to set up and is a completely reasonable approach if you plan to build only one boat to a design.

Because using a specific part also makes it easier to describe this particular process, we'll discuss this method using the outer stem. It's an ideal candidate for this method.

To prepare the inner stem area, see Chapter 8, "'Outbone' and Rails, Then Off the Jig."

Carefully tape over the inner stem, keelson, and adjacent planking thoroughly, well past the limits of the outer stem, with 2″ clear packing tape. You do not want to glue the outer stem to the boat, at least not at this point.

Assemble your tools and parts nearby. You'll need a good handful of drywall screws long enough to go through all the veneers with plenty of thread left to hold in the inner stem along with a matching number of roughly 2″-square plywood pads (each drilled in the middle for a screw) or fender washers.

Take the stack of outer stem veneers and locate where the stem should end on the keelson from the full-sized pattern or lofting. Always leave extra past the keelson and sheer; you'll trim these off later. Drill a clearance hole through all of the veneers at the keelson end, then drive a drywall screw, with a plywood pad or fender washer under its head, through all the veneers into the keelson, firmly fixing this end to the hull. If the screw drives hard, stop and back out the screw. Drill into the stem with a smaller, tapping drill to make driving the screw easier rather than risk breaking a screw.

Start bending the stack of veneers. You are going to be doing most, if not all, of the bending by hand. When you have bent the stem a comfortable amount (in other words, you can still hold it in place with one hand), drill a clearance hole and drive a drywall screw with its plywood pad. Continue working your way down the stem past the sheer. Use a wooden hand-screw to keep the veneer layers aligned and centered over the inner stem. You also may be able to clamp to the inner stem beyond the sheer, another good reason to start bending at the keelson.

Draw a big fat V with a permanent marker on the one side near one end. This will tell you, once you have the stack smeared with glue, whether any of the veneer strips are flipped or out of order. *Carefully* unfasten the veneers and remove them as one bundle to a flat surface. You do not want to have to shuffle pieces or fiddle with drilling new holes once you've got everything coated with glue.

Apply glue to the veneers and reattach the outer stem. Drive the screws in the same order that you did on the dry run, which should automatically align the veneers.

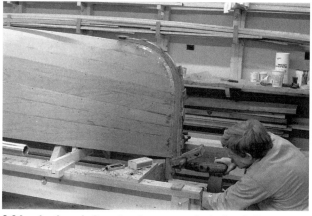

3.6 Laminating a hefty outer stem over a planked-up hull.

Removal, clean-up, and planing to final thickness

Let the part cure for at least 24 hours. Transfer all crucial marks to the part, then free it from the form. Clean up the glue from the form, laminating blocks, or boat, and remove any tape.

Scrape most of the excess glue or epoxy off the laminated piece with a well-sharpened scraper. Hand plane one face flat, making sure that the face is square with the edge that was against the laminating form or jig. The plane also will remove drools of glue that are too big for the scraper.

When the one face is flat, run the part through the planer until it is trimmed down to the desired thickness, starting with the flat face down. Be careful not to catch the curved part on the side of the machine or other obstacles. You can change the angle of the part as it goes through, but be ready to hit the stop button or the clutch if things start looking too hairy, to keep from breaking your part (see Photo 6.11).

If you don't have access to a planer, after one face is flat and cleaned up, mark the final thickness with a marking gauge or try square and knife. If the waste is more than ¼″ thick, cut most of it off on the bandsaw. Finish up by trimming to the score lines on the fore and aft sides, using the same technique you will use to cut the bevel on the inner stem (see Chapter 6, "The Backbone, and Lining Off").

STEAMBENDING

There typically aren't many pieces that require steambending in a glued-lapstrake boat. However, if your plans call for steambent parts, here is an explanation of the general process.

Selecting the wood

We use white oak or ash for steambent parts. Oftentimes, the wood you can acquire easily will be kiln-dried. A piece of this stuff sawed out and popped in the steam box will bend about as willingly as hardened steel, no matter how long you cook it. If you can find someone offering green wood, you'll find that it bends much easier straight out of the saw. However, if kiln-dried is all you can get, submerge the pieces of wood in a tub of water for a day or two. It makes all the difference.

Building a steam box

We don't do a lot of steaming, so our steam box is pretty simple. Plain pine boards screwed together form the basic box. Cut dadoes in all four boards at the back end, and in three boards on the front end with the sliding door. Or, if you prefer, the back could be screwed on and the door attached with hinges and a latch.

Making the box. Before you assemble the box, tack the two sides together. Lay out and drill for the ½″ or ⅝″ dowels that will form the inside racks. Drill for the dowels at the front at least 2″ back from the door. (John didn't and has regretted it ever since.)

Assemble the steam box dry; don't use any glue or caulking. You want the box to leak a little, allowing new steam to enter without building up an exciting amount of pressure. Drill a ½″ hole in the box's bottom to allow former steam to drain away. If you find you are losing more steam than water through this hole, plug it and drill a smaller drain hole.

Cut the rack dowels 1″ or so longer than the width of the box. Push them through the holes and leave them loose so you can remove a row to accommodate thicker pieces.

Cut the door so it slips easily in the dadoes. It, and the box, are going to swell up a fair bit.

Assembling the steam boiler. The time-honored boiler for a small steam box is a *new* 5-gallon gas or kerosene can. It will be a sad, desperate day when all such receptacles are plastic. If you can't hunt down a metal can, a domed teapot with a lid only on the spout will also work.

While you're at the hardware store, buy a length of heat-resistant washing machine hose along with whatever fittings you'll need to attached the hose to your boiler. (If the washing machine hose won't fit, auto parts stores sell heat-resistant radiator hoses that might.) Also buy a brass nipple that fits the hose or the fitting on the hose. If there is a fitting on the hose, get some extra washers for it. Nipples are tapered, and the hose fitting will be tight before the nipple edge seats against the fitting's standard lone washer.

Drill a hole in your box a little smaller than the nipple's diameter and screw the nipple into it.

We normally fire our boiler with a backpacking stove that burns white gas or kerosene. Any stove that will drive a healthy boil safely will do.

3.7 A simple (dare we say "crude") steam box arrangement using a camp stove, a brand new gas can, a length of washing machine hose (propped up so condensing water will drain), and a pine box with dowel shelves.

Steaming the wood

You may want to round up an assistant or two to help during the frenetic moments when the steamed wood comes out of the box. Clamps, quick reflexes, and ingenuity will have to suffice if you're working alone. In any case, plot your moves and make sure everything you will need is set up close at hand—before the pieces are done.

Place the pieces in the steam box, spacing them evenly on the racks.

Starting with boiling water from the kitchen stove speeds things along. You don't necessarily need a lot of water in the steam box's boiler; an inch or two of vigorously boiling water is plenty, so long as you don't let it boil dry. Fill the steam boiler and attach the hose. Fire up the burner. It will take a few minutes for steam to appear in the box.

A useful rule of thumb for steaming: Cook the pieces one hour for every inch of thickness. For an example, it takes about twenty minutes in the steam box to render an Ellen's ⅜" white oak floorboard frames pliable. Pull out a piece and try to bend some curve into it with your gloved hands. If it bends easily, surprisingly so compared to its behavior before steaming, the pieces are ready. Don't cook them for too long—they will heat-harden, and become difficult to bend. Start with the pieces requiring the most gentle curves and finish up with those that survive the toughest curves.

A hot piece of wood is not something to dawdle with. Start bending it in your gloved hands as you stride to the boat or form. Lay the piece in position and clamp in place. If the piece is one, like an outer stem, that will be held to the proper shape after it is permanently fastened in place, simply clamp the piece in place and let it cool. If, like a floorboard frame, it must hold its shape more or less on its own, you must overbend the piece by bending it past the desired curve and holding there for several seconds, then letting it relax into position.

Let the steamed parts set overnight before releasing the clamps or blocks holding them.

STATIONARY SANDING

A handy way to clean up parts—either shaping them or final sanding—is with a belt sander turned on its back and clamped to the workbench. Clamp the handle of the belt sander with wooden hand-screw, and clamp or screw the hand-screw to the bench top. Some belt sanders have an attachment for holding the sander on its back.

Clamp or mount the sander on the corner of the bench so that the front roller is just about even with the edge of the bench. You'll need all the room you can get around that front roller for sanding parts with tight curves.

You'll find the stationary sander great for shaping ¼" patterns—and for final sanding of many parts, after those that need them have received chamfers or bullnoses.

When you start building the interior of the boat, set the sander up again for trimming, shaping, and final sanding of parts, as you fit and cut them to their final shapes. The sander is also indispensable for shaping bronze plate into hardware.

Shape-sanding curved parts

Reasonably tight curves. Smooth out any bumps as much as you can with hand tools. Run the part over the smaller roller, moving a steady speed to take off an even amount. Don't pause or dawdle. By moving quickly, you'll feel any remaining bumps and hollows. Stop and remove the bumps, since the small roller only makes them worse. You should feel the part travel smoothly over the roller as you pass it briskly over the machine.

Shallow curves. For parts that have curves that are too tight to sand on the flat of the sander but too gentle to sand easily on the front roller, make curved pine inserts to fit between the belt and the platen. For a 4x24 machine, two inserts are useful. Both are 6½" long; one is ½" thick, the other ¹³⁄₁₆". With the thicker insert, which gets the most use, the belt just barely slips over the rollers.

Mark the curve you want, saw the insert out on the bandsaw, and clean it up.

3.8 A belt sander positioned on its back on the workbench makes a compact stationary sander.

3.9 A curved insert placed between the belt and the platen helps you to reliably shape curved parts.

Finish up by sanding with a fine grit, then rub a soft pencil over the curve to serve as a lubricant for the belt. Stick the insert to the sander's platen with 1″ double-sided sailmaker's tape. Replace the belt and turn the machine on. Be ready to adjust the tracking knob quickl, and ready to turn the machine off if the belt goes too far sideways. If you can't get the belt to track, your insert may be thicker on one side. Check by tracing around one side on paper or smooth plywood. Flip the insert over, line up the straight baseline, and compare the curves.

FINISHING THE EDGES OF PARTS

You'll want to do something to most of the corners on your boat. Sharp corners look lubberly and are nasty to knock a shin against. They also won't hold paint or varnish. The corner treatments you choose add measurably to the elegance of your boat.

Breaking edges: Simple roundovers

For the simplest corner treatment, take a file or a piece of sanding belt and break the edges, then finish up by hand sanding. On the right boat, or in the right places, this looks surprisingly nice for such a simple job. You'll want to do at least this much to all edges, even those that are not visible, because paint and varnish adhere much better to a rounded edge.

You must break and round over the edges of the planking as well. This is done after the hull is built (see Chapter 8, "'Outbone' and Rails, Then Off the Jig," and Chapter 9, "Building the Interior").

Bullnosed and chamfered edges

On our boats, we stick to simple bullnosed and chamfered edges. More complicated fancy shapes may look great at first, but they often lose their appeal after a few rounds of sanding and finishing. They may hold up acceptably on household furniture or the interiors of larger boats but are not terribly practical for a small open boat. For simpler boats, consider bullnoses; on fancier finer boats, chamfers. How you combine the two, and how big you make them, is a matter of taste.

If you rout the edges, additional shaping by hand—with spokeshave, plane, scraper, rasps, and sandpaper—will eliminate the impersonal machined look. Also, gently round over the sharp edges of chamfers with sandpaper or sanding sponge. This process is a balancing act between maintaining the attractive clean sharpness of a well-executed chamfer and adjusting it slightly to produce edges that will keep paint and varnish past the first week of use. Evenly shape and smooth bullnoses to pleasing contours.

In general, the bigger the chamfer, bullnose, or other corner treatment (keeping things in proportion), the lighter and finer the part will appear. Removing wood from the corners will reduce the boat's weight more than you might think, possibly by several pounds. You'll have

an idea of how much vessel you won't have to lug around when you sweep up the pile of wood chips.

Planing lumber.

Chapter 4

Milling Solid Lumber and Scarfing the Planking Plywood

ORGANIZING THE PROJECT AND ORDERING WOOD

Before we dive into woodworking, we'd like to take a minute or two to offer a few thoughts on how to organize the project, in its entirety or in part, as well as explain how to figure out how much lumber and plywood to order.

For most people, including many professionals, building a boat is a process of making one or two parts at a time, buying only as much wood as you need to build each portion of the boat, such as the backbone (transom, keelson, and inner stem). However, if you would like to organize your boat project in a more comprehensive way, consider the following suggestions based on the methods and systems we have worked out over the years.

The Ellen, the boat we're going to build as our primary example, has more than a hundred pieces. Unless your memory is perfect, lists are the way to go. Later on, after you've cut that expensive 2″ mahogany plank into little pieces, you won't suffer the descending stomach elevator: "Oh @#!, I missed that second inner stem piece…and I'm out of wood!" Not having this experience is worth every second you spend figuring things out and writing them down. If you take a little time to make up a master parts list now,

John's Master Parts List

John sets up his master parts list with the following categories:

Part name.

Number of parts. *Total needed.*

Thickness, rough. *Specified in quarters of an inch, with species.*

Thickness, final. *Planed thickness.*

Width, rough. *Finished width plus extra for milling and machining (e.g., 2¼″ finished should be at least 2½″ rough).*

Width, final. *For only those parts requiring ripping to precise width.*

Length. *Add at least 2″ to the length you take from the drawings or lofting.*

Number of blanks. *The number needed before machining.*

Work notes. *Short notes on the operations required, after milling, to make each final part. It's especially helpful to note resawing requirements here.*

you can order exactly what you need (with plenty of extra added for insurance), and relax.

Making a master parts list

Round up every piece of information you have on the boat: specifications, drawings, lofting, full-size patterns, instruction booklet, notes, sketches. Work at a table large enough to spread out the drawings flat. (Note: If your boat must be lofted, do it before attempting the list.)

Set up the categories for your list. (See box, "John's Master Parts List," for some suggestions.) As you do this, think about other lists you may want later on: stock type (for a lumber order), cutting, ripping, planing, etc. If working with a computer spreadsheet suits you, you may find its ability to sort and re-sort the master parts list very handy.

Begin by going through the specifications and writing down the dimensions and recommended wood species for all parts. Search the drawings and construction booklet (if there is one) to make sure you've found every part. Some plans have the specs right on the drawings so double-checking will be easy, although those specs can tell you only the bare bones of what you need to know about the parts.

Use everything you have to fill in the rest of the list. This means lots of paper shuffling. While making the list, check the accuracy of the plans. Double-check everything. If the specs give a dimension for a part, check the drawing or full-sized pattern. Compare views in the drawings and between the full-sized patterns and the drawings.

It is vastly preferable to find any errors in your plans now, rather than later while you're holding a piece of gorgeous, expensive wood that just proved to be an inch short.

The designer's full-sized patterns or your lofting are likely to offer the most accurate information. The specifications also can be considered very reliable, but watch for typos.

On the other hand, don't expect the scale drawings to offer perfectly reduced renditions. These are illustrations of how to build the boat, and they will not—cannot—scale up accurately. For example, the mere width of a line on the drawing may translate to $\frac{1}{8}$" thick at full size. Paper swells and shrinks as the humidity changes, and this movement is noticeable—on the order of several sixteenths of an inch for a drawing several feet long. Trust the measurements written on the drawings before trusting your ruler.

Don't use the scale drawings to obtain your working measurements unless you have absolutely no choice. Then check your results against known parts of the boat, and give yourself plenty of extra wood.

As you fill in the measurements for the parts, use a scale ruler to determine if the drawing is at least close to the measurement written down or drawn somewhere else. If it's off, decide whether it's close enough or needs

additional head-scratching.

For many parts, you will use the drawings to give you a general idea of how big a part ought to be, within several inches or a foot, as you will be doing the final fitting in the actual boat. No matter how carefully you build your boat, it will not be exactly like the plans.

Don't try to figure out precisely exact measurements and fits now. Plan for plenty of extra; you'll cross-cut accurately and/or trim to fit later.

As you make the master parts list, think about how you will make each part and jot down the major construction steps. You also may want to decide how you will group and make some of the smaller parts so you can determine what size rough blanks are needed.

When the list is finished, and you've ironed out any discrepancies or figured out strategies to work with them later, you are ready to make a cutting list, a stock list, and a lumber order.

The cutting and stock lists

Create a cutting list by sorting the master parts list by rough thickness and species, rough width, and length, in descending order. You may want to sort this list into other useful lists (see box, "John's Milling Lists").

You can condense the cutting list to a working stock list by deleting the "Number of parts," "Thickness, final " and "Width, final" columns.

John's Milling Lists

You can sort and juggle the elements of the cutting list to create other lists that will help you organize the milling of your lumber.

Planing list: Sort the main cutting list for final thickness and rough thickness, in descending order.

Ripping list: Sort the main cutting list for finished widths, in descending order. (There will be parts that do not have finish widths because you will be cutting curves from them. These can be deleted from this list.)

Resawing list: Sort the main cutting list for those parts listing resawing under "Work notes."

The lumber list

First find the obvious boards. For example, the Ellen has a 1" (¼) keelson that is 6" wide and 12' long. This is a nice size to order. After you have written down the larger pieces, you will be left with a bunch of smaller pieces. How do you figure out the boards you need to efficiently get out these pieces? The easiest way is with what we call board diagrams.

John likes to use ¼" graph paper held horizontally and

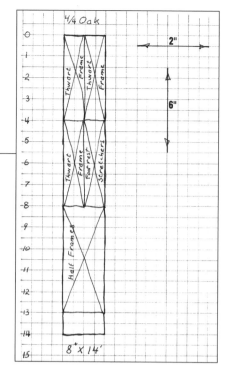

Fig 4.1 Board diagrams help group smaller blanks into boards that a lumber company sells.

set up so that the horizontal squares equal 2″ and the vertical squares equal 6″ so that he can fit 16′ boards on the paper. See the sample diagram, Figure 4.1. If this drives you crazy, keep the vertical and horizontal measurements at equal proportions and find or make larger sheets of graph paper.

Create your boards by adding together pieces from the list. This process takes a certain amount of fiddling, erasing, and caffeine. Give yourself some room to adjust things later on. If the list says 1¾″, draw it as 2″. Leave between 6″ and 1′ at the end of each board as well, as cheap insurance against checks, warping, knots, bad grain, and mistakes. Leave more room to adjust when matching color and grain pattern.

You can use your board diagrams again when you cut the lumber apart, so label them clearly and add helpful notes.

ORDERING YOUR WOOD
Solid lumber

John's lumber ordering list shows the number of pieces, stock type, board width, board length, lumber grade, and millwork to be done by the yard.

When you've finished the board diagrams, collect all the boards together on a final ordering list for the lumberyard. Review and make sure that you've ordered plenty of extra. Condense the list some (and make the yard's job easier) by making identical two boards of the same stock that are close in size.

This brings up an important point. After you have laid out your board diagrams and ordered your lumber, the yard will send you whatever boards it has in stock that are as close as possible to your order. If you order 10-footers and all the yard has is 12-footers, that's what you'll get. John has frequently ordered several 6″ mahogany boards and re-

ceived the equivalent board footage in 12″—or even 18″—boards instead. If you have your lists and board diagrams at hand, you won't be stuck standing in the driveway wondering if what they sent you will work while the driver hands you the bill.

Order the lumber lightly dressed on both sides. The lumberyard crew will run the boards through their huge two-sided planer, removing about 1/16″ on each side, and most (if not all) of the saw marks. This costs a little more per board foot but has several distinct advantages. When the lumber comes off the truck, you can see at a glance if they sent you acceptable boards. When you are ready to lay out your pieces on the wood, you will have a smooth surface to mark on and will be able to see the figure of the wood for pieces where that matters. You can get right to marking and cutting without having to arm wrestle large pieces of lumber through a planer that is usually too light-duty. The yard's planer can plane the boards flatter than a small shop planer. Unless you own or have access to an 8″ or bigger jointer, this will be a big help.

Plywood

Though most of the head-scratching required in ordering your wood involves solid lumber, you will also need to order your plywood, often from a separate supplier.

In the good old days, determining how much planking stock you needed for a small boat was fairly straightforward: if your boat had sixteen planks, then you needed sixteen boards to make them, or eight boards if you were going to resaw them. Our "boards" are uniform manufactured sheets measuring approximately 4′ by 8′. We must determine how many of these sheets we need as well as how to rip, cross-cut, and scarf them into the panels from which planks can be cut.

• Calculate the panel sizes needed for one side of the boat, then double it for both sides. When you make the planks, you'll stack two panels together on the planking

How to Calculate Board Footage

At some point, you may want to figure out board footages for your boat's wood, especially if you would like to know how much it's going to cost. Use the following formula:

$$\frac{\text{thickness} \times \text{width} \times \text{length} \times \text{\# of pcs}}{12 \text{(for lengths in feet)},}$$
$$\text{or } 144 \text{(for lengths in inches)}$$

For example, here's a floorboard frame blank measuring ¾″ × 3½″ × 4′:

$$\frac{1.25 \times 3.5 \times 4 \times 1}{12} = 1.458 \text{ (1.5) board feet}$$

53

What Size Is That Board...Really?

Much of the wood you'll need will come as rough lumber. You can expect the boards to measure close to the size they are reputed to be. A 2 " (¾) by 6 "-wide board should be exactly that—with the following exceptions.

Wood coming from other countries often will be cut to metric dimensions. For example, 1 " (¼) mahogany is often 30mm, or about 1⅛", thick. Many other woods are cut to 25mm, or ¹⁵⁄₁₆ "+. A standard sheet of marine plywood often measures 125 mm by 250, a tiny bit bigger than 4' by 8'.

Rough lumber from other countries or from a local person operating a bandsaw mill can vary quite a bit in thickness due to less-precise sawing.

If you order wood that has been milled in any way, your piece of wood will be smaller than its given dimensions, as anyone who's ever bought a 2×6 from the lumberyard knows. Apply a tape to that particular piece of spruce/fir, and you'll get 1½ " x 5½ ", the lumber's nominal size. So far, so good. But hardwoods usually are planed to order. If you request your wood dressed on two sides, hit or miss, the nominal size will reflect only a decrease in thickness, and this typically will be a lesser amount than that found in softwood lumber like the spruce/fir 2×6. If you order a 2 " (¾) by 6 " white oak board dressed on two sides, it is likely to have a nominal size of about 1⅞' x 6 ", with rough-sawn edges. You also can request that the lumber yard dress four sides if you want the edges straightened.

If you have any doubts about the actual size of the boards you will receive, call the yard and ask. If the person on the other end of the phone is having a bad day and tries to make you feel foolish for asking, let that be his or her problem. Your job is to eliminate nasty surprises when that lumber truck pulls into your yard.

---

table and cut out identical pairs after spiling.

- To determine the total width of the panels, you'll need to measure around the girth of the largest section from the centerline to the sheer, then add at least 30% to 45% to allow for laps and curves.

  We round this number to the nearest 24 " increment because panels this size are much easier to work with than plywood's full width. And we round up: a little extra plywood in the shop is insurance or stock for the next boat, whereas one sheet short means two or three weeks wait and extra handling charges.

- To determine the length of the panels: Measure the length of the longest plank by measuring around the sheer in the plan (top) view—not the profile—of the lines or construction drawing with a flexible ruler or, less elegantly, a tape measure. Match this length to the appropriate scale on a scale ruler to come up with the length on the full-sized boat.

  On most boats, this will tell you all you need to know about the length of the panels: a 15' boat usually needs

two 8' sheets, a 10' boat needs a sheet and a half, an 18' boat will typically need two and half sheets.

For some boats, you may want to do a little more layout work to determine where to crosscut some of the sheets to use the plywood more efficiently. For example, making 14' panels for the 12' Ellen planks could require four sheets of plywood, but if you lay out the panels carefully, the planks can come out of three sheets. Here's how:

1. After measuring for the longest plank, measure for the shortest one, the garboard. Bend the flexible ruler around the curve of the keel on the profile drawing and add for the extra length where the plank will land on the stem and transom.

2. Determine the length of a plank in the middle of the hull by measuring the length around the curve of a diagonal, found on the plan view of the lines drawing (see Figure 1.2, page 7). Make sure the diagonal runs through the stem and the transom. If the diagonal runs through the sheer, the length of the diagonal will be shorter than the length of a plank. The Ellen planks can be cut from two 24 "-wide panels, so you can use a diagonal close to the middle of the girth of the midsection; diagonal 3 works fine.

Figure 4.2 shows how to lay out the various lengths to determine where to make the crosscut. Make one cut in the middle between the layout marks so each panel has a little extra length (if possible).

ORDER OF OPERATIONS

While you wait for the lumber and plywood to arrive, you may want to do a little more paperwork and set down some helpful notes about the order of operations for the whole parts-making process. Figure 4.3 shows John's basic order of operations chart. Use it for inspiration and

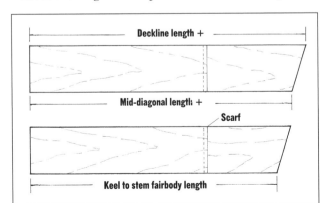

Fig 4.2 Lay out to determine the panel sizes that use the planking plywood efficiently. You'll need to do this only for some designs.

adapt to suit; John makes most boat parts before building a hull, and the chart reflects this.

The chart leads you through the tools in orderly fashion. Note that all the table saw operations are grouped near the beginning of the shaping section, other tools near the end. The belt sander appears earlier than you might think, as it is needed to shape patterns for pattern routing. It and the routers stay set up for final shaping and finishing. (See Chapter 3, "Some Very Useful Techniques.")

A few hints on arriving at the best order of operations:
• Complete necessary gluing operations as soon as possible. For most parts, there are many operations to do after they're glued-up. Gluing-up early lets you group these blanks with the others. Good examples of this are the inner stem and transom. Although epoxy sets up in a few hours, it cures for days or weeks afterward. The longer it has to cure, the stronger it will be. It's especially important to glue-up the planking scarf joints early for this reason. Most gluing jobs require clamps, and there are never enough clamps to do everything at once. Starting early means that all of your pieces will be glued up by the time you're ready for them.
• Resaw early. Because resawing is so similar to machining, it is nice to do it early in the process. When you clean up the big pile of chips and sawdust, you won't

have to do it all over again a little while later.
• Certain parts require doubling back up the operations chart. For example, some floorboards must be shaped and routed as double-thickness blanks, then resawn to make matched pairs.

It's helpful to tack the operations chart to the shop wall. Speaking of which, that's enough paperwork. Your lumber and plywood are out there, in the shop, waiting. It's time to start turning that wood into a boat.

Making Solid-Wood Blanks and Scarfing Plywood

Collect your plans and working lists, along with board diagrams if you have them. Find your hearing protectors, safety glasses, and dust mask. Solid wood should be cut into pieces of manageable size, and the plywood must be scarfed together to make pieces that are long enough for the planks. Though the first involves cutting pieces apart and the latter gluing pieces together, both operations result in "blanks" that are ready for their parts to be laid out.

In small shops such as ours, it often works best to reduce the solid lumber to smaller blanks, then scarf the

Fig 4.3 Solid-Wood Parts-Making Operations Chart
(Note: The plywood planking stock has its own operations chart and is not included here.)

MILLING	TOOLS
Lay out pieces, crosscut, and rough-rip long	Jigsaw, circular saw
Rough rip, short	Bandsaw
Plane blanks	Planer
Straighten edges, rip	Table saw (jointer)

SHAPING	TOOLS
Resaw	Bandsaw, planer (table saw)
Joints: those needing gluing early	Appropriate tools: table saw, routers, drill press, jointer, hand tools
Glue	Clamps
Ripping operations: bevels, dadoes	Table saw
Crosscut parts	Table saw
Oddities: Individual & special	Table saw, and other tools as required
Long curve, rip: Lay out, nail on batten, saw out	Table saw w/jig (jigsaw and hand tools)
Pattern rout: Make patterns, mark, bandsaw, flush trim, pattern trim	Bandsaw (jigsaw), belt sander, router(s)
Drill: Mark, punch, drill, countersink	Drill press (portable drill)
Hand work: Lay out, mark, bandsaw, clean up, bevel	Bandsaw, chisels, planes, spokeshaves, etc.
Shape sanding	Belt sander, clamped to bench

FINAL SHAPING AND EARLY FINISHING	TOOLS
Shape: round, bullnose, chamfer	Hand tools; router(s)

(Note: Some parts must have their edges routed then receive final trimming, dadoes, rabbets, additional shaping, or resawing.)

Final cleanup	Belt, random orbital & vibrator sanders; hand scrape & sand
Prime when possible	Clear sealer or primer

plywood planking stock, which takes up a fair amount of precious horizontal bench real estate, so we'll talk about things in that order. Also, as we noted in the section on organizing the project, John prefers to turn rough lumber into blanks, then into parts, before filling up the shop with a hull. Adapt all or part of our recommendations concerning the order of operations for working up solid wood to suit your project and work style.

MILLING SOLID LUMBER
Laying out

Lay out the pieces on the boards. Avoid knots; they are unsightly, weak, and hard to cut, especially with hand tools. Remember to lay out pieces with the proper grain orientation. Choose straight, clear wood for blanks to be made into thin strips for laminates.

Use straightedges and squares for short straight lines. To mark long straight lines, drive a nail at each end of the line, stretch a string taut between, then make small pencil marks alongside the string. Remove the string and connect the pencil marks with a straightedge.

Mark crosscuts with square. Although using a square against the rough edge of a board isn't terribly accurate, it is good enough at this point, as each piece should be several inches longer than it has to be and will be cross-cut accurately later, if need be.

Check off each piece on the list as you mark it on the board, and write the part's name on the blank. Make sure that you are happy with the grain pattern and direction. If you need to change something, remove the pencil marks with a scraper.

Cutting out

In our small shop, it is definitely preferable to move relatively light tools over heavy pieces of wood rather than struggle with running heavy planks through heavy machinery.

The sequence of roughing out the blanks goes like this:
- Make the crosscuts that span the entire width of the plank, using a jigsaw or handsaw. A circular saw tends to make splintery crosscuts. (Note: Mill the board for the transom intact and crosscut after planing.)
- Make the long ripping cuts with a circular saw and straightedges. Run the narrow side of the saw's base plate against the straightedge so that you can easily see that the base is against the straightedge, and also so that the nails holding the straightedge in place won't interfere with the saw. On narrow boards, nailing on a straightedge for the wider part of the saw base may be impossible. If you have to saw the edge of a plank to make it straight, rest the wider part of the saw base on a second plank of the same thickness.
- Crosscut those newly ripped pieces that require it.
- Collect the short pieces that need further ripping. Cut

these short rips on the bandsaw. In a boat, many pieces are curved and therefore don't need to have an edge jointed and be ripped to a precise width on the table saw; the bandsaw cut is fine. Those pieces that do need to be accurately ripped are easier to joint as small pieces and will be more accurate because all of the internal stresses in the wood will have worked themselves out by the time you are ready to make accurate cuts. This is also why the bandsaw is safer; you don't have to worry about a warping piece pinching the blade and becoming a missile.

You can cut the short rips now, or you can go through all of the boards and cut a big stack of them later.

You could make these rip cuts with a circular saw. If you do, make them when the pieces are as big as possible so there is plenty to clamp and hang onto. A jigsaw will work, slowly, but it's hard on the tool.
- Label both ends of each blank with a permanent marker and note the label on the cutting list. Choose a label that will still make sense after its trips through the planer and other machines.

Machining

Next, the rough blanks must be machined to their finished sizes—ready to be shaped into boat parts. How you proceed depends on your tools.

In the dream shop scenario, there is plenty of room for large, well-maintained tools, including a wide-bed jointer. Separate your pieces into those that must eventually be accurately ripped and those that won't. Those that won't be ripped only need one face jointed to make it flat. For those that will be ripped, joint a face and one edge. In either case, mark the surfaces that have been jointed.

If you only have a small jointer, you can flatten the

4.1 Plywood straight-edges guide a circular saw to true-up the edge of a large plank.

larger pieces with hand planes. This is enjoyable, challenging work. Check your progress with a straightedge laid fore, aft, athwartships, *and* diagonally across the piece. You will straighten the edges with a straightedge on the table saw after planing the pieces to the proper thickness.

Small pieces with only a small curve in them can be pretty well flattened by running them through the planer by making the first pass with the concave side down, against the table.

Planing

Stack the boards by final thickness. (Keep in mind those parts that will be resawn and planed to final thickness afterward.) Label the stacks with the thicknesses written on 3″ x 5″ cards in large, friendly letters. Organize your stack, remembering that the boards should be run through with the flattened side down and the grain running properly to avoid chip-out. Starting with the thickest stock, work systematically from the thickest pieces to the thinnest. Keep the sorted pieces together, along with their label.

Depending upon atmospheric conditions, a piece of wood is usually wetter or drier in the middle than on its faces. After laboriously flattening your blanks, you want to keep them that way. To accomplish this, you need to have the moisture content on both faces the same. After each pass through the planer, flip the board end for end so that the next pass will cut wood from the opposite side, and keep the grain headed in a favorable direction. If the pieces of a particular stack are small, you can get the rush of high productivity by flipping the whole stack.

As much as possible, try to plane the pieces down in one session, taking a half turn on the crank (⅛″ on our shop's planer) after each pass and running all the pieces that need that particular cut through, take another half-turn, run pieces through, and so on. After each cut, you will often have one stack that is at its finished thickness and another stack that is ready to be started with its first pass.

Long pieces are the only difficulty in this approach. In our small shop, it is just plain awkward running long and short pieces together, so they are done separately.

After the blank has been planed, it's wise to write the name of the part on the face of the blank with a soft, dark, number 1 pencil. If you're ripping several parts out of a blank, write the name of each. You'll take the pencil marks off when you scrape and sand the part, which should be recognizable by then.

Ripping

Collect the blanks that need to be ripped. Up-ending boards to read them while ripping at the table saw is not good, so double-check for clear labels on the faces of all planed blanks. If you had access to a jointer earlier, you are ready to start ripping.

If you don't have a jointer, you must straighten an edge. To straighten an edge on the table saw, nail on a straightedge so that it slightly overhangs the board edge not to be cut, and parallel to the edge to be cut. The overhanging edge of the straightedge rides against the saw's fence. Measure the width from the straightedge's "fence" edge to the exposed edge of the board and set up the fence for a cut of ⅛″ or so. Run the piece through to rip the exposed edge. Remove the straightedge.

Turn the board around so the freshly cut edge rides against the fence. Set the fence for the final width (from the ripping list), then run the piece through again. Keep a collection of plywood straightedges near the table saw so you can match one closely to the length of the piece you're about to cut.

You also can straighten edges with a hand plane, though it is time-consuming, if skill-enhancing, work.

Crosscutting

Some pieces need to be crosscut to precise lengths, but many won't, as we are building a curved object. Accurate crosscutting comes a bit later.

Resawing

There are often a number of pieces that need to be resawn before they are shaped in any manner. Other parts will be shaped first, then resawn. Sort out the parts that need resawing before shaping. Most parts will be split in half on the bandsaw and planed to final thickness. (See Photo 8.2, page 147, for a jig for resawing wide pieces.) Others, such as the veneers for a laminated outer stem or midship frame, can be ripped on the table saw. Floorboard frames can be resawed on either the table saw or the bandsaw.

You'll note that when you resaw pieces on the bandsaw that the two pieces often will curl away from each other, in response to differing face and interior moisture levels. Set the pieces on edge with a little space between them so air can flow through. Let the pieces stabilize for awhile, flatten them as best you can, and then run them through the planer to the finished thickness.

A blank resawn into thin strips on the table saw can warp similarly, particularly if you keep cutting on the same side. The edge you are cutting becomes proportionally wetter (or drier) than the edge away from the fence. To help prevent this, flip the piece after each cut and run the opposite edge against the fence. Keep flipping and cutting evenly toward the middle so that the moisture content of the edges stays about the same—and the piece, we hope, stays straight. This depends on the grain, so check again for desirable straight grain and unwanted knots.

As the dust settles

Now you have a shop stacked full of blanks. Some visitors will glance at the lovely piles and ask when you're going start building your boat. Never mind—you know better. The worst of the grunt work is done and it's on to

57

the fun stuff, making the jig, molds, and recognizable parts for your boat. But first, attend to the planking plywood so its scarf joints can cure.

SCARFING THE PLYWOOD PLANKING STOCK

The scarf joint for gluing is a long, angled cut that gives a maximum amount of gluing area and is fairly easy to make. The epoxy keeps the feather edges from lifting, breaking, and possibly pulling the whole joint apart.

John prefers a 6:1 scarf for the thin marine plywood we use on the boats. When he built his first glued-lapstrake boat, he started out with 10:1 scarf joints in the ¼″ planking. The joints were about 2½″ long. Back then, he scarfed each plank individually on the bench. When he bent the first planks over the molds, the scarf joints produced very noticeable flat spots several inches long. So he tried an 8:1 scarf; still a flat spot. On to 6:1; just right.

Preparing the plywood

It is best to scarf the plywood planking stock all at once on the bench. For easier handling and planing, pile all the sheets on a couple of sawhorses and rip them in half lengthwise with a circular saw. Unless your boat's longest planks are nearly 16′ long, you'll probably want to cut half of the sheets shorter so that your planking stock will end up comfortably longer than your longest planks and no more.

(Note: If you skipped the section on ordering plywood in the previous chapter, you may want to take a quick look back for specific information on how to figure out panel sizes.)

A circular saw will make quick work of crosscutting those sheets to the proper length but can also make quite a mess in chip-out. Score the top sheet with a utility knife to reduce chip-out, or use a jigsaw or hand saw instead.

If you plan to varnish some or all of the planking, match the grain of the panels. Set the panels on edge, leaning them up against stationary tools, horses, lumber rack, garbage cans, etc. Shuffle and flip them until you've found the best-looking mated pairs. Label each pair with a big pyramid and a letter of the alphabet (to avoid confusion later with plank numbers).

Sapele plywood often exhibits a contrasty, fairly wild grain pattern characteristic of rotary-cut veneers. It does vary, though, and you can usually find a few sheets with a finer, muted grain pattern. It's worth reserving these sheets for a varnished sheerstrake, or most of the topside planks, if you're lucky and have enough. We tend to feel that a little varnished plywood planking is best—perhaps a varnished sheerstrake, outside or in, or varnished topsides between a painted sheerstrake and painted bottom. But it's strictly a matter of taste.

If the boat is to be painted, you don't have to worry about grain at all. Of course, if you think you might have second thoughts about varnishing that sheerstrake, you will want to match up the best couple of sheets just in case.

4.2 All the plywood for the planking nailed to a bench with the edges staggered, ready for the scarf joints to be cut.

4.3 Lightly waxing the sole of the plane makes cutting the scarfs easier, especially as the blade dulls from cutting the hard glue in the plywood.

Planing the scarf joint

You'll need a solid work surface—a bench or a ¾″ plywood panel set up on horses—that has a sharply cut square edge. Stack all the plywood sheets with their factory edges aimed toward the square edge of the work surface.

Setting up the panels. Set a try-square for the width of the scarf: 6mm = 1½″, 5mm = 1¼″, 4mm = 1″, and 9mm = 2¼″.

Working from the factory edge, score the length of the scarf on each sheet with a utility knife. Press hard enough to make the line clearly visible, but don't cut through first veneer.

For boats over about 15′ long, you'll need to add additional panels with a second scarf joint. You can glue up the second joint after doing the first, but score all the joints at once.

Place one panel on the bench, and line up one corner of its factory edge with the edge of the bench. Drive a single 1″ brad slightly back from the scored line. Swing the back end of the panel until the remainder of the working edge lines up perfectly with the bench edge. If you are working by yourself, moving the panel minute amounts can be tough. Try flapping the panel like a sheet while gently pushing or pulling. The cushion of air supports the panel for a brief moment and allows you to position it very accurately. Once it's there, drive a brad on this side, once again back behind the scored line.

Place the next panel on top, line up its factory edge with the first panel's scored line, and nail it in place. Repeat the process for the remaining panels. Drive a third brad near the middle in every third panel to keep the center of the panels flat.

Accuracy matters. That is why you scored the joint line instead of using a pencil. Take the time to line up the panel edges and scored lines as precisely as possible.

Stacking all the panels at one time for scarfing makes more accurate joints, plus it feels like you're getting the job done quicker.

Planing the joint. For the thin plywood typically used for planking stock, we recommend using a hand plane to cut scarfs. It would seem that roughing out the joint with a power plane would make the job go quicker, but John has found that the time he saves initially is spent sharpening the power plane's blades later. The glue is hard on sharp blades, and it's a lot easier sharpening a hand plane's single blade than the power plane's two or three little blades. If you are using thicker plywood (½″ or more), the power plane is worth the effort because there is so much wood to take off.

Start out with a sharp plane with a lightly waxed sole. Don't kill yourself trying to make the plane super sharp; you're going to dull it pretty quickly. Sharp will do.

Hold the plane at about a 45-degree angle to the working edge of the plywood stack—facing downhill—with the blade positioned to cut the corner of the top panel and the front of the sole resting on the corners of one or two panels below. Plane about halfway to the score line on the top panel, then move down and work on the next panel. The plane will remove wood until its sole rides on the cut of the top panel. You'll note that the width of the cut on the second panel is narrower than that you made on the first panel. Now, plane the third panel. Again, you'll only be able to cut so far before the plane's sole rides on the two other panels and the blade cannot cut. The width of the cut on this third panel will be narrower than that on the second. Move the plane back up to the second panel, and you'll find that you can make two or three productive strokes. Plane off a shaving or two on the third panel, then start beveling the fourth panel.

Keep coming back up to the top of the panels and work your way down again. You will end up with a hump in the middle of the stack. We'll fix that in a moment. For now, make sure that the width of the cuts on each panel are the same from one side to the other. Use long strokes to cut the joint, going from one side to the other. (Aren't

you glad the panels aren't 4′ wide?) Establishing even, parallel cuts will be make your job easier as you approach the finished joints.

Lightly wax the sole of your plane from time to time—it will feel like a fresh sharpening.

To trim down the hump, cut down the slope, still holding the plane at an angle to the direction of travel, starting in the middle of the stack and using increasingly longer strokes as you cut. Work across the panels this way, making sure to lift the plane when backing up, or the back of the plane will crush the thin edge of a beveled panel. When the hump is pretty flat (check with the corner of the plane or a straightedge), go back to planing parallel to the ends of the panels.

Depending on how thick your plywood is, you may have to repeat this procedure several times before the cuts begin closely approaching the score lines. You'll also notice that getting the plane to cut takes a lot more effort than when you first started, even with the wax. It's time to sharpen again.

Set the freshly sharpened plane for a lighter cut than before. Carefully work down the last little bit until the edge feathers, the cut touches the score line, the ply-

4.4 The nearly completed scarfs.

4.5 A few strokes with a sanding block roughen up the faces of the scarf joints and remove any traces of wax to ensure a good epoxy glue joint.

59

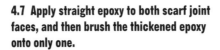

4.7 Apply straight epoxy to both scarf joint faces, and then brush the thickened epoxy onto only one.

4.6 Before mixing any epoxy, nail one panel to the bench with the face of the scarf joint to be glued facing up.

4.8 Carefully line up the end of the scarf joint on the second panel with the score line on the first panel and securely nail the second panel in place, first on one edge of the panels...

wood layers form parallel lines, and the planed surface is one long continuous slope from the top panel to the bottom. Alternate frequently between planing parallel and perpendicular to the edges. You can use a sharp block plane for the final couple of strokes.

The finished slope will be shiny from the rubbing of the plane, along with a trace of wax. Equip a sanding block with 80- or 100-grit and stroke *down* the slope a few times.

Take the stack apart, being especially gentle with the thin feather edges.

Gluing-up the scarf joints

Assemble all the tools and materials you need before you start. You'll need:
- Small finish nails (brads)
- Hammer
- One caul (clamping board): a ¾ " solid board or piece of plywood, 6 " to 8 " wide and 26 " to 28 " long
- Drywall screws, long enough to go through the board or plywood, the stack of planking plywood, and into the bench. A ³⁄₁₆ " × 1" fender washer for each screw is helpful
- Clearance drill, sized for the drywall screws
- Screw gun
- Epoxy
- Two tab brushes and two mixing pots
- Sheets of plastic (or waxed paper), about 6 " × 26 " to 28 ", one for each joint, plus the top and bottom of the stack
- Epoxy-proof gloves

Make that trip to the head and turn on the answering machine. Once you start this process, it's no interruptions until you're done.

Place the first pair of sheets, planed side up, on your work surface (or even the floor). Make sure the joint will be well supported with a broad perfectly flat surface.

Slide one panel out of the way for the moment. Put a strip of plastic under the joint of the other and nail it to the bench or floor, preferably using the existing nail holes. You only need a brad on each side, just enough to keep the panel from sliding out of alignment. Pull the first panel back over the plastic.

Set up the epoxy and related equipage nearby, and stack the remaining panels close to hand.

Mix two batches of epoxy: one straight, one thickened. Thicken with colloidal silica and sanding dust (wood flour) to about the consistency of pancake batter or a touch thicker. (For a varnished hull, use mahogany sanding dust and mix a color darker than the plywood.)

Wet out both scarf joints with the straight epoxy. Brushing over the scored line makes it more visible. Don't fuss; time is somewhat of the essence. Just brush it on evenly. When you clamp this joint, epoxy is going to squeeze out everywhere.

Apply thickened epoxy to the nailed panel with the second tab brush. There is no need for an excessive amount, since this joint will be tight.

Now flip the loose panel over, slide the joint faces over each other, and bring the feathered edge of the loose

4.9 ... then the other edge.

4.10 After all the scarf joints have been glued and the panels nailed in place (with waxed paper or plastic strips between all the panels and the bench), a caul (clamping board) secured with screws clamps the joints tight.

4.11 A scraper works well for removing excess epoxy from the glued joints.

panel together with the score line on the fixed panel. With a glove-covered finger, remove squeeze-out that obscures the scored line. Line up one side perfectly and nail it, then line up the other side and nail it, preferably using the existing nail holes. Gently press down on the top panel at the joint to see if a small bead of epoxy squeezes out. No? Then pull the top panel off and put on more epoxy putty. Lay a strip of waxed paper or plastic over your new scarf joint. Repeat the process, placing the second joint right on top of the first. Continue until you run out of panels, and place a last sheet of waxed paper over the last joint.

Center the ¾″ caul (clamping board) over the joints. Mark ten evenly spaced holes for screws, well clear of the joints. For each screw, drill through the board and planking plywood, but not into the bench. Starting with the four outside corners, one at time, drill for, then drive drywall screws with fender washers to clamp the stack together. Then do the same for the remaining screws.

You will probably sleep better if you peek under the sheets of plastic or waxed paper to reassure yourself that there is plenty of squeeze-out at the sides of each joint. If you see very little or no squeeze-out, take everything apart *now* and clean up all of the epoxy. Re-glue the joints, making sure to use more epoxy putty to ensure that the joints are fully glued, as evinced by ample squeeze-out.

If it's warm in the shop, you can unscrew, un-nail, and clean up the panels after they have cured overnight. It is best to wait at least 24 hours.

Cleaning up

Remove the caul, and gently lift each panel with a flat bar, either pulling the brads up or through the plywood.

Sharpen a good 3″ scraper and clamp one panel to the bench. Remove the excess epoxy by holding the scraper at an angle to the joint and scraping in the direction that presses the joint down. With epoxy, lifting of the edge shouldn't be a problem, but it's better to do it this way. Change the angle of the scraper from time to time to keep from forming "waves" or ripples in the plywood surface. A sharp scraper used with light pressure should skate over the soft wood and bite into the hard epoxy. Periodically run your hand over the joint area—fairly quickly—feeling for any humps or hollows. Check more often as the cleaning-up progresses. If the joint is uneven or the panel is acquiring humps and dips, carefully level the surface with a sharp block plane set for a fine cut.

After you've cleaned up all the panels, you can lightly belt-sand the joint with 120-grit. Keep the sander moving, don't stop in the same place at end of each stroke, and don't stop while the sander is running. Move the sander as if it were a sanding block, but let the weight of the sander do the cutting; don't push down. This is a job to be done with a light touch. If it makes you overly nervous, skip it altogether and sand the joints by hand after the planks are installed in the hull.

Chapter 5

Building Jig and Molds

The Building Jig System

Putting together the building jig is not one of the most glamorous jobs in building a boat, but it must be done correctly. If the jig isn't right, the boat will never look right, and it will be hard to build. Spend some time constructing and setting up your jig properly, and your hull will go together easily, the interior parts will all fit, and your boat will look great, forever.

The glued-lapstrake method creates a lovely, shapely hull but requires a hull-building jig that firmly supports and holds the plywood planks in fair curves while the epoxy cures. The jig system we use is designed specifically for building glued-lapstrake boats—and is the result of John's thinking very carefully about how to make the building (and cleaning up) go much easier than it did on the first couple of boats he built using a more "traditional" setup.

HOW THE BUILDING JIG SYSTEM WORKS

The jig's two side beams do the lion's share of supporting the molds. Two end beams, situated near the ends of the side beams, catch the inner stem and transom. Diagonal braces arise from the side beams to hold the center beam, which in turn holds the molds plumb and in position.

The whole jig rests on legs attached to the side beams. The feet can be screwed to the floor or to wooden sleepers made of 2×8s or 2×10s laid flat.

The side and end beams are not especially remarkable; most building jigs have them in some form. If you are building a few reasonably light, small boats, 2×8s will work acceptably. It's helpful to make the side beams L-shaped, of two pieces of lumber, as this shape keeps them stiffer and straighter side-to-side.

Making the end beams L-shaped is essential. On our boats, the keelson is a flat plank sprung into place over the molds. When the inner stem, keelson, and transom are fastened in place on the jig, there can be a fair amount of pressure on the end beams.

Triangular gussets at each corner hold the jig square. The gussets also hold all kinds of useful items: drills, screws, screwdriver, putty knife, mug, pencil, square, marking jig, and, occasionally but strategically, your posterior.

The center beam's single most important function is to hold the molds plumb. Diagonal braces come up from the side beams to hold the center beam in position, and there aren't many of them. This setup replaces the

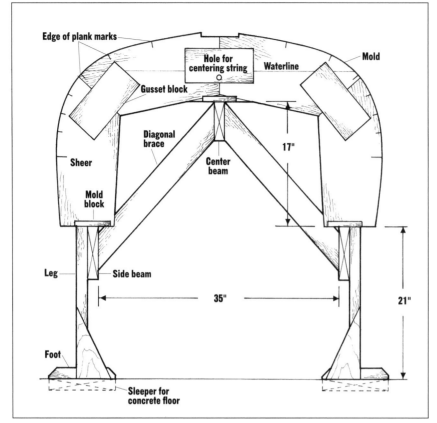

Fig 5.1 A section of the building jig with a mold in place.

act as wooden nuts. The battens and blocks are removed after the epoxy cures—in a day or two—so they can be reused for other planks. If you're really flying, you can hang as many planks in day as you have battens and blocks.

The batten-clamping system is quick and simple, definite pluses where epoxy is concerned. You don't need a hundred clamps, just a few battens, a modest boxful of hardwood blocks, a couple handfuls of drywall screws, and some paste wax.

The time to clean up the excess epoxy putty that oozes out from a joint is immediately after you finish attaching the batten. Because the batten and blocks don't cover the plank edge, it's easy to run a putty knife along the joint, inside and out. You can sit comfortably under the jig and reach almost every bit of the inside of the hull, except right at the molds. The inch-long spots of hardened epoxy that remain at the molds will chisel off

webwork of bracing typically used in traditional jigs, allowing easy access to the inside of the hull.

A 2×6 center beam works well for most boats. The beam needs to be wide enough for the ends of the diagonal braces to bear completely (or nearly so) on it and beefy enough to withstand any attempts by the boat or its builders to move it. You very likely will find yourself grabbing it to haul yourself along under the boat while cleaning up epoxy. For many boats, the easiest way to plane down the garboards at the keelson is by kneeling on top of the hull while it's still on the jig (see Photo 8.5, page 149). If you build your jig strong enough to climb on, you won't have to worry about it racking or shifting while you're building the hull.

Long battens that clamp and hold the plank laps fair while the epoxy cures are an integral part of the building jig system. They allow the molds to be fewer in number and widely spaced, creating less work all around and giving room to clean up epoxy squeeze-out inside the hull. These battens are attached to the outside of the hull, on top of each lap joint. You won't need the clamping battens and their blocks until the second plank goes on, but you might want to make them before setting up the jig, especially if space in the shop is tight.

We clamp each lap joint after applying the epoxy by placing a batten over its entire length, then drilling for and driving drywall screws into the molds and, in-between stations, into small angled hardwood blocks that

readily after you remove the boat from the jig. Once the batten-clamps are removed and the boat comes off the jig, epoxy putty squirted with a modified syringe quickly fills the screw holes.

JIG CONSTRUCTION
Materials

The entire jig is built of materials found at the local lumberyard. Buy kiln-dried wood. Though not an absolute guarantee that the wood won't warp, kiln-dried will put the odds more in your favor.

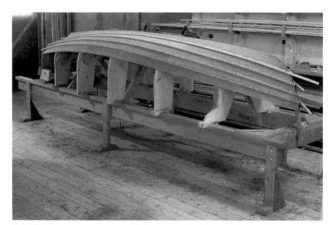

5.1 The jig system uses widely spaced molds and reusable battens temporarily installed on the outside of the plank laps while the epoxy hardens.

In Maine, standard construction lumber can be spruce, hemlock, or fir, none of which are noted for staying straight. If you plan to use your jig more than once, or don't like arguing with independently minded pieces of wood, you might want to make the jig of a more stable, more expensive wood. Our shop jig is made of Eastern white pine.

Setting the jig up and letting it adjust to the humidity of your shop for a week or two, then giving it a coat or two of a thin urethane finish or varnish will do wonders to keep your jig more stable. This is a particularly good idea if you plan to store the jig in the usual less-than-ideal spots: garage, basement, attic. When you break down the jig for storage, the individual pieces will be free to go their own ways. You can encourage a warped jig into alignment with the aid of pipe clamps, but it's worth the effort to minimize the problem.

The "standard jig"

In order to keep things clearer, we'll describe the process of laying out the relevant measurements for the "standard jig" used for the Ellen and all of our designs up to roughly the size of the 18′ Peregrine rowboat (including the 16′ double-paddle canoe Salicornia). This version of the jig will fit many other similar designs. If the standard jig won't work for your boat, you'll need to settle on the right size for the jig and determine some key measurements. Specific suggestions for doing this begin on page 67.

Boats that are much larger or smaller can use the same jig concept. See page 68 for sketches on adapting the jig in these cases.

Making the jig parts

Please refer also to the following section on measurements and the accompanying sketches.

Side beams. The ends don't need to be cut perfectly square unless you are butting two lengths together to

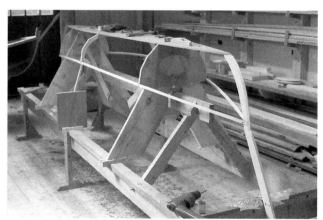

5.2 Bulkheads can be installed on the building jig over the center beam for small boats such as this Harry Bryan Fiddlehead double-paddle canoe.

make each beam long enough. Use a piece about 2′ long, of the same stock as the beams, to make a butt block over the joint.

The top of the side beams must be as straight as possible. If there is a slight curve to the lumber, you can spring it out when you level the jig and fasten it to the floor. If the beam is heavily curved, saw the top edge straight, using a string to establish the line. Plane off the saw marks if they are really rough.

End beams. There are four end-beam pieces, all the same length. Trim one end of all four pieces, making sure they are clean and square. Measure and trim the other end of one piece. Use it to accurately mark the other three with a knife or awl, then cut them square.

Center beam. A shallow curve in the center beam can be sprung into place if it is held up by at least three pairs of diagonal braces. A large curve should be straightened as you did the side beams, but it isn't as crucial. Trim the ends clean and square; this is important for setting up the molds.

Legs. Make the legs identical, as you did the end beams. Although accuracy isn't as crucial here, if your floor happens to be level and you make the legs identical, you won't have to shim any of them.

Feet. Chamfering each end makes stubbed toes less likely.

Diagonal braces. These must be identical. If you spend a little extra time now making them accurately, you will be repaid when the jig goes together effortlessly. We suggest cutting the diagonals on a miter saw. Set up the saw for the proper angle. Cut all the angles on one end, leaving the pieces a little long.

Using the finished brace as a guide, mark the rest by scoring a thin line with an awl or knife on the end to be trimmed; cut very precisely to the line. If you miss and cut a brace too short, make another. Several 2″ squares of scrap plywood screwed on the side of the first brace will help align it with the others.

Gussets. You don't have to fuss much with the gussets, as they are simply triangles cut from scrap plywood. Round off the corners slightly.

Mold blocks. These hold the molds in position at the center beam and side beams. Nothing fancy; just cut 1″ × 3″ spruce/fir strapping to length.

Center beam temporary braces. A pair of temporary braces made of 2×4 stock in the shape of an inverted T will save you lots of grief when it comes time to set the center beam at its proper height and install the diagonal braces. Make the horizontal bottom piece of the T wider than the

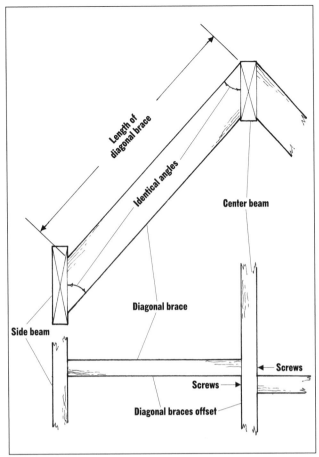

Fig 5.2 Lay out the diagonal brace between a side beam and the center beam on the full-sized pattern or the lofting. Diagonal braces are parallelograms with identical angles at the ends. On a jig that is screwed together, the diagonal braces are offset.

jig and the vertical piece taller than the center beam height. The bottom of the horizontal piece must be straight and the vertical piece attached so that it is perfectly square. Measuring from the bottom, carefully mark the height of the center beam. If you want to add a diagonal piece to make sure that the T stays square, go ahead; just make sure it doesn't interfere with clamping the center beam.

Basic measurements and parts

It's helpful to have all the dimensions and angles for your jig listed on an index card, along with the other information you'll need when it's time to put the whole thing together. Again, because these numbers are for our standard jig, change and adapt as necessary to suit your boat.
- Width between the side beams: 35″.
- Height of the center beam: 17″.

These dimensions have worked quite nicely for a wide variety of boats from 8′ to 18′ long, with beams up to 52″. The narrowest boat we've built, the double-paddle canoe Salicornia with a 28″ beam, required a little leaning and stepping over, but the standard jig still worked fine.

- Length of the side beams: About 1′ longer than the boat.
- Length of the center beam: The length between the first mold and the last, plus 6″.

We adapt the jig for different designs by increasing the length of the side beams with extensions and choosing a center beam (with extension if necessary) that fits. John designs all of our boats with a 2′ mold spacing, which allows us to use center beams cut to standard lengths. We currently have center beams for 8′, 10′, and 12′ hulls, along with 4′ (two-mold) and 6′ (three-mold) extensions. By combining different beams and extensions, we can build boats of any length.

- Height and number of legs: Our jig's legs are 21″ tall. Space them about 6′ apart (e.g., the Ellen needs six).
- Dimensions of the gussets: 12″ on the two short sides of the triangle. Four needed.
- Number of mold-positioning blocks. For each mold, you'll need two for the side beams and two for the center beam. Pieces of 1×3 spruce/fir strapping 6″ to 8″ long work fine.
- Spacing of the molds (station spacing): For the Ellen and all of our other boats, 2′.

Other important measurements

Unless otherwise noted, this information can be found on the full-sized patterns included with our plans. You'll need to measure for these on your plans and full-sized patterns or lofting if you have a design from another designer.
- First station to inside of the inner stem: This locates the forward end-beam. The line of the inner stem's inner face is extended until it crosses the line of the top of the side beams (see Figure 5.3).

    Measure from last station to the inside of the inner sternpost to locate the aft end-beam if your boat is a double-ender.
- Last station to the inside of the transom: This locates the aft end-beam and is measured on top of the gussets, not the side beams, as the transom will be secured to blocks that rest on the gussets (see Figure 5.4).
- Transom angle: This is the angle at which the transom blocks must be cut. It is also the angle at which you usually will trim the top of the transom after the hull is planked up.
- Distance of sheer to jig, at transom: Measure this along the transom's outboard face. You'll use this to set the transom at the proper height on the jig (see Figure 5.4).
- End of the inner stem on the keelson: The point where the outer (forward) face of the inner stem joins the inboard face of the keelson. You'll mark this on the keelson when you make it, but this is an absolutely crucial measurement, so it's nice to have it on a setup card, to double-check when you assemble the backbone.
- Intersection of the keelson and inner stem: The point at which the sharp curve of the stem joins the shallow

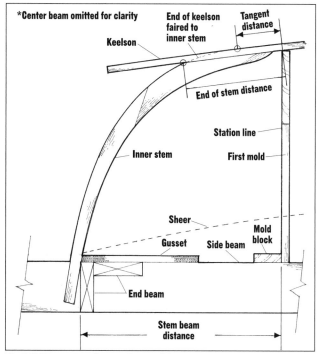

Fig 5.3 Stem, stem beam, first mold.

Dimensions for locating the end beams, assembling the backbone, attaching the backbone to the jig, and trimming the keelson at the inner stem. If you are building a double-ender (with two

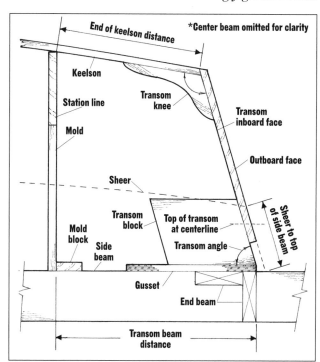

Fig 5.4 Transom, transom beam, last mold.

stems) or a pram (with two transoms), there's no difference in how a stem or transom is measured just because it is on the other end of the boat.

curve of the keelson. This is a very useful point to know when trimming the end of the keelson after the backbone is fastened to the jig. Sight along the drawing to find this point. Close is good enough.

- Location of the full frame (optional): If your design calls for a full frame (or several), we suggest installing it on the jig, much like a mold, and planking over it.
- End of skeg (optional): You only need write this down if the aft end of the skeg is *not* flush with the transom, as is the case with the racing skeg on our Peregrine and Merlin rowboats.
- In case you're wondering, bulkheads normally go in after the boat comes off the jig. We built one of Harry Bryan's 12′ Fiddlehead canoes, which has two bulkheads and a full frame instead of molds, by going over the center beam and setting up the bulkheads and frame as if they were molds. Though this approach works, it is easier to build the hull over open web frames at the bulkhead positions, then attach panel bulkheads to the frames after the hull comes off the jig. Our Somes Sound 12½ has this type of construction.

Fitting the jig to a boat designed by others

If you are building a boat designed by another designer, here's how to adapt our jig design to your boat:
- *Make patterns representing the cross-sections of the center and side beams.* Use ¼″ plywood or stiff cardboard.
- *Mark the location of the top of the side beam in relation to the sheer.* On your lofting or full-sized pat-

terns, draw a line an inch or two above the highest point of the sheer. This often will be at the bow. Check to make sure that this line doesn't cross below the top of the transom (or the sternpost if your boat is double-ended).
- *Determine the best width for the side beams.* On your plans, half of the sections likely will be drawn to the left of the centerline, the other half to the right. Determine the best spacing for the side beams by placing the two side-beam patterns under the ends of the sections, equidistant from the centerline. The width of your mold stock will determine the widths of the "feet" of your molds and thus how much latitude you have in placing the side beams. (To read ahead about making the molds, see page 72.) You don't want the side beams too close together, for then the widest molds will overhang the beams, requiring extensions, and, worse, it will be hard to move around inside the jig while cleaning up. If the side beams are too far apart, cleaning up won't be as much of a problem, but you'll have to make extensions for many of your narrower molds. If you are making your molds of sheet stock, you have a little more latitude on the side beam width spacing, but remember the need to keep clear working space under the jig.
- *Determine the height for the center beam.* The center beam must fit under the keelson at the shortest section by at least several inches. Leave enough space between the keelson and the top of the center beam to fasten

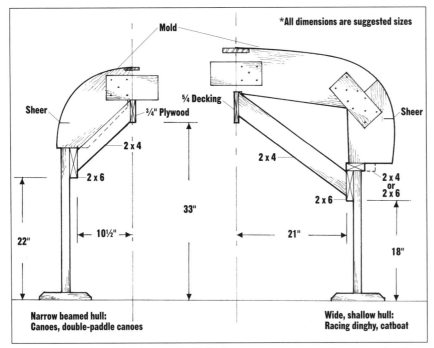

Fig 5.5 Suggested modifications to the jig for long, narrow canoes or kayaks, and wide, shoal, racing dinghies or catboats. Lighter duty boats can be built on a jig built with smaller side and center beams. An L-shaped side beam provides more landing area for the narrow molds at the bow as well as the wide molds amidships.

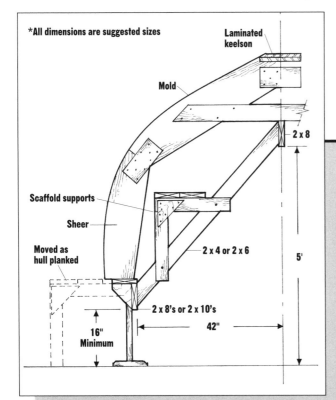

Fig 5.6 The building jig for larger boats requires beefier parts to support the heavier hull and the greater pressure from bending the heavier keelson and planking as well as holding the weight of several people who must climb on the jig to reach the backbone and first few planks.

gusset blocks over the centerline joint, even if they must be narrow on the smallest molds. The top of the center beam is parallel with the top of the side beams.

- *Accurately draw in the locations of the beams on the full-sized patterns or lofting.* When you are happy with the location of the beams, mark the widths of the side beams (both sides of the centerline) and the height of the top of the center beam. Remove your beam patterns and accurately draw the beam sections from the locating marks you made.

- *Draw in the diagonal braces.* You need draw only one because the other side will be exactly the same. Start from the top corner of the center beam and draw a line that ends an inch or so below the top of the side beam. Then mark a parallel line about 3½″ (the width of a typical 2×4) below and toward the center of the boat.

Measure and record the length of one side of the diagonal brace and the angle at which it meets the center beam. The brace is a parallelogram, so its sides will be the same length and the angles top and bottom identical. The braces should be spaced about 3′ to 4′ apart, in pairs.

- *Decide about the legs.* Consider: what height of the center beam allows you to sit comfortably upright, how

Suggested Jig Modifications for Larger Boats

The standard jig is designed for relatively small, lightweight boats. If you'd like to build a larger, heavier boat, consider the following adjustments:

- *Heavier side beams with an L-section.*
- *Evenly spaced diagonal braces that will allow you to attach cleats or brackets for staging, making it possible to reach the first few planks.*
- *The addition of a few more legs.*
- *Bigger gussets on the molds to take the pressure of bending a thicker keelson into place.*
- *Larger transom blocks, more securely fastened; more screws holding the transom to the transom blocks.*
- *Plywood L-brackets fastened to the inboard side of the transom to keep it flat. These can also be fastened to the transom blocks.*
- *Wedge at the bow end-beam to provide a landing for the inner stem. Bolt the inner stem to the end beam.*
- *End beams made of 2×8s instead of 2×6s and built U-shaped instead of L-shaped.*

much height you need to slide under the side beams, and what offers a comfortable working height. Most boats require a pair of legs about every 6′. If your boat is large and heavy, add more.

Getting Oriented

Obviously, the hull will be built bottom-side up. To be perfectly proper about it, up is down, port is on the right, starboard to the left. It may be proper, but it's certainly confusing. For the duration of the boat's stay in the upside-down mode, we follow the following conventions:
- *The keelson (or keel) is up.*
- *The sheer is down.*
- *The bow of any boat always faces the same direction, in our case the back of the shop and the woodstove. (This becomes particularly important with a double-ender.)*
- *Port is to the left as you face forward from the stern, starboard to the right.*

ASSEMBLING THE JIG

It's a little quicker to assemble the jig using drywall screws but, as you can see from the photos, we use bolts to hold ours together. If you plan to build many boats, assembling and disassembling your jig often, you'll want to use the bolts, as drywall screws will eventually strip out their holes. However, the drywall screw approach works fine for several boats.

Laying out

A carefully laid-out jig will go together quickly and make every step of setting up the molds and building the hull straightforward and consistent.
- *Assemble the parts of the jig that will remain permanently together.* Screw the feet to the legs. Screw together the parts of the end beams, including the gussets. The gussets should be flush with the face of each end beam. Screw together the parts of L-shaped side beams (if you're using them), and bolt or screw together the side-beam lengths if they must be joined with a butt block.
- *Measure and mark one side beam.* Stand one of the side beams on edge upright and clamp a bar or pipe clamp at each end, against the floor, to keep the beam from flopping over at an inopportune moment. First, mark a position for the bow end-beam a few inches in from the end of the side beam, then measure off the distance to the first station (from the measurement card) and mark this.

Next, lay out the station spacing. On our boats, the interval between stations is 2′, so we line up the 2′ mark on the tape with the first station and weight it in place. After the tape is positioned properly, run the tape down the length of the side beam and carefully mark and label the remaining stations. Particularly if your plans call for stations set at different intervals, it is worth checking your mental gymnastics by remeasuring on the way back. Lay out the position of the transom end-beam from the last station. Mark a line for each pair of diagonal braces.

Finally, locate the jig's structural supports. The diagonal braces located at the ends of the center beam are easy: the forward one goes 6″ aft of the first station, and the aft one belongs 6″ forward of the last station. Space the diagonal braces approximately 4′ apart, but always at least 6″ from any station line. Space the legs about 6′ apart so that you end up with a pair near each end of the side beams. Because all the weight of the jig, molds, hull, tools, and your person (on occasion) rests on the legs, try to keep the spacing more even than with the diagonal braces. Mark the widths of the legs (3½″) on the side beam so you can see if they will cover up anything important. The legs can be located on a station line, as the molds will go over them. But, the legs cannot be located over the lines for the end beams or the diagonal braces due to screw (or bolt) conflicts. It's wise to leave at least 3″ from these lines to the closest edge of a leg.
- *Transfer the marks from the marked side beam to the other beams.* Clamp the side beams and center beam together in the same fore-and-aft relationship they will enjoy on the completed jig: ends of the side beams even with each othe, and center beam centered between the first and last stations.

Using a framing square, draw the station lines and diagonal brace lines across all three beams. These lines need to be crisp and clearly visible. Draw the lines for the legs and end beams on the other side beam only. Make the end-beam lines particularly dark and visible.
- *Label everything.* Label all the station lines with a permanent marker. Permanently label the end-beam lines with the name of the design. Label the diagonal brace lines with pencil. Make sure that you can't possibly confuse a diagonal brace line for station line or one of the leg lines. It may look obvious right now, but unlabeled lines can quickly become baffling once you start putting the jig together.
- *Unclamp and separate the beams, slightly.* Maintain the beams' original orientation. Mark the end beam and diagonal brace lines on the inboard faces of the side beams. Draw all of these lines down the entire height of the beams using a try-square. Using the same technique, mark the diagonal brace lines on both sides of the center beam.

Now is a good time to label where each brace will go. If you wish to screw your diagonal braces to the center beam, you need to offset them so you can drive the screws. On our jig, each member of a pair of diagonal braces sets directly opposite its partner, as the two are bolted together through the center beam. Indicate where each brace goes by drawing an elongated X on the proper side of its diagonal brace line. Using a try-square, draw a light pencil line ¾" from each diagonal brace line, through each X, for centerlines for the screws. Mark for two screws. Draw similar lines ¾" from the end-beam lines and mark for a couple of screws in each.

A Few Hints on Using Drywall Screws in the Jig

- *When screwing together various parts with drywall screws, drill a clearance hole through the first part, then drive the screw.*
- *When driving drywall screws, stop when the head of the screw is flush with the surface of the piece. Don't bury the heads! It does absolutely no good and will make taking the jig apart later a real pain. If you need to pull things together, use a clamp or two on the pieces. Fender washers under the screw heads are also helpful.*

Putting everything together

- *Fasten the legs to the side beams.* Do the end legs first, then the middle ones. Line up the top of the legs tight under an L-shaped side beam or flush with the top of a single-piece side beam and flush with the vertical line. (You'll level the jig by driving wedges under the feet, later.)
- *Fasten the end beams to the side beams.* Drive *one* screw, with a fender washer, in each gusset, as close to the end-beam line as possible. Make sure the end beams are butted tightly against the side beams; deploy

a pipe clamp or two if things are reluctant before driving any screws.

- *Square up the jig.* At the first and last stations, mark the center of the top edge of the side beams with a try-square. If you are working alone, drive a small nail in each side beam at these points at the forward station. Leave enough of the nail exposed to hook a tape measure.

    Measure diagonally across the jig to these center points, adjusting the jig by tapping (or tunking) with a hammer until both measurements are the same. Check to see that the side beams are fairly straight side to side. If they're too wide, pull the beams in to the proper width with a pipe clamp. If too narrow, push them out with straightedge and a couple of nails. Once the jig is square, drive three more screws in each gusset.

- *Fasten the diagonal braces to the center beam.* Put the center beam and all of the diagonal braces in the middle of the jig where you can reach them. Clamp the center beam near the ends to its T-shaped temporary braces at the height you marked. Line up the tip of the first diagonal brace with the top of the center beam and the diagonal brace line (on the X'd side). Drive *one* screw. Repeat this process with all the remaining braces.

    If your jig is bolted together, attach each diagonal brace pair with its bolt, but don't tighten the bolt completely.

- *Fasten the lower ends of the diagonal braces to the side beams.* Check to be sure that the center beam is still clamped at the proper height marked on the temporary T-shaped braces. Attend to the diagonal braces located at the ends of the center beam first, lining them up with their diagonal brace lines, over the Xs. Drive *one* screw (or barely tighten the bolt) in each.

    Once the ends of the diagonal braces are fastened

5.3 The building jig is squared up by measuring diagonally from the first station to the last.

5.4 The diagonal braces and center beam are installed with the help of an inverted T-shaped temporary brace made of 2x4s.

in place, move the T-shaped braces in toward the middle of the center beam, and fasten the rest of the diagonal braces in the same way. To adjust the height of the center beam, either pull the beam up with a pipe clamp hooked over the top of the upside-down T-brace (turn the jaws 90 degrees to each other) or lower it by pushing down (or have your helper lean or sit on the beam).

Remember, if the center beam is a little lower than the mark, the molds will sit firmly on the side beam and all will be well. If the beam is above the mark, then the molds will be held a little above the side beams and will rock from side to side—not good. Try to pull the center beam down to the proper height. However, if you exert excessive pressure on the beam, you'll distort the whole jig. Fasten the beam as close as you can to the mark for now. When you put the molds on the jig, you can trim the underside of the molds until they sit firmly on the side beams.

• *Level the jig.* The best tool for this job is a water level (see box). Check for bubbles and work any you find out of the water column.

The first task is finding the highest point of the floor. Slide the jig to where you want it. Each person takes an end of the water level and chooses a leg. Pull out the

5.5 A water level made of clear vinyl tubing is used to level the building jig.

water level's plugs. Person A, the "control," moves her end of the water level until the water lines-up the top of the side beam. Person B notes where the water level naturally settles on his end. Is it higher or lower than the top of the side beam? If it's lower, this leg becomes the new control point to measure from, Person A moves to it, and Person B moves on to a new leg. If it's higher, Person A stays put at the original leg, and Person B moves on to a new leg. They work systematically around the jig, choosing the higher leg at each turn.

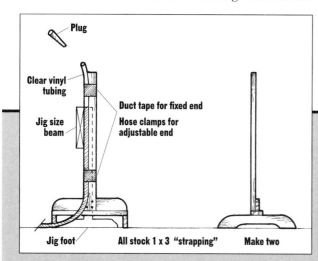

Fig 5.7 If you are working alone, make two simple stands out of inexpensive 1" x 3" "strapping" to hold the ends of a water level.

Making a Water Level

A water level is a simple tool that works elegantly. You'll need a length of ½" vinyl tubing from the lumberyard that is at least 1½ times the length of your boat. Extra length won't hurt, so don't be afraid to buy extra or to buy enough for the longer boat that will be coming after the present vessel. Whittle a couple of pine plugs to fit in the tube ends.

Fill all but about 20" or so of the tubing with water, while being careful not to create air bubbles. You don't have to color the water, but you may want to, especially if you're working alone. We finally ended up coloring ours with professional-strength

food coloring obtained from a cooking store. You won't need much. Plug the ends of the tube. (Note: If you keep your water level full for a long time, things begin to grow in colored water, making the level inaccurate. Drain the tubing and flush it with a little bleach. Try mixing in a little bleach with the food coloring the next time around.)

If you can round up a friend to help with the water level, it will save you a lot of running around the jig from one end to the other. If you're working alone, a pair of stands will keep you saner and the water in the tube (see figure).

To check if your water level is accurate, hold the ends of the tube together and remove the plugs. The water level in each tube should align perfectly. If not, there is a bubble or some debris somewhere in the tube.

5.6 A 2' spirit level and a straightedge are used to determine when the station lines on the side beams and center beam are plumb.

When you are done, you will have a good idea of the shape of your floor, and you'll know the highest part of the jig. Drive screw through that foot.

With Person A holding one end of the water level at the top of the side beam at the highest leg, Person B moves the other end to all the legs and drives wedges or shingles under the feet until the side beam reaches the right height, as shown by the water level. The addition of a Person C to insert shingles while Person B holds and reads the water level is not unwelcome at this point.

When each leg is right, drive a screw through the foot to hold it in place. Once the jig is level, drive a second screw into each foot. If you used sleepers, drive the wedges between the feet and the sleeper, then drive the screws through the feet into the sleepers. If the floor is extremely uneven and the sleeper isn't touching in some places, tap a pair of shingles into the gap and prevent them from being kicked out of place with small nails.

• *Plumb the center beam.* Clamp a plywood straightedge across the top of the side beams on a station line, usually the first station. Holding a 2' level vertically, rest its base on the edge of the station line straightedge and the level's side against the center beam. Move the top of the level until it is plumb.

Note where the station line on the center beam is in relation to plumb. Using a block of scrap wood as a pad, and a hammer or, better yet, a three-pound sledge, tap one end or the other of the center beam to move the station line in the right direction. You'll be surprised at how much force is needed to move the center beam, even though the diagonal braces are held by only a single screw (or slightly snug bolt) at each end. Take great pains *not* to chowder up the end of the center beam—don't even mar the ends. The ends need to be smooth and flat when you center the molds. If you find the center beam extremely reluctant to move, loosen some or all of the screws (or bolts) a quarter turn.

Check with the level again. Tap the center beam until the edge of the level that's held against the

straightedge lines up perfectly with the station line on the center beam. You may have to tap the center beam back and forth a few times, checking with the level each time, to get the station line perfectly plumb. Once that one station line is plumb, all of the stations are plumb. (And your molds will be plumb when you place them against those nice plumb station lines.)

When you're happy that all is perfectly plumb, tighten any screws that you loosened, and drive the second screws into the upper and lower ends of each diagonal brace. (Tighten the bolts on both ends if that applies.) For small boats, two screws in each end has proven to be plenty. However, if your boat will be large and heavy, you might want to drill and drive for third screws, "toe-nailed" in each end of the diagonal braces.

The building jig is now ready for the molds.

Molds

MAKING THE MOLDS

The molds define the shape of your boat. Devotion to detail now will be repaid many times over when you pull a gorgeous fair hull off your molds.

No matter how many boats we build, it's still exciting to see a new design starting to take shape as a stack of molds. It's fun to make molds, and now you'll have something to show those friends who keep razzing you about when they're going to see some "real progress" on your boat.

Materials

We suggest using #4 Northern white pine boards for the molds, or the nearest equivalent if white pine is hard to find or expensive in your part of the world. Unlike chipboard, plywood, and other cheaper alternatives, the pine doesn't split readily when the drywall screws that temporarily secure the planking are driven into the edges. Most screws hold well, reducing the number of holes in the boat and the cussing caused by redriving screws. The molds can be reused, as they aren't essentially wrecked by the construction of the first boat. This may not seem important if you're planning to build one boat, but when you get her done and your friends see how lovely she is (and all of you think about how much fun it might be to race two—or more—boats), you may discover a demand for your molds.

Sheet materials are heavy and awkward, and there is a fair amount of waste, as you'll be cutting out large U-shapes. The pine planes easily when you're beveling each mold for the planks; chipboard and its relatives are murder on hand tool blades and not at all fun to plane. On the other hand, using sheet materials will save you a ration of work making joints.

Measuring the pieces for the molds

Make up a table like the following (used for the Ellen) to record the relevant measurements:

Station	Lengths Upper	Lower	Measured Angle	Miter Angle	Extension, if needed
2					
4					
6					
8					
10					

The first mold (or first and last if you're building a double-ender) is usually straight enough to get each side out of a single board. Use the tape measure to find its length.

The rest of the molds require four parts—two upper, two lower—and three gusset blocks to secure the joints. As you will recall, the boat is to be built upside down, so the upper parts of the molds will form the bottom of the boat and the lower parts, the topsides. If your drawings aren't already oriented with the keel up, you might want to do that now to reduce confusion.

Make a large "angle measurer" from two aluminum yardsticks bolted together through the hanging holes about an inch from one end. Position the angle measurer around a section on the full-sized drawing or lofting, leaving about ½″ between the yardsticks and the closest edge of each section, (see Photo 5.7). If you use 10″ boards, which are actually 9¼″ wide, the center and side beam ideally will be no more than 9″ from the yardsticks. Adjust the angle and position of yardsticks if necessary. If it's hopeless, you'll need extensions to reach the beams. These will be added when you assemble the mold. Extra

5.7 A bevel gauge is used to measure the angle between the yardsticks.

gusset blocks often work well for extensions.

Read the lengths where the yardsticks cross the centerline and the line at the top of the side beam. Because the yardsticks are bolted together with about 2″ of overlap, the measurements you read off will be extra long, which is good. Measure the yardstick angle with a bevel gauge. Use a bevel board to find the angle and record in the measured angle column. Write down the lengths in the appropriate columns. (Note: Because you can't use the side beams to establish the proper width of a mold that is too narrow, measure the half-width of the section at the sheer on your full-sized pattern, double the measurement, and make the mold this wide at the sheer. Note the extensions needed.) Repeat the process for all of the molds. Add up the piece lengths (in inches), multiply by two (to get both sides) and divide by twelve to arrive at the total length in feet you'll need.

The gussets and extensions can be 4½″ wide, half the width of the mold stock, by 10″ long. To figure the length of boards to buy, divide the number of gussets and extensions by two, then multiply by ten (inches), then divide by twelve for the total in feet. Combine the two totals for your shopping list.

Before you launch into cutting up the boards, you need to figure out the miter cuts needed for each mold, using the following formula: 45 − measured angle/2 = miter angle. Calculate this for every station and write the numbers on your table.

Cutting the mold stock

It would be delightful if reasonably inexpensive pine boards came with only small knots—but they don't. Avoid big knots, for they will distort your molds as they dry. Medium knots are acceptable, but make sure that they won't end up exposed along the mold's curved edge. Trying to plane knots as you bevel the laps is a special kind of torture.

To cut the mold pieces efficiently: Place a piece of mold stock on the miter saw. Measure and mark the mold's upper length along the edge closest to the saw's fence blade. Set the saw to the miter angle on your list. Cut so that the side you measured is the longer one. Now measure the same distance along the board edge closest to you, from the newly made cut. Mark a square line. Label the pieces, but don't cut the square line yet.

Keep going until you've done all the molds. You will have a stack of boards with angles cut on both ends. Now set the saw to make a square cut and address your attention to all of the square lines. When you're done, you'll have a large stack of mold parts. Then rip the remaining mold stock in half and crosscut at 10″ to make the gussets and extensions.

If you don't have a miter saw, you must mark the angled lines as well as square lines. You can cut out the molds with a circular saw, handsaw, or jigsaw.

5.8 Fasten the crosscut and mitered stock for half a mold to the workbench, then position the paper or Mylar full-sized pattern over it and hold in place with weights. Transfer the shapes of a section and the jig to the stock by pricking through the pattern with an awl.

Fig 5.8 On a full-sized pattern of the sections, a lap is drawn as two short lines across the section line. The one closest to the sheer—and the one to mark on the mold—is the upper edge of the first plank. The line closest to the keelson is where you'll mark the scored line for the lap on the first plank and where the lower edge of the second plank will fall when it is attached to the first plank.

Assembling and marking the mold halves

Put the upper and lower parts belonging to one half of a mold on a surface that you don't mind driving screws into, such as a plywood bench top or a piece of ¾″ plywood on horses.

Mark the length of the gusset block over the mold's side miter joint by using a compass set to 5″ and marking parallel to the miter. Keeping clear of the gusset area, fasten the mold parts to the bench with drywall screws, pre-drilling for the screws and butting the miter tightly together. Position the full-sized pattern on the wood and hold it firmly in place with weights. Punch around the section, the jig parts, keelson, main waterline (labeled DWL or LWL), and the centerline with a sharp awl. Mark the side-beam position and the sheer with deeper punches.

If you are working from a lofting, as we often are, we suggest that you record the sections on stable Mylar to make your own full-sized patterns, as we do. Trace the shapes freehand with short dashed lines; there is no need to set up battens again.

If your full-sized pattern shows the location of the laps, there will be pairs of marks. Using deep punch marks, record the one in each pair that is closest to the sheer. These are the edge-of-plank marks you'll be working to. Try picturing it this way: Turn the pattern right-side up for the moment. Start near the keel, with the low-est pair of lap marks. The line you want to mark is the up-permost one of the pair available. It indicates the actual upper edge of the first plank: the garboard. The lower line belongs to the next plank, which will overlap the garboard. This is the plank line that you will see on the outside of the hull. The distance between the two marks is the width of the lap joint.

Confusing? Yup. And you're going to be working with everything turned upside down for a good while until the hull comes off the jig. That's why you need to think about it now and make one clear mark for each plank. Draw a small circle around each mark you want to transfer to the mold before punching the mold stock. Take a look at Figure 5.8; it should help.

If your plans don't show the locations of the planks, don't worry. You will determine these once the molds are set up on the jig and the backbone is attached. (See Chapter 6, "The Backbone, and Lining Off" for a preview.)

Carefully lift sections of the pattern to "connect the dots" on the mold underneath for the straight lines for the top of the side beam; top of the center beam; top of the keelson; the centerline; and the waterline. Flag the punch marks for the edges of the planks and the side beams with short pencil lines. Clearly label the sheer and waterline. Remove the drawing.

In most cases, you'll need to cut a slot up to the center-beam line in the middle of the mold so that the mold will fit down over the center beam. Mark this about ½″ wider than the beam so that the mold can be moved from side to side for accurate centering on the jig.

Drill all the gusset blocks for screws. Fasten a gusset over the miter joint with drywall screws and glue. Remove the mold half from the bench, and screw on the matching upper and lower parts, using the existing screw holes. Set the sandwich aside for now.

Mark and pair up the remainder of the molds in the same fashion.

Sawing out the mold pairs

The bandsaw is the best tool for cutting out the doubled-up molds, as the blade of a jigsaw can wander significantly from vertical, overcutting or undercutting the molds' edges.

Saw out the molds' curves smoothly, looking just ahead of the blade to the next punch mark coming up. Let your peripheral vision guide the punch marks the last bit to the saw blade. Try to split the marks, but always leave the marks visible. (Also see the photo of sawing out an inner stem on page 81.) Don't use all of your sawed-off scraps for kindling; save some for when you assemble the molds.

Split the pencil lines for the line of the side beam and the centerline with the saw. Any extra left over these marks adds up quickly, and the molds won't fit together properly. Clean up these edges with a block plane. If you sawed carefully, you should only have to take off the saw-blade marks.

Saw out for the keelson and center beam as well.

If you followed the punch marks closely around the molds' curves, you don't have to trim them. You will be planing the molds into a series of facets when you bevel the laps, rendering any cleanup work done now superfluous. However, if you sawed a little wide of the punch marks, trim off the extra wood with a block plane and spokeshave, checking frequently to be sure that your trimming is square across the edges of both molds.

Project the marks for the sheer, edges-of-planks, and side beam across the edges of both molds with a try-square. Fasten a gusset block on the second mold half.

ASSEMBLING THE FULL MOLDS

Mark the locations of the centerline and side beams on a plywood straightedge. Fasten the straightedge on your screw-accepting work surface. Draw the centerline on the work surface up from the straightedge with a framing square. Measure off the height of the center beam and the waterline. Draw these lines parallel to the straightedge.

Separate the mold halves and set them against the straightedge, lining up their side-beam marks with those on the straightedge. Ideally, at this point the straight feet of the mold will be tight against the straightedge, the waterline on the mold will line up with the waterline on the work surface, and the miter joint along the centerline will be tight. This doesn't always happen. The materials you're using aren't perfect, and any tiny differences that might have crept in will have been magnified twice by sawing the mold halves together. You probably will find that there is a little too much wood somewhere. Double-

5.9 A bandsaw makes a reliable square cut when sawing out the paired-up halves of the molds.

check your cuts and measurements, matching the mold halves on the plan drawings if necessary. Trim judiciously. Along the centerline miter, trim both halves the same so the miter remains located at the centerline. This will be vital when you set up the molds on the jig.

When you're done trimming, drive a screw into each lower part to hold the mold halves against the straightedge, being sure that the side-beam marks are still lined up. Glue and screw a gusset over the centerline joint.

Remove the screws holding the mold to the bench. One mold face has the gusset block on it. The other face, the smooth one, is called the working face. It will be the one lined up with the station lines on the jig.

Boldly label the mold with its number and the boat design.

Your molds may need extensions to reach the side beams, or you may have a mold that is too tall, with a middle that hovers above the center beam. To attach side extensions, first increase the thickness of the straight-edge by screwing on a couple of straight-edged gusset blocks in the side-beam areas. Lay the assembled mold with the working face against the bench, just as you assembled it, then slide the side extension pieces under

5.10 Assemble the two halves of each mold against a plywood straightedge fastened to a workbench. Lay out the width of the side beams on the straightedge and draw a centerline on the bench top.

the mold's lower ends. Insert a scrap of mold stock near the top of the mold to raise it up so that the mold's working face is parallel to the bench top. Position the mold roughly over the centerline drawn on the bench top; push the side extensions and mold feet against the straightedge; and position the extensions so that they reach the side-beam marks. Glue and screw the extensions to the assembled mold.

If the mold is too tall by a few inches, flip the mold over onto its gusset blocks and settle the feet firmly on the straightedge. Slide a scrap of mold stock with a straight edge under the middle of the mold. Line up the scrap's straight edge with the center-beam line. Trace around the inner side of the mold onto the scrap. Remove the scrap, and cut out the scrap inset; glue and screw in place, lining up carefully with the center-beam line. You can be a little above the line, but don't go below it or the mold won't sit properly on the side beams.

If your mold is too tall by more than a couple of inches, raise the mold up above the bench top as you did with the side-beam extensions (working face down). Line up a gusset block of sufficient size on the mold's center-beam line and glue and screw it in place.

MAKING THE MOLDS FROM SHEET MATERIAL

If you choose to use sheet material, ½″ will work fine for most boats. Get a piece of the material you'd like to use, and try driving some drywall screws into it to see if they'll hold. Does pre-drilling help? If not, use thicker panels or a different material. Plywood is likely to be better than chipboard or fiberboard.

Lay out the molds as you would a transom (see Chapter 6, "The Backbone, and Lining Off"). Draw a centerline and the side-beam line, then position your drawing over these lines. Punch-mark one half, flip the drawing over, then mark the other side.

Mark the width of the molds with a compass set to the width you want (8″ to 10″, approximately). Mark a series of arcs around the inside of the section shape. If you draw enough of them, you can cut from arc to arc and not have to bother with a batten. Mark the cutout for the center beam with a framing square.

If you mark out the largest molds first, you should be able to nest some of the smaller ones inside them. Making the molds in halves that will be joined at the centerline allows you to nest the molds closer together.

It may be tempting to skip the bit about cutting out the middle of the molds and just leave them whole. Solid molds will make it difficult to reach most of the hull's interior. It's a trade-off: spend a little time cutting plywood now, or more time swearing over hardened epoxy later.

A jigsaw is the best tool for sawing out the single-piece molds. Molds cut in halves are usually small enough to be sawn out on the bandsaw, doubled-up like solid-wood molds.

INSTALLING THE MOLDS ON THE JIG

Putting the molds on the jig is always a thrill. For one thing, it's fast. For another, your boat is now *really* taking shape—no more visualizing or pretending.

Orienting the molds

Each mold has a smooth face, unencumbered with gusset blocks, called the working face, and it is the one that will be lined up on the station lines. The rest of the mold wants to be on the side of the station line where the boat is bigger. Because the biggest part of the boat is its middle, this means:
- *Forward* molds go on the *aft* side of the station line, and
- *Aft* molds go on the *forward* side of the station line.
- The middle mold, if there is one, must become one or the other. We generally make it a forward mold.

The exception to this is if the molds have *extensions* screwed to them, in which case the extensions go on the opposite side of the station line from the above.

But first, attach the mold blocks

You must install one mold block on each beam (that is, three per mold) before placing the molds on the jig.

Positioning the mold blocks for molds without extensions on the side beams and center beam is easy: The blocks sit opposite the working face of the molds, so blocks on the aft half of the boat go on the aft side of the station lines, and on the forward side for the forward half. (Molds with extensions for the side beams will be opposite this: for mold blocks on the aft half on the boat, put the mold blocks on the forward side of the station lines; for the forward half, on the aft side.) Attach each block with two screws.

Now you may place the molds on the jig. And, enjoy the view of your boat-to-be for awhile.

Fasten a second mold block on the center beam on the other side of each mold to hold them securely. The molds are now square and plumb.

(If you look carefully at the photos of our jig, you'll notice that we use special blocks that fit down over the center beam and hold both sides of the molds. These save a little time if you're building many boats.)

Center the molds

On each carefully smoothed and squared end of the center beam, mark the center of the beam, then draw a plumb line through this mark with a torpedo level.

To hold the mold-centering string, make two centering blocks from scrap wood about ¾ square and 10″ long. About 3″ from one end of each block, mark a score line all around the blocks. The blocks will be installed with this line even with the top of the center beam. Drill the longer portion of the block for two screws that will fasten the blocks to ends of the center beam. Mark a second score line on each block at 1½″ above the first line. Cut a small notch in each block at this line to hold the string at the proper height. Finally, drive two short drywall screws into each block on the same side as the screw holes. Leave the heads proud about ½″ to form a cleat for the string.

Install the centering blocks on the ends of center beam, making sure to put them on the same side of the line in the middle of the beam. Otherwise, the string will be angled slightly across the jig and all the molds, and the transom will end out of alignment.

Drill a hole in each mold for the centering string. First locate the height of the center of the holes, which wants to be the same as the "string height" on the centering blocks. Set a block of wood of the right thickness on the mold blocks, and mark a line on the mold. Where the pencil line and mold's vertical miter joint intersect is the center of the hole. Drill 1″ holes with a spade bit. Before you start drilling, check to make sure that the bit won't hit any screws in the gusset block. Pull any that look close and re-install them elsewhere.

Thread the string through all of holes in the molds. A needle made of wire with a looped eye is very helpful. Pull the string taut and make off to the screw head "cleat."

Center the molds. Before you can start, the taut string must run freely through all the holes. Move any molds that touch the string.

At each mold, sight down the miter joint over the center beam and move the mold side to side until the joint lines up with the string. You will find this method accurate enough that you can choose which side of the string to use. It doesn't matter which side you choose, so long as you use the same side for all of the molds. Make sure that you don't touch the string while centering the molds.

Once a mold is centered, drill for and drive a screw to hold the mold firmly to the side beam mold block on one side of the boat.

5.11 Sighting along the joint at the center of each mold positions the molds accurately on a taut string attached to blocks at each end of the center beam.

5.12 The building jig and molds all set up and ready for the backbone.

After you have centered all molds, drive a second screw in the legs of the molds on the other side of the boat. If you are building a big boat, you will want to put at least two screws into each mold leg. Remove the string and centering blocks. Rub Paste wax onto the molds' edges down onto the sides. Let dry.

The jig and molds are ready. Before you move on to making and assembling the first parts of the boat, the backbone and transom, make the clamping battens and lap-clamping blocks you'll need for planking the boat.

PLANK CLAMPING BATTENS AND LAP-CLAMPING BLOCKS

The clamping battens and lap-clamping blocks are an integral part of the jig system. You won't need them for a little while—not until it's time to attach the second pair of planks—but you may want to make these now while you're still in "jig" mode.

Making the clamping battens

Please see the general instructions for making battens on page 34 if you haven't already made your clamping battens and used some of them when working up your rough lumber into blanks and parts. Don't forget to wax the battens well and let them dry before use.

Making the lap-clamping blocks

The lap-clamping blocks go on the inside of the plank lap joints to draw them tight and fair and easily accommodate the various angles at which the planks meet. (see photo, page 139). Ours are made from scraps of hardwood left over from roughing out the part blanks. Rip out strips 1″ wide with a thickness of ⅛″ less than the width of the laps (e.g., for a ¾″ lap, the strips should be ⅝″ thick).

Each block must have a hole in its center. Drill the holes through the edge of the strips before cutting up the strips. Either lay the holes out and then punch and drill, or set up a fence on the drill press. Mark the fence for the first hole on each strip and the center-to-center spacing of the holes. Our blocks are about 3″ to 4″ long. Center-

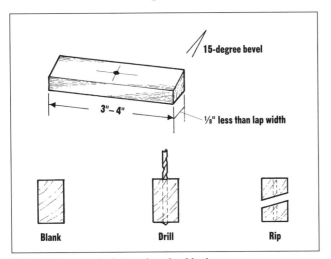

15-degree bevel

3"– 4"

⅛" less than lap width

Blank **Drill** **Rip**

Fig 5.9 A close-up look at a clamping block.

ing the hole sideways is crucial; as for centering it on the block's length, close will do.

Drill the strips with a ³⁄₃₂″ drill.

Rip the strips in half at ½″ with the blade set at 15 degrees to make two beveled strips.

The blocks must be waxed with paste wax so they can't be epoxied to the boat. It is much easier to wax the whole strip than to do each little block.

Crosscut the beveled strips into individual blocks, midway between the drilled holes. For a helpful guide, place marks on the table saw's crosscut fence spaced half of the blocks' center-to-center distance of the holes on both sides of the blade slot. Try cutting the strips in gangs of two or four. You can also cut the blocks apart on the miter saw or bandsaw.

How many clamping blocks?

We put two blocks between each pair of molds (about 8″ apart) and between the first and last molds and the bow and transom; therefore, on the 12′ Ellen, we use twelve blocks per lap. Occasionally, you'll need a third block to pull together two stubborn planks. This most often happens at the ends of the boat, especially on the garboard and the adjacent plank. Hulls with lots of tumblehome also benefit from a few extra blocks in the right places.

If you plan to build more than one boat, make jillions of these little blocks. They get lost, the holes strip out, the wood splits, or they are swept up in a pile of shavings. Puppies find them irresistible.

Fastening the backbone to molds: Keelson to last mold.

Chapter 6

The Backbone, and Lining Off

In glued-lapstrake construction, the basic framework of the hull often is divided into two groups. The inner stem, keelson, transom, and transom knee and, in many cases, any "full" frames (those run from sheer to sheer) are assembled before the planking is attached; the outer stem, keel, and skeg (plus deadwood if any) go on after the planking is finished. We call the inner stem and keelson the backbone, and include the transom, transom knee, and any full frames with these. The outside parts have become known around the shop as the "outbone." We include the boat's rails with outbone parts in the building process, as they are easier to put on the boat while it is still on the jig.

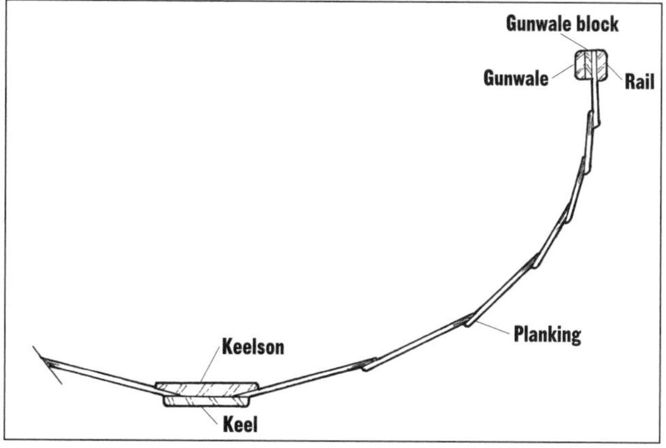

Making the Parts for the Backbone and Transom

You have some latitude when choosing the woods for the inner stem, keelson, and transom, but these parts must be made of woods that will glue well with epoxy, as they will be glued to each other, then the planking glued to the resulting assemblage. We often used cosmetically imperfect Honduras ("real" or New World) mahogany for the inner stem and keelson, reserving lovely pieces of mahogany for transoms, which are invariably varnished. You can also use mahogany relatives such as khaya ("African mahogany"), Spanish cedar, Douglas-fir, or Philippine mahogany (carefully chosen) for these parts. We often use white oak for the transom knee; ash and other hardwoods are also possibilities. (See also Chapter 2, "Materials and Tools," for wood selection considerations.) Our boats' full frames are typically laminated from white oak or ash.

Check your plans for the designer's wood recommendations.

Fig 6.1 A hull section showing the keelson, keel, planking, gunwale, and rail.

(diagram labels: Gunwale block, Gunwale, Rail, Keelson, Planking, Keel)

INNER STEM
Making the blank

The inner stem blank can be made of several blocks of wood glued together and the shape sawed out, or it can be laminated out of a stack of veneers over a curved jig. The sawn blank is a little easier to make and is plenty strong enough.

Sawn blank. Lay the piece for upper half of the stem over full-size pattern or the lofting. Make sure to leave several inches of wood above the sheer for fastening the stem to the jig. In the Ellen and other boats we've designed, the curve on the inner stem continues past the sheer and crosses the line of the jig. It is important to have enough wood to cut out this curve properly, so that the stem is held in the proper fore-and-aft position on the jig.

Trace around the upper piece, then remove it and position the lower piece. The joint will be cut where the two pieces overlap; mark this on the block from the line traced along the aft side of the upper piece. Trace around the lower piece and remove it.

To hold the two blocks together for gluing, you'll need to cut a notch for a clamp in the upper edge of the lower block, opposite the middle of the joint and with the "clamping face" parallel to the joint. Lay out the notch on the drawing, then mark for it by placing the drawing over the block, lining up the outline of the block, and punching with an awl.

Bandsaw for the joint and notch, then clean up the joint's mating surfaces with a sharp block plane, just removing the saw marks. You can glue up these pieces as is, taking care to keep the blocks lined up, or use splines (see box, page 82) or biscuits. Most of our boats' inner stems have a double spline joint. If you use a plain butt joint, shape and bevel the stem, then drive a couple of screws into the joint.

The stem for a larger boat or one with a sharply curved bow must be made of three or more blocks, but the procedure for building it is much the same.

6.1 The blank for a sawn inner stem, made of two pieces, is clamped together while the glue hardens.

Laminated blank. Cut out the wood strips, and glue-up the laminated stack using the general instructions given in Chapter 3, "Some Very Useful Techniques." Typically, the laminated blank is formed over the inner stem's inner curve (taken from the full-sized pattern or lofting). Once the glue cures, you must clean up and flatten the blank as the general instructions describe before proceeding to lay out the inner stem's shape upon it.

Layout

Orient the glued-up sawn inner stem blank so the sheer is up. Place the full-sized pattern over the blank, and line up the blank's traced outline by feeling through the paper. Try not to locate the cutting outlines too close to the edge of the blank, which will make it hard to mark and saw out the shape.

If you laminated your stem blank, the stem's final inner curve was formed when you glued-up the blank. Line up the pattern's inner curve line with this edge, sheer up. Obviously, you won't have to mark or cut along this line unless irregularities require correction. Otherwise, laying out and shaping a laminated inner stem proceeds in essentially the same way as shaping the sawn stem.

To avoid distortions, make sure the paper lies perfectly flat. Placing additional blocks of wood of the same thickness as the stem under the drawing helps.

When you have the paper pattern close to where you want it, hold it with one weight, then finely adjust its position. When you're satisfied, add more weights to keep the pattern firmly in place.

Punch through the paper with an awl along the stem's outline and its rabbet line (the line that forms the inboard end of the bevel), spacing the marks about ½″ to ¾″ apart. Also mark the following: the sheerline; the line of the jig; the joint between the keelson and inner stem; the waterline; and the location of the edge-of-plank marks (punched deeper than the others). As you will recall from making the molds, the edge-of-plank-marks are the ones closest to the sheer of the pairs shown on the pattern.

Don't remove the drawing when you are done punching. Peel sections of it back to reveal the blank below. Connect the dots for the straight lines of the sheer, jig, and waterline with a ruler, checking the drawing to make sure you are connecting the right punch marks. Draw a circle and a short tail on each lap punch mark. Draw the joint between the stem and keelson (usually a straight line).

Now you can remove the drawing. Label the jig line and sheerline so you don't confuse the two.

Sawing out the shape

Don't bother with a batten when connecting the dots that define the stem's curves. Quickly sketch along the punch marks so they show up better, but follow the punches, not a drawn line, when you bandsaw out the shape.

Set up the bandsaw for a perfectly square cut and

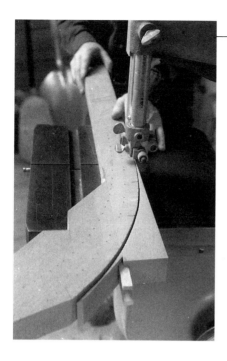

6.2 Saw out the shape of an inner stem on the bandsaw so that the cut just touches the dimples made by an awl.

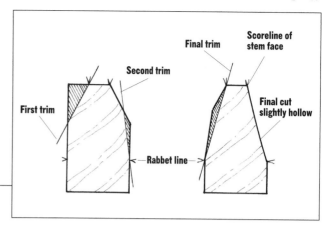

Fig 6.2 Beveling the inner stem in three steps assures a precise angle. This same method can be used anywhere a bevel needs to be cut.

saw out inner stem's profiles. Saw just to the edge of each punch mark, then take off just the saw marks with a spokeshave or plane. The more accurately you can saw out the shape, the easier the hand tool work will be. If you have to take off any more than the saw-cut grooves, check frequently for square. Trim the edges until a series of halved punch marks remains.

This procedure works for many parts you trim with hand tools.

Sand the inboard face until the sweep of the curve feels good under your hand. (Pieces of cloth sanding belt are helpful here.)

A little more layout

Once the inner stem's profiles are cleaned up, draw lines for the edge-of-plank marks across the forward face. These lines are crucial and will be hard to redraw later, so mark them with a knife blade or an awl to make sure they won't be accidentally sanded or scraped off.

Also mark the ends of the sheer, waterline, and jig lines on both the inboard and outboard faces of the stem. Connect these lines on the unmarked side.

Lay the stem on the bench, unpunched side up. Flip over your pattern. You will be able to see just the ghosts of the lines, but it should be easy to follow your punch marks. Draw the lines of the sheer and jig on this side of the pattern.

Cut out small diamond-shaped holes on the sheer and jig lines so you can line up the paper drawing with the lines on the inner stem. Feel around the edges of the stem to position the pattern properly. If you have to favor one edge, favor the outboard (forward) one. Check to be certain that the pattern is still lined up with the sheer and jig lines, then weight it. Punch the rabbet line and remove the pattern.

On your drawings, find the width of the face of the inner stem's outboard face. For most boats, this will be a constant width. Set a marking gauge so that, when used from both sides, the space between the scored lines is the proper width. You also can use a try-square for this job.

Beveling

Pre-cutting. Removing a majority of the wood from the bevel is the first step. To do this on the bandsaw: Using a bevel gauge and ruler, measure the angle near the sheer. This will be the bluntest angle along the length of the stem. If the angle is less than 45 degrees, set the bandsaw table for a degree or two less than the angle. Frequently, the angle is steeper than 45 degrees. In this case, set the table at 45, usually the maximum the table will go. Lay the side of the stem on the table with the score lines (on the outer face) near the blade. Cut the bevel close to the scored line (about 1/16"). When you finish the cut and flip the inner stem over, you will see that the cut follows close to the prick marks near the sheer and moves gradually away as the stem angle becomes steeper (sharper) near the keelson. Repeat the cut on the other side.

You can skip the bandsaw and remove all the wood by hand if you wish. Start with a drawknife or a wide, heavy chisel. Mind the grain as you work, especially around the glue joint. Avoid the joint as much as possible until you are nearly done with the rough cutting. Trim the joint area by cutting with a chisel from the rabbet toward the stem's forward face. Angle the chisel whichever way works best.

Final trimming. Hold the inner stem to the bench with clamps, as they are more secure than a vise. To hold the stem vertically, screw two wooden hand-screws to the bench (see Photo 6.3). To hold it horizontally, apply two quick-action bar clamps (see Photo 6.4).

Clamp the inner stem in the vertical position near a corner of the bench. You must be able to clearly see the score lines on the forward face as you work. Trim the bevel to the score lines but don't cut to the rabbet line, yet. The best tool for this job is the spokeshave. Do both sides of the stem.

6.3 Slash marks made with a soft pencil clearly show where the chisel cuts as the inner stem is beveled.

6.4 Scooping cuts made with a chisel hollow out the finished bevel.

Now clamp the stem flat (horizontal) on the bench. Using the spokeshave, trim the bevel just to the rabbet line. If you are having trouble seeing how much you are cutting, take a soft pencil and draw closely spaced slash marks perpendicular to the rabbet line. As you cut, you will see the pencil lines shrink toward the rabbet line. Remember not to cut past the marks. The scored lines and punch marks will help you here; if you do trim just a little bit past a line, a vestige of these will remain, unlike a pencil mark. File away this little fact for later use when beveling the transom and the keelson.

When you finish trimming to the rabbet line, the bevel should have two sloping sides meeting at a ridge near the middle (see Figure 6.2). Keeping the stem horizontal on the bench, draw slash marks, and start trimming off the ridge with a spokeshave or chisel. Set the

spokeshave for a fairly light cut until you gain confidence in your ability to hold the tool. Find yourself trimming too much off one edge? If you have shaped the blade of your spokeshave to a slight curve, you can move the middle of the spokeshave over to the other side of the cut (see Chapter 2, "Materials and Tools"). The deeper part of the blade will cut more and even things out. Trim until the pencil slash marks are almost gone at both the scored forward face line and punched rabbet line.

Spline Joints

To make a spline joint, you first cut a dado into each piece, then make the spline that will connect the two. Glue is applied to both dadoes, and the spline inserted into the dadoes. The whole assemblage is clamped firmly together. Splines help to register the pieces, keeping the faces flush with one another. They also increase the amount of gluing surface area, making for a stronger joint.

All the parts for the Ellen, for example, need ¼" splines, so it is possible to set up the tools once and run all the parts over them. As a rule of thumb, gauge the size of the spline by dividing the thickness of the pieces to be joined by three. For example, a ¼" spline is perfect for a ¾"-thick transom. However, there are always exceptions. For a 1½"-thick inner stem, it is better to make two ¼" splines, spacing them ½" apart rather than make one ½" dado and spline.

The sizes for the splines and dadoes we've given here generally fit the parts for the Ellen and boats of similar size. Use these as guides for your project.

To cut the dadoes, set the depth of the table saw's dado blades at about twice the thickness of the dado.

Before you cut the dadoes into your pieces, do a test on a piece of scrap. The test piece is also handy for checking the fit of the splines. You also can cut these dadoes with a slot-cutting bit in a router. This method works nicely for large pieces that are difficult to handle on the table saw.

Splines should be a little narrower than the total depth of the two dadoes—by about ¹⁄₁₆"—so that the visible joint always closes up tight. Trim the splines so that they are a slip-fit in the dadoes, not too loose and not so tight that they must be driven in with a mallet. Make your splines a little fat, then trim them to fit. Set up a couple of feather boards on the table saw to keep the spline piece against the fence while trimming them. You'll probably need to cut several test pieces.

With the dadoes cut and splines made, you are ready to glue. With the good joints you have undoubtedly made, we suggest using a resin glue such as Weldwood because it makes the least visible glue joint. If you're feeling unsure about a joint, you can use epoxy, but the glue line will show more.

Take a straightedge and check to be sure that the bevel is flat or slightly hollow. There's still a hump in the middle? If it is large, draw another round of slash marks and trim carefully with the spokeshave. If it is small, use a chisel positioned flat-face down and perpendicular to the rabbet and score lines to pare off thin shavings. Use a slight scooping motion to hollow out the bevel slightly. It's best to stop well short (¹⁄₁₆ ″) of the score and rabbet lines and finish up with a sharp scraper that has a shallow convex curve filed in it. Once again, slash marks will be very helpful.

You should now have one side of the inner stem beveled nicely. Repeat the performance on the other side. You will be using these same techniques when beveling other parts on the boat, so your patience at gaining skills now will be amply rewarded later on, especially when you confront the considerable length of the keelson.

A chamfer looks good on an inner stem's inboard corners. The side of the inner stem near the keelson can be a good place to carve your initials, and perhaps the year, for dedicated refinishers to find. Give the surfaces that will be exposed inside the boat a next-to-finish sanding and set the inner stem aside until the rest of the backbone is ready for it.

TRANSOM

The geometry of the transom is a real mind-bender—all the more so because you must make the transom early on and therefore must envision three-dimensional curved shapes coming together in thin air. Not to worry. As you work, it will all start to make sense.

Making the blank

Most of the time you will need to glue two or more boards together for your transom. For example, the

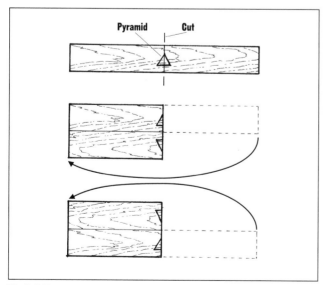

Fig 6.3 Marking a builder's pyramid on the crosscut line helps orient the pieces of the transom blank for a pleasing grain pattern.

Ellen's transom is made of two pieces 10″ wide and ¾″ thick. These can be either butt-jointed or splined. You could also use biscuits if you have access to a biscuit jointer. All of these options require starting with two perfectly mated edges.

If you plan to varnish your boat's transom, cut its pieces from a single board for the best color match possible.

Mark your board where you would like to crosscut it and pencil a builder's pyramid over the line (see Chapter 2, "Materials and Tools"). Mark the best face for outboard if you plan to varnish it. If you plan to varnish both inside and outside, mark the best face for outboard, because all of it will be seen, then look at the inside to determine which portion should be the one to show above the seat.

The pyramid helps you orient the pieces. Flip one piece end-for-end while keeping the pyramid face up and match the edges until you like what you see. The grain pattern and the color, particularly, match very nicely when you line up the boards in this way (see Figure 6.3).

If you want a better idea of how the wood will appear when varnished, swipe a little thinner or denatured alcohol over the surface to highlight changes in color and pattern. Let the solvent evaporate thoroughly before proceeding.

The pyramid halves will be on the same end and pointed either at or away from each other. When the two boards are lined up *without* flipping, the grain may work nicely, but the color match may well be all wrong. When you are happy with the way the pieces match, draw (with a soft pencil) a large pyramid, pointing up, right over the joint.

Cutting the joint. There are several ways to cut the joint between the boards, but the one we're going to recommend is the slickest John has ever seen—and it's easy to do. He found the instructions in Robert Waring's *Woodworker's Essential Shop Aids and Jigs*, a book to drool over if you like clever, well-made jigs and making your own tools.

You'll need a router fitted with a straight bit; for example, John uses a ¾″-diameter bit. Fasten two straight 2″ × 2″ cleats that are at least several inches longer than the combined width of the two transom boards on top of two sawhorses. Clamp the boards to the cleats, leaving a 2″ gap between them. Clamp a plywood straightedge along the "gap edge" of one board, locating it so that the router bit will trim off about ¹⁄₁₆ ″. Check to see that the clamps are tight, then trim the edge. Getting an even cut will be much easier if you've fitted your router with a rectangular base. If the base of the router is round, be sure that the same point on the base contacts the straightedge. Because the chuck is never perfectly centered in the base, turning the router so different points contact the straightedge produces an undulating cut that will mean gaps in your joint.

Now move the second board until the gap between the pieces is ¹⁄₁₆ ″ less than the cutter's diameter. Clamp

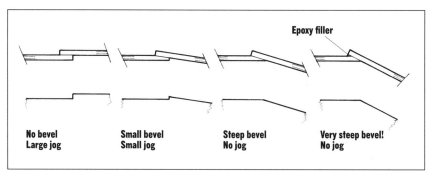

Fig 6.4 Planks joined at different angles show how the jogs in the transom are formed.

6.5 Using a router and straightedge to cut the butt joint in the transom pieces makes a nearly invisible glue joint.

it in place. If you cut from right to left on the first pass, cut from left to right on the second. Make a steady, firm, smooth cut. Any jiggling away from the straightedge will put dimple cuts in the second piece. If you do make dimples, move the second board a little closer and make another pass. Don't worry about the first piece; the cutter will whisk by without affecting it.

Before you ask: *No, you cannot cut both planks at the same time. It is a very bad idea. John tried it. Once. Don't.*

Unclamp the second piece and push up against the first to check the fit. The joint should be so perfect that it almost sucks together. The line between the two pieces seems to vanish.

One very large advantage of this system is that even if your straightedge has warped a little, the router cuts the identical curve in both planks so the joint is perfectly matched.

You can glue this joint as it is, or you can register and reinforce it with a spline or biscuits. We prefer splines, using them in transoms, as well as inner stems, breasthooks, and rowing seats (see box, "Spline Joints").

If You Do Not Have Plank Widths for Your Boat's Transom (Yet)

If your transom's outline is not a series of facets, either because you lofted the boat or are working with plans for a traditionally constructed lapstrake boat, you need to skip ahead to the section that explains how to define plank widths for the transom, part of the process called lining off (see page 103) and complete that little job—then return here to continue laying out and shaping the transom.

If you plan to carve a name in your transom's outboard face, offset the dadoes inboard (away from the pyramid). This way, if the name or hail must go over the joint area, you will not cut down into the spline.

Laying out

Set the glued-up, cleaned-up, and sanded transom blank on the bench outboard face up, top of transom away from you. Mark the desired center for the transom (soft pencil, please). Using a framing square, draw the centerline, perpendicular to the glue line. Of course, your glue joint is perfect and almost invisible, but you still want to build the boat with the glue joint, and primary grain direction of the wood, parallel to the waterline. It's a subtle thing, but the transom will always look a little off if you don't. If the two boards happen to age slightly differently, the joint line will definitely show. If you're really worried about this, you can stain your mahogany before varnishing to minimize any color differences.

We have assumed varnish in the preceding discussion, as we rarely build a boat with a painted transom. If you're planning to paint, you don't have worry so much. Then again, you might want to set the transom up properly just in case you change your mind about the varnish. Unless the wood you're using is really ugly, you may find it awfully hard to paint the transom when the time comes.

Dig through your plans to find the full-sized pattern, which usually shows only half of the transom. (If you lofted your boat, pick up the necessary information from the developed transom. The easiest approach is to trace the shape onto Mylar from the lofting.) If you have a paper pattern, cut two diamond-shaped holes on the centerline near the transom's top and bottom. One of these holes needs to be located on a horizontal line: either the drawn waterline, which is desirable, or top or bottom of the transom. Don't use any lines between the drawn waterline and the top of the transom, as you're going to mark the line by punching holes in the wood, and this tends not to enhance a varnished finish. Locate the pattern on the centerline, with the bottom of the transom near the edge of the blank.

The planking lands on the transom in a series of facets. Some of the facets have small jogs between them,

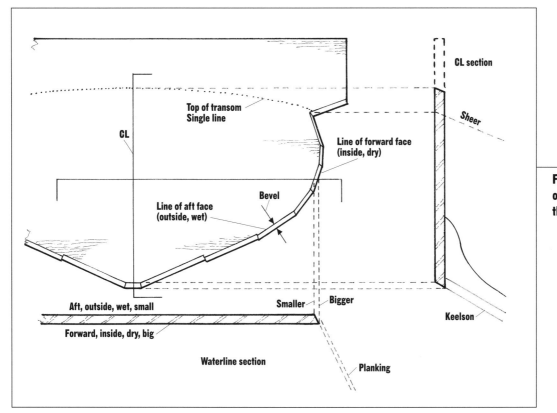

Line labels within the figure:

Top of transom
Single line

CL section

CL

Line of forward face
(inside, dry)

Sheer

Bevel

Line of aft face
(outside, wet)

**Fig 6.5 Transom lay-
out showing what all
the lines mean.**

Aft, outside, wet, small

Smaller

Bigger

Keelson

Forward, inside, dry, big

Waterline section

Planking

some don't. When the angle between the two planks is small, there will be a jog; when the angle is steeper, no jog appears (see Figure 6.4). Your pattern will show two nearly parallel sets of facets. The outer line is the forward—or interior—face of the transom. The inner, smaller shape shown is the aft—or exterior—face. You need to mark both.

This is a good place to mention one of the most common stumbling blocks in the transom-making thought process. The outboard face of the transom is the smaller of the two planking lines shown on the pattern. For whatever reason, common logic wants the bigger shape to be the outboard one. *It's not.* Quiet your mind and remember the following:

• Aft = small; wet; inside line.
• Forward = big; dry; outside line.

For the most part, you can mark all the corners: where the facets meet the jogs, where the facets meet each other, and the jog at the top of the transom. The top of the transom is a curve. Mark with punch marks as you did the inner stem's curves.

Mark the top of the transom now, but deeply bury the urge to apply a saw to that attractive curve. You do not want to trim the top of the transom until just before the boat comes off the jig, at the earliest. You're going to need all that "waste" wood to secure the transom to the jig.

On some of our boats, the garboard is fairly wide. To make this wide plank look nice at the transom, it can be encouraged to follow the design curve of the transom, rather than a straight line like the rest of the planks. This

is especially elegant if the transom has some hollow in the garboard, as one version of the Ellen does. The plywood will be somewhat (sometimes very) reluctant go into the curve, but a proper allocation of many screws will pull it in and keep it there. Mark this as you would any curve.

Punch the points with the awl. Double-check to make sure you have gotten them all. Then, as with the inner stem, lift portions of the drawing, without moving it, to connect the dots along the facets with pencil and ruler. Sketch pencil lines over the punch marks of the curves, just like you did for the inner stem. It's particularly important to do this connecting before removing the drawing from the transom, because the punch marks alone look particularly confusing and random. Also, if you miss a point you can lay the drawing back down and punch the mark.

However, if you're rereading this after you've just pulled off the pattern and are now aiming your Anglo-Saxon vocabulary at a couple of missed points, go fish a few tacks out of the kitchen drawer. Line up the pattern as closely as you can by using the center and horizontal lines, then carefully register the pattern by placing the tacks in the holes you can match with certainty. It's best if at least a couple of these are near the points you missed. Check the centerline and other known marks to make sure the pattern's correctly positioned, weight it well, then punch the errant marks and draw any necessary lines.

You may find it helpful to flag the punch marks before trying to connect them. Draw short pencil lines facing into the center of the transom on the aft (smaller) face and lines facing out on the forward (larger) face. The lines on the aft face will prove useful later on when you are beveling the transom and planking.

When all the punch marks are connected with pencil lines and labeled, remove the drawing and flip it over so you can do the other half of the transom. Draw the centerline and your horizontal reference line on the back of the paper. (A window makes a good instant "light table.") Line up the pattern using the center and horizontal lines, and hold it in place with weights. Punch all the holes. Be systematic, as using the previously punched holes makes it pretty much impossible to tell whether you've missed a hole. As you did on the first side, pull back the pattern and connect the dots before you remove the drawing for good.

Remove the drawing and extend the lines of the jog at the top of the transom out to the edge of the blank. If the waterline crosses the transom, neatly score or punch along it deeply enough that you won't lose the line when you sand the transom.

Cutting out

The best tool for the job is a bandsaw, although a jigsaw will suffice. If you lack a bandsaw, you can lay out the transom (along with the inner stem and keelson, if you wish) and take them to the shop of a good friend. Cutting on the bandsaw is much easier and more accurate than using a jigsaw, so this trip will be worthwhile.

You are going to cut to the outer line, the forward or interior face. Mark it clearly with little Vs drawn out from the line. Keep this idea clearly in mind: When you finish cutting, there should be the penciled plank lines of the aft face closely paralleling your newly cut edge. The cut you make should be square.

On the bandsaw, the job goes easier if you first make a rough cut around the shape of the transom about an inch or so away from the outer line. Next, make short cuts from the rough-cut edge to the inside corners of the jogs (on the outer line). You can also cut to the other corners (where there are no jogs), though this isn't essential.

Now cut along the outer line, splitting the line. On the starboard side, you'll have no trouble reaching all the corners of the jogs. However, unless you are using a large bandsaw (36″ or so), you won't be able to cut into some of the corners on the port side. Do as much as you can, then finish up with a jigsaw with a fresh, sharp blade. Keep the cut as square as possible.

Unless you strayed from the line, there is no need to clean up the saw cut. Take a look at your newly freed transom. Do you still have a pencil line running more or less parallel to the cut? Good. Oh… No penciled plank line? Somehow you managed to cut to the inner lines. The bad news: You're going to have to make a new tran-

6.6 Using a jigsaw to rough-cut the bevels for planks on the transom.

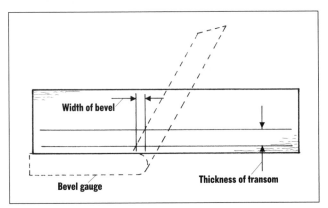

Width of bevel

Bevel gauge

Thickness of transom

Fig 6.6 How to lay out to measure the angle of a bevel when you know its width.

som. The good news: You already have a blank for another boat with a smaller transom.

Beveling

With a handsaw, make short angled, cuts into the jogs and at each corner. At the top of the cut, the saw blade should almost touch the punch mark, and at the bottom. it should almost touch the corner of the bandsawed edge. Don't cut into the punch marks!

Trim excess wood off the bevels with a jigsaw. Measure the angle of the bevel where the bandsaw-trimmed outer line and inner line are farthest apart, usually the garboard. You can measure this with a bevel gauge and thin metal ruler in the same way as you did the inner stem (see page 81).

Or, you can lay out the bevel on a straight-edged scrap (see Figure 6.6). Use a marking gauge or try-square and awl to accurately score two lines the thickness of the transom apart. Next, lay out the width of the bevel at its widest and score perpendicular lines across the first two lines with try-square and awl. With the bevel gauge, measure the angle of the two opposite corners of the little rectangle you've created and find the angle on the bevel board (see Chapter 2, "Materials and Tools").

Set up the jigsaw for the proper angle and trim the bevel with a slow, smooth cut, keeping between ¹⁄₁₆″ and

⅛″ from the pencil line.

John's tool of choice for final trimming of the bevels is a 1¼″ chisel, sharpened until it shaves the arm nicely. Give it a good stropping on your palm (see Chapter 2, "Materials and Tools").

With the transom clamped to the bench aft side uppermost, trim the bevels, working from the bottom of the boat toward the top. Trim the bevels in much the same way as you did the inner stem. Trim to the inner pencil line, then to the outer sawn edge, leaving a ridge in the middle. Use pencil slashes across the bevel to help you see where you're removing wood. You don't want to take off much along the lower, sawn edge, because you split the line in half when sawing out the transom. Once you have the middle ridge, draw more pencil slashes across and trim off the ridge. You should generally hold the chisel with the flat part down (against the wood), using a slicing motion to take the wood off and maintain control, which is particularly important as you need to stop cutting *before* you get to the jog in each lap, not after.

If your transom has some hollow at the bottom, you will need to hold the chisel with the bevel down so the blade can go around the curve. You can still use the slicing motion. John also likes to finish all the cuts with the blade's bevel side down, because all of his chisels are ground in a slight curve. Cutting this way makes the bevels on the transom slightly concave, ensuring a good landing for each plank. If you test the bevel with the straight edge of the chisel and find it still convex, cut perpendicular to the length of the bevel in a scooping motion—just like you did on the inner stem. A little wax on the chisel makes the beveling job go easier.

Finish up the beveling so that just the last bits of the pencil slashes remain. It bears repeating: Don't cut off your marks. This is particularly important with the transom. If you cut off too much on one side, your transom will be lopsided and the planks won't fit properly.

Before you set the transom aside for a bit, mark the centerline on the forward face. Now is a good time to carve the transom.

Set the transom aside until it's time to set up the backbone on the jig. You'll finish sand it after the hull is done.

KEELSON

For smaller boats like the Ellen, you can get the keelson out of a single piece of wood of a length readily available. For longer boats, you'll either have to pay a premium and be lucky enough to find a board of sufficient length or sharpen up your plane and limber up, for you'll be getting plenty of exercise.

Making the blank: scarfing a long keelson

You can skip the trip to the health club today. An enormous amount of wood needs to be removed for a proper

6.7 Trim the ridge in the middle of the bevel by making controlled slicing cuts with a chisel held flat-face down. Pencil slashes clearly show where the chisel is cutting.

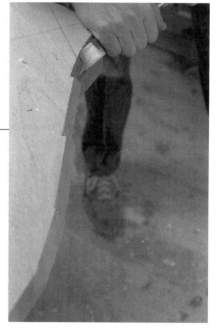

6.8 Trim a concave curve of the bevel for the garboard plank with the beveled side of the chisel against the wood.

scarf joint in the keelson.

John likes to use an 8:1 scarf. This joint is essentially the same as the joints in the planking stock (see Chapter 4, "Milling Solid Lumber and Scarfing the Planking Plywood Stock"), just longer and with a few differences. After cutting the ends of the keelson pieces to be scarfed, score the length of the scarf on both. Tack them together, lining up the upper piece on the score line of the lower.

Mark the slope of the joint on both edges of the keelson pieces. With a hand saw, make a series of cuts, parallel to the scored lines and spaced about ½″ apart, down to the angled pencil line marking the joint. Every once in a while check the other side to be sure you don't cut over the line. Stop about 1″ from the end of each piece.

6.9 A series of handsaw cuts is the first step in making a scarf joint for a keelson.

6.10 Roughly chopping off the waste with a chisel and a mallet.

With a large chisel and mallet, chip out most of the waste, starting from the lower ends of the pieces and working up the slope. Remove waste in at least two chips so that if the grain is playing tricks, you won't end up with large chipped-out holes in the joint or, even worse, a split.

Once you're removed a majority of the waste, set aside your mallet and turn the chisel flat side down. Remove more waste by paring across the joint, downhill. On a wide keelson, you will have to work from both edges toward the middle, unless you have an unusually long or large chisel. (See your favorite fine tool catalog for patternmaker's chisels.) When you have the joint pared down pretty close to the line, finish up with your trusty plane and finally a few swipes with a sanding block loaded with 80-grit.

Glue-up the scarf in much the same way as you did the planking stock, nailing the pieces in position. Instead of screwing the top board down to hold the joint, simply clamp it. Check that the keelson is straight by sighting down the edge or using a plywood straightedge.

Laying out

Before marking, sand both edges and the inboard face one step short of finished, to 80-grit.

At this point, the keelson should be a straight-sided, planed board. You'll need to lay out the following: the centerline and stations inboard and out; the widths for the keelson's shape; the widths for the rabbet lines for the area to be beveled to receive the planking; and the locations defining the end of the inner stem, the stem bevel rabbet line, and where to cut off the aft end for the transom.

Marking the centerline. Set a try-square to a distance just shy of half the width of the keelson blank. Use it and a very sharp pencil to mark a line down the length of the blank. Turn around and draw an identical line from the other edge of the board, resulting in two closely spaced parallel lines at the center of the blank. Flip the board over and do the same on the other side.

This method is very accurate. If you mark the centerline with a single line from one edge, it is very likely to be off no matter how careful you measured. It's also easier to line up two parts or punch a centerpoint in the narrow space between two lines, rather than trying to guess the middle of a fat pencil line (see Chapter 2, "Materials and Tools").

What To Do if the Keelson Has Warped a Little

Uh, oh. You've just discovered that the keelson has warped a little, and the straight edge you so carefully marked with a string and sawed out now has a slight, but distinctly un-straight, curve. Should you lay out the centerline with a string? You don't have to. You can use the try-square method and spring the keelson in place on the jig. The mold notches and temporary drywall screws hold it in place initially; once you've got the garboards glued in place, that keelson isn't going anywhere.

It's very rare to have a keelson warp so badly that it can't be encouraged into place with gentle firm persuasion. If yours has, we don't recommend forcing it into position, for fear that the pressure will wrack the jig or, no matter how wide the garboards are, the keelson will take the boat along with it as it springs back into its natural curve when freed of the jig. Make another one, and use the warped board for small parts.

Laying out the stations. The best tools for this job are an 18″ metal ruler and a 1″ tape measure.

Use the ruler to lay out the distance from the end of the stem to the first station, which will be on your full-sized pattern or lofting. Mark and label both. Line up the tape on the measurement for the first station (as you did when laying out the stations on the jig), and hold it with a weight (see Figure 6.7). Run the tape down the length of the keelson, and carefully mark and label the remaining stations. Use the ruler to lay off the distance to the end of the keel-

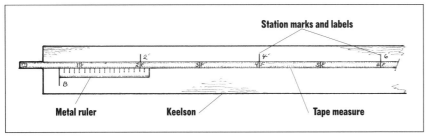

Fig 6.7 Using a ruler and a tape to lay out the end and the stations on the keelson helps to avoid measuring errors and measurement creep.

son from the last station. In the case of the Ellen and our other designs that are not double-ended, the end of the keelson is also the inner face of the transom.

Check your measuring on the way back to the forward end, especially if your stations are at differing intervals. Draw square lines at the stations and the ends on the outboard face and an edge, then flip the keelson over and draw them on the inboard face as well, except for the aft end at the transom.

Make a healthy dimple with a centerpunch wherever a station crosses the centerline on both sides of the keelson. The pencil lines will be sanded or scraped off, but the indented marks will survive. You'll need the marks for locating the keel; end of the inner stem; thwarts; and floorboard frames as well as any sailing parts, deckbeams, or bulkheads your boat may have.

At the forward end of the end of the keelson, lay out the width of the inner stem's forward face. Repair to your full-sized pattern or lofting, and find the measurement from the end of the keelson back to the inner stem's rabbet line along the top of the keelson. Lay out this measurement on your keelson blank and draw a square line through this point, then mark the half-thickness of the inner stem.

Note: When you bend a batten around (in a moment), you likely will not be able to touch the points at both the face and rabbet of the stem. Go to the wider mark and fair it later in on the jig.

Finding the points that define the keelson's shape.
With the Ellen and other similar designs, most of the keelson side is straight. At the ends of the boat, the angle of the plank is steeper, and so the keelson must be narrower and taper to the transom and stem. To spring a batten and define the proper curves at the ends of the keelson, you will need the end points for the keelson, plus the keelson half-widths at the two stations nearest each end. You should already have the end points, but you may have to do a little work to get the half-widths at the stations.

Get out your full-sized patterns or lofting and take a look at the two forwardmost sections. Does the line forming the top of the keelson inter-

sect with the section line or does the keelson end before it reaches the section line? If you have an intersection of keelson and section line for both stations, you're all set. Pick up the half-widths, and transfer these to the keelson blank.

However, you may find that keelson and section line intersect neatly at the first station, but not at the second. This is a common situation. Pick up the half-width for the first station, then deal with the difficulty presented by the second.

Take a ruler and extend the line of the top of the keelson until it does intersect the section line. This intersection is your second station point, and the distance from the centerline to it is the half-width you need.

You now have your end point and the half-widths at the two forward stations—and a little problem. That second station's intersection point will be located out past the edge of the keelson blank, in free space. Because holding a batten to a point that exists only in thin air is quite impossible, you need something more tangible. A small square stick serves nicely. Transfer the second station's half-width by laying the stick on the full-sized pattern or lofting with one end touching the line of the section, then subtract the width of the batten. Clearly label this shorter distance with a V.

Once you're done with this process at the bow, turn your attention to the stern. Make a point-defining stick for that end as well, if necessary.

Defining the keelson shape with the batten.
Temporarily screw or nail the "point-defining" sticks at the appropriate stations, with the V-mark on the centerline. (Be sure to place each stick on the "middle" side of its section line—same as the molds.)

Tack the batten to the keelson at one end to the two known points, bend it around the "point-defining" sticks, and tack it to the points at the other end. Let the middle go where it may. Trace the outside of the batten to mark the keelson's outline. (See Figure 6.8; it will help clarify matters.)

There's no need to get overly fussy with this. You'll be beveling the keelson down to the final width and

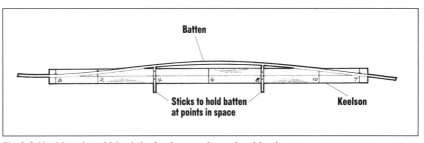

Fig 6.8 Marking the width of the keelson at the ends with a batten.

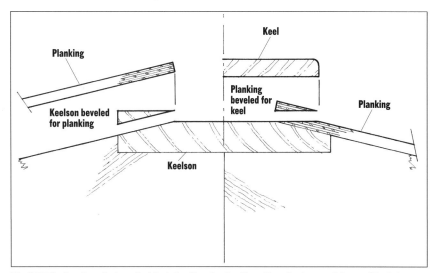

Fig 6.9 The keelson is beveled to take the planks, then the planks are trimmed to take a plank keel.

shape once it is on the jig.

When you're done, remove the batten and point-defining sticks, and duplicate the process to mark the other side of the keelson.

Laying out the rabbet lines. In traditionally built boats, the rabbet is often an angled cut made in the keel and stem to receive the plank edges. The keelson is a totally separate interior piece that is usually not a major structural member in small boats. In bigger boats, the keelson typically sits on top of the frames.

In glued-lapstrake boats, the keelson forms the boat's backbone. The garboard (first) plank lands directly on the keelson, which is beveled along its length to accept the planking at the proper, ever-changing angle. In our boats, which have a flat keel, the overlapping plank edges are planed flat to the keelson to accept the keel after the hull is complete. The hull is intact without a keel, though the boat benefits greatly from the addition of one.

When you bevel the keelson, you will need to know where to stop, where the inboard edge is. You've already met this line on the inner stem; we call it the rabbet line.

The full-size patterns should have both the keel and keelson drawn on them, and you can get the widths for the rabbet line from these. In our plans, the rabbet line widths are noted in the offsets as well. Pick up the widths with a compass and mark both sides of the centerline on the outboard face (the bottom) of the keelson. Tack a batten to the points and mark the line.

There is a complicated interplay among the width of the keel, the thickness of the planking, and the angle at which they all meet at the stations. Although the rabbet line may curve in and out, the batten should still touch all the marks. If the batten won't go to a mark, get it as close as you can and let the batten be your guide. But don't worry about making the batten fair.

If things seem very strange, double-check your measurements. It's alarmingly easy to mis-measure.

Attending to daggerboard or centerboard trunk tenon holes

In many sailing designs, the lower ends of the posts belonging to the daggerboard or centerboard trunk are cut to form small tenons that fit into the extensions of the slot through which the board passes (see Chapter 9, "Building the Interior" for a preview).

Warning: The location of the holes for the trunk tenons on the keelson will be different from those that mark the end of the board slot on the keel. It's advisable to work from a full-sized drawing for these details. If your plans don't have one, make one. When you loft a boat, draw the daggerboard or centerboard trunk on the profile drawing.

Once you're confident of where they should go, mark and drill the tenon holes.

Final cuts

Trim the outside shape of the keelson with a jigsaw. After making sure that you have a sharp blade, set the saw's foot to the angle between the keelson and the transom, and carefully trim the aft end of the keelson. Make *sure* that the angle is going the right way. If you trim it the wrong way, stick the scrap back on with epoxy and trim it the right way after the glue dries. If the scrap is long, trim it so you can hold the scrap on with tape while the epoxy cures. Use a clamp and a couple of blocks (one top, one bottom) to align the little offcut with the keelson. (Yes. Experience speaks.)

For many designs, including the Ellen, you can leave the stem end of the keelson long, then trim this after attaching the inner stem and putting the entire backbone on the jig. If your boat is a double-ender, leave both ends long, of course. Keelsons (or bottoms) that fit into a notch in the stem(s) must be trimmed to a precise length before the stem can be attached.

Flip the keelson inboard side up and treat the straight corners that didn't get trimmed when the keelson was tapered with a bullnose or chamfer, to your taste. A small chamfer often looks good on smaller boats. If you expect a lot of hard wear on the interior and won't be adding floorboards, a moderate bullnose will hold paint longer.

TRANSOM KNEE

You can shape the transom knee by pattern routing (see Chapter 3, "Some Very Useful Techniques"), then cross-

6.11 A laminated full frame being guided through the thickness planer. Note the ready hand on the feed roller clutch.

cut the short end to the angle of the transom. The knee also can be cut out on the bandsaw and cleaned up on the stationary sander (see Chapter 3, "Some Very Useful Techniques") or by hand.

If your boat's transom knee will not be completely buried under a seat, a small chamfer or bullnose looks nice.

LAMINATED FULL FRAMES

Our lightweight Peregrine and Merlin rowboats have a laminated full frame that resides in the midships area. Your boat may have a single frame much like these or several (many) spaced along the hull. We recommend making these now and installing them after the backbone is together and on the jig—before planking the hull.

The laminating jig for the frame should be set up to the frame's inboard curve. (See Chapter 3, ""Some Very Useful Techniques" for general information on laminating.) Once the glue is dry, clean up the frame and plane it to thickness. Take the frame's outboard shape and key marks, including the edge-of-plank marks, from the full-sized pattern. Mark the edge-of-plank marks clearly with deep punch marks. (If you lofted your boat, you'll have the outboard shape, but no edge-of-plank marks until you line off the hull, after the full frame is installed.) Saw out the frame's curve on the bandsaw, in much the same way as you did the molds. You'll plane for the planking when you put the planks on, treating the frame like another mold. If you have edge-of-plank marks, mark them clearly on the frame with dark lines on the frame's edge and one face.

If your full frame has sprung back very little, you can mark the proper beam (width) on the frame at the sheer. Then mark out the curve of the hull on both sides (port and starboard), lining up with the mark of the beam you just measured and the centerline at the bottom of the frame.

If the full frame has sprung back a lot, measure its proper width between the inboard edges from the full-sized pattern or lofting, and pull the frame back to its proper width at the sheer with a pipe clamp. Hold it in place with a plywood straightedge screwed to the "legs" of the frame. Mark the frame's outboard shape as described above.

If your boat will have risers

After sawing out the frame, mark the position of the riser (usually to be found on the scale drawing) showing the riser's width. Then you can treat the interior corners with a pleasing bullnose or chamfer, skipping over the place where the riser will attach.

Putting It All Together

ASSEMBLING THE BACKBONE AND TRANSOM
Preliminaries

Set the keelson on three horses with the inboard face up. The horses must be tall enough to allow the inner stem and transom to clear the floor when they are attached to the keelson.

Re-mark the centerline on the inboard face of each end of the keelson, using the punch marks you made earlier.

Set the transom on some clean protective cardboard on the bench or a couple of horses, also with the inboard face up. If you haven't already, mark the centerline on the inboard face.

Using a marking gauge, mark centerlines on the mating faces of the inner stem and transom knee. Carry the marks up around edges onto the visible faces, so you'll be able to see what you're doing when you attach these parts.

If your boat is larger or the keelson heavily curved

There comes a point at which it is no longer efficient, or possible, to pick up an assembled backbone and transom, place it on the jig, and bend it into place. If your boat is large or shapely enough, you will want to fasten

6.12 A scrap piece of plywood used as a tick strip to measure the length of the bottom of the inner stem.

6.13 A hand-screw and two small bar clamps clamp the inner stem to the keelson.

the inner stem and transom to the jig first, then fasten the keelson in place. Simply adapt the instruction following to suit. (Also see the box, "Dealing with a Sharply Curved Keelson.")

Dry-fitting

Inner stem to keelson. Double-check the distance from the first station to the end of the inner stem on the keelson (from your lofting or notes made earlier). This mark should be there from when you made the keelson, but it can become obscured, especially if you make the keelson well ahead of assembly time.

Because it will be very hard to see what you're doing with the forward end of the inner stem, a mark that allows

6.14 Drilling holes for screws with the inner stem and keelson firmly clamped together in perfect alignment.

6.15 Measuring the length of the aft side of the transom knee and the beveled end of the keelson with the plywood tick strip.

you to position its aft end instead is extremely helpful. Transfer the length of the inner stem's base to a small thin piece of plywood, then transfer this to the keelson, beginning at the inner stem mark. Use a compass or circle template to draw a circle with the same diameter as the thickness of the inner stem, close to the point where the inner stem's rabbet line touches the keelson. This will help in centering the forward end of the inner stem.

Clamp a wood hand-screw to the bottom of the inner stem, then lightly clamp the hand-screw/inner stem combination to the keelson using a small bar clamp or C-clamp.

The hand-screw firmly grips the awkwardly shaped stem, and the metal clamp (or clamps) securely holds the hand-screw to the keelson. Other methods of holding the stem are tenuous at best (experience speaks) and can tolerate very little adjustment. This method is marvelously secure. Clamping the pieces this way allows you to locate the inner stem very accurately, which is thoroughly satisfying. You'll use the same method to hold the transom knee to the keelson, then to the transom.

You can now encourage the inner stem into its proper position, lining up on the fore-and-aft marks, centerlines, and centering circle by tapping with a small wooden or light machinist's mallet. Shine a clamp lamp around so you can see clearly whether the inner stem is lined up. When it is, tighten the metal clamp and check the wood hand-screw to make sure it's tight. Add a second metal clamp next to the first to make sure nothing can move.

Gently drill for one screw near the clamps at the aft end of the inner stem. Although the clamps are tight, things can still move if you use too much force. Drive the screw, carefully. Check to see if the stem is still lined up. It moved a little? Not uncommon. Send it back into place with a smart rap or two.

Drill for and drive a second screw at the forward end of the stem with only a little less caution. Snug up the screw, then check the stem alignment again. Drill for the rest of the screws, at least two more. There is no need to drive these screws now.

Back out the screws and set the inner stem and screws on the bench for now.

Transom knee to keelson. Clamp the transom knee to the keelson in the same way you as you did the inner stem. Tap the knee until it lines up with the centerline on the keelson and the knee's aft face is flush with that of the keelson.

Drill for and drive two screws near the ends of the knee, then drill for the other screws.

Transom knee to transom. Using a scrap of plywood again, transfer the combined length of the transom knee's aft face and end of the keelson to the inboard face of the transom. Line up one mark with the bottom of the transom.

Remove the knee. Assuming that your transom will be varnished and that any bungs over screws will be plainly visible, carefully locate and drill tapping holes along the centerline in the knee attachment zone from the inside of the transom. Hold a scrap of wood against the outboard face of the transom to prevent drill blow-outs.

Clamp the knee to the transom, using the hand-screw clamping method. Line up the top of the knee with the mark you just made, and center it.

Using the tapping drill, drill from the outside of the transom into the knee, using one of the holes you drilled earlier, then countersink the hole and drive a screw. Repeat for the other holes, but drive only one more screw.

Remove the knee from the transom and the inner stem from the keelson.

Gluing up

Mix a small batch of the glue. Resin glue is a good choice because it holds well and cleans up easily with a chisel after it has cured to a rubbery consistency, usually a half hour or so, depending on shop temperature. You can use epoxy if you prefer.

Inner stem to keelson. Apply a coating of glue to the base of the inner stem, then push the two screws back into their holes and start them by hand. Check the alignment of the stem; you'll have to remove excess glue with a putty knife to see the marks. After you've tapped the stem into final position, tighten the screws and drive the rest.

Transom knee to keelson. Repeat the process given above with the transom knee. The aft edge of the knee and keelson must be flush.

Transom knee to transom. Gently flip the keelson over while making sure that the inner stem doesn't bang into the floor.

Apply glue to the edge of the knee and the end of the keelson. Push two screws through their holes in the transom as far as they will go. Starting them in the holes in the knee is a little awkward, because it is hard to see around the transom. But this method is the best way to assure that the screws start in the holes already

6.16 Checking the alignment of the transom knee on the centerline of the transom. A small machinist's mallet, this one shop-made, is the perfect tool for making small, accurate adjustments.

6.17 Two screws hold the transom knee in place, so that the other holes can be drilled while the transom is held in a more comfortable position. Note the jog between the bottom of the transom and the bottom of the knee where the keelson will go.

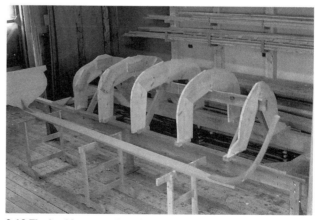

6.18 The backbone, ready to be installed on the building jig.

drilled for them in the knee. Driving a screw into oak without predrilling a hole will result in a split knee or a broken screw.

As with the stem, snug the screws up, tap the knee into proper alignment, then tighten the screws and drive the others into the remaining holes.

Cleanup

If you used resin glue, check the consistency of the glue squeeze-out from time to time. When it becomes rubbery, pare it off with sharp chisel. If you used epoxy, immediately clean up the squeeze-out with a putty knife, then finish the job with a denatured alcohol–dampened paper towel (wear gloves) or use sharp tools after the epoxy kicks.

No matter what adhesive you use, clean up thoroughly before proceeding. You definitely don't want to leave these joints a mess, as it will be difficult indeed to reach these spots once the planks go on.

ATTACHING THE BACKBONE AND TRANSOM TO THE JIG

Generally, it is best to let the glue cure thoroughly after you've put the backbone and transom together, but there have certainly been plenty of times when a tight schedule or the excitement of building a new design has prompted us to install the freshly glued backbone on the molds and jig. If you decide to forge ahead, be gentle with your new backbone.

A reminder: Did you wax the molds? If you haven't, wax the edges and adjacent faces with paste wax and let dry.

Attaching the keelson to the molds

Lay the backbone on the molds, fitting the keelson into the slots. If the slots are tight, remove the keelson and pare some wood off the molds with a sharp chisel. Rewax and let dry.

Begin attaching the keelson to the jig at the midship mold. Line up the punch mark on the inboard face of the keelson with the working (smooth) face of the mold and with the mold's centerline miter joint. If the slot keeps you from centering the keelson, trim the slot.

Using the clearance/countersink bit for a drywall screw, drill straight down through the keelson to the top of the mold, aiming for the middle of the edge. If there are two rabbet lines on the keelson, drill inside these lines, a little to one side of the centerline. If there are no rabbet lines, drill right on the centerline. Drive a drywall screw into the mold.

Line up and fasten the keelson to the rest of the molds, working from the middle toward the bow, then the stern.

As you bend the keelson into place, you'll notice that the distance between the stations marked on the keelson and the molds will differ by an increasing but slight amount. You'll see this most on the first and last molds, and it will be more obvious on boats with a lot of curve to the keelson (see box, "Dealing with a Sharply Curved Keelson"). The top of the molds typically will give some to allow you to locate the punch mark as close to the mold's working face as is comfortable. Don't force it. At this point, you can count on the mold being closer to correct.

Pull the keelson down to the molds by clamping it to the center beam wherever necessary to encourage it to go into place and stay there while you fasten it.

Attaching the inner stem to the jig

Tie or tack the string of a plumb bob to the side of the inner stem, suspending the weight just above the floor.

Dealing with a Sharply Curved Keelson

As a keelson is bent in a curve, the distances between the molds along its arcing surface become greater than the station spacing. For most of the boats shown in this book, the amount of curve in the keelson is relatively small, and the stretching of the spacing is worth noting but presents no real problems with setting up.

However, for a deeper boat of great displacement with sharply curved keelson, the distance between the molds can be measured by bending the keelson (or one layer of laminated keelson) over the molds and marking the keelson along the working face of the molds. You can also use a batten bent over the molds or around the keelson's curve on the lofting to pick up the distances, then transfer these to the keelson stock.

6.19 The inner stem is aligned with a plumb bob, then screwed to the building jig.

6.20 A small square block that rides on top of the straightedge helps set the transom to the proper height.

The goal is to drive one long drywall screw through the waste at the top of the inner stem into the meatiest part of the end beam. Drill through the inner stem in the proper spot. Put a screw in the hole. Kneel down in front of the stem, wielding a charged-up drill with a screwdriver bit. Grab ahold of the stem with your free hand and pull it down until the jig mark on the stem lines up with top of the end beam. You'll have to peer around the stem to see the jig line.

If this is difficult, pull the keelson down with a clamp at the end of the center beam.

Line yourself up in front of the stem, and move your head until the side of the stem next to the plumb bob string appears as a thin line, the very edge of a flat plane. Look at the string. When the string appears to run down the stem "line" from top to bottom without disappearances or gaps, the stem is plumb. Adjust the end of the stem as necessary.

Double-check the position of the jig mark. Double-check the stem and string relationship. Hold your breath. Drive the screw.

Check the alignments again. If you are off by a little, but not much, loosen the screw, move the stem, and retighten the screw.

If there is a lot of pressure on the stem, drill for and drive a second screw. Then remove the clamp from the end of the center beam.

Attaching the transom to the jig

Clamp the transom to the transom blocks using a plywood straightedge that touches both side beams. The straightedge must be narrow enough to end a few inches shy of the sheer. You'll need the distance from the jig to the sheer, from the plans or your lofting.

What's that? Your transom was a close fit on the blank and there's very little to clamp to?

If the scraps from the transom blank are still around, cut a couple of pieces from that or blocks from any wood of the same thickness as the transom. Slide these spacer blocks between the transom blocks and the straightedge, then tighten the clamps. If a spacer block

slips out, move the clamp so that both the transom and block are held firmly against the transom block on the jig. The little spacer blocks can be temporarily attached near the bottom of the transom blocks with double-sided tape or drywall screws.

For the next step of adjusting the height of the transom, you will need a small block of the same thickness as the straightedge, with four smooth, square, and parallel edges and square ends. Set the block on top of the straightedge.

Measure the distance from the jig line to the sheer over the face of the straightedge to the small block. Mark the measurement on the block. With a try-square, draw a line through the mark and carry the mark around to the small block's face and two edges. Mark the block's orientation with a pyramid pointing up.

Check to be sure that the straightedge is still touching both side beams. Then compare the position of the sheer on the edges of the transom with the correct height as shown by the small block by sliding it from one side to the other on top of the straightedge. The transom will probably need to come down. If the transom needs to come down a small amount—½" or less—push it down by hand, one side at a time, loosening the appropriate clamp slightly as you push. It's a good idea to walk the transom down to the proper height by doing a little on each side at a time. After each move, check the height with the small block.

Don't move the transom a large distance with this technique, or you may force a side-to-side bend in the keelson that will put the transom off-center.

If the transom needs to come down a long way, clamp from the forward edge of the end beam to each side of the keelson, just forward of the transom, with a couple of pipe clamps. These will hold the transom down

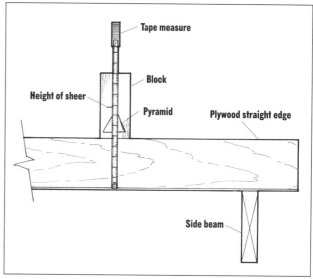

Fig 6.10 Use a straightedge and block to position the transom at the proper height.

6.21 Installing a laminated full frame on the keelson and building jig.

while the clamps on the transom blocks are loosened. If necessary, provide a better bearing surface for the clamps by sticking wedges on the keelson with double-sided tape. If one side of the transom is higher, tighten the pipe clamp on that side to pull it down. This will push up the transom's opposite side, so keep checking on progress with the small block. If the transom seems excessively recalcitrant, check your work. You may have made a part incorrectly (see Appendix A, "Oh, @#!").

Before you make one last check of the transom height, glance down to be sure that the straightedge is still solidly contacting the side beams.

Once the transom rests firmly at the right height, drill clearance holes for drywall screws in the waste wood over the transom blocks and drive a screw in each. If there is a lot of pressure, put in a couple of extra screws, just like you did for the inner stem.

Finishing up

Remove the clamps, plumb bob, etc., and invite over the doubting neighbors to see that your project now looks very much like a boat in progress. Sharpen your planes and spokeshave; you'll be needing them to bevel the keelson, the next step for those of you with boats that do not have a full frame (or several) to install first.

INSTALLING FULL FRAME(S)

If you haven't already done so, mark the location of each full frame on the jig and keelson, drawing clear lines with a try-square. Re-mark the centerline on the keelson on the inboard face where a frame will be attached if it has faded or been sanded off.

Generally speaking, the working face of each full frame should be oriented opposite those of the molds. In other words, the molds have their working faces facing

the ends of the boat, so each full frame should have its working face aimed toward the middle. This way, you'll have plenty of wood available when you trim and bevel the frame for the laps' facets, allowing for good full wood-to-wood contact between the planking and the frame. Though this doesn't matter a bit in terms of strength of the hull—epoxy putty will adequately fill any gaps—when you get done cleaning up the inside of the hull and the word "varnish" pops into your mind, you'll be glad there is very little unsightly epoxy putty under the frame. Besides, it's much more satisfying to plane wood than squish epoxy putty, and you'll be able to beam proudly when asked how you made that frame fit so well, rather than scuff your toe and mumble about puttying the gaps.

The line of each full frame is parallel to the molds, which are plumb. However, because the keelson describes a fore-and-aft curve, the bottom of each full frame will meet it at an angle, unless the full frame is located at the deepest point of the keelson's curve.

The angle between the line of a full frame and the keelson can be picked up either from the lofting or by measuring the keelson on the jig with a bevel gauge and a bullet level. Bevel the bottom of the full frame with a block plane.

Check the width of your full frame at the sheer. If it is still the same as on the full-sized patterns or lofting, all you need to do is mark the sheerline on the face of the frame using a plywood straightedge and on all the edges with a square.

If the frame sprung a little more when you cut its shape out, you'll need to screw the frame to a plywood straightedge to keep it at the proper width until it is firmly installed on the jig, just like you have to do for a frame that had sprung before you marked and sawed it out.

Place the straightedge or cleat on the full frame and line up its lower edge with the sheer marks. Screw one end of the straightedge to the full frame, then drill a clearance hole on the other end. Adjust the frame's width with a tape measure and your hands or use a pipe clamp if need be. When you have the width right, screw the other end of the straightedge to the frame.

On the keelson, mark and drill tapping holes for the screws that attach the full frame. (For a guide, three screws are appropriate for the Merlin and Peregrine rowboats.) Clamp the frame in place; wooden hand-screws are good for this job. Adjust the frame's position until its edge and center are lined up with the appropriate lines on the keelson. Drill and drive a screw in the middle, then remove one clamp at a time, drilling and driving screws each time. Keep checking to make sure that the frame stays lined up.

Because each full frame attaches to the keelson, there's no need for any connection between the frame and the jig's center beam. Connect the ends of the frame to the side beams with rectangles of ¾" plywood about 8" × 12". Lay out and mark the height of the sheer from the jig, at the frame, on the plywood panels. (Find this distance on the full-sized patterns or lofting).

Attach a mold block on each side beam at the full frame position, over the X you drew earlier indicating where the frame goes.

Fasten the plywood panels to the mold blocks. Clamp the ends of the frame in place, adjusting the frame until its sheer marks line up with those on the panels. Once in a while, you'll have to make do with getting the marks as close as possible without putting undue pressure on the keelson or the frame. Just make sure both sheer marks are the same distance from their lines so you know the frame isn't crooked!

Get out a batten that is long enough to go over at least four molds, and check for fairness at every lap. Usually molds are fine, but a full frame occasionally needs a little adjusting. Remove the straightedge holding the bottom of the frame if you used one. Start at the sheer and flex the frame in and out to fair it with the molds. For the rest of the frame, occasionally you will have to trim it with a block plane if it is too big or shim the planking out with a wedge if it is too small. Trim the frame just at the edge-of-plank marks; you'll be planing the frame more later on when you bevel each plank. If you need to line off the molds for the planks, adjust the frame at the sheer now, but trim the rest later while lining off.

Drill and fasten the ends of the frame to the panels below the sheer with drywall screws. You'll need to get these screws out after the hull is all planked up, or nearly so, so be sure that this will be possible.

If you have multiple full frames, repeat the process for each one.

MAKING AND ATTACHING THE KEEL (PERHAPS)

We need to look at two different approaches to keel construction at this point, as one method requires adding the keel before you plank the boat. The other approach, the one we prefer, calls for installing the keel after you finish planking (see Chapter 8, "'Outbone' and Rails, Then Off the Jig").

The before-planking method works well with narrow keels. The garboards are fitted right to the keel. If the keel is very tall, it will be made stronger by the abutting planking.

Using this approach with a wide, flat keel is a mistake. When the keel takes up water and swells, which white oak does very well, it will go in the only direction it can—pushing out of its recessed home, pulling out its screws as it goes. Water can flow between the keel and keelson unimpeded. The boat will not leak, since the keelson and garboards are glued together, but rot will be aided greatly. Not good.

It is much better to install a flat keel after you've planked up the hull. This way the keel can expand sideways without opening up the joint.

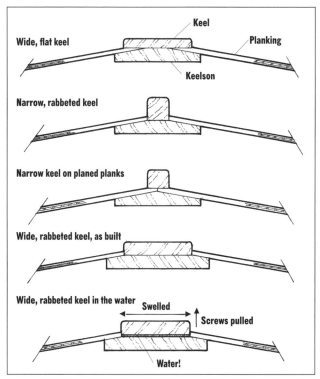

Fig 6.11 Planks can be butted against a narrow keel or trimmed for the narrow keel to be fastened on top. Wide keels must always sit on top of the trimmed planking so they can swell and shrink with no ill effects. A wide keel between two plank edges is thicker and heavier and will squeeze out of the recess when it swells, letting water in underneath it.

Installing a narrow keel before planking

Before you bevel the keelson to receive the planking, mark the widths of the keel at each station with a compass (those punch marks are handy), and connect the arcs with a straightedge or batten, depending on whether the keel of the boat is straight or curved. (You may have already done this because this line is also your rabbet line, where the bevel for the plank stops.) Bevel the keelson (see below). Temporarily screw the keel in place along its lines.

If you want a true rabbet that a square-edged plank will fit into, mark the thickness of the planking on the side of the keel with a compass, then cut the rabbet with a small rabbet plane held with its side against the bevel of the keelson.

In the bow, you will have to make a transition from the rabbet to the planking planed flush at the stem. This may take a little fudging, depending on the shape of your boat.

If you are permanently installing the "outbone" with bedding compound, you will measure and fit the garboard planks to the keel and temporarily screw them to the keelson, then remove the planks and the keel. Plan on leaving the keel behind on the bench when you reattach the garboards with epoxy and the screws; this way, you won't inadvertently glue the keel onto the boat. You can install it permanently with screws and bedding compound once the planking is done and the outer stem installed, in much the same way as we do our wide keels.

If you are gluing the keel in place, you can do this any time before or after the planks are permanently attached.

No Edge-of-Plank Marks on the Molds?

Beveling the keelson requires that you know where the plank edges will land on the molds. If they aren't marked on the molds, you need to finish up the lining-off process you began with the transom (see page 103).

BEVELING THE KEELSON
Preliminaries

The beveling method we use doesn't require a lot of setup—no battens or jigs. It requires some skill, but you will gain this quickly. By the time you finish beveling the keelson, you should be ready for beveling all those plank laps to come.

Properly sharpening and setting of the plane is most important (see especially Chapter 2, "Materials and Tools").

Before you start in, take a minute to mark a few things more clearly:
- Mark the intersection of the rabbet lines and stations on the keelson with punch marks, so these locations don't vanish instantly when planed. Also, mark the intersections of the centerline with the stations if you haven't already done so.
- Mark the plank lines onto the working face of each mold. If you should inadvertently plane off the line on the mold's edge, it will still be there, just around the corner.

Sawing the guide marks

Angled guide cuts made with a handsaw at each mold will show you how much wood to remove by planing. As you plane, the saw cut gradually becomes shallower, offering a clear measure of your progress and reassurance that you haven't removed too much. Also, if you see one end of the saw cut getting much shallower than the other, you'll know to change the angle of the plane to cut the proper bevel.

Cloak about 4″ of the teeth at the end of your crosscut saw with several strips of masking tape. To cut the middle mold on the starboard side, position yourself at the middle mold—as good a starting place as any—on the port side opposite, facing the keelson. Your goal is to make a saw cut perpendicular to the keelson near the working face of the mold. Saw into the keelson, and

6.22 Bevel the keelson first at each mold.

eventually into the mold, letting the tape ride on the first edge-of-plank mark on the mold, until the saw cut just touches the rabbet line and the very edge of the edge-of-plank mark. Be aware that we all tend to rock the saw as we push and pull it, so as you are finishing up the cut, make a conscious effort to saw as straight as possible.

Do all of the molds.

Beveling

Rub the sole of your smoothing plane with a block of paraffin wax. Standing between two molds, with your favored arm outboard, hold the plane at a 45-degree angle to the keelson and mold (see Photo 6.22). Rest the back end of the sole on the mold and the front end on the keelson. The angle of the plane is roughly the angle of the bevel of the keelson. Pull the plane back, still holding this angle, and start cutting the keelson, letting the back end of the plane just kiss the edge of the mold. At this point, concentrate on beveling right over the mold—no extended reaches or contortions needed. You'll be doing the areas over the molds first, then finishing the areas in-between later.

Draw pencil slashes, just as you did when beveling the stem or transom, to get an idea of how close to the rabbet line you are cutting.

When you have cut about two-thirds of the bevel,

6.23 As the bevel of the keelson nears the final angle, trim the curved mold to form a flat facet for the plank to seat on firmly.

6.24 The edge of a plane makes a handy straightedge for checking the bevel.

6.25 Make the final trim of the keelson's cross-grain with the plane blade set for a light cut and the tail of the plane riding on the mold.

you'll note that the cut is approaching close to the rabbet line. This is because the curved mold is actually making the bevel too flat. Turn your plane around so it can cut away from the centerline of the boat, parallel to the edge of the mold, with the back of the plane resting on the keelson (see Photo 6.23). In this position, trim the mold, but don't cut off the edge-of-plank mark.

Continue beveling the keelson in the same manner as before, correcting the angle to that of the newly trimmed mold. You may find that you reach a point when the plane no longer cuts a shaving. Pushing harder won't help. Holding the plane at an angle as you are, you are are actually cutting a shallow fore-and-aft curve. Eventually the curve becomes deep enough that the blade passes through thin air over it. Shoal up the curve by extending the bevel forward and aft of the mold, then continue beveling.

When the saw cut becomes very shallow, tip your plane and use the side corner as a straightedge to check the line along the mold and keelson (see Photo 6.24).

Trim the mold, if you need to. Adjust the blade for a shallower cut, then turn the plane around so its nose faces up toward the centerline and make the final trimming cuts across the grain of the keelson (see Photo 6.25). This allows you to rest the sole of the plane on the edge-of-plank mark, making a series of passes in a fan shape, pivoting on the heel of the plane. Stop when the cut reaches the rabbet. Check with the corner of the plane, trim and check again until plane's corner sits firmly on the rabbet and plank lines, usually with just a tiny ray of light showing between the plane and the keelson.

Move on to the next mold and repeat the process. You'll be using a very similar method to bevel the planking at each mold, so practice now will be amply repaid in the future.

In many texts, the authors suggest using a straightedge to assess the progress of the bevel. If you can, use the plane: it's convenient, straight, and in your hands. You will need a straightedge of some kind if the distance from the rabbet line to plank line is longer than the plane, as it will be on boats with very wide garboards.

At the transom, cut most of the bevel with a block plane. Stand at the stern and plane forward, letting the transom hold the plane at the proper angle. Stop before the plane hits the transom and chips it out. Finish up with a chisel, cutting aft toward the transom.

6.26 Bevel the keelson at all the molds and the transom before beveling between the molds.

6.27 Start the cut to bevel the keelson between the molds with the plane resting on the angle of the closer mold

6.28 The stroke finishes with the nose of the plane seated firmly on the bevel of the farther mold.

6.29 The best tool for checking progress is a well-placed critical eye.

For now, don't worry about beveling the keelson between the first mold and the inner stem. It's easier to get the proper shape after the rest of the keelson is beveled.

Now bevel the portions of keelson between the molds. Face in the opposite direction from that you used when beveling at the molds; i.e., with your favored hand inboard. It's usually easiest to stand in one bay between molds and plane the next, though you will find it better on occasion to stand in the bay that you are planing.

Start with the back end of the plane resting on the bevel at the mold closest to you (see Photo 6.27). Cut this angle until the front of the plane starts to contact the bevel of the mold toward which you are planing. Stop the cut when the forward end of the plane reaches the next mold (see Photo 6.28). Repeat this several times, and you'll feel the plane beginning to make the transition from one bevel to the next. If it's hard to see where you are cutting, pencil some slash marks. Another way to check your progress is to sight down the edge of the keelson, to find the dips at the molds and humps in between. The idea is to plane until the thickness of the edge forms a fair curve from one mold to the next, then from one end of the boat to the other. This will become easier to see after you have trimmed a couple of bays.

Plane the changing bevel until most of the wood has been removed. Set the blade for a finer cut, then concentrate on trimming the edge of the keelson to a fair curve, checking frequently. When you're happy with the edge, draw more pencil slashes and trim the rest of the bevel until the slash marks are nearly gone at the rabbet line and the edge of the keelson. Periodically check with the corner of the plane to see that the bevel is flat or concave athwartships.

This process is an excellent chance to discover the usefulness of a curved plane blade. Not only will it cut a shallow hollow (remember, epoxy likes a gap), you can center the plane over the area you need to cut without worrying about trimming wood from spots that don't need it.

Keeping the bevel flat is more difficult in places where there is more twist in the bevel. The bow and stern are noted for this. In less severe areas, marking with pencil slashes and planing carefully with the smoothing or block plane works fine. In the more extreme areas, the best tool is the spokeshave, also outfitted with a slightly curved blade (see Photo 6.30). You can see the shaving coming out of the tool, so you know where you are cutting, and the small sole fits the twist

6.30 A spokeshave is the ideal tool for trimming a crown in the bevel.

6.31 The bevel is finished when it forms a fair curve at the edge of the keelson

6.32 A thin batten shows just where the end of the keelson needs to be trimmed to fair into the curve of the inner stem.

6.33 A spokeshave works well for beveling the keelson where the plank will twist sharply to meet the stem.

6.34 The backbone ready for the first planks.

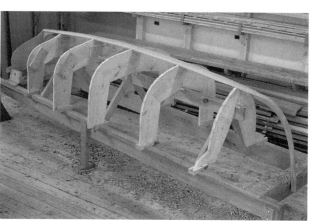

much better than a plane.

For the final trim, keep your tools waxed so they glide smoothly, but don't glom it on. Try buffing out the waxed sole with a small piece of wood; it helps.

At the bow and stern, rough out the bevel with a chisel and plane, then fair the twisting bevel with the spokeshave, testing progress with a scrap of thin plywood or solid wood 3″ to 4″ wide (to represent the planking stock) from time to time. Where the bevel meets the inboard face of the keelson (where you trimmed the width with a jigsaw), you are likely to cut past the jigsaw marks and make the keelson even narrower. Let the test strip and your eye be your guides.

At the transom, it is a good idea to finish the cut by pulling the spokeshave more or less down along the edge of the transom rather than straight aft. The straight aft cut is very likely to chip the face of the transom, a minor disaster if you plan to varnish the transom. If it happens, repair the damage with closely matched epoxy putty. (If you have lived a truly righteous life, this spot will be hidden by bottom paint.)

Beveling the Keelson, Advanced Method

If you're very comfortable with the beveling process, you can do what John normally does:

Bevel the keelson at each mold, then set the plane for a coarse cut and rough-in the bevel for the entire keelson, working between the molds. With the plane set for a thinner shaving, give the bevel a final trim everywhere except the bow and stern. Use the spokeshave as needed. After you've finished that, take a scrap of planking and attend to the final trimming of the keelson at the stem.

Repeat everything on the other side of the boat. At the stem and stern where you beveled to the inboard edge of the keelson, compare to see if both sides look the same. Depending on exactly where your seats and other interior parts go, you're likely to see some or all of these edges in the finished boat, even if you have floorboards.

Fairing the keelson to the inner stem

Trim the keelson to fair it into the face of the inner stem, checking your progress with a thin batten. In Photo 6.32, note the high spot in the middle that needs to be pared down. You also can use the outer stem for checking your work if you have made it already. After you're happy with the keelson to inner stem melding, double-check and refine the inner stem's final bevel.

Finishing up

Wax the portions of the molds that were trimmed when you beveled the keelson. (Let the wax dry before proceeding with planking.) You're ready to plank if the full-sized patterns of your boat's plans have given you satisfactory edge-of-plank marks for the molds, inner stem, and transom. If you have full-sized patterns with acceptable plank locations given, you don't have to go through the lining-off process, but you might want to skip ahead to the part about tacking on the battens to check the run of the planks, and do that, just to make absolutely sure that you'll like what you will see in the finished boat.

IF YOUR BOAT HAS LAMINATED FLOOR FRAMES

Most of you who are building relatively small, light-weight, open or nearly open boats can skip right by the next couple of paragraphs. However, if your boat is a larger and heftier damsel, such as our Somes Sound 12½ daysailer (overall length 15'8"), your design may call for laminated floor frames. Gluing these up over stout bat-

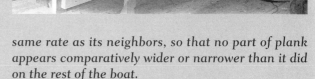

6.35 Lining off for planks is part geometry and part squint-at-her-until-things-look-right.

A Few Guiding Principles for Lining Off

• In general, the faceted shape formed by the series of planks should follow the curved shape of each section as closely as possible. The planks can be wider where the curve is flatter and must be narrower where the curve is sharpest. Not only does this allow you to follow the hull's desired shape more closely, it adds interest and shows the shape of the boat nicely.

• The curve of each lap should be a nice, fair curve from stem to stern, with each plank tapering at the same rate as its neighbors, so that no part of plank appears comparatively wider or narrower than it did on the rest of the boat.

• At the stem, make the planks increasingly narrow from keelson to the sheer, largely ignoring the widths of the planks farther aft unless the pattern makes the curve of the lap unfair or results in the forward end of the plank being wider (bugle-shaped). (A noted exception to this is the garboard on a flat-bottomed boat.)

• Take particular care with the sheer-strake. Because it is normally nearly vertical, it will appear wider than its neighbors, which are viewed at an angle. This is doubly true if the sheerstrake has some tumblehome to it.

Also consider what the rail will do to the sheerstrake. The sheer-strake needs to be wider by the width of the rail because the top portion will be covered by the rail. The exposed portion below the rail should look pleasing in relation to its neighbors. When you make the sheerstrake wide enough to correct this, it will look much too wide before the rail goes on.

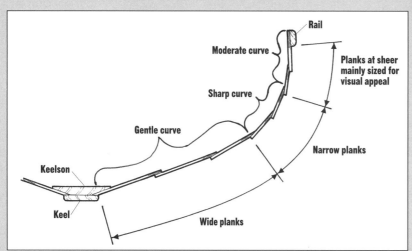

Fig 6.12 Planks can be wider where the section curve is gentle, but must be narrower around the sharper curves.

Fig 6.13 Aesthetics play an important role in determining the widths of the planks near the sheer. Keep in mind that the rail covers a portion of the sheerstrake and the plank below the sheer is usually angled and appears narrower.

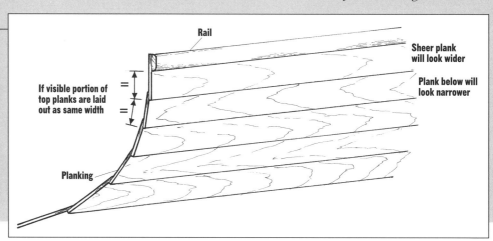

tens tacked to the backbone, transom, and molds is far and away the easiest and most accurate way to make these important, complex-shaped, load-bearing parts.

Set up the backbone and molds for laminating by tacking stout battens along the hull at the edge-of-plank marks. These battens must be stiff enough that they bend very little when the floor frame veneers are clamped to them. Mask the battens, keelson, and molds thoroughly with clear packing tape. Follow the general instructions for laminating given in Chapter 3, "Some Very Useful Techniques." Let the newly laminated floors cure for at least 24 hours. Remove them, and plane to final width. Set the floor frames aside to be fitted, trimmed, and installed along with the other interior parts after hull comes off the jig.

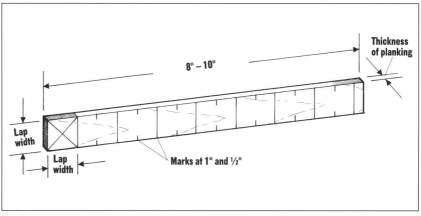

Fig 6.14 Lining off layout tool.

Lining Off

Lining off isn't a particularly difficult job, but it is a little fussy. It's also exciting; like setting up the molds, it gives you a glimpse at what your boat will look like. Lining off is part geometry and part squint-at-her-until-things-look-right. Because taste dictates a fair amount of lining off, there is really no "right" answer for any particular hull. As long as the planks lap each other so they can be glued securely, you'll be in good shape.

GENERAL APPROACH

The standard methods for lining off for the plank widths instruct you to start on the midship section—the largest one—and proportionally reduce the widths of the planks to fit the other sections. This usually works well for solid-wood boats, with their typically thicker and narrower planks. We can, and often do, use fairly wide planks on glued-lapstrake boats. Wider planks and typically thinner plywood planking stock means that it is necessary to watch that the angle between the planks doesn't become too steep.

For this reason, we suggest that you lay out the widths of the planks on the transom first, and make them

proportionally wider to fit around the larger sections in the middle of the boat.

The transom for solid-wood boats typically is cut out in a smooth curve, like the molds, with no jogs. Gains are cut that make the planks flush, just as is done at the stem (see Chapter 7, "Planking"). The builder can locate the plank edges anywhere he or she wants on a smooth transom. For glued-lapstrake boats, the proportionally wider planks and the plywood itself make the gains hard to make. In some cases, the gains weaken the planks. Therefore, for boats designed like ours with no gains at the transom, you'll have to determine where the planks will land before building the transom.

In most open boats, the sections are broadly similar in shape from a point about a third of the way aft of the stem to the transom. Usually the smallest section that resembles the midships section is the transom. This is where steep-angle problems on the laps will show up quickest.

The transom is the one place where you can see all of the planks, and you want it to look good. Laying it out first makes this part of the job much easier.

If your boat is a double-ender, we'll deal with your particular problems in a minute. First, let's line off a hull with a transom.

LINING OFF A HULL WITH A TRANSOM

Begin with the developed transom on the lofting. There is no set formula for laying out the plank widths; work it out using common sense and a critical eye for what is attractive. You'll need to decide how many planks to use before you start, but don't be afraid to change your mind and add another plank if it looks better. If another plank improves things at the transom, it will do the same for the rest of the hull. (See also the discussion of plank angles, page 130.)

Using the layout stick—basic method

On the developed transom on your lofting or plans, draw the keel and mark the width of the rail. Lightly pencil in where you think the planks should go. Recall that planks can be wide where curves are shallow and they must be nar-

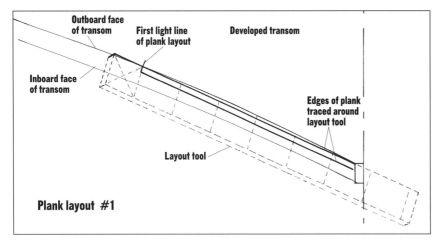

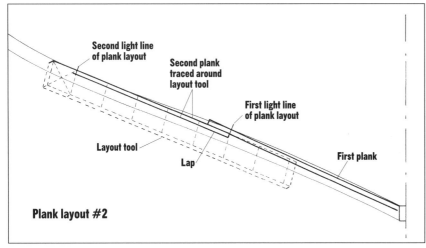

Fig 6.15 Laying out the planks with the plank layout tool.

row where curves are sharp. Other than that, aim for what looks good. You'll probably end up erasing many of these first marks, but they will help you make your final decisions. If you are working on a Mylar tracing, mark the planks on the back of the drawing so you don't erase the curve.

Position the plank layout stick, on edge, on the outline of the developed transom thusly: lap end pointed toward the sheer; inboard edge touching the outline of the transom, lining up the lap mark on the stick with the first penciled line, outboard face at the edge of the keel (see Figure 6.15). The transom's curve should be under the edge of the layout stick. (If it is not, your boat has a reverse curve in the garboard. Read through this basic procedure, then see below on what to do in your particular case.) When you like the width of the plank, trace around the stick except the outboard edge of the lap. Clearly mark the lap using the width of the layout stick.

When you position the layout stick to mark out the next plank, you can see not only the width of the exposed face of the plank, but also the amount of bevel at the lap. You also can see how closely the planks are following the actual curve of the transom.

A few hints:

• The lap end of the layout stick always aims toward the sheer and should touch the transom outline.

• The other end of the stick usually touches on the outside of the previous plank, at the projected lap line, except....

• Where the angle is steep, line up the inboard face of the tool with the top corner of the previous plank. This will create a small gap at the bottom of the lap that is filled with epoxy putty (see Figure 6.4, and also Figure 7.7 on page 130).

• Compare the width of the plank to its neighbor, using the increments marked on the stick.

• Consider the curve in the transom. It often looks and works best to cover (that is, remove) no more of the curve than the thickness of the planking.

• Consider the amount of bevel required in the lap. It's best to avoid steep bevels. They are a little harder to cut (and easy to over-cut); make clamping the next plank in place troublesome; and the gap between the two planks must be filled with epoxy putty. If you must create a gap, don't make it any bigger than a third of the lap width.

Lay out all of the planks along the developed transom.

When you are done you'll have the proper shape for the transom, with the proper jogs and everything.

Garboard plank with a reverse curve

If your transom has a reverse curve (or hollow) in the garboard (and possibly in the next plank), you must decide how to handle this area: whether to follow the reverse curve or not. In general, trying to follow a strong reverse curve with a plywood plank is difficult and creates all sorts of interesting stresses. Straight is easier to build. But it is often much less elegant.

Following the curve. Draw the lap width as two lines perpendicular to the lines of the transom. Mark the lap width using the layout stick. Lay out the thickness of the plank following the curve, and draw a parallel line representing the outside of the plank.

Going straight. Mark out the plank with the layout stick held on edge. The upper end of the stick at the lower lap line) should just touch the transom outline; the lower lap line on the stick also should line up with your sketched line as with planks on convex curves. Trace around the

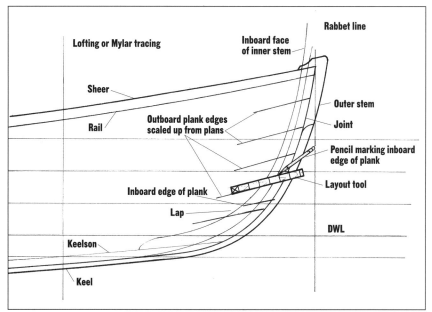

Fig 6.16 At the stem the plank laps are usually scaled up from the plans and laid out to look pleasing. Visually, we like the widest plank width at the keel and the narrowest at the sheer. Remember to draw the width of the rail on the layout, or you will be in for a rude surprise after the hull is planked up. This is an "Oh, [very, very bad word]!" situation.

entire layout stick to where it meets the keel. You will not be beveling this plank for its neighbor. Instead, the next plank will be back-beveled to fit the angle of the garboard. Mark the width of the lap with short lines that are perpendicular to the new, straight plank line you just drew, not to the original outline of the transom.

Projecting to the forward face

After the planks are laid out to your liking, project the lap jogs and corners to the forward face, following angles of the diagonals for planks in-between. You can trim extra wood or fill gaps as you plank.

Attend to the inner stem

Lay out the plank widths on the lofting or full-sized pattern. You'll usually have to acquire these by scaling up from the profile drawing. If, for some reason, the designer failed to give you a profile with plank lines or you're changing the plans, you'll have to work out the plank widths. Obviously, you'll have to draw the same number of planks on the stem as you did on the stern, but beyond that, do what appeals to you. Look at other boat plans and designs, and do the best you can. And don't worry too much; you'll be refining these later in the process.

The lines you draw are the visible plank edges on the outside of the boat. To draw the edge-of-plank marks, the lines to which you need to

measure and cut planks, lay out the lap width with the layout stick *above* (toward the sheer) the visible plank edges (see also Figure 1.6 [inner stem, full-sized pattern], page 12).

Prepare the boat's framework

Make the molds, backbone, and transom, and set them up on the jig. Bevel the keelson. Obtain the widths of the keel on the keelson from the offsets or section patterns, and mark.

Lay out the key marks on the molds

Pick the side of the boat that offers the best, clearest viewing perspective from as much distance as you can get in the shop. All of your efforts will be directed at this one side for the time being.

Find a thin ($1/16''$) batten that will reach from below the sheer to above the keel when bent around the biggest mold. Neatly and firmly bend the batten around the developed transom on the lofting, making sure that it contacts the transom edge completely. Transfer the keel line, *outboard* plank edges, rail's lower edge, and sheer from the transom to this "story stick."

Dig out a scrap of smooth plywood at least a few inches wider than the full length of the transom edge on the story stick and about 4' long.

A simple layout grid of parallel lines marked from the story stick makes it possible to quickly and accurately find the plank widths for all of the sections (molds). Using a straightedge, duplicate Figure 6.17.

Thoroughly remove all of the marks from your story stick after you have completed the layout grid. Bend the story stick around each mold. Record the keel line and sheer. Lay out the width(s) of the rail for each mold. You can do four molds on the story stick. Label each clearly.

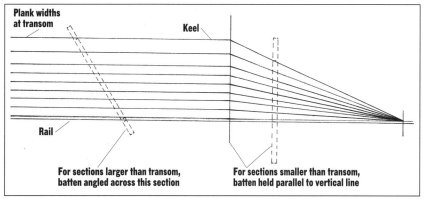

Fig 6.17 The grid for proportioning the plank widths for the molds.

6.36 Using a thin batten to lay out the planks on a mold.

Orient your story stick at an angle on the parallel lines of the layout grid so that the keel and rail width lines for the first mold contact those on the grid. If the distance between the mold's keel and rail lines is too short to reach, move on to the next, larger mold. We'll come back to the molds that are too small in a moment.

Once you have a mold's keel and rail width lines lined up with those on the grid, hold it in position. Transfer the plank widths from the grid to the story stick. Do the rest of the molds recorded on the stick in the same way.

If you have molds that were too small for the parallel lines section of the layout grid, move over to the section where you brought the parallel lines to a single point. Hold the story stick perpendicular to the horizontal baseline of the grid, and move it until the keel line and rail line match the lines on the tapered grid. Then mark the plank edges on the story stick.

Take your story stick back to the molds, and transfer the plank lines to the edge of each mold.

Clean off the stick completely and repeat the process for the remaining molds, if any. You also can cover the marks with strips of painter's masking tape.

Assess and refine the lines using battens

For the next step, you'll need as many battens as you have plank laps. These should be comfortably longer than the hull and the same width as the plank lap joint. Conveniently, these characteristics are shared by the clamping battens, so you can use them for this process.

Starting amidships (simply because it's easier), tack a batten to the molds, transom, and inner stem, lining up its *upper* edge perfectly with the plank lines. (Remember that on the jig, "up" is toward the keelson.) Don't pound the nails flush; you'll be pulling quite a few of them shortly. Do the same for all of your plank lines, working your way

down the hull. Also attach a batten with its upper edge on the lines for the rail (not the sheer!). If there's room for a batten along the sheer, it's helpful but not essential.

Now for the seriously fun part. Step back and look at her from all angles, including upside-down—*especially* upside-down, as that is presently the only way to see your boat as she will appear after she's off the jig and right-side up. The plank lines you have marked and outlined with the upper edge of the batten are the plank edges you will see on the outside of the hull. The lower edges of the battens are the edges of the planks that are visible inside the hull. Tweak the battens until you are satisfied. John finds that the inner stem and station No. 2 usually need a goodly bit of adjustment, whereas the midships mold is often fine. In fact, you often can be quite faithful to the midships mold. And, of course, battens on the transom are never moved.

When you like how she looks and have dragged enough folks into the shop to add their opinions, mark the *lower* edge of the battens on the transom, molds, and inner stem. These marks are the official edge-of-plank marks, the marks you will be working to when you measure and cut out your planks. Mark each of these with a clear little V so there is no possibility of confusion. Label or erase the rail's edge line, so you don't mistake it for the sheer.

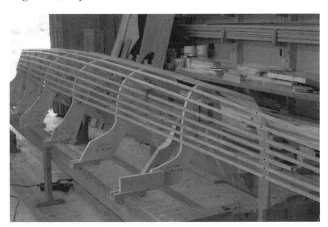

6.37 Battens are used to sight the run of the planks...

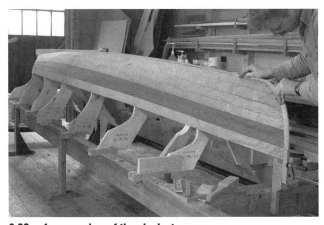

6.38...for a preview of the planks to come.

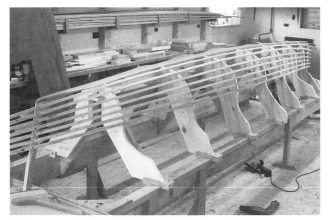

6.39 The lining-off battens on the aft portion of a double-ender, in this case a Salicornia double-paddle canoe.

Transfer the marks to the other side of the hull

Clean off your story stick, and pick up the marks for the keel, edges-of-planks (the ones with the Vs), and sheerlines for each mold. Transfer carefully to the proper locations on the other side of the boat. You don't have to transfer the initial exterior plank width marks; their job is over.

LINING OFF A DOUBLE-ENDER

If your boat lacks a transom, you can follow the same general lining-off procedure. Just start at the midships mold. You may have it easier than the folks with transoms, as many double-enders are also symmetrical forward and aft. However, attach the battens over the entire hull, not just one end, to make sure that you don't end up with any surprises.

Because a double-ended boat has a stem and sternpost, and the planks have gains cut in both ends, you don't have to make any permanent decisions about the location of the planks before the jig, molds, and backbone are set up. You can adjust the battens on both ends to your heart's content when lining off instead of having to work to fixed points on a transom.

Cutting out a plank.

Chapter 7

Planking

The Garboards

It's time to put on the first pair of planks. The first job is figuring out what they should look like by measuring or, to be precise, spiling.

SPILING

Aaak! Spiling: A word that furrows the brows and wrenches the innards of many an aspiring boatbuilder. A perplexing verb, the font of much consternation: "I've read all sorts of books that talked about spiling, but I still can't figure it out."

First, let us offer some encouraging words. In all of John's classes, after he has demonstrated how to spile and the students have had a chance to try it, everyone in the class spiles away happily from then on, with only an occasional "John, can you check this?" They usually have it right. Spiling is one of those operations that proceeds fairly rapidly from total confusion to "Aha!" to "Why did I ever think that was so difficult?"

Let's park the bothersome word "spile" for a moment and consider the situation.

At the moment, you have a backbone resting on a set of molds, beveled and ready to receive the first plank: the garboard. You can see where the plank needs to go. You can follow along the lines of all of the planks with your eyes; you may have established those lines yourself.

On the other side of the shop, you have a stack of scarfed plywood sheets that await life as planks.

That's the problem: How to transfer those lovely, often rather odd, curvaceous plank shapes to that flat plywood.

A jointed plywood pattern is a big part of the solution. This pattern will closely follow the curve of the plank, eliminating one major source of inaccuracy. It also limits the mind-bending necessary. You don't have to try and figure out what the plank "should" look like; the pattern shows the way. And you can put away your tape measure. The simple geometry of the circle makes it possible to transfer the points with a pencil compass.

Consider the circle

Draw a circle with your compass. Now place the pointer anywhere on the circle and draw an arc inside the circle

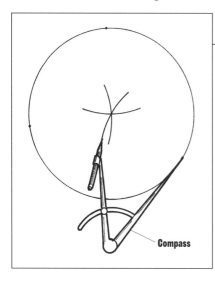

Fig 7.1 How the geometry of a circle works for spiling.

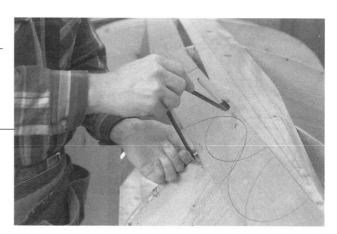

7.1 Place the pointer of the compass on the edge-of-plank mark on the mold and draw a portion of a circle on the spiling pattern.

with the pencil end. Do this again from several different places on the circle. The arcs cross at the center of the circle, the original pointer hole.

Fine. But how does this relate to spiling? This *is* spiling. Think of it this way:

- The original pointer hole represents the edge-of-plank mark on a mold, the keelson, or the previous plank.
- The original circle, or a part thereof, is the arc you will draw on the pattern (see Photo 7.1).
- When you place the pattern on the planking plywood and draw several arcs by placing the pointer on the original arc (circle), you will re-create the original pointer hole, the edge-of-plank mark you wished to transfer.

Spiling is extremely accurate; it allows you to transfer any plank shape, no matter how radical; and it really is simple, once you've bushwhacked the short ways to "Aha!" And spiling isn't just for planking. You can use the same method for precisely measuring many curves in a boat.

7.2 The center of the circle—the edge of the plank—is re-created on the planking stock from the arc drawn on the spiling pattern.

The spiling pattern

A spiling pattern must be made of several pieces so it can closely follow the shape of the plank to be spiled. A pattern that closely matches the curve of the plank being spiled produces much more accurate results—planks that fit the first time, with very little trimming needed.

Many builders make their spiling patterns from strips of ¼″ plywood and butt blocks glued together with hot-melt glue. This method is quick but requires making a new pattern for each plank.

The spiling pattern we use is a little more work to make because it is held together with bolts and screws, but it is fully adjustable and can be reused for at least three or four boats.

The spiling pattern is made up of pieces about 4′ long joined with butt blocks. There are two pivot points, one for each section, near the middle of each butt block. This allows you to change the angle between the sections. You can also twist the butt block to raise or lower the

Important Things To Remember When Spiling

- *Never force the pattern into the shape in which you think it should go. Let the pattern drape over the molds.*
- *Don't be afraid to drive extra nails to hold the pattern firmly to each mold in difficult twisted places. If you must, resort to a screw or two.*
- *Always record the setting(s) of the compass on the pattern.*
- *The butt blocks must hold the pattern sections fixed in position after you remove the pattern from the molds. Remember to tighten all screws in the butt blocks and to use reasonable care when moving the pattern around.*
- *Always remove all marks from your pattern with a scraper when you're finished transferring the marks for each plank, as any leftover marks will be lurking there, waiting for their opportunity to confuse you.*
- *This is a job that rewards accuracy. Work carefully, and you can make a plank that fits perfectly—or very nearly so.*

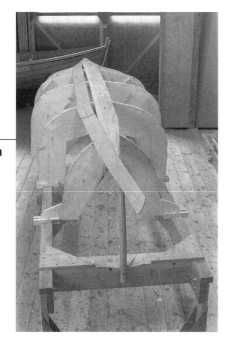

7.3 A spiling pattern made of several pieces can closely follow the curve of the plank.

end of a pattern section as needed. You will find this last feature incredibly useful at times.

Once the pattern is lightly nailed to the jig, at least four screws in each butt block hold the sections firmly in position.

Making the pattern

• Use ¼″ lauan plywood (or similar). Rip pieces about 4″

wide: enough sections to add up to the length of the sheer plus about a foot, and enough 10″-long butt blocks to join the sections together.

For the Ellen and other boats with molds spaced 2′ apart, make the midship section a little longer than 4′ so that butt blocks will not land on top of the molds. (You can work with a butt block over a mold, but it is a nuisance and occasionally can throw things off.)

• Trim the ends of the sections into a curve so they can be moved to different angles. Round the ends of the butt blocks, too.

• Each pivot uses a #10 flathead machine screw with a washer and double nuts. The machine screw heads are on the bottom of the pattern, so countersink them in addition to drilling clearance holes. The attachment screws are #6 or #8 × ½″ pan-head self-tapping screws. These require only clearance holes through the butt block.

• Assemble the pattern with the pivot bolts. The pivots in the butt blocks should be snug, but not so tight that it's hard to adjust the individual sections.

• When you drive the positioning screws, their tips will protrude slightly through the bottom of the pattern. This can help hold the pattern in place, but remember not to slide the pattern or you'll gouge some nice scratches in your planking stock. Place a washer underneath each screw head to reduce the length of protruding screw tip.

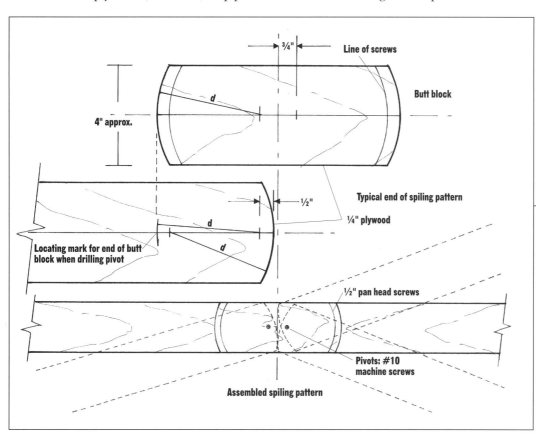

Fig 7.2 Laying out the various parts for the spiling pattern.

Essential Support for the Planks

Even after they've been cut down to 2' wide, the plywood panels for the planking are large and cumbersome, not in the least part because they are also thin. You need some sort of planking table. You must have firm support not only for cutting the planking, but for nailing the shaping battens. This job is exceptionally frustrating if the panels are unsupported, as the plywood bounces up and down, resisting your attempts to drive a nail into it. Also, with bouncy panels it is far too easy for the batten to move off the mark just before the nail takes hold.

The simplest answer is several sawhorses with flat 2x4s or 2x6s laid over them to form an even table. Use a horse about every 7'. Don't use wood you care about; you will be cutting into the "table top." Drive 3" drywall screws to hold the table together and steady, but be sure

to countersink the heads at least ½" below the surface.

If you'd like a more permanent solution, build a planking rack like that shown in the photo at the beginning of this chapter. This rack has turned out to be very stiff and works very well for all the processes necessary for cutting out planks.

We also use the planking rack for gluing-up spars and oars; stacking things to be planed or sawed (as it's right next to the planer and table saw); and finishing parts. Of course, when it's not in use for these laudable purposes, it makes a darn fine level surface on which to pile wood, boat parts, sails, books, boxes, jigs, and what-all. It has supported a temporarily parked hull or two in its day. The rack does come apart easily, should you ever find it more in your way than useful.

Positioning the pattern on the jig

The spiling pattern must naturally follow the path the plank will eventually take over the molds and backbone.

Lay the pattern on the jig and let it drape over the molds. Your ultimate objective is to have the pattern rest close to the entire line of the plank to be measured—but don't attempt to follow the curve exactly.

If you spring or otherwise force the pattern to precisely follow the curve of plank line (called "edge-setting" the pattern), the pattern will straighten out when released from the molds, and all of your carefully transferred marks will be completely wrong. Take your time. Patiently work with the pattern to see where it wants to go, then help it stay there.

7.4 Gently push the spiling pattern down to allow it to lay naturally and squarely on the mold, then nail it to the mold with small finish nails driven at angles.

The pattern may cover part of the plank's lower line. This is fine; we will deal with those hidden marks in due time.

Tack the pattern to the molds with 3d or 4d bright finish nails. A little nailing technique will help keep the pattern where it belongs. Each time you start to spile a new plank, drive the first nail into the pattern at the midship mold perpendicular to the surface. After that, drive the rest of the nails at about a 30-degree angle. It is best to put two nails in each mold, angled toward or away from each other; this holds the pattern tight to the molds. If the nails are upright, the pattern can lift as you bend it to adjacent molds.

Don't try to make the whole pattern fit right away; attach it section by section, starting with the midship section. Drive the first nail into the midship mold, then press the ends of the midship section of the pattern down against the molds to see where they wish to go. If all looks good, drive a nail into the mold immediately aft of amidships. Drive a second nail in these two molds, making sure the pattern is tight to the beveled facets on the mold.

Move to the forwardmost mold that the middle portion of the pattern touches. Push the pattern to the mold, letting it twist where it will. Support the rest of the pattern with your hand, so its weight will not affect the section you're working on. You also can rest the edge of the pattern on a nail driven into a mold farther forward. Remove the positioning screws on the ends of the butt block, allowing the two portions to pivot and releasing the midship portion so it lays perfectly naturally upon the mold. Nail the pattern to the mold.

On boats that possess transoms, the aft portion of the pattern is pretty well supported by the molds—for the first couple of planks, anyway—but a perch (drive a small nail) for the forward portion of the pattern often is required.

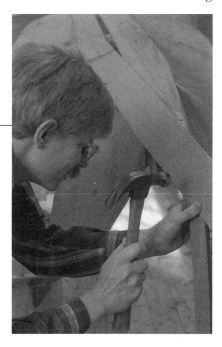

7.5 The spiling pattern must be securely nailed— or even screwed— to the stem because of the sharp twist of the hull at the bow.

After securing the midship section of the pattern, turn your attention to the aft end of the boat, because this stretch is normally easier than the forward end (unless your boat is double-ended, in which case it's a toss-up). Securing the more obliging parts of the pattern also cuts down on the variables influencing the behavior of the harder-to-place portions.

Remove the positioning screws from the ends of the aft butt block while holding onto the aft portion of the pattern piece so it doesn't slide off the molds. (Loosen both aft butt blocks to free both aft pattern pieces if your boat is long enough to require them.) To see where the pattern section wants to go, hold it against the molds as best you can with two hands. Try twisting the butt block to see what influence this has. Remember, you want the pattern to follow the curve of the plank as closely as possible without forcing the issue, so try to rest both ends of the pattern portion an equal distance from the upper plank line, without allowing the middle of the pattern to cover the line (see box, "Pattern Positioning Tips").

Working from the middle of the boat toward the stern, nail the pattern to each successive mold, each time making sure the pattern is naturally bending and twisting to where it lands squarely on the molds. Try pushing the pattern to the molds and releasing it several times to be certain it wants to land in the same place. Don't hold the pattern as you push it against a mold; push it with a couple of fingers or, where the twist is harder, the heel of your hand. The idea is to help the pattern find its own spot on the mold. The whole pattern must touch the mold—not just one edge.

Nail the pattern to the transom, just as you have to the molds.

The plank you're measuring is likely to develop a strong twist as you approach the bow, especially as it's the garboard. The nails through the pattern into each mold must be steeply angled and driven in pretty deep. You might even want to nail the pattern to the keelson between the molds. Hold the end of the pattern to the stem with a wooden hand-screw, then nail it in place. If it's really a handful, drive a screw or two into the stem. (This job is easier on a long, lean rowboat than a short, round dinghy.)

After nailing the pattern in place, drive at least two positioning screws into each end of the butt blocks. You'll see that this holds the pattern in a fairer curve, especially in areas with quite a bit of twist.

Peer underneath the pattern at each mold. Is the pattern tight to the each mold's beveled facet? If not, you'll have to pull some nails and re-lay and re-nail the pattern. Your plank will do exactly the same thing as the pattern and make the hull unfair at that point, so it really is worth re-doing. (Sigh.)

Transferring the points to the pattern

For this job, you'll need a rigid compass. Marking a dark line on a plywood pattern with a sharp hard pencil puts a surprising amount of stress on the compass. One that bends will frustrate your pursuit of accuracy. Also make sure that the setting knob prevents the legs from moving no matter what, and also check that the pencil can't move. A good compass from a supplier of quality woodworking tools will set you back a bit, but once you use it, you'll not regret the cost.

Record the primary arc before you do anything else. Set the compass for a comfortable distance and record it on the pattern. Roughly 4″ is usually about right. Firmly

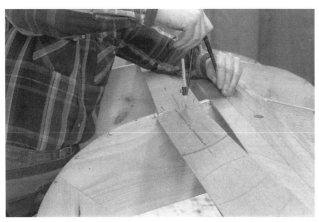

7.6 The primary arc is recorded on the spiling pattern with two arcs that look like a set of parentheses.

7.7 After the plank is spiled, mark the working face of the molds, the station number, and a pyramid—with the letter or number of the plank inside—on the pattern.

stick the point of the compass into the pattern—any-where—and draw an arc. Then stick the point in the middle of the first arc and draw another through the first pointer hole. If you should ever need to reset the compass, you'll need to find these pointer holes, so make them bigger if they are hard to see.

Clearly label this pair of arcs, so you don't remove them by mistake.

Begin transferring the points at the midship mold. Put the point of the compass in the punch mark at the station line on the rabbet line (or centerline, if you don't have a rabbet line) and draw an arc on the pattern, sweeping down from the edge and right back up again. Don't stint on your arc drawing; longer is better and more accurate.

The garboard is often rather wide, considerably wider than the pattern, so many of the edge-of-plank marks for the garboard's lower edge will be visible on the molds. Stick the compass on the line, near the working edge of the mold, and mark another arc on the pattern, again from edge to edge.

At every mold, mark the pattern with arcs, from the rabbet line (or the centerline) and the edge-of-plank mark, if visible.

Wineglass Transom?

If your boat has a wineglass transom with the end of the garboards encouraged to follow the curve, the garboards must be made a little wider than their straight cousins. (One version of the Ellen has just such a curve, including our Iris.) To deal with this, spile the lower edge of the plank the same way as you have done at the molds. After the spiling pattern has been removed, come back to the transom and measure the true width of the curved plank with a strip of paper or thin cardboard that bends easily to follow the curve. You will eventually transfer the width to the plank-width measuring jig (see page 115), and lay out the plank on the planking plywood just like any other.

Mark all the points you can with the primary compass setting, no matter how short the arc.

At the transom, put the compass pointer as close to the aft face as you can without accidentally splitting the wood, and draw arcs for the upper and lower edge-of-plank marks on the pattern, just as you did at the molds.

At the stem, the garboard's shape becomes more complex as it changes from the easy, gentle curve along the keelson to the much harder curve of the stem. To record the shape accurately, mark several points forward of the first mold, and record the stem's curve above and below the pattern, about ⅛″ from the patterns' edges.

For these measurements, press the compass pointer into the corner between the forward face of the stem and the bevel for the plank.

A good rule of thumb: The sharper the curve, the more points needed to measure it.

If the edge-of-plank mark shows below the pattern, draw an arc for it as well. Usually, the edge-of-plank mark is covered by the pattern and will be dealt with in a moment.

Once you've finished with the "standard" compass arcs down the length of the keelson, plus the transom and stem, turn your attention to those places in which your compass was too short to reach the pattern or where the arc you could draw was awfully small. Set the compass for a second, bigger radius, say half again as much as the first. Check that it will work on the molds that need it, then record and label this second distance as you did the first.

On those points needing a second, healthier arc, you'll end up with double arcs, making it obvious which is the larger. Label any large arcs that stand alone, as it is easy to forget which are standard arcs and which are large.

You can set the compass aside for now. If you have edge-of-plank marks on the molds that are hidden by the pattern, also ignore these for the time being. Get out a pencil and mark the station lines with short lines on each

Planking

edge on the pattern. Make similar marks at the transom right along the aft face.

Important note: Place your stem and transom marks exactly; you need to know precisely where the boat ends fore and aft. These marks are not rough where-to-cut-the-plank-off lines. You will be cutting the plank long, and trimming it to fit after it's installed. These lines are essential for marking the widths of many planks.

At the stem, if the lower edge-of-plank mark is under the pattern, trace the curve of the stem on the back of the pattern, then look for the edge-of-plank mark on the face of the stem. Mark it on the pattern, labeling it with a small V. This is a technique you only need to use on the garboard plank. For the remainder of the planks, you'll measure at the stem the same way as at the transom; we'll discuss this in detail once the garboard is on.

Label the forward end of the pattern with an "F," the aft end with an "A." Make these large and clear; it's easier to turn a plank end for end than you might think. Be consistent with labeling, and make sure that everyone working on the boat understands what the labels represent.

Label the station lines with their proper numbers.

Draw an authoritative pyramid pointing up, near the midship station. Remember, "up" on the boat during the time it is on the jig is toward the keelson, toward the sky.

Finally, mark the letter or number of the plank in the middle of the pyramid. The planks go on in order from keelson to the sheer, thus: G = garboard; followed by 2, 3, 4…; S = sheerstrake.

Check over the whole pattern to be sure that you've marked everything you could (except, of course, those hidden edge-of-plank marks) and secured the butt blocks with the positioning screws (two, or maybe three, on each end). Did you record the larger compass radius if you used one?

Stack and line up two panels of planking plywood on the planking table. One of the delights of making planks is creating two identical planks from one effort at spiling.

When you are sure that you have marked the pattern completely and driven enough positioning screws to ensure that the sections can't move, gently and carefully pull the nails, starting at the ends and working toward the midship molds. Grasp the pattern securely before pulling the last couple of nails so it won't fall off. Carry the pattern to the planking plywood and gently lay it down.

Before you leave the pattern to rest for a little while, take a minute to drill a small hole (big enough for a pencil

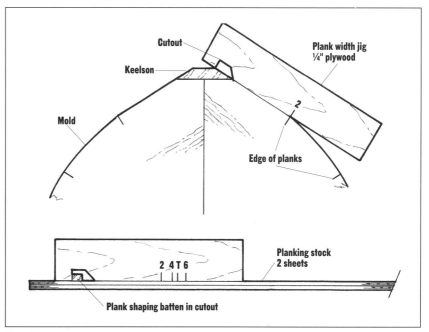

Fig 7.3 Using the plank width measuring jig to record a plank width on a mold, then transfer the measurement to the planking stock.

tip) where the edge-of-plank mark intersects the line of the stem. Lift the bow end of the pattern or flip it over.

Capturing those hidden edge-of-plank marks

For the molds where you weren't able to mark the lower edge-of-plank marks with the compass, you need to make a plank-width measuring jig, which is simply a tick strip made with a cut-out designed to fit over a batten. Use a piece of thin plywood about 3″ wide and several inches longer than the greatest width of plank you need to measure. Cut one of the long sides straight. Cut a saw kerf near one end perpendicular to the straight side and a little taller than the thickness of your plank-shaping battens. Cut a notch large enough to go over a batten (see Figure 7.3). Note that there is only one vertical edge of the notch, making it impossible to rest the wrong side of the cut out against the plank-shaping batten. (See below, "Connecting the Dots: Shaping the Plank," for a look ahead at plank layout and cutting.)

To measure the width of a plank at a station, place the jig on the edge of a mold's working face, and line up the saw kerf of the cutout with the rabbet line (or centerline). (In case you're wondering, after the garboard you'll be lining up the saw kerf on the line scored for the plank lap.) Mark the edge-of-plank mark on the side of the jig. Label the mark with the mold number.

When you are done, you will find all the forward plank widths on one side of the measuring jig and all the aft plank widths on the other.

Garboard planks are usually wide on glued-lap-strake boats. Typically only one or two plank widths will need to be measured this way, and these are normally near the stem. Save the measuring jig; you'll be needing it

7.8 Using the plank-width measuring jig on a mold. (Note: This is indeed a later plank; position the jig over the keelson's bevel to measure for the garboard.)

for the remaining planks.

Positioning the pattern on the planking stock

Place the pattern so that the plank you draw out will have its edge close to the edge of the plywood panel, at least 1/2″ away. Estimating by eye, set the pattern in a likely location, then place it permanently by checking with the compass. Use the recorded primary arcs to set the compass, then walk along the pattern, putting the point of the compass at the top of each primary arc (the point farthest from the edge) to see where the pencil lands. Move the pattern as necessary, gently; you do not want to disturb the alignment of the pattern's sections at this point. If you do, you'll have to get out the scraper, clean all the marks off, and start spiling all over again.

Double-check all arcs with the compass to make sure the pattern is in the right place, then weight the pattern to keep it from moving.

Re-creating the plank shape on the plywood

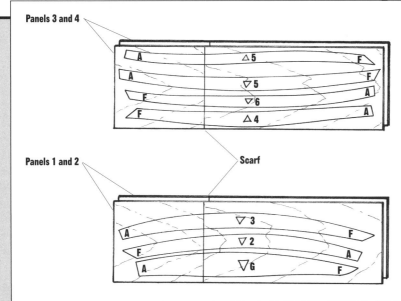

Panels 3 and 4

Panels 1 and 2

Scarf

Fig 7.4 Various shapes of planks laid out to use the plywood panels efficiently and stagger the scarf joints.

have a similar curve, but each will have a little less than its predecessor. Nest the planks with the middles as close together as possible (see Figure 7.4).

For the remaining planks, things can get a little tricky. Usually plank number four or five is relatively straight. It can look pretty serpentine, twisting in a long "S" curve, but it occupies a relatively narrow rectangle. Put this plank along one edge of the panel, then do the best you can to nest the rest of the planks together. Again, try to get the middle of all the planks as close to the edge of the panel and to each other as possible.

There is only one more monkey wrench to throw in the works. It is best to stagger the scarf joints so they don't fall on top of each other. It's not as critical with a glued-lapstrake boat as it is with a solid, wood boat, but it's still worth doing.

If the scarf joint is near the middle of the panel, you can simply place the first plank toward the left edge, the second near the right edge, and so on.

For planks with a scarf close to the end of the panels, make the first plank, then flip the pair of plywood panels over. Lay the next plank out flipped end-for-end.

Thinking Ahead:
Fitting All of the Planks on the Planking Stock

Laying out the planks would be a simple job if you could tell what they were going to look like ahead of time. Unfortunately, unless you have plank patterns, you can't. However, most boats follow the same general trend in plank shape, so it is possible to plan ahead to some extent. It can be nice to have an extra panel of plywood sitting on the shelf, however.

Here's one efficient strategy. Usually, the edge of the garboard that attaches to the keelson is pretty straight, so start by putting it along one edge of the panel. The outboard edge is heavily curved (the middle is wide, the ends narrow). The next two planks

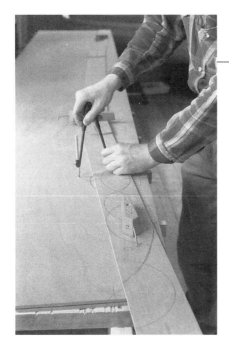

7.9 Laying out the plank shape on the planking stock.

7.10 With the spiling pattern close by, mark the station numbers, bow and stern labels, and pyramid on the plank-to-be.

Now for the fun part.
- Check to be sure that the compass is set for the primary (smaller) width on the pattern. Sharpen the compass's pencil.
- Choose an arc on the pattern. Draw three arcs on the plywood by sticking the point of compass on the chosen arc in three places: the left side near the pattern edge; the middle; and the right side near the pattern edge. The three arcs drawn on the plywood should intersect neatly. If only two of the arcs intersect, the compass is set to the wrong distance.
- If all is well, repeat the procedure for the remaining primary arcs. Then re-set the compass for the secondary, larger width (if you have one) and transfer those points as well.
- If your arcs don't cross perfectly, check the compass spread against the correct recorded arc. If that matches up, there are two possibilities: The compass distance may have crawled and you didn't catch it. Or, the compass flexed, changing the distance, usually for the greater.

What to do? Mark out the other arcs first. If all the rest seem fine, you can fair around the inaccurate point with the batten. If most of the other marks are also off, get out the scraper, erase the pattern and plywood, and re-spile the plank. Guesswork and fudging just won't solve this problem.
- Now transfer the lines for the stations, stem, and transom to the plywood panel. Also, stick a pencil in the hole you drilled at the inner stem for the edge-of-plank mark and make a dot or small circle on the plywood.

Check again to be sure that you've transferred all the marks, then remove the weight holding the pattern in place. Lift and slide the pattern, moving it away from you to expose the plank while keeping it lined up with the marks. Transfer the labels onto the plank: pyramid,

plank identity, station numbers, and "F" and "A." Draw a V on the dot that marks the lower edge-of-plank mark at the inner stem.

With a ruler, draw straight lines at the stations and transom. Freehand-in the curve of the stem.

Take another look. Everything there? Good. You can put the pattern away in a safe place until you're ready for plank number two, and get out a couple of battens, a circular saw, and a router.

Connecting the dots: Shaping the plank

Battens connect the points transferred in the spiling process into fair and pleasing curved lines. You can use the battens just for defining the plank's shape, trace along them and remove them, then saw along the lines with a jigsaw or handsaw, then clean up with a hand plane. However, we suggest that you employ the battens as cutting guides for a rough cut with a circular saw, followed by a final trim with a router. This is accurate and fast, and also leaves a nice, clean edge on the planks.

Bend a batten along the upper edge-of-plank marks,

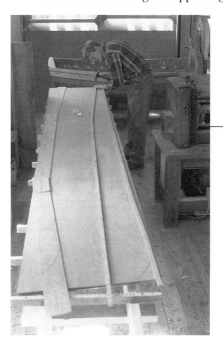

7.11 Starting at the midship station, nail a batten to the spiled points to define one edge of the plank.

placing the batten on the "plank" side of the marks. Use small brads to lightly tack it in place. (Yes, indeed, this means that you are to drive small nails through your new planks-to-be.) The brads should be just long enough to go through the batten and into two layers of planking stock, but not through the second layer. With ½"-thick battens, ⅞" brads will work fine for 6mm, 5mm, and 4mm plywood. Although the ⅞" brads stick out a little through the second layer of 4mm plywood, they hold better than ¾" brads. A light tap with a hammer or a quick stroke with a file renders the nail points flush. This is important, as you will see in a moment.

Fairing

Don't drive the nail heads flush yet. Spring the ends of the battens, then check the whole batten for fairness (see Chapter 3, "Some Very Useful Techniques"). All curves should be fair: no humps, no flat spots. This doesn't mean that each side of the plank necessarily will be one long, sweeping curve—many will have far more interesting (bizarre) shapes—but the plank edges must flow easily along fair curves. Remember, no one will ever know if you are exactly on a mark on the station or the plans, but everyone will see that the plank edge is unfair.

Often when a batten looks unfair, it is one point that causes the trouble. Pull that nail and let the batten relax to a sweet and fair curve. Still not right? Then you'll have to pull more nails. Don't be afraid to put the batten back to the point at which you pulled the first nail and see if pulling the nails at the stations to either side of that point will fix the curve.

Small changes (1⁄16" to ⅛") can be made to one station—if it works—but bigger changes should be distributed over several stations so that the change to any one station isn't more than about ⅛".

7.12 Springing one end of the batten.

7.13 A circular saw fitted with a jig that follows a batten rough-cuts the planks.

One great advantage of building a lapstrake boat upside-down is that your first planks will be underwater most of the time. As an added bonus, the garboard will have its upper edge trimmed and hidden under the keel (at least on our boats; check your plans). You'll be an old hand at fairing with a batten by the time you get to the the visible planks above the waterline, especially the sheerstrake.

Adding the missing plank widths

Once the first batten is fair, it's time to attend to the plank widths that are missing because the planking pattern covered the marks on the molds. You should have marked these widths on the plank-width measuring jig. Find it and line up the proper width at the first "missed" station. Be sure to keep the vertical edge of the jig's cut out tight against the outside edge of the shaping batten. Mark the width on the planking plywood. Repeat the process for the rest of the missing marks.

(Please read on page 34 if you need the width of the plank at the transom.)

The second batten, and finishing up

Nail another batten along the lower edge-of-plank marks, again inside the marks. Spring the batten ends and check for fairness.

When you're happy with both battens, walk down the length of the planking plywood panel, driving the heads of the brads down and putting more brads between stations if the stations are more than a foot apart.

Make one last check (just in case) of the battens' fairness, and you are ready to cut out the first pair of planks.

CUTTING OUT THE GARBOARD

The method we prefer cuts out planks in two steps. The first cut is made with a circular saw with an attached jig that follows the batten. The jig is set up to cut the plywood about 1⁄16" proud of the batten. After that, the planks are trimmed neatly flush with a router. If this process doesn't suit you or your equipment, please see the following section for an approach that uses smaller, quieter tools.

Useful Procedural Hints

- *Putting a little paste wax on the bottom of the circular saw and the router makes the job go more smoothly.*
- *Do not use a plywood-cutting blade in the circular saw. The blade's tiny teeth will make cutting the curves nearly impossible. A standard rip blade is best.*
- *Watch that the saw doesn't wander away from the batten. Cutting the curves is hard work for saw and it is easy to stray from the batten.*
- *If the saw blade binds and works hard as it cuts the curves, put a little more set in the blade's teeth using a pair of pliers.*

Sawing out with a circular saw

The circular saw's jig is made from a piece of Plexiglas fastened to the base of the saw with machine screws. There is a slot in the plastic big enough for the blade guard to swing through. Two plywood discs on either end of the slot act as guides, riding against the batten. Each disc attaches to the Plexiglas with two screws. The first goes through an off-center hole drilled in the disk, the second rides in a curved slot that arcs around the first screw. Put a washer under the head of the second screw so the guide doesn't move when you tighten it.

Set up the jig by placing a straightedge against the guides while holding the blade guard out of the way. Adjust the guides until the straightedge is parallel to the blade and about $^1/_{16}"$ away. If your planks have tight curves to them, make this distance greater so the blade won't hit the batten.

Sometimes the garboard is wider than the Plexiglas

7.14 Two discs attached to the bottom of the circular saw jig ride against the batten to hold the blade a set distance from the batten.

7.15 The bearing of a flush-trimming bit rides on the batten when trimming the plank to its final shape.

base. In that case, attach another batten of the same thickness between the nailed battens, on the plank-to-be, and let the base ride on that. This creates more holes, but only requires a few nails and makes the job go much easier.

Cut both edges of the plank with the circular saw, then carefully flip over the double planks and batten assembly.

Trimming with a router

Set up a router with a flush-trimming bit. Smaller-diameter bits (say, $^1/_2"$) work best because the bearings are smaller. The bearing and its retaining screw or nut must be thinner than the thickness of the battens, or you'll hit the planking table. You can't hang the plank over the edge of the planking table with the battens affixed underneath, since the plank will rest at a cockeyed angle and be in danger of slipping off the table altogether. The head of the nut or screw can be filed thinner.

Put a clamp somewhere on the plank sandwich to keep it from sliding. If you are making 4mm planks, file the little tips of the brads flush with the plywood. Flush trim the planks even with the battens, and you're done.

If you haven't gotten your quota of jig-making in this month, you can make an oblong Plexiglas base for the router. Put a knob on it, if you like. This makes hanging onto the router easier, though it is certainly not essential.

The trickiest part of a plank to fit is at the bow where it meets the stem (and at the stern where it meets a sternpost, should you have this condition). If you are unsure about how things will fit, leave the plank edges between the first (or last) station and the stem untrimmed. This will give you about $^1/_8"$ of plank to fiddle with to make the ends look just right.

7.16 To test-fit the garboard, start at the midship mold and line up the edge of the plank with the mark on the mold, then nail it to the mold through the lap area.

Final attentions

Remove the battens with a flat bar. Be gentle—you are going to use these battens over and over. If they hold a nice curve, you will come to revere and cherish them. Make sure not to move or separate the plank pair. Remove one batten, and, if no brads have pulled through the batten and are left holding the two planks together, put two or three in, using the old brad holes. Then take off the other batten. Mark the stations, stem, and transom on the edges of both planks. Carefully turn the plank pair over, resting it on edge. Reproduce the pyramid and plank identity, stations, and forward and aft labels on the unmarked plank.

Lay the plank pair back down and trim the ends of the planks with a jigsaw, cutting ¾″ to 1″ beyond the stem and transom lines.

Separate the planks.

Quieter option: Sawing out with a jigsaw and trimming with a hand plane

Nail the battens in place at the stations, spring the ends, and check them for fair. Draw a line alongside each batten to mark plank edge. Remove the battens. Hold the two panels together with short brads driven in the plank middles, away from the edges. Cut out the planks with a jigsaw, making sure to save the pencil lines. Saw the ends off long, leaving at least ¾″ to 1″ beyond the marks. Trim the plank edges smooth with a block plane until the pencil lines are nearly—but not quite—gone. As you trim, check frequently with a try-square to be certain that the plank edges are square.

FITTING AND FASTENING THE GARBOARD
A dry run: Test-fit first

It is a supremely good idea to check the fit of the garboard plank. This is true of any plank, but doubly so of the garboard.

Always test-fit the plank that belongs on the same side of the boat that you measured on. That way, if there are any differences from one side of the mold to the other, they won't compound any errors and create more confusion. (Of course, there *shouldn't* be any differences, but….) Find this plank and rest it on the molds, facing in the right direction, with the "F" at the forward end.

Because a plank balances nicely on its middle, this is always a good place to begin attaching it. Make sure that the pyramid is in front of you, pointing up. Line up the station line on the plank with the working edge of the mold and the lower edge of the plank with the edge-of-plank mark on the mold. Drive a 3d or 4d smooth finish nail through the lap area of the plank into the mold. Nail holes in the lap will be filled, usually completely, when the next plank goes on. Nail holes in the middle of the planks are hard to see, easy to miss, and mean more holes to fill when you do find them, preferably before launching.

Moving aft, skip a mold or two, then tack the plank in place on a mold. Go aft to the transom and nail the plank so that its edge is hard against the notch chiseled out for it. This is an absolutely fixed point; you will work the aft section of the plank until it runs easily to this point.

Now go forward, skip a couple of molds past amidships, and tack the plank in place on a mold. Due to the amount of twist to the plank at the bow, you will need to nail the plank to each of the molds immediately aft of the stem, about halfway to midship. Angle the nails to hold the plank firmly to the molds, as you did with the spiling pattern.

Hold the end of the plank to the stem with a wooden hand-screw. In the case of the Ellen and many other designs, the plank end won't go willingly, but it will go. Does the lower edge of the plank match up with the line on the stem? Can you easily push it there and tighten the clamp to hold it? Generally, it will go. If it won't because the plank lands above the mark, pull the nail on the first mold, adjust the end of the plank until it is on the line, and tighten the clamp firmly. Then push the plank edge at the first mold to get it as close as possible to the

7.17 After the plank is tacked to several molds, check the alignment of the lower edge with the mark on the stem.

7.18 A wooden hand-screw holds the sharply twisted end of the garboard to the stem.

7.19 Adjusting the alignment of the plank at the first mold is often easier after the end of the plank is clamped to the stem.

original mark and tack it in place.

Before you force the plank into place with excessive zeal, look for the layout points from spiling, where the three arcs cross, to see if your plank faired out wider or narrower than the measurement. If the plank is wider, the edge should land below the edge-of-plank mark on the mold. If it is narrower, the edge should be above the mark.

If the end of the plank is below the mark on the stem, but is on the marks on most of the molds, you can trim the edge of the plank right at the bow until the plank edge touches the marks at the stem. When you pull the plank off, make sure to trim that edge until it is fair all the way to the forward end. You're likely to encounter the above situation if you left yourself some room for adjustment by not flush-trimming the forward end of the plank to the cutting batten.

On the other hand, if the plank hangs down over the marks on the molds when lined up with the mark on the stem, you can trim the plank edge to fair into the end of the plank at the stem. In this case, it's best to mark the amount of discrepancy on the plank and plane it off on the bench, where it is easier to trim and see if the edge is fair. But do this only after careful consideration. Once you've trimmed the edge, you can't put it back.

Trimming the plank up to ¹⁄₁₆″ or ¹⁄₈″ is fine, but if you need to take off any more than this you should look carefully for possible measuring errors.

What if the plank meets the edge-of-plank marks perfectly on all of the molds, but is too narrow at the stem? This happens fairly often, and if the discrepancy is about ¼″ you can fix the problem by moving the end of the plank up or down to halve the error. You can either adjust the width of the end of the second plank to compensate, or you can fill any unsightly cosmetic gaps between the planks and/or at the keelson with epoxy putty.

Once you've settled the forward end, tack the plank to the rest of the molds, as close to the lines on the molds as you can while allowing the plank to lie flat on each

mold. Sometimes the plank bulges up. If you can *easily* push it down with a finger, all should be well. Tack several nails along the keelson to hold the plank down.

If the plank bulges a lot and is hard to push down, pull some of the nails along the bulge to allow the plank to relax. Check your measurements. You might have made the plank a little wide at one station, in order to achieve a fair edge. Nailing it to the edge-of-plank mark on the mold will result in a bulge.

Check the bevel of the keelson, especially in the bow area. If the planking touches the lower (inboard) part of the keelson but not the upper (outboard) part, the keelson needs to be trimmed. If the top touches but not the bottom, you've trimmed too much already and the gap will have to be filled later on with epoxy. Remember not to drive the screws too hard in this area when you attach the plank permanently. Check by looking to see if the plank's lower edge runs fair. If it dips after the nearest mold, ease the screws until the lower edge is fair.

7.20 A compass makes quick and accurate work of marking for screws along the keelson.

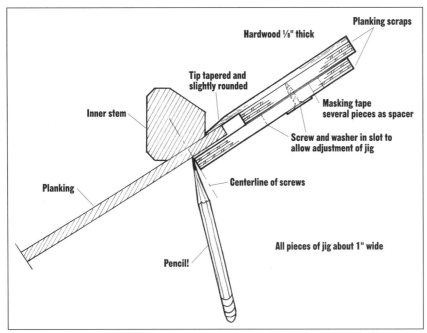

Fig 7.5 A simple jig for accurately locating the screws that fasten the plank to the inner stem.

Labels in figure:
- Planking scraps
- Hardwood ⅛" thick
- Tip tapered and slightly rounded
- Inner stem
- Masking tape several pieces as spacer
- Screw and washer in slot to allow adjustment of jig
- Planking
- Centerline of screws
- All pieces of jig about 1" wide
- Pencil!

Marking for screws: Preliminary fastening

The plank should now be tacked in place at each mold and at strategic points along the keelson and into the transom as well as clamped to the inner stem. Mark for the attaching screws with the compass by picking up the distance from the edge of the keelson to the center of the keelson bevel from the "unplanked" side of the boat at each mold, and transferring these center points to the attached garboard. Connect the points on top of the garboard; a flexible yardstick works well.

You can freehand a line down the middle of the bevel along the inner stem. (Figure 7.5 shows a simple jig for accurately locating the center of the inner stem bevel if you plan to varnish your hull.) Mark for screws 3″ or 4″ apart. Use the same bronze or stainless screws you'll be installing permanently for this preliminary fastening. Attach the plank to the inner stem by drilling for and driving a few screws. Now you can remove the clamp.

Next, drill and drive a screw into the keelson along the line at every mold. Eventually you will install screws about every 6″, but if you drill all of the holes now, little geysers of epoxy putty will squirt through every one of them when you glue on the plank. This makes a mess, and also tends to glue the screws in place, which you do not want, as they must be removed later. The few screw holes you drilled are just to help you replace the plank in the right

7.21 For boats that will be painted, a hand and its fingers work well to form a marking gauge that can reach around the overhanging end of the plank to let a finger ride along the face of the stem while the pencil marks for the screws at the bow.

7.22 This adjustable jig is used for marking for screws that hold the planks to the transom, then later can be set for marking where the planks will be trimmed flush with the outboard face of the transom.

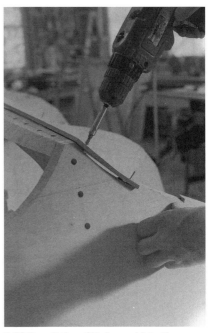

7.23 To pull the stiff plywood into the curve of a hollow transom, start at the lower edge of the plank and methodically drill and drive closely spaced screws, one at a time, to work the plank into the curve.

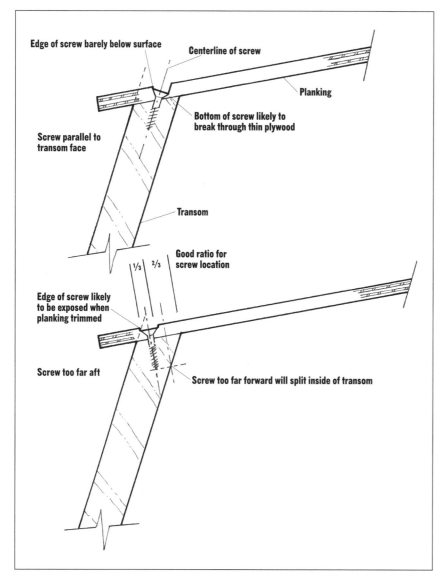

Edge of screw barely below surface

Centerline of screw

Planking

Bottom of screw likely to break through thin plywood

Screw parallel to transom face

Transom

Good ratio for screw location

1/3 2/3

Edge of screw likely to be exposed when planking trimmed

Screw too far aft

Screw too far forward will split inside of transom

Fig 7.6 Carefully locating screws to be driven into the transom eliminates common difficulties.

7.24 After fitting the first garboard, check the fit and fasten its mate as well.

spot when the time comes.

Mark and drill for the screws into the transom. See Photo 7.22 for a marking gauge that does this job well. For a straight garboard (no hollow), three screws is usually plenty.

Drill for the screws, particularly at the transom, perpendicular to the face of the planks, not parallel to the face of the transom. Because the planks are thin, screws driven at an angle will break through the inside face while standing proud on the outside face (see Figure 7.6). If there is much pressure on the plank at all, the screw will break through the plywood, leaving a plank end with a very ragged hole waving gently in the breeze.

Because the screws are driven at an angle, set the transom marking gauge for about a third of the thickness of the transom, measuring in from the aft face. Screws driven in the middle of the beveled edge of the transom are likely to break through the inboard face.

If the transom has hollow in the garboard, carefully pull the plywood down into place by drilling and driving each screw, about 2″ apart, starting at the lower edge of the plank. Don't put too much pressure on any one screw, for fear of stripping the threads or pulling the head through the plywood. One builder of an Ellen clamped curved cauls to the end of the plank to help bend it into the curve of the transom.

Don't worry about the ends of the plank extending an inch or two past the ends of the boat. These will be trimmed after the hull is planked up.

Once the plank is screwed in its final position, reach under and trace the edge of the keelson onto the inside of the garboard. Remove the plank.

Attending to the other garboard

If you trimmed the first garboard at all, attach it to its mate. Trim the second plank to exactly the same shape as the first. Take the plank pair apart, then test fit and preliminarily fasten the second garboard in the same manner. Work to the same edge-of-plank marks on the molds that you did with the other plank. Remember the places where the plank hung over and where it was shy, and put on the second plank exactly the same way.

Cutting gains

Now that you have two perfectly fitted garboards, you're ready to cut your first gains.

A gain is a joint cut in the face of one or both planks that is the width of the lap and that allows the proud edge of the plank on top to become flush with its neighbor at the stem. This is always done at the bow, for the typical boat with a stem and transom. Gains are often cut at the transom in a solid wood boat, but it is difficult to make a strong or good-looking joint when using the wider and thinner planks typical of glued-lapstrake boats. The joints tend to crack, especially on the planks just under the sheerstrake, particularly if the boat suffers regular hard thumps from un-neighborly companions at the dinghy dock. Many people, including us, prefer the looks of proud plank edges at the transom.

(Note: If you are building a pram or any other boat with two transoms featuring proud plank edges, you can skip this little discussion about gains.)

Plywood's alternating grain direction requires some special consideration when cutting gains. The easiest and strongest way John has found is to make a tapered half-lap joint in each mating surface; that is, one in the plank already on, and one in the plank ready to be installed.

The garboard only needs to have one gain for receiving the next plank. Future planks will require a gain

7.25 Half-lap gains work well for the plywood planking used in glued-lap-straking.

on the "attaching" edge and another on the "receiving" edge. We will come to that shortly. For now, address yourself to a garboard's forward end that rests on the bench:

- Set a marking gauge for the width of the lap joint, and mark this on the garboard's lower, outboard face, along the whole edge (see Photo 7.26).
- Clamp or nail a ¾″ straightedge along the score line made by the marking gauge, leaving the lap exposed. Gains should be about 10″ to 12″ long; shorter for fatter, rounder-ended boats and/or thinner planking; longer for leaner, gently curved boats and/or thicker planking. Mark the length of the gain with a pencil.
- Hold a dovetail or back saw against the straightedge and cut a kerf from nothing at the aft end of the gain to

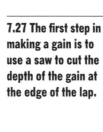

7.27 The first step in making a gain is to use a saw to cut the depth of the gain at the edge of the lap.

7.26 A marking gauge (this one shop-made of oak and a nail) is a good tool for marking the width of the lap on the outboard face of the planks.

7.28 Rough-cut most of the waste from the gain with a chisel.

7.29 Finish the gain with a few strokes of a rabbet plane.

7.30 A completed half-lap gain.

7.31 All the epoxy materials and supplies you'll need for gluing the planks.

chisel's cutting edge a little, first away from the straightedge, then towards it. This will leave a peaked ridge running down the middle that removes easily with the chisel held straight. Don't try to make the "slope" smooth now; all you want to do with the chisel is remove most of the excess material. Finish up the joint with a rabbet plane (see Photo 7.29). Usually a few strokes does the job (see Photo 7.30).

• Do the other garboard in the same manner.

ATTACHING THE GARBOARDS

Well, finally.

Rest the garboards, inboard face up, on sawhorses near the jig. Most of the tools you'll need should be distributed about the jig area already, but make sure that all of the necessary drill bits are either in a drill or close to hand. (A block of wood with holes drilled in it to hold drill bits is a big help.) Check to see that you have enough screws for the whole run down the keelson. Set up your epoxy station: pumps, wood dust, colloidal silica, stir sticks, little yogurt containers (or official epoxy mixing containers), throwaway brushes, putty knife, old cap, clamp lamp. Half a pizza box makes a great drip-catcher for the epoxy pumps. (See also Chapter 2, "Materials and Tools"). Don an apron or old shirt and gloves or barrier cream. Make sure that you have everything now, before the chemical clock starts ticking.

If you trimmed any portions of the molds during the fitting process, wax these areas and let dry. Of course, if you neglected to wax the molds earlier, do them all now.

Mix up a single pump batch of straight epoxy. (This is for a boat roughly Ellen's size or smaller; mix a two-pump batch if your boat is significantly larger.) Use the throwaway brush to wet out the areas of the inner stem, keelson, and transom that will be under the garboard plank you've chosen. Don't slather on the straight epoxy; paint it neatly, just enough to dampen the surface. Also do the mating surface on the garboard plank. Don't forget the stem and transom surfaces.

If you are working with a partner, he or she can mix

the bottom of the middle veneer at the end of the plank (see Photo 7.27).

• With a sharp chisel, hog out most of the wood alongside the saw cut (see Photo 7.28). You'll find the glue lines quite hard to cut. To cut out smaller chips, tip the

7.32 Epoxy putty about the thickness of peanut butter works well for gluing the planks to the backbone.

How much putty is enough? You're aiming for enough to squeeze out healthily inside and out, letting you know that there are no starved spots inside the joint. Don't scrimp; make more if you need it (and for the garboard, you very likely will). If it seems like you're putting on too much and the putty threatens to blurch onto the floor, scrape off the excess by running the putty knife at an angle, riding the blade near the handle along the outside edge of the keelson.

Put on your nailing apron if you haven't already. Pick up the plank, flip it over, and lay it on the keelson. Aim well; the more you slide the plank around in the epoxy putty, the bigger mess you will have to clean up. Line up the edge of the plank with the midship mold and edge-of-plank mark, and push or lightly hammer a nail into the existing holes in the plank and mold. Line up the plank with the next mold aft, and tap in its nail. With gentle, careful application of a manual screwdriver, drive one screw into the pre-drilled hole in the keelson. Make absolutely sure that you are driving into the existing hole. If you aren't, nothing else will line up and you'll have to pull the plank off and try again, rather quickly.

Once the first screw is in, the remainder go in easily. Work your way aft, then forward, tapping in nails and driving screws with the manual screwdriver until the whole garboard is held firmly in place. If you had spots that were beveled a bit too energetically, remember not to overtighten those screws.

Drill, countersink, and drive the rest of the screws along the keelson.

You should have a nice, fat bead of epoxy putty squeezing out along the inside and outside edges of the joint. If there is an awful lot of squeeze-out, you'll have a little extra mess to clean up, but you know the joint is well-fed. (You can put on a little less putty on the other side.) If there are places where you don't have squeeze-out, check the other side of the plank to see if there is any there. Sometimes the epoxy only goes one way. Press on the spot with your fingers. If you see the putty moving, then you know the joint is full, but there's just not quite enough to squeeze out. It will be fine.

up a two-pump batch of epoxy putty while you wet out. By the time this person is nearly finished mixing the putty, you should be done wetting out, and can contribute whatever straight epoxy you have left to the putty mixture. Hang onto the wet throwaway brush, since you'll be using it in a minute.

Mix the two-pump batch thoroughly and thicken this with colloidal silica and wood dust until you achieve a putty like peanut butter. Spread the putty on the backbone with a putty knife, then brush out evenly.

Evenly distribute the putty along the inner stem, keelson, and transom with the putty knife, using a swiping motion. Don't try to spread it evenly with the putty knife. Use the throwaway brush to smooth the putty out.

7.33 A putty knife makes quick work of getting the epoxy putty on the backbone; a brush will be used to evenly spread the putty.

7.34 Carefully aligning the plank as it is laid on the molds keeps the epoxy putty mess to a minimum.

7.35 Tighten the screws only until they are snug and a small bead of squeeze-out appears along the edge of the plank.

7.36 Use a putty knife to scoop up the epoxy putty squeeze-out.

If you have good squeeze-out on one side, but a small gap between the keelson and plank on the other, you can wait to fill the voids until after the epoxy has kicked. If the gaps are on the outside of the hull, you can fill them with putty leftover from later planks by masking the affected areas with regular masking tape and forcing epoxy putty into the gap with a putty knife. If they're on the inside, it's easier and cleaner to putty the gaps after the boat is off the jig.

If you don't have squeeze-out on either side, and you don't see fluid movement when you push down on the plank, it's time to pull some screws, open the joints with wedges, and force more epoxy between the plank and keelson.

The Gospel of Epoxy Putty Removal

Thou shalt clean up excess epoxy putty forthwith, or live to repent thy hastening on with the planking up of thy vessel.

The time to clean up the excess epoxy is immediately after attaching a plank. People who have had the opportunity to clean up even a small amount of hardened epoxy are passionately thorough about removing every molecule of accessible epoxy as soon as humanly possible. Those who have had a chance to clean up a whole boatful of hardened epoxy are putty-knife-thumping preachers.

Clean up now

After you've admired your new garboard, do yourself a big favor and clean up the excess epoxy putty. You'll need a firm but flexible putty knife, a small scrap of plywood for holding the goo, and a hat you no longer care for.

There is a knack to removing the putty, which you will soon learn. Generally speaking, you want to shovel up the putty, not spread it around.

To keep the putty from riding up on the edge of the planking while you shovel it up, first clear it away from the edge. Rest the side edge of the putty knife on the plank or edge and pull it toward you to plow the putty away from the edge.

Keep your putty knife very clean by regularly scraping the excess off onto the plywood scrap.

Run down the whole outer joint. (Don't forget under the plank at the stem and transom.) Grab a clamp lamp and the old hat and climb under the hull to do the inside. You will have to scrape more than shovel to clean near the inner stem, but aim for a neat microscopically thin layer of putty if you can't get it all. The stem area will be easier to clean on subsequent planks. Do the best you can, though; scraping and sanding hardened epoxy putty down in this tight corner is not much fun.

Don't forget to clean up any putty that is partially covering screws.

If the putty is getting more sticky and gummy by the minute, scrape it off as best you can. If possible, cool off the shop a little to give yourself more time for the next plank.

You can clean up more of the epoxy residue by wiping with a paper towel dampened with denatured alcohol

7.37 A thorough cleaning of the epoxy putty that has squeezed from the lap on the inside of the hull makes the final cleanup for finishes go much easier and quicker.

(wear gloves). We don't normally bother with this, largely because we generally plank up a boat in few days. If you're working on your boat over a fairly long period, the epoxy has longer to cure and you may find this a worthwhile extra step.

Painter's Masking Tape Makes Cleanup Even Easier

In our eternal search for ways to make working with epoxy cleaner, we tried taming squeeze-out inside the boat by taping off the inboard face of each plank just outside the pencil line marking the keelson or lap joint. We cleaned up with a putty knife as usual after installing each plank. Once the hull was off the jig, we pulled the tape. The tape came off easily (for the most part), and left an almost perfectly clean surface, except for a thin line of epoxy along the plank edge that came off easily with scraper and file. We also tried taping along the inner stem. This proved to be a pain to remove, but still easier than chiseling and sanding hardened epoxy putty.

If you use the tape, be doubly sure to clean the excess epoxy off very well. If the boat will be on the jig for weeks (or months) instead of days, pull the tape after the epoxy hardens, as you build the hull.

Garboard number two

You may attach the second garboard as soon as the first garboard is all cleaned up. Before you apply the epoxy, check to be sure that the second plank won't hit the first at the bow. Trim the first plank so that the second plank fully contacts the inner stem. A flexible-bladed Japanese saw is a very handy tool for trimming the plank ends.

BEVELING THE GARBOARDS' LAP JOINTS

The procedure for beveling the lap joints is similar to beveling the keelson: cut the bevel at each mold and the transom, then cut and fair the bevel between the molds.

Before you begin, carry your bench, block, and rabbet planes over to the sharpening stones and sharpen all of the blades until they shave you nicely. Don't kill yourself over each blade; the glue in the plywood is diabolically hard and you will be revisiting your stones often. A slight curve in the blades is as useful here as it was for beveling the keelson.

Beveling at the molds

Bevel the laps at the molds with your favored hand outboard, just as you did on the keelson. Find the position that is as comfortable as possible, but make sure that the aft end of the bench plane skates across the mold as you

bevel the lap so that you maintain the proper angle (see Photo 7.38). If you try to work with the plane's forward end pointed toward the mold, the aft end, which is fairly heavy, hangs out in space and gravity causes you to cut the bevel too flat and too wide. Which brings us to rule number one of beveling the laps:

Don't cut over the scored line. Every shaving you take off above the scored line is making the bevel all wrong. The next plank will not attach properly, which isn't fun for the boatbuilder and certainly doesn't help strengthen the hull.

Planing the bevel is a precise operation. Yes, you can fill gaps and overplaned areas with epoxy putty, but striving to do it right will make the next plank much easier to hang. Unless you have a fair amount of experience with a hand plane, you will not find beveling the laps easy. The thin plywood and glue lines conspire against you. But keep working at it. Once you have mastered beveling the laps, you will have achieved a high degree of proficiency with a very useful tool and have accomplished the most difficult job in building a glued-lapstrake boat.

Establish the bevel you are going to plane by resting the plane with its aft end on the mold, forward end on the planking. Holding this angle, pull back the plane toward you and make several passes, cutting until you've beveled about two-thirds of the lap.

The mold's original curve should be untouched at this point. The bevel you just cut is too flat, but now that you've taken off the corner of the plank, you can trim the mold in same way as you did when beveling the keelson. Turn the plane perpendicular to the plank edge and trim the mold toward the edge-of-plank line. Try not to cut off the edge-of-plank mark on the mold. (Is it marked on the

7.38 A plank lap is first beveled at each mold, much the same way the keelson was beveled.

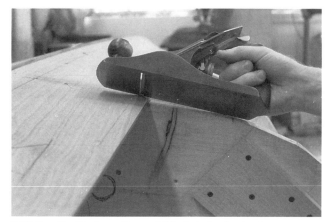

7.39 Beveling the lap will go quickly, but stop to check progress before the cut reaches the lap score line.

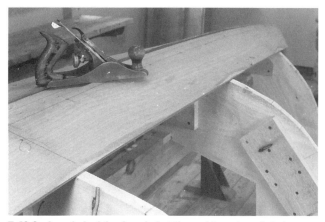

7.40 Garboard plank lap beveled at the molds and ready to be beveled between the molds.

working face, too? If not, take a minute and mark it as well the rest of the molds.) If you can't see where you're cutting very well, either on the lap or the mold, use pencil slashes.

Now check the angle of the bevel, using the corner of the plane as a straightedge. Trim the bevel and mold until the plane's edge touches from the scored line on the plank to the edge-of-plank on the mold. Very slightly concave between the marks is fine.

Bevel at all of the molds and at the transom. As you near the end of each, try doing the last few cuts with a block plane set for a finer cut than the bench plane.

Beveling between the molds

Begin at the lap between the first and second stations. (Don't worry about the area from station No. 2 to the stem; we'll do this last, after finishing the rest of the lap.)

Position yourself so that your favored hand is now inboard. Hold the bench plane on the mold closest to you to establish the angle, then cut at this angle until the plane's forward end meets the angle of the second mold. Let the plane lean into the new angle. After a couple of passes, you'll feel the whole plane twisting to cut the changing bevel from one mold to the next, just as you did

on the keelson. As usual, pencil slashes will help you see where you're cutting.

The planking is much thinner than the keelson, of course, and as you cut, it can bend. Try not to push down on the plywood very much. If the blade is not cutting, try waxing the plane's sole a little. It will often feel like you freshly sharpened the plane. Sharpen the blade often, though, because you don't want to lean on the plane to compensate for a dull blade. If you do bend the plywood, it will change the angle of the cut. The plane will cut higher up on the lap than you really want, leading to a flatter bevel than you intended. If you aren't careful, this will lead to the forbidden activity: cutting above the scored line.

Normally you can cut about half to two-thirds of the bevel with the bench plane before it stops cutting effectively.

The block plane is the best tool for finishing the bevel. You need a plane you can easily hold in one hand so that you can support the plywood with the other. You can do this in two ways:

Method one. Hold the block plane in one hand, and reach under the plank with the other to support it (see Photo 7.41). This is the easiest and safest method. Its only disadvantage is that you can only bevel right where your supporting hand is—about 8″ to 10″ of lap. You have to interpret exactly what you want the bevel to be in each successive spot, rather than following the changing bevel. We'll talk about what to look for in a moment.

Method two. In this approach, both hands move with the plane. Your favored hand holds and guides the plane at the correct angle. The thumb of your unfavored hand pushes down on the front end of the plane, and the remaining four fingers reach around the edge of the plywood and push up. In this position you can cut the entire bevel from mold to mold. Keep your fingers well clear of the plywood edge, which can give you a nasty splinter.

Try starting off with the first method, followed by a stroke or two along the bevel length using the second method.

7.41 A small block plane that can be held in one hand finishes the lap bevel while the other hand supports the thin planking.

Levels of Bevel

The angle between the garboard and second plank is likely to be fairly moderate, so your bevel can safely be cut to the scored line. Later on, there are likely to be exceptions. It would be good to look ahead at these now.

The sketches show several different degrees of bevel in cross section and boatbuilder-eye views. The first is a moderate bevel, such as you will probably encounter on the garboard plank. The bevel cuts through the first three veneers and just begins to make inroads on the fourth of a five-veneer panel.

The second bevel is one you won't likely see until the second or third plank. This is the steepest angle you can cut that will still go all the way to the scored line. The bevel just touches the last veneer, leaving a thin, square edge. Don't plane all the way down to a feather edge. It is far too easy (trust us) to catch the edge with the putty knife and break it. Chunks missing from an otherwise sweeping plank line on the inside of the hull are quite noticeable. A square edge is much tougher and will make epoxy clean up, sanding, and finishing go along much better.

The third sketch shows how to handle the steepest bevels. The bevel is at the proper angle, but it does not reach the scored line. When the next plank goes on, it will land along the bevel but there will be a gap, which will be filled with epoxy putty. This joint is very strong, creates a deep shadow line, and still leaves a fair plank line on the inside of the hull. This sort of bevel occurs on the Ellen near the sheer on the aft end of the boat, and on many other boats with fewer planks including the Shellback dinghy and Nutshell pram.

Checking for fairness using the plywood's glue lines

On the keelson, you were able to sight along the edge to see whether the cut formed a fair curve from mold to mold, telling you the bevel was right. You can't do that with the planking so easily because the plywood is so much thinner. Instead, you can use the glue lines in the plywood.

The glue lines act like contour lines on a map. Each beveled slope that you've cut at each mold is different, and shows a different pattern of lines to reflect this. When you bevel between the molds, the pattern of the glued lines will gradually shift from what you see at one mold into the next. Seeing the changing bevel angles in the glue lines will become automatic once you've looked at and refined an assortment of different bevels. Wrapping your mind around the concept can prove interesting at first, especially if you're reading about it without a plank to bevel in front of you. This is definitely one of those things that is easier to understand while you're

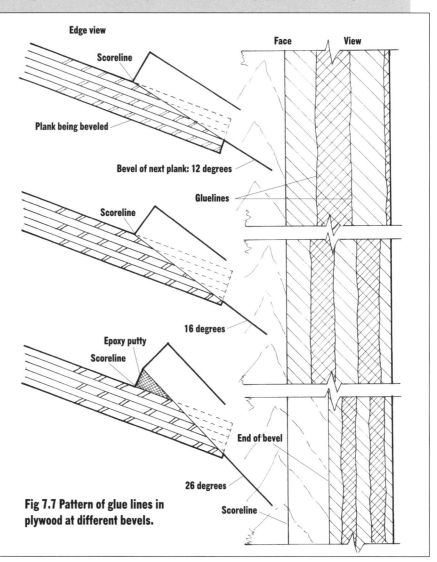

Fig 7.7 Pattern of glue lines in plywood at different bevels.

actually doing the work.

So, for starters, please inspect Figure 7.8. In this example, mold A exhibits four glue lines, while mold B has three. The bevel at A is steeper than the bevel at B. If you are right-handed, you would be working from right to left. The goal is to see the bottom glue line die out and disappear fairly quickly, then see the third glue line gradually approach the plank edge. As you approach mold B, the distance between the glue lines will increase.

If you were to bevel this lap area for real, you would start by making some pencil slashes across the bevel so you can clearly see how close to the scored line you are cutting, and figure out where you want to cut. Because you may have planed the bevel correctly in your initial passes with the bench plane, it's also likely that you would encounter the following:

The area at mold B has three glue lines; that at mold A, four—but the area in the middle, between the molds, only shows one or two glue lines, even though you've cut the bevel quite close to the scored line. This is a pretty common situation, especially when you're first learning how to bevel the laps. It means that the bevel is too flat. To remedy the situation, you need to take off more at the plank edge.

On the other hand, if you see more lines than you want or the lines are too close together, the bevel angle is too steep and you need to take off some more closer to the scored line.

Useful Rule of Thumb: The steeper the bevel, the more glue lines are visible and the closer together they are.

As you can see in the pictured example, the glue lines run very nearly parallel to each other. To help show the pattern on your boat, use a yardstick to draw lines from the glue pattern at one mold to the next. If you have an extra glue line at one mold, as does our example, draw a line parallel to the other glue lines to see where the extra glue line ought to reach the plank edge. In this case, the fourth glue line touches the plank edge just after the "A" mold.

Finishing up the bevel

Beveling the laps is where the curved plane blade really shines. By positioning the plane's edge close to where you

want to cut less, the meaningful portion of the blade will be over the area that needs trimming.

Finish up with the last stroke of the plane just touching the scored line. All the glue lines you want to see should be exposed. This can be tricky. Employ a technique very similar to that used in beveling the inner stem and keelson: After roughly planing the bevel with the bench plane, hold a block plane with a curved blade at a little steeper angle than the final bevel wants to be and plane along the plank edge to expose the pattern of glue lines without having to worry about trimming past the scored line. Then draw pencil slashes, and plane with the lower edge of the plane very close to the plank edge so you won't cut there. Where the pencil lines are cut tells you the angle at which you are holding the plane. When the bevel is done the pencil slashes will be mostly gone. The finished bevel will have a slight hollow, which is perfect. The next plank will sit firmly upon it, leaving a slight bit of room for epoxy.

As you plane the lap, check to see if you are cutting a flat or slightly concave bevel, using the corner of the plane as a straightedge. If you have trimmed down to the scored line and as far as you want to at plank edge but

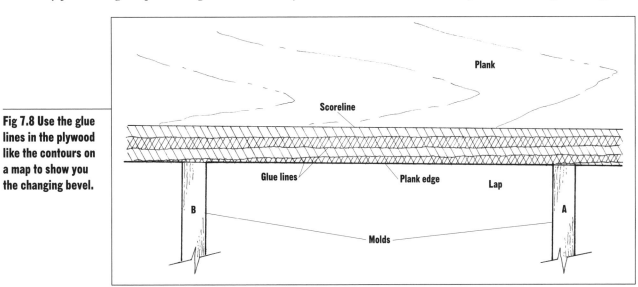

Fig 7.8 Use the glue lines in the plywood like the contours on a map to show you the changing bevel.

7.42 A rabbet plane bevels the lap in the gains.

the bevel is convex, you need to trim off the hump. Using a plane to cut the angle just right will be almost totally a matter of blind luck. A spokeshave (with a curved cutting edge on the blade, like the planes) is the tool for this job.

Pencil slashes will help you see where you're cutting, but with the spokeshave the real clue is where the shavings emerge from the tool's throat. Small adjustments in angle are easy to make because your hands are so far apart.

One trick is to let the edge of the spokeshave's sole (next to the blade on the "uphill" side) ride along on scored line, ensuring that no wood is trimmed there. The blade will begin cutting at the hump. Each pass will let you hold the spokeshave at a slightly steeper angle, until the last one takes off nearly the last of the pencil marks. This is a very controlled way to correct the bevel. Make sure that the spokeshave is very sharp. There is no way to keep the plywood from bending if you push down.

Finish beveling along the laps on both sides, except for the region between the first mold and the inner stem.

At the gain

You will need a rabbet plane to cut inside the gain. The process is the same as for the rest of lap, except that the bevel is changing from the angle at the first station to no angle—flat—at the bottom of the gain at the bow. The pattern of glue lines is a little hard to read. At first, as the bevel angle becomes smaller, the glue lines will spread apart and disappear. Then, at the start of the gain, the

Sheathing the Bottom and/or Garboards with Cloth

Because we prefer to rely on a flat, replaceable oak keel on most of our boats, we rarely have had occasion to protect a boat with abrasion-resistant cloth. It can be a good idea for flat-bottomed craft that will be hard on their bottoms.

We like Xynole cloth, available from Defender Marine (see Appendix B, "Resources"). This cloth is thinner and lighter than typical fiberglass cloth. It is cottony soft, drapes well, and cuts nicely with sharp scissors. The cloth swells some after wetting out, and it does not become transparent. The cloth is a little harder to wet out than fiberglass, but it does not share that material's tendencies toward lifting and bubbles. Xynole cloth isn't cheap, but for small boats its ease of use and longevity balance the equation for us. That, and no itchy, glass fibers.

Here's how to do what we did when we sheathed the bottom and garboard of a couple of flat-bottomed double-enders: Harry Bryan's Fiddlehead double-paddle canoe and Steven Weld's American River Skiff rowboat.

- *Attach the garboards, then bevel for and fit the next plank. After setting aside the second plank, prepare the hull for the cloth by planing the garboards flush with the bottom and stems; removing the screws into the bottom and into jig from garboard; beveling and rounding over the chine; and breaking the edges of the planking at the stems.*
- *Optional step: Mask off the lap bevel on the garboard with regular masking tape, taking care to run the tape*

7.43 Sheathing the bottom and garboard plank of a Harry Bryan Fiddlehead double-paddle canoe with Xynole cloth.

precisely along the score line. (On the Weld boat, John didn't use the tape and found the process went just as well and the gains worked better.)

- *Pick a time when the shop is reasonably cool, or use a hardener with a generous working time.*
- *Lay the cloth over the boat and trim to about 6" below the edge of the garboard.*
- *Starting at each end, roll the cloth toward the middle of the boat.*
- *You'll need one of those flat plastic squeegees sold by epoxy suppliers, a throwaway brush, and a quart yogurt container with a vertical slit cut several inches down the side.*
- *Drink a diminutive cup of coffee, visit the head, let in the dog. Find your respirator and put it on.*
- *Mix epoxy putty and fill the screw holes.*

glue lines will come back into view as the plane ventures deeper into the tapered rabbet. This job is largely done by feel and the help of a scrap of plywood or a thin wide batten about 2″ wide and about 3′ long to test the lap bevel.

Line up the edge of the rabbet plane with the scored line at the first mold. As you push the plane ahead to cut the bevel, follow the scored line, which will turn into the lip of the gain. As with the scored line, you don't want to cut any wood right in the corner of the gain, so the plane's edge need pass only close to the edge of the gain, not ride against it.

At first, use the test batten frequently to help tell you where you need cut and—equally important—where not to cut. Don't forget the pencil slash marks. And finally, you'll be glad of epoxy's gap-filling qualities here, if nowhere else.

Don't forget to wax those molds, again

After you finish beveling, give the freshly cut mold surfaces a neat swipe with a little paste wax. Don't get the wax on the planking.

7.44 The sheathed bottom and garboards ready for the remaining planks.

- Roll the cloth out on forward half of the boat, smoothing until flat.
- Wet out the cloth with epoxy in small batches. Pour the epoxy in long puddles on the cloth, and spread it with the squeegee. Push manageable small amounts over the edge and down onto the garboard to avoid drips onto the floor. You can do small areas near the bow with the tab brush, but with practice you probably will find that you can use the squeegee nearly everywhere.
- Cut the cloth along the top edge of the gains with scissors. Wet out the cloth in the gain, using the brush.
- Before wetting out at the bow, trim the cloth so it just overlaps on the face of the inner stem and plank ends, not onto the side of the garboard. The outer stem covers the overlap. Wet out the first side with the brush, then lay the second layer over it and wet this down.

Plank On!

Many of the steps for putting on the garboard will be repeated for the rest of the planks. And because the garboard is without a doubt the most difficult plank, things will get better and easier from now on. You'll find this whole planking stuff a snap by the third or fourth plank. (We know this from John's week-long hull-building classes: on Tuesday, people look distinctly perplexed as they consider the garboards; by Thursday, it's "Plank coming through!" There are planks everywhere, being measured, cut, fitted, and installed by people who have definitely Figured Things Out.)

From the moment you start to bevel the garboard to receive the next plank until you have cleaned up the last bit of squeeze-out, everything you do to put on this second pair of planks will be repeated for the rest of the planks until you reach the sheerstrake.

- When the entire half of the boat is wetted out, mix up a single-pump batch of epoxy and make sure that all areas are wetted out well, especially the cloth about an inch below the edge of the plank.
- Squeegee off the excess with moderate pressure. Clean the squeegee by pulling it through the slit in the yogurt container (thanks to Ted Moores for this idea). The idea is to get the ratio of epoxy to cloth down in order save weight. You'll fill most of the cloth weave later with microballoon putty.
- Do the other half of the boat the same way.
- It took us about four hours to do a 12′ double-ended canoe. With the shop at 70 degrees, the epoxy had kicked to the soft plastic stage after about five hours. At this point, we could easily cut the excess cloth at the plank edge line with a utility knife without disturbing the cloth attached to the planking.
- If you used masking tape, cut with a utility knife along tape edge on the score line and remove it after the epoxy has cured a bit more, but is not rock hard.
- Once the epoxy has kicked well, sand the plank edge and attach the second planks as usual.
- When you've finished the hull, fill the cloth weave with microballoon putty. Scuff the cloth surface with 80-grit. Tape off below the cloth with regular masking tape. Mix the putty to a consistency that will not run, but that is thinner than peanut butter. Spread this on evenly with a wide (6″ or 8″) putty knife. Fill in several thin layers, sanding a little between coats. Don't glom it on; you'll be sanding forever. Epoxy is hard stuff.

The Rest of the Planks
SPILING

You spile the second plank in almost exactly the same way you did the job on the garboard. A refresher:

- Nail the spiling pattern in place on the jig.
- To measure the upper edge, put the compass point on the score line of the garboard's lap at each mold. (You'll do the same thing with every plank afterward, except the sheer.)
- Most of the marks needed for the plank's lower edge will be visible on the molds, but there will be more molds that require use of the plank-width measuring jig than there were on the garboard.
- Mark the stem just like you did the transom on the garboard plank, with two arcs at the edges of the pattern, rather than tracing the stem's shape on the back of the spiling pattern. If it's heavily curved, just freehand-in the approximate shape.
- A reminder: Forward molds go on one side of the plank-width measuring jig, aft molds on the other. The stem (bow end) goes on the "aft mold" side of the jig; the transom or sternpost (stern end) goes on the "forward mold" side (see box, "Transferring Stem and Transom Widths Using the Plank Measuring Jig").
- Until spiling becomes second nature, writing down a list of the steps for ready reference will help ensure that you don't forget something. Much better than scraping the pattern clean and re-spiling….

If the transom bevel is off

As you spile and test-fit the planks, you may find that the bevel you cut in the transom isn't quite right. This will almost always mean that the angle is too steep. To get an idea of how much to trim, look at the gap on the outboard side of the transom. You can even set a compass to this distance if it's more than ⅛". Mark the distance on the inboard face of the transom.

To fix: Hold the plank end away from the transom, employing a friend or a block of wood. Mark the bevel with pencil slashes and trim with a sharp chisel, lightly waxed. Start cutting on the inboard edge, and work the new bevel down until nearly all of the pencil marks are gone.

Important: Never, ever trim the outboard edge of the transom.

The points that form the transom's outside perimeter are absolute fixed points in space that define your boat. Trimming the outboard edge will change the shape of the transom, and it's likely to look very odd and to lose

---

Transferring Stem and Transom Widths Using the Plank Measuring Jig

When you lay out the widths of the plank on the plywood, the plank-width measuring jig (see earlier, "Capturing Those Hidden Edge-of-Plank Marks") must follow the angled stem and transom lines that you marked from the pattern. From the sketch you can see that one corner of the cutout touches the plank-shaping batten and the other doesn't. If the side of the jig where the corner touches is marked, your plank will be the right width. But if you marked the other side, your plank will be too narrow by the distance the angle creates between the cut-out and the batten.

To record the plank width, hold the measuring jig along the same line that you marked on the pattern. Holding the jig as you did on the molds with the cutout on the scored lap line will be a little awkward, but it is important to do it properly. If you can, turn the measuring jig over so the cutout is on edge-of-plank mark and you mark the width at the plank lap score line.

7.45 Trimming the transom bevel with a chisel as a plank is being test-fitted.

Fig 7.9 At the ends of the plank, the plank-width measuring jig touches the shaping batten at an angle. If the measurement for the bow and stern are on the wrong sides, the plank will be cut too narrow.

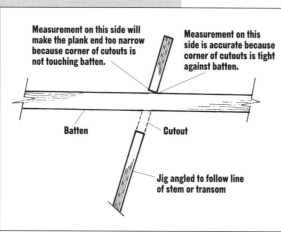

Measurement on this side will make the plank end too narrow because corner of cutouts is not touching batten.

Measurement on this side is accurate because corner of cutouts is tight against batten.

Batten

Cutout

Jig angled to follow line of stem or transom

7.46 The shapes of planks to come can be interesting and surprising.

7.47 Spiling and fitting the second plank is usually easier because there is less twist to the hull. (Note: The gain is already cut in this plank because in production mode, John makes planks and cuts gains all at once using Mylar patterns or "phantom planks" (see below).

its lovely bilateral symmetry.

You will find a slicing cut very helpful, particularly when trying to cut end-grain, which you will find as you approach the sheer. We're sure you can guess which planks tend to have problems with the transom bevel.

Trim the transom bevel, test the plank, then trim again. It's the best way. When the angle is just right, measure it with a bevel gauge and trim its twin on the opposite side of the transom. If you plan to build another boat, record the angle on your full-sized pattern as a reminder.

Occasionally, the transom needs trimming in a place where you can use a block plane. Once again, a sharp, fine cut and pencil slashes make the job go easier.

If the angle at the transom happens to be the odd one that is too flat, remember: Don't trim the outboard edge. Make some wedges to fill the gap. These don't have to be perfect; just enough to hold the plank at the proper angle. When you drive a screw into the transom, the epoxy putty will fill any gaps. Remember to make the identical wedges for the other side of the boat.

To make a nicer job of filling the gap in the bevel, and not have to worry about a little wedge falling out, cut a strip of matching wood a little wider than the angled edge of the transom and a little more than the thickness of the gap at the inboard side of the transom. Make another for the other side of the transom. Glue the strips to the transom with five-minute epoxy, holding them in place with tape.

While the epoxy hardens, you can cut the gains in the planks. After a half-hour, trim and bevel the glued strip, and nail on at least the aft end of the plank for a test fit. Trim and test until it's just right, as you did above. Measure the angle and trim the filler piece on the other side of the transom to match.

Attach the plank as usual.

CUTTING AND FITTING

Lay out the plank on the plywood panels and nail on the battens. This time, and from here on, both battens must be fair curves. Getting a batten fair is one of the arts of glued-lapstrake construction, so don't be afraid to try different things. Nothing is permanent until you apply that saw.

Spiling with the adjustable pattern tends to be extremely accurate, so you can flush trim the whole plank to the batten. If you feel unsure about how your second plank might turn out, give yourself a little wiggle room by not flush-trimming the plank forward of the first mold, just as you may have done with the garboard.

Test one of your new planks on the boat on the same side you spiled. Trim where you need to. At this point, you don't have to drill for any screws. It is easy enough to hold the plank in place with nails and fingers, so wait to drill for screws until you fasten the plank on permanently. This eliminates the problem of epoxy putty squirting through the holes.

7.48 A block plane can be held in one hand for trimming a plank to fit its neighbor, freeing up the second hand to hold the plank.

When fitting and attaching planks, always line up on the edge-of-plank marks on the molds (as much as you can), not the score line for the lap of the previous plank. The edge-of-plank marks are located at the same point on both port and starboard sides of the mold—or should be. Working to the lap score lines can allow the planks to creep, not always at the same rate on the two sides of the hull.

When you're happy with the fit, pull off the plank and bring it back to the planking table. If you trimmed the plank, remember to nail it to its partner and trim with the block plane until the two are identical. Make sure that the curves are still fair. If there is a lot of wood to trim, you can re-nail the battens in place, fairing in the changes, and flush-trim the pair with the router.

Gains

With a marking gauge, mark the lap on the lower edge of the outboard face of both planks, then do the inboard face's top edge with a compass also set to the width of the lap. This pair of planks, and those that follow, except the sheer, must have a gain cut in the upper inboard "attaching" edge as well as the lower outboard "receiving" edge. Draw a dark, squiggly line over the areas to be cut out for

7.49 If a plank needs to be trimmed, most likely it will be at the bow where the gains must fit together. Here the gains have been cut before fitting, but the plank also can be fitted before the gains are cut.

gains. Double-check to be certain that you've marked the right places. You'd be surprised how easy it is to cut the gain on the wrong side of the plank, or to put the straightedge on the wrong side of the score/pencil line

7.50 Putting a plank in the Gain-O-Matic.

7.51 Cutting the gain with a router in the Gain-O-Matic.

Power Gains

Now that you've learned to cut gains by hand, we'd like to introduce one of John's favorite shopmade jigs: the Gain-O-Matic. This set-up allows you to cut the gains with a router equipped with a straight bit the same size as the width of the lap. This approach is highly favored by folks who love using their routers and is worth the effort if you plan to build more than one boat. However, we recommend strongly that you become proficient at cutting gains by hand before trying the powered approach. The router is very fast; faster than your "Oh, @#!" will be, particularly if you haven't become thoroughly familiar with the look of a proper, well-cut gain.

The Gain-O-Matic (G-O-M) consists of two main parts, a base to hold the end of the plank and a track at an angle that guides the router cutting the gain.

The base is a simple rectangle of ¾" plywood. The track is made of two L-shaped pieces of scrap mahogany fastened flush on top of the edges of a piece of ¼" or ½" plywood cut narrower than the base and 6" or 8" inches longer. A rectangular Plexiglas base for the router sets on the track with about ¹⁄₁₆" of slop.

A 1½"-wide strip of plywood attached to the bottom of the track near one end holds the track at an angle and determines the length of the gain. To lay out the position of the spacer, first draw a line on the bottom

7.52 Trimming the top edge of the new plank at the bow will make a pre-cut gain narrower, and the lower edge of the previous plank will need to be trimmed with a rabbet plane to make the exterior edges fit tightly together. You can pre-cut the gains if you are sure that you won't have to trim the plank edges more than 1/8".

(see Appendix A, "Oh, @#!").

If you think you might build another boat, make plank patterns by tracing onto Mylar (available from architectural and graphic arts suppliers in rolls.) now, before cutting the gains. Also, go around the jig with a backsaw and cut a shallow kerf in the molds along the plank edges.

This will allow you to precisely position the next boat's planks. Remember to do this for all subsequent planks.

Cut the gains just as you did on the garboard:

After you've cut the receiving gain as you did for the garboard, flip the plank over for the attaching gain and fasten the straightedge along the marked pencil line so that you can see all of the line. This should make this gain a tiny bit wider than its counterpart on the previous plank, thus ensuring that the plank edges fit tightly together on the outside of the hull. This is a nice aesthetic touch, and essential if you plan to varnish the hull. (Small gaps on the interior caused by cutting this gain a little too wide are easily filled with epoxy putty after the hull comes off the jig. Try to get the gains close, especially near the sheer, if you're varnishing the interior, however.)

ATTACHING THE PLANK(S)

Before you can attach plank number two, you'll need your collection of well-waxed clamping blocks and battens. Please see Chapter 2, "Materials and Tools," and Chapter 5, "Building Jig and Molds,") for how to make these, if you've skipped ahead.

Unless you have lots of well-directed help or plenty of experience, work on one plank at at time.

of the track 6" from one end. This is where you will position the end of the plank. If you are using a spacer with a thickness equal to that of the planking (in the case of the Ellen, ¼" or 6mm), locate the spacer twice the length of the gain from the line locating the end of the plank. For boats such as the Ellen, John makes the gains 11" long; the distance to the spacer is therefore 22".

Before you attach the track to the base, cut out a 3"-wide slot from the plank end line toward the closest end of the track, spanning the distance between the L-shaped mahogany pieces.

One end of the base is located on the plank end line and fastened with drywall screws through the Ls of the track about 1" from the end of the base. The other end of the base must be at least long enough to support the spacer. Drywall screws holding this end also go through the Ls of the track and are about ½" from the spacer, on the side toward the plank end line.

Although the track spacer is attached with glue on John's G-O-M, it could be screwed on to make it possible to change the spacer's position for different gain lengths.

Four other identical spacers, the same thickness as the planking stock, hold the track flat from side to side as it holds down the plank. Screw these at the base's four corners, making sure that two are under the track spacer.

The base spacers must be of the same thickness as the planking, so make them easy to change.

Put a straight bit of at least the same size as the lap width in the router and set the depth so it will just cut through the plywood of the track when the router, on its Plexiglas base, rests on the track's L-shaped channels. Cut a slot in the track plywood, running the router first tight against one channel, then tight against the other. Be careful not to cut the track in half. (Small blocks screwed to the Ls make convenient stops.) Mark a pyramid on one edge of the router base and on the matching track channel so that you'll always know how to put the router in the jig the same way.

Now you're ready to cut some gains. Try out your new G-O-M on a few scraps first to determine the proper depth for the cutter. Write the depth down on the G-O-M.

Insert the plank, and line up the scored or pencil line for the lap with the edge of the slot. Tighten the four long drywall screws. Drive small finish nails through the track into the plank and into the base at each end of the base to hold the plank firmly in place. The finished gain should look exactly like a hand cut-gain.

7.53 Wetting the lap.

7.54 Spreading the epoxy putty.

7.55 Fastening the end of the plank to the stem.

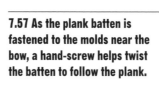

7.56 Like the spiling pattern and the plank, a plank batten is first attached amidships, but with a screw into the mold.

7.57 As the plank batten is fastened to the molds near the bow, a hand-screw helps twist the batten to follow the plank.

Set a plank on the sawhorses and check to be doubly sure about which side it goes on. Apply epoxy to this plank just like you did the garboard: Wet out the plank's landing areas on the garboard, inner stem, and transom, then do the matching areas on the plank. Remove the little screw driven into the gain on the garboard. (Putty over this, and you won't remember it until you try to drive a clamping screw through the batten into the stem, and find the screw. We finally made up a reminder sign for those days when we are moving a little too fast for our own good.)

Mix up a nice batch of putty and spread it on the garboard lap, stem, and transom. You'll need less than

you did for the garboard-to-keelson connection, and this new amount should be about right for all of the remaining planks.

Pick up and flip the plank. Starting at the midship mold, tack the plank in place at all the molds. Move to the bow, and drill, countersink, and drive permanent bronze or stainless screws to hold the plank to the stem, including one through the plank's receiving gain. Countersink this last screw (carefully) so you will be able to plane the bevel in the gain with the screw in place. Don't drive a screw at the attaching lap joint. (As you will recall, you just removed a screw in the garboard's underlying gain; again, this area will be held in place by a batten.) If there is copious squeeze-out along the joint at the gain, scoop this up with a putty knife. Move to the stern, and permanently screw the plank down, avoiding both lap joints here. You won't need a screw below the plank's scored lap line, since a screw placed just above the line holds well enough.

Locate the screws about half of the lap width above the score line. If the plank is wide, as it often is at the transom, drive another screw halfway between this screw and the middle of the attaching lap. If you plan to varnish your hull, attention to screw spacing is vital. The epoxy putty "bungs" over the screw heads will be eminently visible, so give some thought to attractive spacing.

Time to change drill bits. You won't need the countersink. You will need a clearance drill bit sized for drywall screws and a Phillips driver bit. Two drills make life easier. So do two drill operators: one to position the clamping batten and drill clearance holes, the second to insert and drive screws. (A helper is not essential, however.) You'll also need drywall screws: 2″ for the molds; 1⅝″ for the battens; and 1¼″ for the stem and transom, unless your boat is significantly larger than the boats we are covering in this book.

It's helpful to put a pile of 2″ screws at each station, and a pile of 1¼″ screws at bow and stern. Carry the 1⅝″ screws along with a good handful of (waxed) clamping blocks in your nail apron.

To make the job of trimming the planks for outer stem easier later on, trim the plank about ¼″ proud of the stem. Clean epoxy off the saw with a little solvent. (Wear gloves.)

Pick up a waxed clamping batten and set it on the lap at the midship mold. Make sure that the edge of the batten is flush with the edge of the plank, then drill for and drive a 2″ drywall screw through the batten into the mold. The clearance hole must go through the batten and both planks. (A 3″ length of 1″ masking tape wrapped around the bit makes a handy depth gauge.) Work your way forward, fastening the batten at each mold. Take

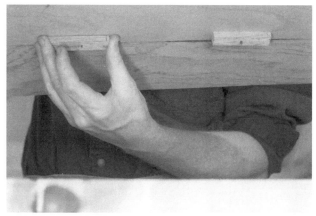

7.58 Lining up the hole in the clamping block with the point of a drywall screw takes practice.

pains to keep the batten flush; if it overhangs the edge of the planking, cleaning up the epoxy putty will be difficult and tedious. You may find twisting the batten into place difficult near the bow. Clamp a wooden hand-screw to the end of the batten, and use it as a handle to *gently* encourage the batten into the proper orientation. A helper can be useful here. Don't force the batten harshly, or you'll break it. (If it breaks, see Appendix A, "Oh, @#!). Generally, the battens are more amenable in this regard as you work your way toward the sheer. Drill the same clearance hole at the stem, but fasten the batten with one of the 1¼″ drywall screws.

Head back aft and fasten the batten at each mold. At the transom, pause to consider the problem. You can follow the angle of the transom with the drywall clamping screw, but it is best not to. Putting this screw in perpendicular to the planking makes replacing it eventually with a permanent bronze or stainless screw much easier. Drill the same clearance hole and drive a 1¼″ screw, with care.

It is reasonable to worry about splitting the wood of the transom. Take some of the pressure off by aiming to miss on the inside of the boat if you have to miss at all. A couple of glued-back-together spots will never show on the inside, since the first planks are usually under a seat at the stern, but they won't do much to enhance the looks of a varnished transom. If you do drive a screw wrong, it's usually best to leave it in place, so long as it's performing its clamping function. You'll remove the screw when you remove the batten, then you can redrill at a more promising angle for the permanent screw.

Lay out the screws for clamping blocks about 8″ apart between molds. (This is for our 2′ mold spacing; change to suit your spacing. That ever-convenient gauge, a fully spread hand, works just fine. However, if you're planning to varnish, set a compass for 8″ (or another consistent measurement) and mark from the screw driven into each mold. That way the puttied screwholes will line up, as do the clench nails or rivets that fasten steam-bent frames in traditional lapstrake boats.

Drill clearance holes at each mark through the batten and planking while holding a small scrap of hardwood against the planking on the inside; this helps prevent dreaded drill blow-outs, which look awful and are a pain to fix and fill. Push a 1⅝″ screw into each hole. Grab a clamping block and orient it so that the angled side faces you and the fat side faces down. Holding the block by the ends in one hand, line up the tip of the screw with the hole. Drive the screw. The block wants to spin, so drive slowly until you learn how to hang on or you'll pinch your fingers. Don't put your finger over the screw hole.

There's a knack to this, which you will develop fully. Don't wind them up too tight—remember epoxy's gap-loving nature. Check to be sure that the plank fully contacts all molds, and that the batten runs fair.

Reverse Curves and Block Orientation

If your boat has a nice reverse curve near her transom, turn the clamping block around so the fat side faces up. This will fit much better. You probably won't need to do this for more than a few places near the stern and for more than a couple of planks. Switch back to normal block orientation when the hull shape allows it.

Fig 7.10 Orientation of the lap-clamping blocks for different angles of planking

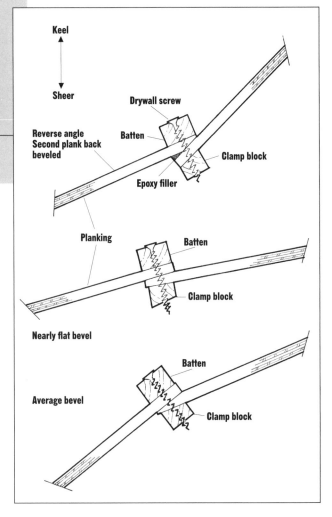

Clean up now

Remember that bit about cleaning up the excess epoxy thoroughl, before moving on to the next plank? Don't forget it now. Grab your putty knife, board, hat, and clamp lamp and remove all the putty you can.

When you come in the shop the next morning to check on your growing hull, use a sharp scraper and file to clean up any more epoxy that has oozed up into the corner of the lap joints on the outside of the hull. The epoxy should be rubbery at this stage and will cut very nicely. There shouldn't be much of this afterthought squeeze-out, but the little bead that sometimes forms is significantly less fun to remove after the epoxy hardens. It's harder to work on the interior, but if you have a few places that you'd like to see cleaner, it is definitely worth giving it a try.

If there are two of you, it is possible to hang both planks in a pair, then clean up. But don't try this until you're absolutely certain that you will be able to remove the excess epoxy from the first plank before it progresses to the sticky goo stage—or beyond.

Onward

Now you can attach the other plank. Run the batten for the second plank just up to the first plank's batten; this way, you won't have to trim either batten. A helper can

7.59 Use care when cleaning up the epoxy inside the hull: the thin edge of the beveled plank can break if the putty knife is wielded with a heavy hand.

tell you where to stop while you adjust the batten from amidships. If you're working alone, measure the distance from amidships to the first plank's batten and mark the distance on the second plank's batten.

When you attach the second plank, remember to check the bow (and stern, if you're building a double-ender) to be sure that it lines up with its partner. Adjust and fudge a little if necessary.

After that, bevel the laps. Then measure, cut out and test-fit, then cut the gains on plank pair number three. Fasten the first one and clean up, then the second one and clean up. Bevel the laps. Measure, cut out and test fit, then cut the gains on plank pair number four. Fasten the first one and clean up, then....

Once you've gotten through your first couple of planks—which are the hardest not only because they're your first, but because they're actually the most difficult and sometimes downright obstreperous planks on the boat—you'll fall into the rhythm of planking. Nothing will change substantively until you reach the sheerstrake.

We usually leave the clamping battens on for at least twenty-four hours (at normal room temperature).

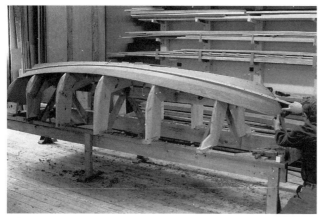

7.60 Fitting the third plank.

7.61 Cleaning epoxy putty in the bow.

7.62 Planking up a double-ender.

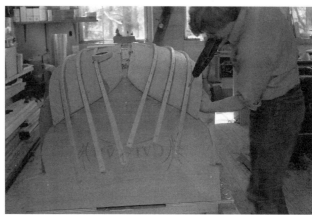

7.63 A look from the stern as planking progresses on an Ellen.

7.64 Beveling the lap on a 10' Achates dinghy.

7.65 Many hands have many tools, and opinions, as a class planks an Ellen.

When you start re-using battens, you'll notice that many of the existing holes won't be in the right places for the new plank. Just drill new holes where needed. You can use holes that fall within a couple of inches of the exact location for the clamping blocks if you're not varnishing the hull. If it's farther than that, mark and drill new holes to keep the clamping pressure evenly distributed. If you are varnishing, keep your screws neatly lined up by marking and drilling new holes.

The battens can survive a surprising number of holes. Ours look like Swiss cheese. Check to see if the holes are making the batten unfair or, more likely, ready to crack. Save the more fragile battens for the gentler curves. If you made several pairs of battens, you probably won't have to worry about this until your second boat, if then.

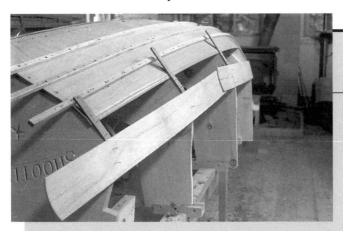

7.66 Using phantom planks to spile a plank.

7.67 The phantom plank used on the molds and transom.

Hyper-Planking

In the first glued-lapstrake boatbuilding class John taught, a major bottleneck showed up pretty quickly. He divided the class into two teams, so people wouldn't be tripping over each other. Unfortunately, one team wound up watching while the other spiled and made a pair of planks. John could have put the idle folks to work building other parts of the boat, but he really wanted everyone to concentrate on planking the hull. There was room for the second team to work on the other side of the hull, but there was a little problem in that they had no plank to spile from, as the first team was still making that pair. The second crew badly needed a surrogate plank, and thus was born an innovation that has proven most productive, not only for classes but for our own building operation.

Take a look at the empty space where you'd like your plank to go. There are the marks on the molds—but these indicate the actual edge of the preceding plank, not the upper edge of its lap joint, which is where you must measure from. There is also the question of cutting the proper facet on each mold for the plank so the pattern will lay the same way as the plank eventually will.

To solve his class's problem, John took short 1" × 6" strips of planking stock, squared up an end, scored the lap width at the end, and beveled the lap to about one veneer thick at the very tip. He made one of these for each mold and the transom. For the stem, he marked the lap on a strip and cut a rabbet to represent a gain, then countersunk for a screw in the rabbet and trimmed the strip to 2" long. These little plank bits were instantly dubbed "phantom planks."

Fig 7.11 Bevel the tip from the scored line of the lap to the last veneer on the phantom planks that are nailed or screwed to the molds and transom. Cut a rabbet, like a gain, in the phantom plank that is screwed to the stem.

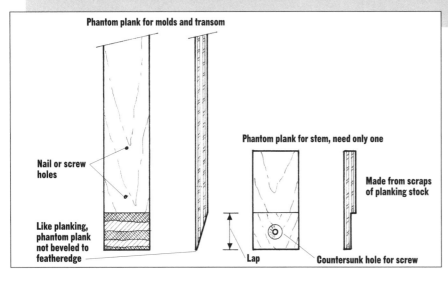

Phantom plank for molds and transom

Nail or screw holes

Like planking, phantom plank not beveled to featheredge

Phantom plank for stem, need only one

Made from scraps of planking stock

Lap

Countersunk hole for screw

7.68 The phantom plank used on the stem.

To use:

- Phantom planks only can be used on molds that have been faceted from beveling the lap of an earlier plank, or by using the phantom planks for this operation (see below).
- Nail or screw the phantom planks with the beveled edge at the edge-of-plank mark on the molds, transom and stem. On the stem and transom, take particular care to follow the edge-of-plank line exactly.
- Bevel the molds with the block plane using the phantom planks as a guide.
- Attach the spiling pattern as close to the score lines on the phantom planks as possible and spile as usual using the scored lines and the upper edge of the gain. Use the plank-width measuring jig to take off the widths from the scored line to the edge-of-plank line on the molds.
- Mark and cut out the plank pair as usual. Test-fit on the phantom planks. Trim if necessary.
- If the lower edge of the new plank varies from the edge-of-plank marks on the molds, draw the new line on the molds and mark with a V.
- Remove the new plank, and the phantom planks. Cut the gains, and install as usual.

When John builds a new design or a one-off hull, he uses the phantom planks to spile and make all the planks, except the garboard, before attaching any of them. Just like when making a "production" hull, this allows him to cut out a pile of planks, set up and cut all the gains, then attach the planks one after another without interruption. John test fits each one before gluing, makes any changes to both planks in the pair, then traces one of them on Mylar for a pattern.

It is very likely that you will not want to use phantom planks on your first boat. But you might try them on your second to make things go quicker. And if you find yourself teaching a class or helping a bunch of friends or a group to build some boats, you'll find phantom planks to be pretty handy.

THE SHEERSTRAKE

This is it. Once the sheerstrake goes on, you've pretty much made the decision about the boat's sheer. You can adjust a little, but not much (see Appendix A, "Oh @#!"). So look carefully now, especially upside down. Is the curve pleasing—just enough, not too much or too little?

Checking that sheer

If you lined off the molds with battens, then you've already seen what the sheer and sheerstrake look like—pretty well, anyway—and can make the sheerstrake with confidence. If you are building to plans that have the laps marked on full-sized patterns, it would be worthwhile to tack a batten at the sheer as well as one on the edge of

7.69 Beveling a gain for the sheerstrake on the extended Iain Oughtred Grebe, GEM.

the second-to-last plank to see what the sheerstrake will look like before you make it. You can also leave the sheer untrimmed after sawing out the plank, then make the final trim after fitting the plank. It's not unusual for a new design to need a little extra "spring" added at the bow; try adding ¼" to ½" to the height at the stem.

Lest you think it's just us simple wooden boat builders who need to fuss with the sheer, we'll briefly relate a tale of woe that involves an extremely famous builder of very expensive fine yachts made of that other material. These folks were building very large custom sailing yacht, a completely new design. They essentially went directly from design computer to a building shed in which the hull barely fit. The crew worked away for many months, installing all of the fine cabinetry, complicated systems, engine, etc., then put on the decks. Eventually, they pulled the well-on-her-way-to-completed vessel out of the boat shed to attach the keel. Everyone stepped back to give her a good look-over, for the first time, and pretty much what everyone said was "Uh, oh" or, rather, the more pithy, heartfelt nouns, verbs, and adjectives that fully express the realization that a very large, very costly problem is sitting in front of you.

The boat had the classic droopy stern and powder-horn bow that don't show up on two-dimensional draw-

7.70 Attaching GEM's sheerstrake.

ings. In these days of computer lofting and CNC-cut parts, a good eye liberally applied is still a valuable boat-building tool. A person experienced in lofting knows how to anticipate and fix these problems by giving a little more spring to the batten drawing the sheer, just how much depending upon the size of the boat and the amount of sheer. Another useful tool is a carefully made half model built to the same scale as the lines drawing.

Note: The yard was able to add 18″ to the sheer at the bow, but the boat was so close to completion that nothing could be done about the stern, and it droops to this day.

Measuring for the sheerstrake

It's finally time to measure for the sheerstrake. (Oh boy, last plank!) If you try to lay the spiling pattern on the hull to measure it the way you've done all the others, you'll notice a problem: it won't go unless you trim it to fit around the transom's "ear," some of the molds, and the end beam at the stem. If you think you'll never build another boat, you could trim the pattern. But there is a better way.

Position the pattern so you measure the curve from the marks for the *sheer* on the molds. This simple change works just fine. Measure the widths the same, using the plank-width measuring jig.

Obviously, the sheer doesn't need to have a line scored for a lap joint, bvecause there isn't going to be another plank. Just mark the lap width on the inside, attaching edge with the compass, as you've been doing all along. And remember to cut only one gain. (See Appendix A, "Oh, @!#," if you get carried away.)

Once you've made the sheerstrake and test-fitted it, you can attach it just like the rest of the planks.

An important note regarding full frames

If you are planking your boat over a laminated full frame and plan on installing closed gunwales along the inside of the sheerstrake, mark the frame for the gunwale while test-fitting the sheerstrake and cut the rabbet for the gunwale after removing the sheerstrake. Take pains to clean the epoxy out of the rabbet in the frame when gluing the sheerstrake on. (See Chapter 9, "Building the Interior.")

WHILE THE HULL IS STILL ON THE JIG....

Although it would be fun and immediately rewarding to pull that lovely new hull right off the jig as soon as the sheerstrake's epoxy has cured, it's worth waiting until you've completed several important operations that go along much better and easier while the hull still resides on the jig—namely, fitting and attaching the "outbone" parts (keel, outer stem, skeg) and the rails. If you can't wait to see what your boat will look like right-side up, climb under the hull with a pencil and trace along the working faces of the molds to mark the station lines on the planking. Find

7.71 Planked-up Ellen hulls, off the jig after a week-long class for a short photo session. The hull on the right will go back on the jigs for installation of outer stem, keel, and rails.

a helper, read ahead on page 162, pop off the hull, turn her over, set her out in the sun, and enjoy a nice long look. Then carry her back in the shop, flip her back over, and replace her on the jig just as she was.

Attaching the outer keel and stem.

Chapter 8

"Outbone" and Rails, Then Off the Jig

CONSIDERING THE OUTBONE PARTS

For any small boat that sees real use, the keel, outer stem, and skeg should be made of a tough, dense wood such as oak that can survive the indignities of life on the boat's very bottom.

As previously mentioned, we prefer a wide, flat keel that is bedded and screwed over a keelson, as this construction suits the life of a small boat so well. Such a keel allows the boat to sit upright on a beach or float; offers more protection to the bottom of the boat; and makes sliding the boat around much easier. Although we have built boats designed by others that specified narrow keels, our customers usually request that John redesign the backbone with a flat keel, especially if they plan to beach their boats regularly. We will cover the construction of wide keels in greater detail in this book, but if your boat design features a narrow keel and you're happy with it, we don't suggest that you change it.

Regardless of the shape of your keel, we recommend that you not attach it or the outer stem, skeg, and rails with epoxy or a tenacious goo like 3M's 5200 if you would like to be able to remove these parts someday. Instead, bed these parts well in bedding compound and fasten them with screws.

What's in a Name? Rails, Gunwales, Inwales, Outwales, Rubrails

Rails? Gunwales? Let us give you our definitions for the two strips of wood that run along inside and outside of the sheerstrake of an open boat. No one appears to agree on what their names should be. For the sake of clarity, we will refer consistently to the outer strip of wood as a rail, and the inner one as a gunwale. (Ruth has a little trouble with this, coming from a canoeing background, but she lost.)

Rubrails are sacrificial strips fastened along the hull, usually well below the sheer, where they will do the most good. These should be installed after the hull is off the jig.

You may call these parts whatever you want after you close this book.

Making and Attaching the Keel, Skeg, and Outer Stem

MAKING THE KEEL

Keel shapes vary widely from design to design, influenced by physical laws, performance goals, and personal taste. It may be one-part, two-part (keel and keelson), wide, narrow, shallow, deep, square, beveled, curved, rabbeted, shaped— or a combination of several of these characteristics.

A wide keel, at the very least, must taper in width from amidships to the stem. Curving the entire length of the keel is no more difficult, looks elegant, and saves weight.

We recommend using the table saw with a guide for cutting long curves in thick lumber and hardwood. That's the job ahead, so it's time to clean all that stuff off the saw.

Laying out

Lay out the centerline on the planed stock using a string. At the stations, employ a framing square aligned from the centerline, then mark the widths of the keel at the stations, as you did for the keelson. Mark the centers of the holes that will be drilled for the ends of the daggerboard or centerboard trunk slot, if you have one. Use a punch to mark the centers after laying them out with pencil and ruler, including the intersections of the centerline and the stations.

You can drill the holes for the trunk before resawing if you are making two keels. Drill these holes after resawing if you're making a two-part long keel.

Bend a batten around the width marks on one side of the keel and spring the ends fair, as you did when fairing the cutting battens for the planks. Hold the batten in place with small finish nails, 3d or 4d, smooth, not galvanized. You will find nailing into the oak difficult, to say the least. You'll be glad to know that the nail only needs to go into the keel stock far enough to hold the batten firmly. The heads can project up above the batten all you want. After nailing the batten in place, check for fairness.

Cutting out

You can cut out the keel with a jigsaw, or it is usually small enough to cut out on the bandsaw. Mark along the edge of the batten with a pencil, remove the batten, and saw the curve out, saving the line. Plane the curve smooth. Repeat for the keel's other edge.

John cuts out keels using a method called pattern ripping. He also uses this method for cutting out small spars and stock for laminated spars. If you wish to do this, drive extra nails into the batten along the keel's edge-to-be so that they are spaced 1″ or less apart.

You'll need to make a simple L-shaped jig of ¾″ birch plywood (or similar) for the table saw (see Photo 8.1). Note that the vertical part of the jig, which clamps to the fence, projects ¹⁄₁₆″ below the horizontal part. This makes setup easy. In addition to the jig, an outfeed table or a good helper is essential for this operation.

With the stock—or a scrap of the same thickness—laid flat and pushed against the fence, there will be ¹⁄₁₆″ clearance between the horizontal part and the stock. At the middle of the exposed edge of the horizontal part, use a square to draw a line perpendicular to the edge. You'll be setting up the jig so that this line is over the highest point of the saw.

Clamp the guide on the fence. Use wooden hand-screws, C-clamps, or any other clamp that will stay firmly clamped. Beware of bar clamps: they are notorious for vibrating loose. You do *not* want this jig coming loose. Bring the fence over until the edge of the horizontal part of the jig is flush with the left side of the blade. The top of the blade should be a little below the bottom of the jig.

After making sure that the jig is firmly clamped to the fence, start the saw and slowly raise the blade to cut about ¹⁄₁₆″ into the jig. Shut off the saw.

On the bandsaw, trim the keel stock to about ⅛″ from the batten. This makes the cut on the table saw safer, and results in a finished keel that is cleaner, with fewer burn marks.

Run the keel stock through the saw, holding the batten against the edge of the jig. The batten will contact at one point—usually—and this point should be right on the mark over the center of the blade, or a little closer to you.

Hang on firmly to the piece as you cut. Don't go too slow, or you'll burn the wood and overheat the blade—but don't go too fast, either.

The biggest hazard with this method is thin offcuts that fall down flat on the table, then vibrate over to the blade. The blade snatches one and—BANG!—drives it between the blade and the jig. Very exciting. If you see such a piece forming, shut off the saw, remove the offcut, and then resume sawing.

After you saw out one side, remove the batten, attach it to the other side, trim on the bandsaw, and saw away.

Resawing

If your keel needs to be resawn, find the exact middle of the keel's edge by marking parallel lines from each face using a compass (see Chapter 3, "Some Very Useful Techniques").

8.1 A simple L-shaped jig allows the table saw blade to precisely follow the long curve of a batten.

8.2 Resawing a keel-shaped blank to make two thin keels.

You'll need to make a resawing jig for the bandsaw, as the keel is thin and wide enough to require the jig to keep the piece vertical while you saw it. If you are putting floorboards in your boat, you'll be pulling out this jig when it's time to resaw all those cedar planks.

The vertical portion of the jig is a pointer made of ³/₄ " plywood by making two crosscuts on the table saw with the blade set at 45 degrees. A ³/₄ " plywood triangle holds the pointer vertical. Positioning the pointer opposite the tips of the bandsaw blade's teeth allows you to steer the keel stock as you saw it in half.

The jig's ¹/₄ " or ¹/₂ " base makes clamping to the bandsaw table easy and also makes adjusting the width of the cut easy and very accurate. Loosen the clamp nearest to you when setting up for the cut to move that end back and forth. The other clamp, at the back of the machine, acts as a pivot point, and the pointer moves half the distance you move the end. Wooden hand-screws work best for clamping the jig to the bandsaw table.

A keel is long enough that you'll want to resaw about halfway, stop the saw, pull the keel out after the blade stops, and resaw from the other end until the cuts connect. This way, the piece never becomes too awkward to handle.

Thickness-plane the resawn pieces smooth. If one half needs more shaping because it belongs to the opposite end of the boat, mark the new measurements, then bend and attach a batten and cut out as you did before. If you used the pattern-ripping method, lower the long-curve jig on the table saw fence to the reduced thickness of the resawn keel, and saw out the shape.

Finishing the keel

There will likely be some burn marks on the keel's edges. Clean these up with a sharp block plane or scraper.

If you need to plane the keel flat because it has cupped, mark the station lines on both edges (so you won't lose them when planing the faces), drill the trunk holes if necessary, and plane away. Don't worry about the center-line; you won't need it except when attaching the skeg, and it's easier to mark this again when necessary.

A nice, round bullnose will help keep the keel's edges

from being torn up and give the bottom paint a better chance at staying around for awhile. Set your new keel aside for the moment until the outer stem is ready.

MAKING THE SKEG

Typically, the skeg is a long triangle that can be made from a rectangular blank large enough to make two skegs, or a skeg and a tiller. You may use white oak or a equally tough, rot-resistant wood or marine plywood of sufficient thickness (including a blank glued-up from leftover planking stock).

Straighten the edge that will become the skeg's bottom (the "water" edge), then crosscut the angle between the bottom of the skeg and the transom. Lay out the lengths

Tapering a Skeg

To taper the skeg:

- *Mark the tapered thickness of the skeg at the bottom ("water") edge of the skeg at its widest point, where the bottom edge meets the cross-cut.*
- *Place the long edge of the skeg (its top) on the bandsaw table. With the uppermost corner (the bottom) touching the blade, tilt the table until the distance between the blade and the top of the skeg on the table is the same as the distance from the edge of the blank to the tapered thickness line (see photo).*
- *Write the angle down. You'll need this angle when you cut the curve for the keelson, or the skeg will wind up tipped to one side.*
- *Cut the taper by watching that the blade cuts just above where the skeg touches the table.*
- *Clean up the taper with a hand plane, holding the skeg with several thin cleats screwed to the bench.*

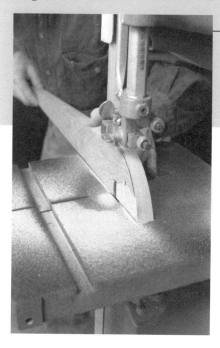

8.3 Rough-cutting the taper of the thickness of a skeg.

147

and widths of the skeg, and draw a diagonal line from one end to the other. Cutting this line by nailing on a straight-edge parallel to it and ripping on the table saw provides the straight, flat edge required for tapering the thickness of the skeg, which looks elegant and saves a little weight (see box). If you are not planning to cut a taper on the sides, you can trim this line on the bandsaw. Mark and cut the curved ends of the skeg.

If your boat's skeg will be protected by brass half-oval (see Chapter 13, "Fitting Out"), you can simply break the sharp edges with a piece of sanding belt. If the skeg will confront the world naked, roundover the edges well.

Making the Outer Stem

The blank for the outer stem can be laminated with multiple veneers, steam-bent from a single piece, or glued-up from several blocks. We tend to prefer the laminated version, made with white oak, but your boat's designer may well favor another method.

Laminated blank. The technique for laminating an outer stem is the essentially the same as that for laminating an inner stem, full-frame, or similar part. Please see the general instructions on laminating in Chapter 3. Most builders, typically set up the laminating form to define the inside curve. Some of John's students set up the adjustable laminating jig (described in Chapter 3, "Some very Useful Techniques") to define the outside curve, and it worked. This approach makes an outer stem with a continuous, uncut outer veneer, but requires that you accurately shape the inside curve to fit the inner stem.

Steam-bent blank. If your outer stem tapers in width like the Ellen's, it will be easier to shape and then to bend when steamed if you trim the taper on the straight blank. Because the outer stem is fastened to the boat, you don't have to worry too much about springback. Bevel the outer stem's sides after steaming and bending to shape. (See Chapter 3, "Some very Useful Techniques," for general instructions on steambending wood.)

Sawn blank. This blank goes together just like one for an inner stem (see Chapter 6, "The Backbone, and Lining Off"). Sawn blanks work well for boats with a large outer stem.

Shaping

Our boats' stems taper from an eye-pleasing width at the sheer to the thickness of the thin keel. The side not defined by the blocks or form must be marked and sawed out using the full-sized pattern or lofting.

A laminated outer stem will have sprungback to some degree, necessitating a little adjusting when marking out the taper. If you're using full-sized patterns, move the sheets around as you mark so that the front or back

8.4 Cutting the terminus of the outer stem bevel with a shallow gouge.

of the stem always lines up with the same line on the drawing as you mark the other line with the awl. In other words, when you reach a point where the stem and line wander away from each other, move the drawing until they line up again.

Saw out the outer stem on the bandsaw, in the same way as you did the inner stem. Clean up the sawn edge. Use a thin batten to help you see that the curve is smooth. Once you've accomplished this pedestrian task, you can turn your attention to the more artistic aspects of shaping the outer stem. Many outer stems are beveled for all or part of their length. Exactly how much and where you bevel yours can be somewhat a matter of personal taste, but remember that the outer stem is the point at which your boat meets the water, and a nicely beveled angle with a generously rounded front edge creates smoother flow and less fuss than a simple wide square edge. Once you're above your boat's functional waterline, you can safely put your personal stamp on the boat by shaping an outer stem that pleases you. In our designs, we normally stop the outer stem bevel even with the second lap, below the sheer. In other designs, Doug Hylan's Beach Pea peapod and Harry Bryan's Fiddlehead double-paddle canoe, for example, the outer stems are beveled from the keel to the sheer.

Many of our boats have brass half-oval molding installed on the outer stem for additional protection. We recommend the practice highly for boats that will eventually hit something unyielding. If you'd like to do this, be sure to leave a flat landing zone a touch wider than the half-oval you will be using. Most of our boats, including the Ellen and the fast rowboats, use $1/2''$ half-oval. (For installation instructions, see Chapter 13, "Fitting Out.")

Use a marking gauge to mark the width of the forward edge of the stem, then cut the bevel, usually with a spokeshave, working first to the scored line on the front, then to the back edge (the inside of the curve), and finally cut the bevel from front to back. This process will be familiar from the shaping of the inner stem. When you're happy with the shape, do a final cleanup with a sharp scraper.

PREPARING THE HULL FOR THE KEEL AND OUTER STEM
Planing for the keel

Remove the screws that fastened the garboard to the keelson, so you won't attempt to plane their heads off. You can either leave the screws out completely (the epoxy is plenty strong enough) or countersink the holes and put the screws back in after you've finished planing.

Lay out the keel widths at each station with a compass from the punch marks on the centerline at each station. Draw large arcs nearly to the edge of the raw edge of garboard planks. As you plane, the arcs will grow smaller and tell you how close you are getting to the final keel width. In the flurry of planing, you may plane off an arc completely. For this reason, put punch marks where each arc crosses a station line.

You know the drill by now. Working in much the same way as you beveled the keelson or planking, plane the planking at each station, periodically checking to see that your cut is flat or concave, not convex, with the corner of bench plane. Waxing the plane is wonderfully helpful during the whole job.

Once the planking is planed flat at all the stations, plane in between until the edge of the flat forms a fair curve through all the stations. John usually does this by eye but if you want a helpful guide, tack a batten around the punch marks at the stations and draw a curve. You also could plane most of the planking flat, then lay the keel over the hull and line up its edges with the punch marks. Hold the keel in place with weights and trace around its edges.

Finishing up the outer stem area and transom

By the time you have finished planing for the keel, the epoxy should be cured enough for you to pull all the remaining battens off the planking. Climb under the hull and knock off any clamping blocks that remain stuck. Mark the station lines on the planking by running a pencil along the working edge of each mold.

Back outside the hull, pull all screws holding the hull to the jig: stem to jig; keelson to molds; and transom to transom blocks. Remove the transom blocks from the jig as well.

Now you can trim the ends of the planks at the stem and transom.

At the stem start out with the bench plane and remove a majority of the plank ends in a series of facets along the stem. Make sure you are cutting square to the face of the stem and stop about 1/8″ from the face at each facet. Next, using a block plane set fairly fine, trim the facets until they just touch the face of the inner stem. To make sure you are trimming square with the face, feel the amount of planking left to trim on each side of the stem—your fingers will tell you instantly which side is higher. Trim that side, then feel the edges again. Keep working this way until planking feels flush with the stem. This sounds tedious but it goes quickly and, best of all, reliably keeps you from plow-

ing into the stem face or making the face angled.

Trim all of the facets flush, then trim in between, finishing up with a very light cut over the whole stem. Sanding with a hard sanding block finishes the curve nicely.

At the transom, set the transom marking gauge so that it is flush with the face of the transom and mark the planking all around the transom. Trim the planks close to the line with a hand saw, staying mindful of the transom's angle so that you don't run the saw into its face. Trim the planking stubs with a block plane. You don't have to worry about making the planking perfectly flush down to the last whisker now. You can take care of that when you sand the transom. But get it close, since it is easy to sand a gouge

8.5 Planing the projecting corner of the garboard planks flush with the bottom of the keelson to take a plank keel.

8.6 Frequently check progress when trimming the plank ends to ensure the joint for the outer stem is square.

8.7 Trim the plank ends about 1/8" from the transom face with a handsaw.

8.8 Trimming the plank ends flush with the transom sometimes requires holding the plane in odd postures to keep the plane blade from chipping out the plank edge.

into the face of the transom while sanding the harder planking ends.

Before you install the outer stem, fill the countersunk screws in the planking with epoxy putty. It's less than efficient to fill these holes after the outer stem goes on. You use any extra putty to fill the countersunk holes along the keelson and the transom, but be careful about filling the holes that belonged to the screws that held the keelson to the molds; the molds are still under there! It often works out best to fit the keel dry while the boat is on the jig, then set it aside until the boat is off the jig. You can then fill all of the remaining holes with epoxy before permanently installing the keel.

Mask off the screw holes along the stem, keel, and transom areas with hole-filling tape (see box). Fill the holes with epoxy putty, holding the putty knife at a low

8.9 Drilling a roll of tape on the drill press to make hole-filling tape.

Making Hole-Filling Tape

A few years ago we were having another one of those "there must be a better way" discussions, this on the subject of filling holes with epoxy putty. We had tried mashing the putty in with a putty knife. We quickly tired of cleaning up cured epoxy around the holes, so we tried taping off carefully around every hole. We gave that tedious process up forthwith; there are better forms of unpaid recreation. We solved the problem of filling the little screw holes with a plastic syringe, which you will meet after the boat is off the jig. For the larger countersunk screw holes, what we needed was masking tape with holes in it, holes of slightly larger diameter than the countersunk screws in the boat. Holes that might be made with a drill press. . . .

Aha! Thus was born the Brooks Boats hole-filling tape. To make your own:

- *Acquire an ordinary roll of 1" masking tape.*
- *Chuck a ½" Forstner bit in the drill press.*
- *Turn the table until the drill bit just misses it. Clamp a 1"-square cleat to the table, positioning it under the drill bit.*
- *Hang the roll of tape on the cleat and drill holes through*

the tape. Six holes around are about right. It takes a fair amount of pressure to get the bit to cut the tape. The sticky "chips" don't seem to clog the bit, but periodically little bits of tape will attach themselves to the cutters. Pull the bit up and clear the cutters. Don't let the tape heat up too much; it will stick together and harden enough to be nearly useless.

- *After you have drilled all the holes, cut through a few layers of tape midway between the holes with a utility knife. If you cut almost all the way across, but leave the last ⅛" or so attached, the first piece you pull off will lift the corner of the next one slightly, and so on. Very handy.*

8.10 To mask off the screw heads that will be covered with epoxy putty, use hole-filling masking tape with holes cut with a Forstner bit.

8.11 Trim the epoxy putty flush with the planking using a file and a sharp scraper.

angle to keep from pulling the putty out of the hole. Keep the putty on the tape, and scrape the residue down to a thin layer. The thickness of the tape allows the holes to be slightly overfilled. After the putty cures to the rubbery but not sticky stage, scrape (file if necessary) the putty flush with the planking.

After trimming the filled holes, file and scrape, then sand the planking near the stem, keel, and rails well with 80-grit. Coat these areas with sealer or thinned varnish and let dry. Also seal the backs of the keel, outer stem, rails, and skeg (see Chapter 12, "Painting and Varnishing").

Fit and attach all of the outbone pieces dry first, then remove them, slather on the bedding compound, and reinstall them permanently. Grappling with an outer stem, keel, or rail that is greased with bedding compound and innocent of useful screw holes is a good way to swear off boatbuilding for at least the rest of weekend, if not longer.

DRY ATTACHMENT OF THE OUTBONE PARTS
Fitting and fastening the outer stem

Locate where the joint between the keel and the outer stem will be and mark it on the planking. If the joint is not shown on the construction drawing or full-sized pattern, go ahead and locate it where the sharp curve of the stem settles into the gentler curve of the keel.

Hand-hold the outer stem in place, starting at the sheer with a clamp just below the planks, and mark the joint location. Cut a miter joint unless your plans specify otherwise.

Begin attaching the outer stem by drilling for and driving a screw just above the sheer. (Remember that "above" means toward the keel, as the boat is still upside down on the jig.) Before you drive the rest of the screws, figure out where you will need to drill for the fastenings for installing hardware: painter eye, towing eye, forestay fitting, etc. Avoid these spots when you drive the screws to attach the rest of the stem. (If you don't plan ahead, we guarantee that you will drill straight into a screw or screws, probably while trying to install the towing eye. Though this is not a total disaster, it's hard on drill, boat, and the boatbuilder's patience.) Also, if you plan to install brass half-oval, use the same spacing on the stem as you

will on the half-oval. After you plug the screws in the stem, punch a small mark in the first one to help you find it after the boat is painted. If you drive your first screw for the half-oval well above or below this marked screw, you know you will miss all of the rest. (For example, for ½" brass half-oval, space the screws 4" apart.)

Work from the sheer up toward the keel, pulling the stem tight to the bow with each screw. Oak splits easily, so be very careful when driving screws near the ends of parts. Keep the last screw at least 1" back from the joint if the stem is thin, and drive it snugly, but not firmly, home. After you have fitted the keel, a last quarter turn or so on this screw will bring the miter joint expertly tight.

Where the Planking Joins the Outer Stem

There are likely to be places where the width of the planks and inner stem—the "outer stem landing zone"—is not the same as the width of the outer stem.

Where the outer stem is wider, hold a wide chisel with the ground bevel against the planking and slide the chisel along the planking to pare off the projecting edge. Don't worry about correcting the outer stem's bevel at this point, just take off the excess wood next to the plank ends. Clean up the bevel after you remove the outer stem from the boat and clamp it to the bench.

Where the planking is wider, score along the sides of the outer stem with a sharp knife. After you remove the outer stem for sealing, bevel the corner of the planking to the score line with a small block plane, then soften the aft edge of the bevel with sandpaper.

8.12 Hold the outer stem against the bow by hand to mark for the miter joint for the keel.

8.13 The finished miter joint between the outer stem and keel.

8.14 Prop the aft end of the keel up with a block of wood to fit the miter of the outer stem, and drive the first screws.

Fitting and fastening the keel

Laying out and cutting the miter joint on the keel's forward end is the first job. If you are building a sailboat and have already drilled the holes for the trunk slot, lay out the miter carefully so the station marks on keel and hull line up, keeping the trunk holes properly placed. If you are building a rowboat, lining up the station marks so they are close will suffice.

After you cut the miter, block up the middle of the keel with a short piece of 2×4 or 2×6 so that the top of the keel continues the curve of the outer stem in a straight line, instead of following the curve of the keelson.

Fit the joint with a sharp block plane. Once you are happy with the joint, drill for and drive a screw at a slight angle to pull the joint together.

Drill for and drive one screw at each station, moving the block aft to let the keel contact the keelson. If the boat will be getting brass half-oval on her keel, set the screws at about twice the width of the half-oval from the keel edges. This location is about right for most of our boats, regardless of the half-oval intentions. The keel may cup at the edge or bulge in the middle if the screws are too close to middle or edge, respectively.

Now mark out the location of the rest of the screws, about 8″ apart down the keel.

Drill only as many holes as absolutely necessary during this dry fit because when it comes time to install the keel for good, the bedding compound will ooze up through all holes, creating a mess that must be removed thoroughly before you can glue in bungs.

Once the keel is fastened in place, scribe the taper of the sides of the outer stem on its end with a utility knife. After you take the keel off, you will bevel it to these marks, tapering the bevel aft until it dies out after a couple of feet.

Fitting and fastening the skeg

While the keel is in place, you can scribe and fit the skeg. You can also drill for its screws and fasten it in place if the jig's center beam is not in the way (which it will be if you are building one of our Peregrine rowboats with the winged racing skeg, for example).

To scribe the skeg, raise it just above the keel on the ends with two blocks of equal thickness. Scribe the curve with a compass.

Cut the curve on the bottom of the skeg on the bandsaw, being sure to tilt the table to match the bevel on the skeg's side, if there is one. Refer to the card where

8.15 The skeg rests steady on small blocks positioned at each end while it is scribed for the curve of the keel.

you wrote the angle down, or use the same method you used to cut the angle in the first place: Set the edge of the skeg firmly on the table next to the blade. Angle the table until an even ray of light shows between the side of the skeg and the bandsaw blade. Lock the table. Lay the skeg on its side and check to make sure that you are cutting the right way.

Smooth the curve with a block plane or spokeshave, and fit the skeg to the keel. A clamp lamp directed at the joint from behind will help you see gaps.

If you can install the skeg now, drill for and drive all of its screws to make sure that the skeg stays properly aligned on the centerline.

If you have a shaped keel and you need to re-mark the centerline, you can still use a compass. Draw lines from each side of the keel until they cross, changing the spread of the compass to accommodate the keel's changing width. Mark three or four crossed lines, then connect them with a ruler. Use a circle template to draw a series of circles, the thickness of the skeg, from the centerline. Use the circles to line up the sides of the skeg as you fasten it in place. (A helper is useful here.) If you plan to attach the skeg later, mark the circle edges with punch marks. The screws will pull the skeg back into nearly perfect position, but it's nice to be able to put it back exactly right with a couple of taps from a small mallet.

Now take it all apart

Now that you've gone to all that work to put these parts on the boat, unscrew everything: skeg, keel, and outer stem.

Set the parts up on sawhorses and coat only their mating surfaces with sealer or thinned varnish. Don't do the rest; you'll just have to sand it off when you trim all the bungs. Resist the temptation to skip this invisible step; sealing the wood on all sides helps it manage moisture in a civilized manner. If you leave the backs unfinished, water will eventually reach them, creating swollen, warped parts prone to rot. The wood will also draw the oil out of the bedding compound, drying it out and aiding the water's progress. Clean up any drips on the "good sides" after fastening the parts in place.

Goo, Glorious Goo

Boatbuilders love squeeze-out. We've talked about this when using epoxy, and the principle still holds when working with bedding compound. Your cabinetmaker friends will cringe and wail in horror, but don't let them shame you into stinting on the bedding compound. Good, healthy squeeze-out means that there's plenty of bedding compound in the joint, and this will make you feel much better when your boat is floating at the dock. Just clean up the squeeze-out and put the excess that hasn't skimmed over back in the can.

PERMANENT ATTACHMENT OF THE OUTBONE PARTS
Outer stem

Bedding compound is formulated for big boats and is therefore too thick for small boats. You'll need to add turpentine or paint thinner, thinning the compound from putty to mud. You are aiming for a goo thin enough to brush, but thick enough to linger behind in your joints in a meaningful way. It should almost, but not quite, run off the stick you mix it with.

Brush a thick layer of bedding compound on the back of the outer stem. Push a screw through the first hole near the sheer and match it up with its hole on the inner stem. Drive the screw, and you will be rewarded with beautiful oozing squirts of bedding compound out both sides. Push the next screw in its hole, turning it by hand until you're sure that you've found its hole, then drive it with the screw gun. Keep driving screws, double-checking the outer stem's alignment on the boat as you go. Adjust the alignment of the outer stem with a mallet. Leave the last screw about a quarter-turn loose, as you did before, if you are also installing the keel.

Keel and skeg

If you are building a sail boat with a daggerboard or centerboard trunk and/or a mast step, you probably will not want to attach the keel and skeg now. We recommend attaching trunks and mast steps by driving screws through the keelson into the logs of the trunk; this is the way the Ellen is built. This method is stronger than driving the screws from above, unless the keelson is fairly thick. It also allows you to easily replace the keel when necessary. Trunks were notorious for leaking, but epoxy and modern sealants make it much more likely that you'll need to replace a worn-out keel before rebuilding a leaking trunk.

If you are building a rowboat, you can go ahead and reinstall the keel. Set the skeg aside for now.

Brush bedding compound liberally on the keel. Set the keel on the hull, blocked up as you did for the

8.16 After the dry fit, you can permanently install both the outer stem and keel with bedding compound. On sailboats, wait for the trunk to be installed before fastening the keel on permanently.

8.17 Trim the top of the transom while the hull is upside down on the jig, where there is plenty of light to see and gravity to help you.

initial fitting. Carefully drive the first few screws, tightening the screw next to the miter very gently to avoid splitting the wood. Snug up the slightly loose screw in the outer stem.

Lower the keel onto the hull and drive all the predrilled screws. Check to be sure that the keel is lined up with the proper punch marks, then drill for and drive the rest of the screws. Scoop up the excess bedding compound with a putty knife, then remove the residue with a paper towel dampened with thinner.

All of the screws for the skeg should have been predrilled, so installation is simply a matter of applying bedding compound and driving screws. Alignment of the skeg is critical; employ the mallet for final adjustments. You can install bungs now, or wait until after the rails are on.

TRIMMING THE TOP OF THE TRANSOM

Trim the top of the transom now, while the hull is held rigidly in place on the jig. It's also easier to see and cut along the awl marks with the transom upside down and "facing upward."

Set the jigsaw for the angle between the transom and the jig: the same angle as the transom blocks. Cut about 1/8" outside the awl marks. Trimming the transom this way, the weight of the saw will make it cut into the waste wood if it wanders. Smoothing the curve later on with block plane and sanding block goes nicely, and the little bit of extra wood will give you a chance to refine the curve a touch if your eye tells you to do so.

Making and Attaching the Rails and Gunwales

If your design is an open boat like the Ellen, you can install the rails before the boat comes off the jig. If your design has decks, you will install the rails after you put on the decks so the rails cover the edge of the deck (see Chapter 10, "If Your Boat Has a Deck"). Because we are concentrating on open boats, we'll tackle the rails now.

Trying to put the rails on an empty open hull is like fighting with an octopus—there's nothing solid to hang onto or work against. It's a little harder to explain how to install the rails at this point, since we also must talk about installing the gunwales, breasthook, and quarter knees somewhat ahead of schedule. But if you'll bear with us, and do some head-scratching and planning now, the whole job really will go much better.

The rails usually are fastened twice: from the inside through the planking, which we'll do now; and from the outside into the gunwales, which will have to wait until the gunwales are going in. The rails and gunwales are inextricably related. Even if you prefer to put off the actual creation of the gunwales until just before they're needed, you must decide what sort of gunwales you want—"closed," simple straight single pieces that contact the hull completely, or "open," with spaced blocks that hold the gunwale away from the hull, allowing water to escape from the inverted boat—since this affects the screw spacing for the rails. Closed gunwales are easier to build; open gunwales are arguably more elegant. It's really not a bad idea to make the gunwales and the rails at the same time, since they require many identical operations. You'll be needing the gunwales very soon after the boat comes off the jig.

Some designs do not have gunwales. For these, the rails are held on only by the screws through the planking, as well as those into the stem and transom. You also will drive screws in the breasthook and quarter knees later on.

Fig 8.1 The screw patterns for fastening the rails and gunwales on for boats with closed or open gunwales.

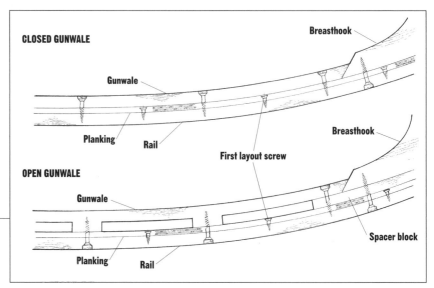

CLOSED GUNWALE

Breasthook

Gunwale

Planking   Rail

First layout screw

Breasthook

OPEN GUNWALE

Gunwale

Spacer block

Planking   Rail

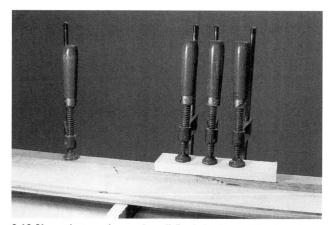

8.18 Clamp the two pieces of a rail firmly in place while clamping the scarf, or the long, tapered joint will cause them to slide away from each other.

MAKING THE RAILS AND GUNWALES
Getting out the stock

We typically use white oak or ash for rails, though we have also used Honduras mahogany, cherry, black walnut, and even Eastern spruce on boats destined for reasonably cushy lives.

Using the wood efficiently is an interesting challenge in making the rails and gunwales for most of our boats. The Ellen's rails, for example, are ½″ × 1½″ × 14′. Ripping these from 1″ stock means that a lot of wood becomes chips when it is planed to ½″. The smallest stock that can be planed to 1½″ thick for ripping ½″ thick is 2″. Sawing 2″-thick hardwood is a real workout for the smaller saws most of us own.

However, 1½″ stock works nicely. For the Ellen example, rip out a blank that is 3½″ wide, using a circular saw guided by a straightedge (see Chapter 4, "Lumber and Scarfing the Planking Plywood"). Plane the blank to 1⅜″, then rip the blank into two 1½″-wide pieces. Resaw each piece, then plane the resulting strips to ½″ thick.

Scarfing and gluing the rails and gunwales

You make scarf joints in the rails and gunwales in the same way that you did the keelson.

It is difficult to clamp rails and gunwales by nailing, and the resulting unsightly holes would be visible, so we suggest using clamps to hold the scarf joints together while the glue cures. Clamp the halves to your workbench firmly but not tightly, fine-tune the alignment of the joint, then tighten the clamps. Next clamp a caul tightly over the top of the joint (see Photo 8.18). A scrap of the rail stock makes a perfect caul.

Use resin glue for a strong, nearly invisible joint in oak; epoxy will work better if you're not one hundred percent sure that the scarf joint is tight.

To keep the rail or gunwale from becoming glued to the workbench or caul, use 2″-wide clear packing tape. Squares of ¾″ plywood distributed over the planking table make a good scarf-gluing "bench."

Be sure the edges line up perfectly, This is as important as making sure the glue joint lines up exactly right. Use a straightedge, or feel the edges of the joint until the two pieces line up, flush.

Finishing the rails and gunwales

Once the glue has dried, clean up the rails, then shape the corners with bullnose or chamfer and sand to suit. If you're making closed gunwales, you can do the same for them.

If your boat has oarlock socket blocks, you may want to wait on shaping the top edges of the rails and gunwales until after they are installed on the boat and the top edge of the sheerstrake has been sanded.

If your boat has open gunwales, clean up the glue from the scarf, and assemble the necessary items: gunwales, gunwale blocks, glue, clamps—and pencil and paper.

MAKING OPEN GUNWALES

The gunwales and gunwale blocks don't require gluing-up a fancy joint, just butt joints, but figuring the spacing of the gunwale blocks may require some work with a calculator. Once again, we'll use the Ellen as example, giving some concrete numbers to aid in understanding the process.

John glues the gunwales as a pair to the gunwale blocks to make a sandwich. The gunwale blocks are made thick enough for two, plus extra for a fat saw cut. On the Ellen, the finished gunwale blocks (and the spacers under the quarter knees and breasthook) are ⅜″ thick, so the blocks must be at least ¹⁵⁄₁₆″ thick. (⅜″ block + ⅜″ block + ³⁄₁₆″ for sawing apart and final trim).

Making Open Gunwales: An Alternate Method

John's system of making open gunwales makes glueup efficient and results in a neatly finished pair of gunwales. However, if you find some of the operations required to be a little intimidating, here's another approach:

- *Make the gunwale block stock to the block's finished thickness, then crosscut the blocks to length. (This stock also can be used for spacer blocks if your boat has them; see page 193 and Figure 8.2.)*
- *Lay out for the gunwale blocks as you would for the sandwich method, but mark both gunwales.*
- *Glue the blocks in place, then clean up around them with a block plane after the glue hardens.*
- *Rout the gunwales' lower, inside edges. You'll deal with the upper edges after the gunwale is installed.*

Figuring out how many blocks and how far apart

- Measure the length from the forward side of the inner stem, around the sheer to the aft side of the transom, using the plan or water lines view—or the boat. (Ellen's rail length is 146⅝″.)

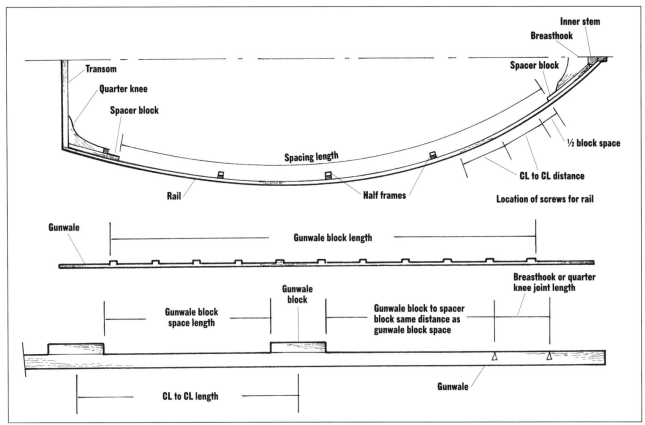

Fig 8.2 Various measurements for calculating the gunwale block spacing on open gunwales, and using the spacing of the blocks to locate the screws for fastening the rails.

- Subtract from this the depth of the inner stem (fore and aft) at the sheer, and the thickness of the transom. (Ellen's inner stem depth is 1½″; transom thickness, ¾″.)
- Also subtract the length of the spacer blocks under the quarter knees and breasthook. Determine these by measuring the length of the quarter knee and breasthook along the sheer and adding 2″ to each. (Ellen's spacer blocks are 11″ long; total, 22″.)
- We call the result the *spacing length*. (Ellen's spacing length is 122⅜″.)
- Decide how long you would like the gunwale blocks and roughly how far apart. These days, we typically use 2″ blocks spaced 6″ to 8″ apart. (Ellen's 2″ blocks are spaced approximately 6″ apart.)
- The center-to-center distance equals one space plus one block (Ellen's center to center distance is approximately 8″).
- Now, to find the number of blocks:

$$\frac{\text{spacing length (inches)}}{\text{approximate center to center distance (inches)}} - 1 = \begin{array}{l}\text{number of blocks (N),}\\ \text{rounded up or down to}\\ \text{the next whole number}\end{array}$$

For the Ellen:

$$\frac{122.375''}{8''} - 1 = 14.2969 \text{ (14 blocks)}$$

- You no doubt noticed the "approximately" in reference to the space. Now that you know the number of blocks, you can calculate the space and the center-to-center distance, exactly:

$$\frac{\text{spacing length (inches)} - (\text{N} \times 2'')}{\text{N} + 1} = \text{space}$$

Or, for the Ellen:

$$\frac{122.375'' - 28''}{15} = \begin{array}{l}6.292'', \text{ or } 6\,^{5}/_{16}''\\ \text{(multiply .292 by 16 for 16ths)}\end{array}$$

$6\,^{5}/_{16}''$ space + 2″ block = $8\,^{5}/_{16}''$ center to center distance

Laying out and marking

You need to mark only one gunwale. Please put away that tape measure. You must accurately mark the same distance repeatedly, and this is best accomplished with either a large compass, a thin plywood tick strip, or the gunwale block measuring tool (see box). The tick strip or measuring tool will also save the center to center distance, so you'll be all set when you lay out the location of the screws for the rails.

On the edge of the gunwale, pencil a mark and an "F" several inches from one end; this is where the joint to meet the breasthook will be cut and is now officially the forward end. The several inches is insurance. Lay out the centerline-to-centerline distance for the first block and put a large X on the aft side of the mark and label it #1. Lay out the centerline-to-centerline distance again, mark an X and #2, then repeat until done. You should have enough left over for one more center-to-center distance plus 2″, plus a few inches for insurance for the quarter knee joint.

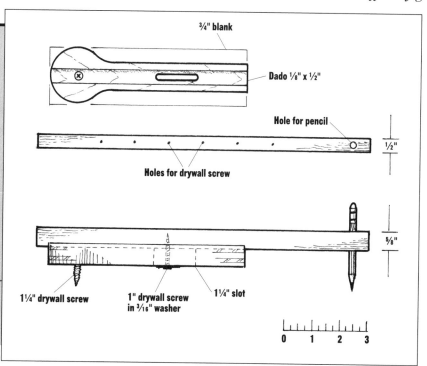

Gunwale Block Measuring Tool

This tool is made of ¾" plywood and scrap mahogany (or similar). Rip the pencil bar out of the mahogany. Cut a dado for the pencil bar in the plywood, then cut a slot an inch or so long in the dado. Drill a hole for the pencil and another for a drywall screw. Bandsaw the plywood into a shape that fits your hand nicely, put a drywall screw in the point hole, attach the pencil bar with another drywall screw with a washer, and stick a pencil in the hole.

Fig 8.3 A simple jig for laying out the gunwale blocks and the screws for fastening the rails.

Gluing-up

Lay the gunwale flat, X-markings facing you, on a long bench or on a long length of 2x6. Gather your gunwale blocks and the other gunwale. Get out all the clamps you have and count them. Mix up some resin (or epoxy.) Apply the glue to one side of the same number of blocks as you have clamps. (If you're using epoxy, wet out this number of blocks as well as the landing sites on both gunwales with clear epoxy, then butter one side of the blocks with epoxy putty.) Starting at one end, place each block on the gunwale (glue side down) so it lines up with its mark and is over the X. Apply glue (or epoxy putty) to the upper surface of the blocks and place the second gunwale on top, carefully, being sure that its forward end is even with that of the other gunwale. Put the clamps on gently at first, adjusting the blocks to keep them lined up with the gunwales (as much as possible). After deploying all of your clamps, go back to the first and tighten it up

firmly but not excessively. Some glue will have squeezed out by now, and the blocks should no longer slide around. (Clean up as much epoxy squeeze-out as possible.)

If you have fewer clamps than blocks, repeat the gluing-up process several times, waiting for each batch to dry thoroughly before proceeding with the next. Brace the upper gunwale up out of your way with a piece of scrap wood, so you can easily reach inside to spread the glue (or epoxy) for the next batch.

When the gunwales and blocks are all glued-up, remove the clamps and take off the excess glue or epoxy with a scraper.

Finishing up

Hand-plane the blocks flush with the gunwales on one edge. If you have access to a planer, clean up the edges by taking off about ¹⁄₁₆" off each, starting with the side that wasn't hand-planed—so that the hand-planed side runs along the bed of the planer. If you don't have a planer, hand plane both edges smooth.

Choose the nicer of the two edges for the upper, visible one, and remind yourself with a builder's pyramid. At this point, you can bullnose or chamfer the outside bottom edge of the gunwales. You can also shape a smaller chamfer or bullnose on the inside edges, around the spaces, top and bottom. Be sure not to bullnose or chamfer the ends where the gunwales will contact the breasthook and quarter knee spacers, if your boat will have these.

Don't worry about the upper, exposed edge of the gunwale now; you'll rout this after installing the gunwales, sanding the upper edge of the sheerstrake, and locating the oarlock blocks.

8.19 Gluing a pair of gunwales to thick gunwale blocks to make a sandwich that will be sawn apart.

Separating the gunwale pair

Mark the middle of the gunwale blocks using the compass and parallel line technique used when resawing the keel, then bandsaw the two gunwales apart. Give each block a light tap with a hammer to be sure it's firmly glued.

Set up the table saw for the final thickness of the gunwales and blocks, setting up fingerboards at the front and back of the blade to hold the gunwale against the fence as much as possible. This is a tricky operation. Go carefully. Don't stand right behind the blade, where you'll be the target if a block should come loose and be thrown by the blade. If the blocks are thick enough that the saw will cut off thin waste pieces (instead of just sawdust), put the dado insert in the blade hole in the saw so the pieces fall down through the larger opening and do not jam. Trim the blocks halfway along the gunwale and turn off the saw. Then take the gunwale out of the saw, turn it end for end, and trim the remainder of the blocks.

After the gunwale is sawn to the proper thickness, clean up the glue on the inside of the gunwales with chisels and scrapers. You also can sand everything but the upper edge. Set the gunwales aside to await sealing and installation in the hull.

LAYING OUT THE RAIL SCREWS
Rails with closed gunwales

On a boat with closed gunwales you can set the rail screws about 8″ to 10″ apart without worrying too much about what will happen when you put the gunwales on. You need only concern yourself with making sure that the rail and gunwale screws miss each other, and that the bungs for the screws are evenly spaced so they look good.

Start by determining where the first and last screws in the gunwales must go, based on the length of the breasthook and length of the quarter knee plus 1″ or so. (Note: Our boats with closed gunwales do not use spacer blocks with the breasthook and quarter knees, as do those with open gunwales.) Mark these on the outside of the sheerstrake, close to the sheer.

To figure out the proper spacing:

Measure the distance between the first and last gunwale screws (in inches). Divide by the approximate distance you want between the screws. We'll use 9″ in our Ellen example. Round the result to the nearest whole number, then divide the total distance by this to get the exact distance between the screws.

For example: Divide the distance along Ellen's gunwale between first and last screws, 125″ by 9″ to get 13.89; round this to 14, or 13, then divide the gunwale distance, 125″, by 14 to get the exact screw spacing: 8.929″, or 8$\frac{15}{16}$″; or 125 by 13 to obtain 9.615 or 9$\frac{5}{8}$″. Write this number down so you'll have it handy when it comes time to install the gunwales.

When you have the magic number for screw spacing, measure half of this distance forward from the first gunwale

8.20 Trim the gunwales to the final thickness on the table saw using stategically located feather boards.

screw location at the bow and mark it with a circle. Unless your breasthook is unusually long, this will be the first screw location aft of the stem for a screw driven through the planking to secure the rail. Marking it with a small circle is a reminder that this mark is to be drilled for a screw.

Use the simple rail and gunwale measuring tool (see box) or a large compass to mark the remainder. Circle the marks as necessary to clarify which ones should be drilled.

Go around the boat with your compass and mark the heights of the screws (usually half of the rail height). There. It's finally time to start drilling some holes and driving screws. You may skip the next bit, meant for folks attaching open gunwales, and get right to work.

Rails with no gunwales

Boats without gunwales require closer screw spacing, on the order of 4″ to 5″. Gluing the rail on also helps stiffen the sheer for these boats with minimal structure in this area.

Simple Rail and Gunwale Measuring Tool

Take a scrap of wood about $\frac{1}{2}$″ *square and drill a hole for a pencil near one end and a small hole for a finish nail near the other, spaced apart by the desired screw spacing. Finely adjust this quality tool by bending the nail. If you need a tool capable of more adjustment, use the gunwale block measuring tool mentioned earlier.*

Rails with open gunwales

Open gunwales also require some planning before you drive screws in the rails, as these should be centered nicely in the spaces between the gunwale blocks as they will show through the varnish. (You can putty the screw holes and paint the planking between the gunwale blocks, but we prefer to varnish the planking areas along with the rails and gunwales.)

You should have the measurement between blocks still set on your gunwale block measuring tool. As you will recall, this is also the rail screw spacing.

Before we can discuss the screw layout for the open gunwales, we need to explain briefly how the breasthook and quarter knees are built using spacer blocks. If your boat's design doesn't use spacer blocks, you'll be measuring to small "ears" cut into the breasthook and quarter knees themselves.

Instead of shaping the breasthook and quarter knees with "ears" to receive the ends of the gunwales, we prefer to use separate pieces that we call the breasthook and quarter knee spacer blocks. These are attached to the hull, then the breasthook and quarter knees are fitted and glued to them (see Chapter 9, "Building the Interior"). The spacer blocks are the same width as the gunwales, to provide a strong landing spot for the ends of the gunwales. Open boats, especially open glued-lapstrake boats with their minimal frames, are prone to twisting. To limit this, the gunwale parts must be joined tightly and firmly together into a strong, rigid framework. The joint between gunwale and the breasthook and quarter knees can be a weak spot, especially if the breasthook and quarter knees are thin. The spacer blocks solve this problem.

There are two important distances on open gunwales: the center-to-center distance of the gunwale blocks, and the space between the blocks. The layout tool should be set for the center-to-center distance, which is the space between the blocks plus the length of one block.

To lay out the first screw for the rails, which will be midway between the first gunwale block and the breasthook spacer block, measure the length of the breasthook spacer block from the inside face of the inner stem and mark it on the outside of the sheerstrake. From this mark, measure half of the gunwale block *space* distance. Mark and draw a circle around this point, which is the location of the first rail screw. Starting from this point, use the measuring tool to mark the rest of the locations for the rail screws. To double-check your spacing, measure the length of the quarter knee spacer block from the inside of the transom plus half of a gunwale block space, just as you did in the bow. If this distance is within an inch of the marks you made with the layout tool, you're close enough.

Note: To hold the rails securely at the bow, layout for a screw halfway between the first screw and the stem. Do the same at the stern between the last screw and the transom.

Set your compass and go around the boat to mark the heights of the screws (usually half of the rail height).

ATTACHING THE RAILS
Boats with closed, open, or no gunwales

Once you have the screw locations marked on the hull, it doesn't matter whether your boat has open or closed gunwales, or none at all; the method for putting the rails on the boat is exactly the same.

You will need two tapping drills. One should be sized for drilling into the wood of the inner stem and transom. Tape this for the longer screws that fasten the ends of the rails. Size the other for the normally harder wood of the rails and the softer bronze screws that you will be driving through the planking into the rails. Tape this well for these shorter screws.

You will also need combination bits (clearance drill, countersink, and counterbore), and screwdriver bits to match your screws. You will have to change the length of the drill bit, or use two different bits: one set for the end screws, which will be plugged; the other for the screws through the inside planking, which should be countersunk flush with or slightly below the surface.

Drill a hole with the short tapping drill for each screw along the sheerstrake edges.

Measure the angles between the planking and the stem with the help of a plywood scrap (see Figure 8.23), and that between the sheer and the stem. Mark these angles on the forward ends of both rails. Two bevel gauges will allow you to easily mark all four sides of each rail.

Clamp each rail securely to a horse and trim with a hand saw. Clean up with a sharp block plane. If the plane isn't cutting well, try a little wax on its sole.

Now, to fit the joint. You must suspend the rail's aft end so that the forward end meets the curve of the sheer and continues it in a straight line. One good way to do

8.21 Measuring the vertical angle between sheer and stem for the rail.

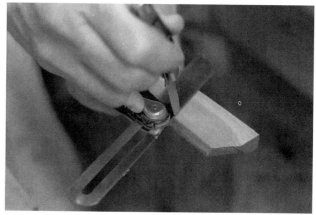

8.22 Marking the vertical angle on the rail.

8.23 Position a scrap of plywood on the side of the outer stem to help measure the horizontal angle between the plank and stem with a bevel gauge.

8.24 Marking the horizontal angle on the rail.

8.25 Support the aft end of the rail with a piece of small line or string hung from the ceiling or a stepladder while fitting and fastening the forward end.

8.26 Trimming the end of the rail with a small block plane that fits comfortably in one hand makes it possible to fit the rail without having to remove it to the sawhorses.

this is a line hung from the ceiling. Use a loop and an adjustable knot such as a clove hitch or rolling hitch so that you can adjust the height of the rail as you work. You could ask a helper to hold the rail, but this person is likely to be less steady and patient than the string. A stepladder also works nicely.

Bring the end of the rail up to the outer stem and lightly clamp it in place. Adjust the rail's aft end until forward end is flush with the sheer for 8″ or so. If the joint is almost tight, the best way to refine it is to plane a little off the points that touch the outer stem. Make pencil slashes to see where you're cutting. To maintain control, trim slowly with a slicing motion. Use the sole of the plane to check for flatness. You can cheat a little by hollowing out the middle of the bevel with a chisel, thus ensuring that the edges will be tight.

If there are big gaps between the end of the rail and the outer stem, you need to scribe the angle with a compass. Make sure to remove all pencil marks made when you marked the measured angles. Trim the rail to your scribed pencil lines, erase the lines, then make your final fit and adjustment.

Once the joint is tight and clamped firmly in place, drill for and carefully drive a screw or two into the inner stem. Offset the two screws forward and aft to avoid splitting the end of the rail.

Chuck up and adjust the drills and driver bits for the small bronze screws, and crawl under the jig with the drills and one screw. Drill for and drive the first screw through the planking and into the rail through the tapping hole you drilled earlier. Pull this screw and crawl back out again. Pull the long screws into the inner stem, and unclamp and unhang the rail. Set it on horses and butter the sealed mating side and the joint with bedding compound.

Put the rail's aft end back in its sling or step. Clamp the rail in place, drive one of the forward end screws gently home, then drive the other screw, if there is one. Climb back under the boat and re-drive that one bronze screw. Now the end of the rail won't shred if someone inadvertently bumps the aft end of the rail.

How you proceed at this point depends upon how many clamps you can round up. If you have plenty, you can clamp the whole rail in place before driving the screws. Collect your box of screws, the drills and bits, that essential clamp lamp, a putty knife, a small scrap of plywood, and a handful of paper towels, a couple of which are dampened with thinner. Climb back under the jig. Work your way along the boat, making final adjustments so the rail is flush with the top of the sheer, then drill for and drive the screws, using the predrilled holes.

If you like a mess, you'll love this job. Wipe the bedding compound off your fingers often. Gravity works, and the bedding compound should enthusiastically dribble and drool from the joint. Swipe up the drips with a putty knife and collect them on the scrap plywood before they hit the floor or jig, before you sit in or grab onto a soft, wet pile.

If you're a bit shy on clamps, attaching the rail will be a slightly more athletic endeavor: clamp as far as you can, climb under the hull, drive those screws, crawl back out, move the clamps, climb back under….

When you reach the stern, climb out, swap drill bits, and drill for and drive the long screws into the transom, aiming carefully.

Repeat the process for the other rail. Thoroughly clean the oozing bedding compound from both rails, then wipe down the planking and rails with a rag or paper towel dampened with thinner to remove the residue. The bedding compound will continue to ooze slightly for the next few days, but it will eventually solidify enough to stop.

If you prefer to glue the rails on with epoxy, proceed as usual: coat the landing areas on rail and sheerstrake with clear epoxy, then putty the rail with epoxy putty. Clean up well.

Trim the ends of the rails flush with the transom.

Fitting rails to a double-ender

A double-ender typically has an outer sternpost similar to the outer stem. To make the rail fit tightly against it:

Mark a short line on the bottom of the rail and on the hull, several feet forward of the sternpost, at a point at which the rail contacts the hull. Measure from this line, along the hull, to the joint between the planking and sternpost, keeping the width of the rail in mind to obtain an accurate length of the rails. Mark this distance on the rail. Measure the angles between the planking and sternpost, and sheer and sternpost. Mark these on the rail just a little beyond the distance line just marked.

Cut the joint at these marks, then trim with a sharp block plane. The joint is perfect when it fits tightly along the sternpost and there is a small gap—$\frac{1}{32}$ " or less between the rail and planking just forward of the sternpost. A screw driven through the rail into the inner sternpost will close this gap. If you cut the aft end of the rails a little short, see the box for a fix.

To avoid a mess, fit the whole rail dry with screws at the bow into the outer stem and clamps elsewhere. Remove the rail, butter it with bedding compound (or epoxy putty), and fasten permanently.

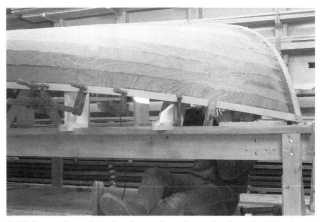

8.27 Clamp the rail to the sheer along the entire length of the boat, then fasten it from inside the jig after it is coated with bedding compound and fastened at the bow.

8.28 Adjusting the rail's height from inside the hull.

Or try a quicker approach. Fit the bow and remove the rail. Apply bedding compound (or epoxy putty) to the rail except for the last couple of feet. Clamp and fasten the rail to the point where the bedding compound stops. Trim and fit the aft end of the rail, then butter the last couple of feet and fasten in place.

Neat Trick Department:
The Amazing Rail Stretcher

Aaargh. You trimmed too much, and now there is a gap between your double-ender's sternpost and the end of the rail. Unfasten the rail for several feet, then use a block plane to trim the back of the rail (the face that fits against the hull), tapering the thickness of the rail to the end. This has the effect of moving aft the sharp knuckle that fits into the joint between the hull and the outer sternpost and thereby "lengthening" the rail. Fit and fasten the rail back in place. The taper will likely be unnoticeable or will actually make the rail look more elegant.

Remember to give the other rail the identical treatment so they will look the same.

Off the Jig
REMOVING THE HULL FROM THE JIG

You are probably more than ready to get your hull off the jig and see what she really looks like, properly oriented with the world. Find yourself a helper, and set your boat free.

Make certain that you've traced along the working side of the molds to mark all of the station lines on the hull. Check your plans to see if any molds should stay in the hull; unscrew these from the jig. Remove all remaining screws and/or nails holding the boat to the jig, including those at the stem. Pull gently on the sheerstrake at each mold. Moderately alarming popping noises are normal. Pull up at the stem and transom, but not too hard. (See Appendix A, "Oh, @!#.) If pulling does not do the trick, firmly tap around the edge of all molds that are still stuck.

If the hull doesn't come loose, you either missed a screw or nail, or forgot to wax the molds. Check again for fastenings and pray that the offending screw is not under your newly installed keel. If the boat remains attached to the molds, unscrew the molds from the jig and lift off the boat with whichever molds insist on coming along for the ride. Find the problem areas, and work the mold loose if you can do so without damaging the hull. It is better to sacrifice the mold(s) than the hull, so take a saw and chisel to a mold if you must. Usually, a smart wallop with a mallet will suffice. You can do the same sort of operation if you do have a screw still doing its job under the

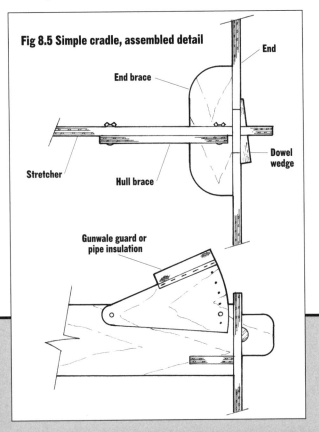

Fig 8.5 Simple cradle, assembled detail

End

End brace

Dowel wedge

Stretcher

Hull brace

Gunwale guard or pipe insulation

pending on the size of your boat, and the wedges from a length of 1¼" or 1½" doweling. Exact sizes are not critical except where the stretcher fits in the slot in the end and the end brace fits in the slots in the stretcher. Make the ends taller for short boats. Make the stretcher longer for wide boats and wider for heavy boats. Make larger triangular hull braces for a hull with a lot of deadrise or a deep keel.

If you are clever, you'll make the curve of the end reversible so that the ends can be marked out nested together on the plywood and one cut shapes the edge of two ends. Make the wedges from several feet of doweling so there is plenty to hang onto while you make the tapered cut on a bandsaw, then crosscut the wedges to length.

Pad the hull braces with short lengths of scrap gunwale guard (see Chapter 13, "Fitting Out") or pipe insulation.

A simple cradle that breaks apart for storage is very handy while working on the boat and afterward.

Making a Simple Cradle

This simple cradle holds rowboats, small sailboats, and motorboats securely while you install the interior. The main parts of the cradle are locked together with wedges cut from doweling, and the hull braces are secured in place with bolts and wing nuts. The cradle comes apart into a flat stack of pieces.

Make most of the parts from ½" or ¾" plywood, de-

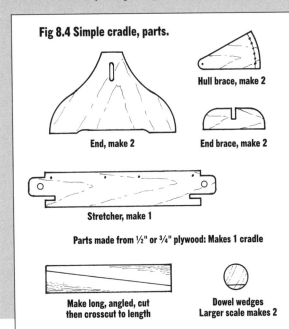

Fig 8.4 Simple cradle, parts.

Hull brace, make 2

End, make 2

End brace, make 2

Stretcher, make 1

Parts made from ½" or ¾" plywood: Makes 1 cradle

Make long, angled, cut then crosscut to length

Dowel wedges Larger scale makes 2

8.29 Lifting the hull off the molds is normally a two-person job.

keel: Remove the attached mold, then you can try cutting and filing the screw flush. However, drywall screws are steel and very hard, and you likely will find yourself taking the keel off to remove the screw.

Set the newly freed hull on a couple of saw horses or, if you like, in the simple cradles shown. Cradles aren't necessary for relatively lightweight, open boats like the 12′ Ellen at this point; you may work on the boat, upside-down or rightside up, while it sits on sawhorses You will need cradles to securely hold the hull when you begin installing interior parts.

Lifting the hull off the jig by yourself

Working alone? You'll need two pairs of hull supports made of 1″ × 3″ strapping if your hull is about the same weight as most of the boats we're discussing in this book. Make the supports of 2×4s with cross-bracing if your boat is significantly heavier.

Cut four legs that are a few inches taller than the top of the molds. Cut two cross members that are comfortably wider than the hull. The legs will be screwed into the inside of the jig's side beams and the cross member rested on top. Notch the tops of the legs, and the bottom of the cross member so that the cross member will sit

8.30 A hull can be lifted from the molds by one person by picking up one end at a time and supporting it on a brace that looks similar to the π symbol.

firmly in the tops of the legs. You'll also need a separate length of 2×4 that is slightly longer than the boat's beam.

Fasten the legs to the inside of the side beams. At the bow, the legs can be positioned outside the hull. At the stern this isn't always possible, and the legs are too tall to stand up under the hull. Measure the distance from the floor to where you can drive a screw into the side beam. Mark this on the beam and the leg. Drill the leg for a screw, then fasten it to the beam with one screw. Do the other leg the same way. This allows the legs to pivot under the hull, then be raised upright.

Place the two cross members within reach at bow and stern. Keep your cordless drills, a few screws, the beam-wide length of 2×4, and a couple of wooden hand-screws handy near the stern. Raise the hull at the bow high enough to clear the tops of the legs and slide the cross member into its notches. Lower the bow onto the cross member. Pick up the hull at the stern and insert the length of 2×4 under the hull and on top of the center beam. Rest the hull gently on this temporary support, making sure that everything is centered and balanced. Lift the support legs until they are vertical, then lift the hull enough so you can slide the cross member into its notches. Clamp the legs if necessary, and drive another screw in each to secure them. There's no rush; with the bow support secure, the stern support will stay upright.

If your hull is fairly heavy, it would be better to hoist it forward and aft with tackles rigged from the ceiling. Keep most of the weight off the supports until you securely fasten the stern legs.

You can now take the molds, center beam, and diagonals apart. Once you've cleared away everything but the temporary supports and the jig's side and endbeams framework, you can slide a pair of horses into the middle of the jig and lower the boat onto these. European-inspired horses made of 2×4s or 2×6s described in Chapter 2 fit perfectly between the side beams of our standard jig.

Once the boat is safely on the horses, remove the support legs and take the rest of the jig apart.

Handling larger boats

If your boat is too big to pick up and flip over without mechanical advantage, a simple system consisting of two circles of line run around the hull and through blocks works well. Even if several people working together can pick up the boat, controlling the boat as you turn her over is another game entirely. A rig such as this turns a potentially hair-raising situation into a controlled, calm, and actually fun operation. You'll still want plenty of able-bodied helpers available for the initial lifting and positioning of the ropes and tackle—and to take pictures. A good rigging book such as Brion Toss's *The Complete Rigger's Apprentice* will help you set up a hull-turning rig for your boat properly and safely.

Larger and heavier vessels such as a Somes Sound 12 ½ will need a beefier cradle to support the hull.

Rightside up

The moment when the hull comes off the jig can be an intensely private time. We enjoy looking the whole hull over, evaluating how the shape and planks look, trying to get an idea of what the finished boat will look like if she's a new design.

You've done it. Enjoy your new hull. After you've invited the neighborhood in for a look, take the jig apart and store it away for your next boat. Before you put away the molds, check your plans again to make sure that none are needed while fitting the interior parts.

After your guests have departed, flip the boat back upside down on a pair of horses.

FILLING THE HOLES

At the moment, the sun shines brightly through the dozens of holes in your boat's hull made during the building process. Filling these with epoxy putty is a not a bad job at all. The keys are to keep the epoxy exactly where it belongs and to search carefully and fill all of the holes now. The more often you have to stop and fill newly discovered holes as you work on the boat, the grumpier you will become.

Using a putty knife to squash epoxy putty through the screw holes either requires a tedious taping job (even using the hole-filling tape), or results in a hull covered with patches of hardened epoxy. We've done it both ways, and we sat down and figured out how not to do it again. Using a syringe modified for hole-filling makes this job actually fun.

Clear the space under the boat, and lay down news-

8.32 Filling a screw hole in a lap with a trimmed syringe.

paper or plastic if you don't want epoxy globules landing on your shop floor. Set the boat upside down on saw horses tall enough to allow you to peer easily under the boat at regular intervals—or to allow a helper to sit under the boat.

Go over the outside of the hull and mask off large holes and gaps. Use the hole-filling masking tape over countersunk screw heads that need putty (see the box earlier in this chapter, "Making Hole-Filling Tape"). Check the lap joints for gaps and depressions, and mask these off with tape along the bottom, top and sides. Don't bother masking the small screw and nail holes; the syringe makes this unnecessary. Look carefully for tiny blow-outs connected to nail holes, and open these for filling by giving them a quick scrape. It's annoying to find (and have to fill) these tiny holes later during the final scraping and sanding.

Mixing the epoxy putty for the syringe takes a little fiddling with proportions. You want putty that squirts smoothly and easily, but hangs together and doesn't run through or fall out of the holes; it will be about the same as that for attaching the planks. Generally speaking, this putty wants a higher proportion of colloidal silica to wood dust than that used for gluing planks so that it's smoother. If you are planning to varnish your hull, putty that is considerably darker than the unfinished planking will look better.

Mix a "one-pump" batch of epoxy putty and fill the syringe about two-thirds full. Starting near the keel, position the syringe neatly over a screw hole, hold it tightly against the hull, and push the plunger gently. Stop the flow by pulling the plunger back, then twist the syringe off to one side, making a neat little blob. Look under the boat to make sure the hole is filled com-

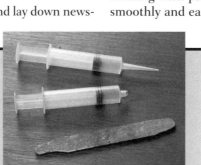

pletely. There should be a drool of epoxy suspended from the hole. If there isn't, reposition the syringe and squirt in a little more. It's helpful to have someone watch for exuding epoxy and tell you when to stop, at least until you get a feel for how much to squirt. Use a clamp lamp to light the boat's interior, but keep it away from falling epoxy putty.

There is a definite knack to this operation. Your first efforts probably will feature epoxy putty squirting out the side and too much putty flowing out before you can stop it. If you've created a huge blob, neatly scrape off the excess with the putty knife and apply it to a masked hole. Fill all the screw and nail holes using the syringe.

We crawl under the boat and swipe off the dangling epoxy stalactites while they're soft. If the epoxy turns too sticky on you, leave them to cure, then snap them off with a chisel after you flip the boat rightside up.

Fill the larger holes and gaps with the extra putty using a good flexible putty knife. Holes that are tiny and don't go all the way through the hull can be filled with a quick swipe of a little epoxy putty on the putty knife; just make sure to scrape the excess off thoroughly.

When you're done, clean your syringe and putty knife by soaking them briefly in vinegar, rinsing and wiping dry.

As the epoxy putty cures, it passes through a stage at which it is stiff, rubbery, and no longer terribly tacky. A fingernail firmly pressed into a hole blob leaves a dent. At this stage, the extra putty removes easily with a very sharp scraper or chisel. Exactly when this stage occurs depends on the temperature and brand of epoxy. If you have to postpone final cleanup of the hull, don't panic; you'll need to exert a little more effort to remove the fully hardened epoxy putty, but it will come off.

CLEANING UP THE HULL EXTERIOR

If you've attended to our preaching about putting epoxy only where it's needed and removing all excess before it can even think about curing, the job of cleaning up the inside and outside of the hull won't be bad at all. If you got a little over-eager and a touch careless, you will be putting in your time now, but our standard removal techniques should work. If your boat was put together by a bunch of friends too far into their six-packs, scan through the first suggestions, then check out the last resort: removing epoxy with a heat gun.

The tools for this job are an assortment of files and a set of very sharp scrapers. Epoxy is hard on sharp edges, but files can be cleared and scrapers can be sharpened. Sanding comes after the hull is scraped clean of residual epoxy.

We start with the screw and nail hole blobs. To remove these, take either a standard mill bastard file or a four-in-one hand rasp. We differ here on the best tool; Ruth prefers the flat files and John likes the rasp with a

bit of masking tape on the forward end for a painless fingerhold. We also differ on technique. John prefers to file his blobs from the top down, whereas Ruth likes to saw into hers from the side, then finish up with a couple of quick top-down strokes. Regardless of approach, the goal is to remove the excess putty, leaving a neatly filled hole flush with the plank surface. You shouldn't need to do much if you were able to pare them down with a scraper or chisel earlier. Use the file card/brush often. We file all the filled holes, then turn our attention to the laps.

No matter how carefully you cleaned up your laps, there will almost always be sections where a tiny amount of putty squeezed out later. A flat file works wonderfully well for filing the inside corner of the laps, but try everything you've got. When filing against the hull, don't get too aggressive or you'll file a groove in the wood. The files generally work best, but use a small scraper where needed, making sure that it doesn't chatter along the edge of the planking. Watch your hands near the plank edges; it's easy to start a splinter and drive it into your flesh.

Scrape the hull clean of all epoxy, using the larger scrapers, sharpening them often. Sapele has somewhat confused and interlocking grain, so change direction as necessary.

Removing epoxy with a heat gun

Although we consider the heat gun the weapon of last resort, you can remove extraordinary amounts of cured epoxy with one. Use just enough heat to soften the epoxy, and keep the gun moving. Wear a respirator!

Once the epoxy is heated, there is no need to hurry. When heated, epoxy chemically changes and turns white. It has lost all of its strength and is easy to scrape off. Thoughtful consideration of this fact suggests employing due care in the matter of how much heat is applied to the laps and other joints that are meant to stay glued together with epoxy.

Procedural Alert: About the Inside of That Hull

Wait! Stay those scrapers! You need to measure for and permanently mark key points for the interior parts before you clean the station lines off the hull. We'll talk about these measurements at the beginning of the "Building the Interior" chapter, then cover cleaning up the inside of the hull.

Final attentions to the hull

We like to tackle the grunt work of filling and sanding the outside of the hull as soon as possible. Even though there are a few more holes to be drilled through the hull, it's nice to move the hull along toward finishing. However, if you'd rather wait to fill and sand until after installing the interior parts, just flag this page and come back to it.

8.33 Trimming bungs flush.

Making and installing bungs. If you have access to a drill press, you'll be pleased when it comes time to make bungs for plugging the countersunk screws in the transom, outer stem, rails, and keel (if you've installed it at this point). Collect scrap wood at least ³/₄ " thick that matches the various parts. The manufacturer of your countersinking bit should make matching bung cutters (also called plug cutters). Chuck the bit in the drill press and cut more plugs than you need. Use a moderate speed: too fast and the wood burns; too slow and the bungs are ragged. Snap the bungs out with a screwdriver.

If you can't use a drill press, make the bungs by cutting a hole the same size as the outside diameter of the bung cutter in scrap of wood. Clamp the scrap to your bung stock. The hole keeps the cutter from vibrating and chattering. Make plenty of extras, and store the bungs by species in separate cups.

Use a short length of doweling to wet the inside of each countersunk hole with carpenter's yellow glue and insert the bung, lining up its grain with that of the surrounding wood. Tap the bung home with a hammer. Let the glue dry for at least an hour. Begin trimming the bungs with a chisel held bevel-side down and a mallet. Trim about half of the length of the protruding portion to see which way the grain is running up or down, then trim it to just a whisker about

the surface with one or two more cuts. Make the final trim by hand with the bevel side of the chisel up (see Photo 8.33). Use slicing motions to keep from damaging the surrounding wood as you trim the bung smooth and flush.

Dealing with cosmetic flaws. We fill the cosmetic depressions, scratches, and other flaws now, using surfacing putty (see Appendix B, "Resources"), which is meant for bare wood only. This stuff dries instantly—on the boat and on your putty knife. Remove a small amount at a time to a scrap plywood "palette," and keep the can tightly closed otherwise. Fill deep pits with several applications. Scrape the putty evenly over area of wild open grain. Check your scarf joints, too.

Wherever you plan to varnish, white surfacing putty is out. You will have fill cosmetic flaws in these areas with epoxy putty. Mix it dark, to match the surrounding wood, which will darken when varnished.

Sanding and breaking plank edges. Break and gently round the plank edges. The tool shown in Figure 8.6 makes short work of this job. Break the edges of the planks at the transom with a file and finish with sandpaper.

Sand with 80-grit to fair the surface, following behind with 100. Padded blocks are best for most of the

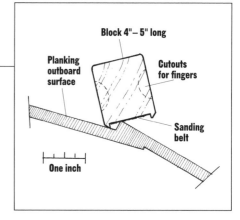

Fig 8.6 Sanding block for breaking the edges of the planks.

Planking outboard surface

Block 4"– 5" long

Cutouts for fingers

Sanding belt

One inch

Making a Flexible Sanding Block

A piece of scrap mahogany or plywood, ¹/₈ " (3mm) x 2¹/₄ " x 9³/₄ ", serves as the sanding block's pad. Glue four small blocks, ¹/₂ " x ¹/₂ " x 2¹/₄ ", across the width of the pad, one at each end, and the last two about 3 " from each end. Loosely screw two handles, ³/₄ " x 1" x 4", on edge, one at each end, to the middle of the blocks, parallel to the pad's long edge. Cushion the pad with leather or a worn sanding sponge (see Chapter 12, "Painting and Varnishing").

Cut 9" x 11" sheets of sandpaper into four long pieces. Load the block by folding the ends and stapling to the small end blocks.

8.34 Sanding the curved top of a transom fair and smooth with a flexible sanding block.

planking. Folded sandpaper and a few thin medium and fine sanding sponges take care of the remaining areas except for the edges. Catch and remedy any remaining blobs or holes now, for you will be applying the first coat of finish after this sanding.

Shaping and sanding the transom

Before you address sanding the face of the transom, flip the hull rightside up and clean up the top edge with a block plane, followed by a flexible sanding block (see box). We like small radius curves at the upper "corners" of the transom; cut these with a chisel. Break and slightly round both edges of the top of the transom to be hand- and finish-friendly.

Flip the boat back upside-down so gravity can help with sanding the face of the transom. John prefers to do most of the sanding with a belt sander. Rub your hand over the transom to find the high spots. Sand these first, then sand the whole transom, keeping the sander moving at all times. Finish up with a random-orbit sander or by hand with a sanding block loaded with 120-grit.

(Important: If you carved a name in the transom, you've already done the major sanding and mainly need to clean up around the edges. Attacking the carved transom with a belt sander is not a good idea.)

Marking centerline of mast on bowseat.

Chapter 9

Building the Interior

Interior Design and Layout

Now that the hull is on its own, and you've taken the jig apart, double check your plans before you put away the molds. You may need to keep the station No. 2 mold (and perhaps others) handy while you work on fitting parts in the interior.

It is extremely tempting to dive right in with a file and scraper and clean up whatever epoxy remains inside the hull. We commend this impulse. However, before you do anything that might erase the station lines on the inside of the hull, you must permanently mark key points for locating the interior parts. Before we tackle that, let us spend a few moments describing how we build a typical interior for our boats. Our approach has much in common with many others. Our goal throughout this chapter is to show you techniques and jigs that will serve well for installing the interior parts of any glued-lapstrake boat, be they simple or elaborate.

OUR INTERIOR SYSTEM

A glued-lapstrake hull is amazingly strong (see Chapter 14, "All Done"). It needs little, if any, framing to keep the

hull together and the water out. The plywood planking can be nearly half the thickness of a similar solid-wood boat, but this means that the glued-lapstrake hull will be flexible. Flexibility is not necessarily a bad thing, but it does need to be limited in the places where you don't want it.

On John's first couple of open glued-lapstrake boats, he installed the thwarts with laminated knees attached to the gunwales. The thwarts also rested on riser cleats and were scribed to fit the sides of the hull. This arrangement reduced the flexing to an acceptable amount, but building the thwarts this way was tediously time-consuming and the thwarts-to-hull joints quickly opened up, admitting water and encouraging rot. Varnishing and painting the boats were lots of work, as the thwarts could not be removed easily.

John therefore designed a system of half-frames and blocks with fore-and-aft risers to carry thwarts and seats. Carrying the thwarts and seats on risers is not a new idea, but a traditional lapstrake boat typically has an abundance of full (sheer-to-sheer) frames to hold the ris-

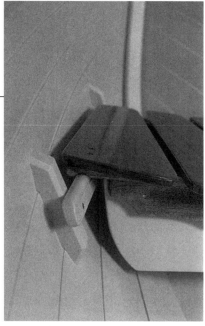

9.1 In the bow and stern, where there's no need to stiffen the gunwales, the risers are fastened to riser blocks glued to the hull.

ers. Half-frames serve this function in a glued-lapstrake hull but are shorter, running from the sheer down several planks, and are spaced farther apart than traditional frames. There is no need for half-frames at bow and stern, so the risers are fastened to shaped blocks called riser blocks. Together the half-frames, riser blocks, risers, thwarts, and seats stiffen an open glued-lapstrake boat while adding minimal weight.

The riser system makes fitting the seats and thwarts easy, as they don't touch the hull. In simpler boats, the thwarts and seats often rest directly on the risers. For fancier boats, the seats can be made of thin panels attached to cleats that rest on the risers. The risers also can accommodate a rowing thwart that can be moved between middle and aft positions, adjusted to suit each rower, or removed entirely for sailing or carrying gear.

For our open sailboats, John designed a removable mast partner that is bolted to a reinforcing cleats on the gunwales. Locating the partner at the gunwale gives the mast plenty of support, and transfers the force from the sail to the rail/gunwale system, which is designed to take it. For a sailboat, twisting is more of a concern than flexing. The half-frames help counter the twist, but the breasthook, rails, gunwales, and quarter knees (along with securely fastened bow and stern seats) do more.

This interior system creates a strong, light boat, but its hidden benefit appears when you pick up a paintbrush. The seats, thwarts, and risers as well as the partner, daggerboard cap, and floorboards (if you have them) are installed in the hull *after* finishing. This means no more varnishing the underside of thwarts while twisting upside down, and running your hair (or nose) through the varnish. The boat's hull is almost completely open and clear for painting. Not only does this approach work for the initial finishing, but for the life of the boat. When the time comes to refinish, simply take everything apart.

You can very easily clean, inspect, repair, and refinish all parts and surfaces. Much better for the boat, and much, much better for the painter.

Many boats, including some of our designs, have bulkheads to carry seats or decks, floor timbers to hold a cockpit or cabin sole, or seats and thwarts carried on cleats attached to the hull. As we go along, we'll cover these options, and others as well.

A cautionary note

Don't immediately dispense with frames and other structural members specified in your plans after reading this discussion of typical interiors for our boats. It is extremely likely that your boat's designer had very good reasons for designing the interior the way he or she did. Some designs for glued-lapstrake construction do require more internal framing than the open sailboats and rowboats that we're focusing on in this book. Planing powerboats, planing sailboats, boats with heavy keels, and boats lightly built with very thin planking are a few good cases of this. For example, we built a 12′ round-bilged outboard tender meant to take a 15-hp motor. To keep her light for lifting with a davit, we built her with half-frames plus floor frames along the bottom. It wasn't enough support for the forces she encountered while motoring at speed. She needed laminated full frames running from gunwale to gunwale.

If you'd like to adapt our interior ideas to your boat, consider the forces involved carefully. If you have doubts, consult the boat's original designer (if you can) or another knowledgeable person.

What's That You're Sitting on?

In this book, thwarts are planks that extend across the boat, primarily intended for rowers to sit on. Canoes have thwarts also, but these are for bracing the hull and its paddlers. Seats are surfaces for sitting located in the bow and stern. The bow and stern seats are sometimes called the sheets, but let us not confuse things any more than they already are.

MARKING THE STATIONS

Important: Do this before you do anything else to the inside of the hull.

After removing the hull from the jig and filling the holes, turn the hull over and immediately mark the stations and crucial points for some of the parts in a permanent manner, before the pencil lines are lost. It is all too easy to put off this vital task while getting caught up in more exciting jobs.

Get out your awl, try-square, and punch. Mark each station as follows, using the penciled lines you traced along the working face of each mold before you took the boat off the jig:

- a punch mark on the centerline on the keelson (that is, if you didn't do it when you built the keelson);
- punch marks where the trunk will cover the centerline, near the edge of the keelson or even on the garboard so they won't be covered by the trunk logs;
- a punch mark at about thwart and seat height (close is good enough at this point);
- a neat vertical score line at the sheer, made with an awl and a try-square.

If you work carefully, you can scrape off most of the worst of the epoxy while leaving most of the penciled station lines on the inside of the hull. You'll lose the lines at the laps where the epoxy squeeze-out was inaccessible when you built the hull but will preserve the lines on the rest of the planking. But it's wise not to rely on this; make the permanent marks with punch and awl now, then clean up the epoxy.

CLEANING UP THE INTERIOR

Gaze into your lovely—empty—hull. Never again will it be so free of objects. Never again will it be easier to wield scraper, sandpaper, and brush. The sheerstrake, inner stem, and upper transom as well as the areas under the trunk and half-frames must be sanded and sealed if these regions are to receive parts that will be bedded and screwed, not glued in with epoxy. Do yourself a huge favor and get the entire interior ready for painting or varnishing now, before the parts go in.

A sharp chisel makes short work of the lumps of cured epoxy putty that were hidden by the molds. Files remove epoxy easily. A half-round or triangular file and a couple of short files are very useful in the laps. Try a thin medium sanding sponge in tight spots, such as around the inner stem.

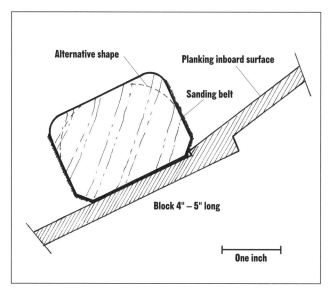

Alternative shape

Planking inboard surface

Sanding belt

Block 4" – 5" long

One inch

Fig 9.1 A small block with a chamfered edge works well for breaking edges on the inside of the hull.

Fill any lingering holes, screw blow-outs, little gaps in the lap fills, and other reasonably major imperfections with epoxy putty. If you don't have many places to fill, five-minute epoxy putty is fine. Otherwise, mix up a batch of regular epoxy putty. Mask off with the hole-filling or masking tape to limit the mess. Let the patches harden overnight, then file and scrape per usual.

If you will be painting the interior, neatly fill all cosmetic blemishes with a filler that sticks to wood such as surfacing putty (see Appendix B, "Resources"), making several trips around to fill the holes thoroughly, since the putty shrinks when it dries. (Do not putty in areas that will receive glued parts.) There is no need to sand between fillings, but try not to put on more putty than you need.

For a varnished hull, you may be able to find a fast-drying one-part filler of an appropriate color, but we usually rely on sawdust and epoxy putty. Small blemishes actually hide better in the busy grain pattern of a varnished hull.

Break and slightly round the plank edges well with a folded bit of cloth-backed sanding belt or with the sanding belt wrapped around a specially shaped block made just for this purpose (see Figure 9.1). Sand the entire interior with 80-grit on a padded block. We find hand-sanding the interior to be as fast as machine-sanding unless the hull is flat-bottomed, large enough, or has very wide planks.

INTERIOR LAYOUT AND MEASUREMENT

An empty hull is a particularly frustrating object to measure in and around—very little is straight or constant. But mark and measure we must. Figuring things out ahead makes life simpler and the results much more accurate.

Making a crucial measurements card

We strongly suggest making out an index card that contains all relevant dimensions for the parts attached to the hull, as well as the thwarts and seats. Otherwise, you'll have the frustrations John did when he built his first boat. (Put the plan in the bottom of the boat. Refer to it for the distances. Check each number three or four times, as each time it seems to change a tiny bit because you're measuring the drawing with a straight ruler in a round hull. Put the drawing away. A day or two later, pull the drawings out and shuffle through them again to find that crucial measurement you've just realized you forgot. Swear.)

It's so much better to sit down with the plans spread out on a flat workbench and write everything you'll need to know down on a card. You'll need two main types of measurements: the fore and aft location of each part ("horizontal") and, if the part isn't on the sheer or the bottom, the height below the sheer or above the bottom ("vertical").

Sometimes it feels like half the battle of building a boat is figuring out where the various parts go. After that, building and installing the parts is almost easy.

Horizontal measurements

For parts that on are on the sheer, such as oarlock blocks or half-frames, or parts situated below the sheer whose location isn't super crucial, such as riser blocks or riser cleats, you can work on the construction drawing's plan view. For most parts, simply measure the distances along a straight line from the rail's end at the transom to the relevant point at the sheer. Measuring from the stern on a transomed boat is convenient, because the transom offers an easy place to hook the tape measure when you're ready to transfer the measurements to the hull. The only exception to this are parts near the bow, such as the riser blocks, since the tape measure will start to bend. Make these measurements from the joint between the inner and outer stems at the sheer.

For a double-ender, measure for the parts from the 'midship station on the drawing.

For the parts not on the sheer or bottom that must be located precisely, such as thwarts and seats or bulkheads the locations should be laid out in a straight line, perpendicular to a station line. Work from the construction drawing's plan view.

Vertical measurements

Most of necessary heights can be measured from the sheer. Take these from the construction plan's profile drawing or from the lofting. It is important to remember that you are taking these measurements straight up and down and to lay them out the same way in the boat. If you lay them out from the sheer along the inside of the hull, you will be measuring at angle or along the curve of the hull and come up short, leading to annoying little problems like a thwart that floats a half-inch above the trunk that is supposed to support it.

Tactics for making specific measurements

Thwart and seats, along with their supports. Don't fret at this point about making the positions of the supports for the thwarts and seats super precise. If your boat has risers, locate the riser blocks or half-frames so the forward and aft edges will rest a couple of inches from the edges of the thwarts and seats. There should be plenty of room for the thwarts and seats to be located exactly where they are wanted later. Plan to make each riser or riser cleat plenty long, then trim to fit after installing the thwarts and seats.

For single-panel thwarts and seats, measure from the aft edge of each thwart to the nearest station; aft edge of the bow seat to the closest station; and forward edge of stern seat to closest station. For bow and stern seats made of panels that rest on supporting cleats, measure for the position of the supporting cleats. The panels can be adjusted to suit when you assemble the seats in the boat.

If your boat has risers, first align a ruler with the top of the thwart or seat to draw a line over the riser block or half-frame, then measure the vertical distance from the sheer to the top of each seat or thwart at the riser block or half-frame, then add the seat or thwart's thickness as well as that of a support cleat, if any, to this number. The result will be the riser height.

Our boats' half-frames end on the plank laps. Some half-frames will be longer than others, so write down the number of laps each frame contacts.

If the lines drawing of your plans show the center of buoyancy, you may want to measure for this from the nearest station along the keelson and mark with a distinctive punchmark. It can help with the adjustment of the thwarts for proper trim after the boat goes in the water, should that prove necessary.

Oarlock socket blocks. Measure and record the distances from the aft side of the transom to the center of each oarlock socket, working from the plan drawing. For extra insurance, also measure and record the distance from the closest station line to each oarlock socket.

Mast step and partner. If you are building a sailboat, you'll also need the locations for the mast step and partner. For both of these, measure from the nearest station to the center of the mast. For the mast step, measure along the top of the keelson. Take pains to measure and mark precisely—a small error can change the rake of the mast dramatically, altering the boat's appearance and balance. Work from a full-sized pattern or the lofting if you can. If you don't have either, it is worth plotting the locations by drawing the hull profile full-sized for three or four stations near the mast. Measure and mark out the precise location of center of the mast in the partner on this full-sized drawing. Measure the angle between the waterline and the center of the mast from the profile drawing, and draw this angle on your full-sized drawing. You can then precisely measure the location of the mast step on your drawing.

Beams. You'll need the beam (the distance, not a wooden part) at the first and last stations, measured at the sheer, so you can brace the hull to the proper width when you fit and install the breasthook and quarter knees. You'll also need the midship beam for fitting thwarts, seats, and other interior parts. (Note: In some designs, you can hold first and last station molds in place with a few nails or screws to keep the ends at the proper beam.

Bulkheads. If there are bulkheads in your boat, measure and record the distance from the side of the bulkhead that faces the middle of the boat to the nearest station. This way, you can spile the bulkhead's bigger face of the bulkhead, then bevel the edges to fit snugly in the hull.

Deckbeams. If your boat has deckbeams, record their locations. If there are many deckbeams they are often spaced a consistent distance apart, except for special

9.2 Measuring from the stern of a transomed boat to lay out the half-frames, riser blocks, and oarlock blocks.

ones at the ends of the cockpit or cabin. When there are only a few deckbeams, they often must be located individually from the station lines.

Transferring horizontal measurements to the hull (laying out)

First, spread the hull to the proper beam amidships, using 1 ″× 3 ″ strapping with blocks screwed at the requisite widths. If the sheerstrake has a lot of flare to it, cut the blocks at an angle so that their corners won't dig into the sheerstrake. This spreader is easy to put in and usually will stay on its own.

Check to be sure that the hull isn't twisted. Set two plywood straightedges on their edges on the sheer near the ends of the boat. Line them up with the station lines or the transom so they are perfectly perpendicular to the boat's centerline. Sight from the bow or stern to see if the two top edges are parallel. Adjust the boat in its cradle by the bow or stern until the edges line up nicely. Make sure that the hull is well supported by the cradles; otherwise, the weight of parts, tools, and boatbuilder can quickly put a twist in the hull. It's good idea to check for twist occasionally in these early stages, particularly before installing the gunwales.

Armed with your measurements card, you are now ready to work on the hull. You'll need a tape measure, sharp pencil, try-square, punch, straightedge, and an awl.

If you're working on a double-ender, you'll need to deviate a bit from the instructions given below. Clamp a straightedge to the rail at the midship station and measure all distances from it. To lay out the parts in the forward half of the boat, line up the aft edge of the straightedge with the score lines of the midship station at the sheer and clamp in place with wooden hand-screws. To lay out the parts aft, move the straightedge until its forward edge lines up with the midship station lines and

reclamp. Running the tape parallel to the centerline from the straightedge usually works best.

Riser blocks, half-frames, oarlock sockets (with or without) blocks. Determine the positions horizontally by measuring along the sheer. For the forward two riser blocks, start at the joint between the inner and outer stem. For the rest of the blocks and all of the half-frames, as well as the centers of the oarlock socket blocks, measure from the aft side of the transom by hooking the end of the tape over the end of the rails. Mark with a pair of punch marks.

Riser cleats for thwarts and seats. Lay out along the sheer for one end from a measurement on the sheer, as you would a riser block.

Center of buoyancy. Mark with a double punch-mark on the keelson.

Mast step. Lay out the center of the mast along the keelson from the nearest station.

Mast partner. To lay out the center of the mast at the sheer, clamp a straightedge across the boat at the closest station, lining it up square to the boat's centerline (see box, page 174). Measure the distance to the mast's centerline and mark it on the sheerstrake with a scored line and a punch mark, to distinguish it from the station marks.

Bulkheads (if any). Lay out for the bulkheads in the same way as the mast partner at the sheer and from a station plane inside the hull along the keelson.

Deckbeams (if any). Install the deck cleats before laying out (see Chapter 10, "If Your Boat Has a Deck"). Locate and mark the position of a major deck beam, such as the one at the end of the cockpit, using the same method used for locating a mast partner. Clamp a straightedge here, checking for square from the stem and/or stern. Locate the other deck beams, measuring from the straightedge, parallel to the boat's centerline. Punch marks on the deck cleats and distinguish with penciled Xs on the side of the punch mark where the beam goes.

Transferring vertical measurements

We'll describe how to locate parts vertically as we install them.

Daggerboard or Centerboard Trunk, and Mast Step

Many modern daggerboard and centerboard trunks, including ours, are made up of a frame of logs, posts, and top cleats with plywood panels attached. These trunks

Laying Out from a Station Plane Inside the Hull and Checking for Square to the Centerline

Lay a straightedge longer than the widest portion of the hull flat on the gunwales. Line it up with the score lines of the station from which you need to measure and hold it in place with weights or gentle clamping pressure. Don't bend the straightedge. Check to be sure that the straightedge is square to the centerline (see below).

Sight along the edge of the straightedge, moving your head fore-and-aft until the edge splits the station punch marks on the keelson and planking. Hold a ruler or tape measure with the blade parallel to the centerline, then align your measurement on the end of tape or ruler with the edge of the straightedge while checking to be sure that you are still lined up with the punch marks. This sounds difficult but is surprisingly easy.

This approach allows you to mark where necessary inside the hull: on the risers, keelson, planking, etc.

This technique is essential for laying out for bulkheads and the thwarts and seats (which we will cover in a little while).

Is the Station Line Square to the Centerline? *It's a good idea not to assume that a straightedge laid on the sheer at a pair of station marks will be square to the centerline. The mold at that station may have warped a little and become slightly twisted. To double-check: Measure from the stem to the point where the straightedge crosses the sheerstrake on both sides of the boat. The straightedge is square to the centerline when both measurements are identical.*

Fig 9.2 Measuring from a straightedge clamped on a station: hold the tape measure or ruler parallel to the centerline to accurately lay out the position of parts such as the mast partner.

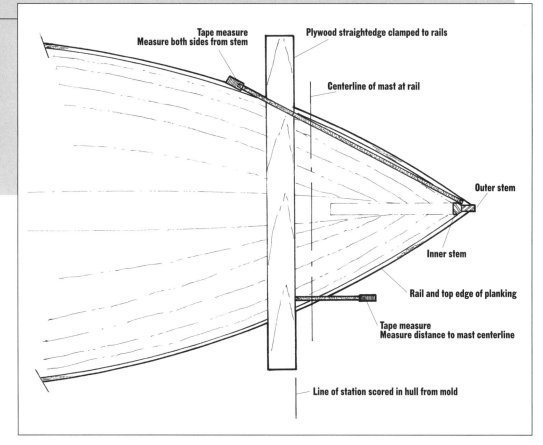

Tape measure
Measure both sides from stem

Plywood straightedge clamped to rails

Centerline of mast at rail

Outer stem

Inner stem

Rail and top edge of planking

Tape measure
Measure distance to mast centerline

Line of station scored in hull from mold

are light and easy to build. When glued up with epoxy, they are also strong and completely waterproof. Sailors of generations past cursed with boats possessing persistently leaking trunks would have rejoiced and instantly embraced this newfangled approach.

Here's a quick overview of the method we recommend for building your boat's trunk: Machine the various logs, posts, and cleats in lengths longer than needed, then fasten them to a pair of panels that have been cut precisely to size and shape. Fasten the two halves of the

trunk together, dry. Mark the various parts for their finished lengths, then take the trunk apart. Trim and sand the parts. Scribe and cut the logs to fit the curve of the keelson. Finally, reassemble the trunk with epoxy and clean it up.

THE TRUNK PARTS

Posts. These vertical members at each end of the trunk are rectangular, and should be thick enough to allow at least ⅛" clearance between the board and trunk. Make these plenty long so that the bottom ends can be trimmed to form the tenons that fit in the board slot in the keelson, which will align the trunk with the boat's centerline.

Logs. These fore-and-aft members are attached to the trunk's panels to form the trunk base. Our friend Ellen, sailing in her *Ellen* (the original), tested the boat's daggerboard trunk for us one day by finding one of Maine's fine submerged glacial boulders, at speed. She landed nose-first in the bow, but she was fine and so was the boat. The only damage was a modest ding in the daggerboard. We make our trunk logs beefy and suggest you do the same, even if you live in a place with soft mud or sand bottoms. Daggerboard and centerboard trunks live very stressful lives.

The trunk logs for our small boats, such as the Ellen, are thick to form a wide base and have the outboard side beveled to reduce weight. A rabbet cut in the top edge receives the panel's bottom edge. If you decide to forgo a rabbet, you can make the logs thinner but remember to cut the curve of the keelson into bottom edge of the side panel, as well as the logs.

The logs of our trunks project several inches past the ends of the trunk, which helps strengthen the vulnerable points where the trunk posts and keelson meet. In stitch-and-glue V-bottomed boats with epoxy putty along the centerline, we have seen cracks radiating out from the ends of the trunk posts. The same forces are at work on glued-lapstrake bottom, though the results may remain hidden longer. Fitting filler blocks between the projecting ends of the logs strengthens the whole trunk assembly, eliminating a couple of nasty water and dirt traps, and simplifies the job of scribing the logs to the keelson.

Top cleats. These are simple cleats, usually rectangular or square in cross section, that fasten to the upper edge of the panels. Bullnose the outer lower edge and finish the ends attractively.

Side panels, port and starboard. Make these of sapele marine ply. For trunks in which all of the pressure of the daggerboard or centerboard will be borne by the frame, the side panels' main job is to keep the water out. They can be fairly thin: the Ellen's 6mm panels for example. For boats with a centerboard that will pry against the panel, you'll undoubtedly find that your plans call for thicker plywood.

Top cap. This covering board, largely decorative on daggerboard trunks, is essential to keep the water out on most centerboard trunks. Generally, it's best to screw-fasten the top caps on daggerboard trunks. It makes refinishing easier, especially if you plan to varnish just the cap. Centerboard caps must be made easily removable to allow access to the board and the trunk interior.

Making the parts

Your plans should clearly show sections for the trunk cleats, posts, logs, cap, and filler blocks (if you have them). Many of these pieces can be sawn out in long lengths and roughly crosscut to make part pairs.

Because the side panels define the shape of the trunk, they must be accurately shaped. John always works from a full-sized pattern taken from the lofting. If your plans have patterns for everything but the trunk, it is worth drawing it full-size on paper or a sheet of ¼" plywood.

After rough-cutting the shape of the two panels, fasten them together with strong double-sided tape or brads and trim the pair until identical. You also can make a ¼" plywood pattern and use it to make perfect copies by flush-trimming with the router (see Chapter 3, "Some Very Useful Techniques").

ASSEMBLING AND FITTING THE TRUNK

Mark the outside surfaces of both panels with a pyramid so you won't inadvertently screw parts to the wrong side. The first round of assembly is a dry fit only; use screws and keep the glue on the shelf for now. Working on the bench instead of in the boat makes assembly easier, and it's also kinder to your back.

Assembling the trunk, first round

Attach the side panels to the logs, then to the top cleats, leaving plenty of overhang for marking and trimming. Next, lay out for the screws that fasten the panels to the posts, making sure to offset the screws so that a screw driven in one side won't hit a screw driven in from the other. Fasten one side panel to both posts.

If your trunk has filler blocks for the logs, measure and cut the angles at the posts. On many trunks, the posts are parallel, so if you make your angled crosscut in the middle of the filler block piece, you should end up with two perfectly fitted filler blocks. Fasten the other panel to the posts. Drill for long screws from the logs into the posts and filler blocks, and from the top cleats into the posts.

9.3 Fastening the trunk panels to the logs and cleats.

Using a pocket knife or utility knife, mark the ends of the posts for trimming, and mark out the tenons that will fit in the slot in the keelson. Clearly mark the portion of the post to be cut away for the tenon. (It is awfully easy to become confused at the bandsaw and cut off the tenon portion.) Also mark the ends of the logs and cleats for trimming. Also mark the parts' orientation: pyramids on the cleats and logs, and "A" and "F" on the posts. The posts' tenons make up and down obvious for them.

Take the trunk apart. Trim the cleats on the table saw, and the ends of the posts and logs on the bandsaw. Rout and/or sand projecting ends and edges.

The trunk logs must be scribed to the hull before you can permanently assemble the trunk. But gluing the whole trunk together at once with epoxy leads to a sticky mess. On our boats' trunks, you can glue the cleats to the side panels, and the posts to *one* panel. Keep in mind that you will have to drive screws from the inside of the panels when attaching the logs. For a trunk with panels that run to the bottom of the logs, the cleats and logs can be glued to the panel but not to the posts. This way, the logs and panels can be trimmed to the curve of the keelson without the post tenons getting in the way.

Fitting the trunk to the hull

Collect the trunk logs and their filler pieces (if any), and set the rest aside.

It is much easier to scribe the logs to the hull without the rest of the trunk in the way. Fasten the logs and fillers together so that you have a trunk bottom sans top. (If your boat's trunk has no filler pieces, screw the logs to temporary spacers that match its posts.)

Place the logs on the keelson over the holes for the posts and slot, with the pyramids on the top edges facing forward. Scribe the curve of the keelson onto the logs in much the same way as you did the skeg. This time, because the curve of the hull is concave you don't need spacers at the ends. Set the compass for the widest part of the gap in the middle, then mark the entire length of the logs on both sides and the ends. Hold the logs in place by hand with just enough pressure to keep them stationary. Don't bend the logs down.

Disassemble the logs and fillers. Saw close to the line, leaving enough wood to plane the curve smooth. After sawing the logs, hold the fillers in place and trace the curve. Trim these on the bandsaw. Screw the logs and filler pieces back together.

Now trim the logs to the lines with a block plane. As you've done on other parts, hold the plane at a slight angle so that when you trim to the line, the inboard edge of the logs is a little fat. Trim both logs to the line, draw pencil slashes, and trim the inside edges until the surface between the two outside edges is flat or slightly hollow; just a little bit of pencil marks should be left at the outside edges.

9.4 Scribing the curve of the keelson onto the trunk logs.

Note: When the keelson doesn't have much curve, the amount of wood to take off the logs is too small to rough-cut on the bandsaw. Cut the curve entirely with a block plane.

Scrape the pencil lines off the sides of the logs. Set the logs on the keelson to test the fit. Usually they need to be trimmed somewhere. If the gaps are small, take a couple of shavings off the high spots with a block plane. If the gaps are large, rescribe the logs and plane at the bench.

Assembling the trunk, final round

Once the logs fit the keelson well, you can take the logs back to the bench, take them apart, and put the whole trunk (*sans* top cap) together for the last time, with epoxy. Follow the same steps you did when assembling the trunk dry, and the standard drill for gluing with epoxy: wet out both surfaces with straight epoxy; coat one surface with thickened epoxy; screw the two pieces together; clean up the squeeze-out.

Clean up the squeeze-out *thoroughly* inside and out. This is one time we'll recommend that you finish cleaning up with paper towel dampened in denatured alcohol. Wear gloves!

Finish up by plugging all of the screw holes: deep ones with bungs (see Chapter 8, "'Outbone' and Rails, Then Off the Jig"), shallow ones with epoxy putty. Use the hole-filling tape.

Clean up any residual epoxy after it has hardened overnight. Trim the bungs. Sand the trunk with 80-grit. Putty and seal (or prime) the trunk before installing it. (Sanding and painting the trunk while it is out of the boat is much easier. You can prime and first-coat the trunk as well.) Set the trunk aside until the hull is ready.

You can try the top cap on the trunk to see how it

looks, but it should not be trimmed until after the trunk and thwarts are installed in the boat if the cap butts against a thwart.

INSTALLING THE DAGGERBOARD OR CENTERBOARD TRUNK

If your boat has a centerboard trunk, it's a good idea to drill the trunk for the pivot pin before installing in the boat and then test the centerboard in the trunk to make sure everything works properly. (See Chapter 11, "If Your Boat has a Sail," for how to make the board.) You might also want to take a few minutes to make and install the plates that cover the ends of the pin on the trunk and keep the water out, as getting at them now will be much easier. We make ours from ⅛ " bronze plate in a pleasing oval shape (See Chapter 13, "Fitting Out" for general instructions). Planking stock will do, also.

Copper tube inserts reduce wear in the holes in the trunk cap intended for a lifting lines or such. You can install these now, and finish the cap later. Round the tubes' visible edges with a flaring tool.

Cutting the slot for the board

Before you can install the trunk, the slot in the keelson needs to be rough-cut. Connect the edges of the trunk tenon holes with lines drawn with a yardstick. Jigsaw out the slot about ⅛ " from the line. That's it for now; you can clean up the slot by flush trimming with a router after the trunk is in.

If you prefer, you can clean up the slot with hand tools. Tackle this job after dry-fastening the trunk in place. Trim most of the wood with a wide chisel, then finish up with rasp. Tape over the end of the rasp so you can use the inside of the trunk as a guide. Smooth the slot with a piece of sanding belt.

Attaching the trunk

Because John finds it easier to drive the screws into the keelson with the hull upside down, he rigged up a little clamping jig for the trunk (see Figure 9.3). If your boat's trunk is long, you may want two of these jigs. If the trunk is large enough to admit pipe clamps, use those once the clamping jig has drawn the trunk up close to its final position.

9.5 Fastening the trunk through the bottom of the keelson while a special clamp made of all-thread and blocks holds the trunk in place.

Dry-fit the trunk, trimming the slot in the keelson for the tenons with a chisel, and drill for screws. Drop the trunk and put several beads of 3M 101 or similar sealant

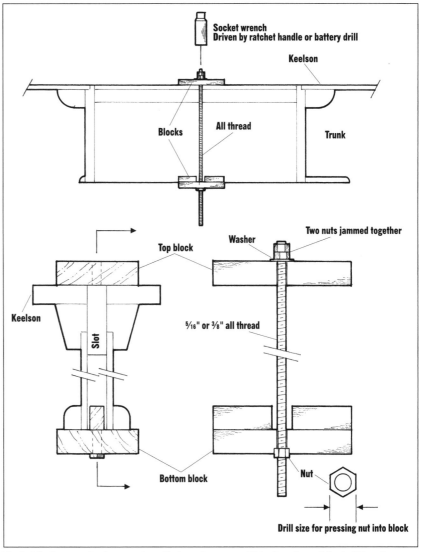

Fig 9.3 A shop-made clamp using all-thread, nuts, and blocks of wood for holding the trunk in the boat.

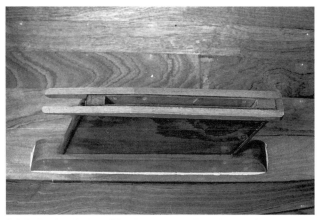

9.6 A nice bead of caulking has squeezed out from under the logs of the installed trunk.

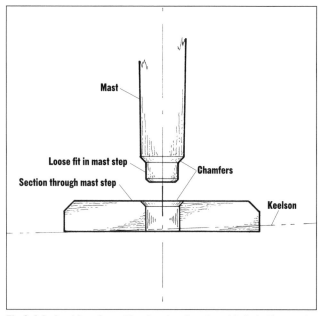

Fig 9.4 A shouldered mast heel and a chamfered hole in the mast step keep the end of the mast from rattling, and they won't bind together when wet and swollen.

(see Chapter 2, "Materials and Tools") in a circle around the base of the logs, putting on enough to thoroughly seal the joint and provide a lovely little bead of squeeze-out all around the edges, inside and out. Wind up the trunk and drive the screws snug but not completely tight, without delay. Tighten the screws after the sealant cures firm enough for trimming.

We hear murmuring out there. Yes, you can use 3M 5200, if you never, ever plan to remove the trunk for repairs. The 101 and similar sealants provide just as watertight a seal, but it can be undone with reasonable persuasion. Read the instructions on the sealant you choose. Sealants such the 101 can be chiselled away cleanly after it cures for a few days. If you decide to use 5200 or its kin, clean up all squeeze-out immediately, as chisels bounce right off many of these sealants when cured.

After the sealant cures well, flush trim the slot with a router—if you haven't cleaned it up by hand already.

MAST STEP
Mast step...or mast stuck?

Small-boat masts must go in and out of the boat when required, often for every trip. They also must stay firmly in position when in use. This is a bit of a design dilemma. If you make your mast and step with a perfect slip-fit, allowing just enough for ample varnish, you're in for a surprise after a fine rambunctious sail that soaks the mast step and heel. There you'll be, leaning out precariously from the dock, wrestling with a mast well-stuck in the step. If you try to fix this problem by leaving plenty of slop in the heel-step fit, the mast will rattle around when it's dry.

To solve this problem in our

boats, John modified a mast step designed by L. Francis Herreshoff for his H-14 (see Figure 9.4). The hole in the step is chamfered to take a mast heel with a chamfer above the tenon. The tenon can be quite a bit smaller than the mast-step hole, because all of the compression and side forces bear on the chamfers. The mast cannot become stuck when it and the step swell, as the fit of the

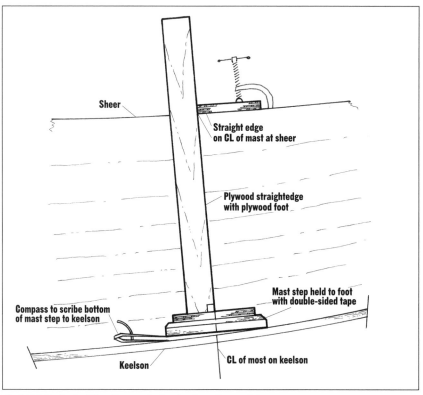

Fig 9.5 A jig for holding the mast step in place for scribing.

chamfers is not affected. The mast is always held snugly, yet can be easily removed. (See Photo 9.47 of John measuring for bow seat on page 204, for an Ellen mast step in position.

Making the mast step

Often the mast step is fairly simple block of wood with various corners bullnosed. Sometimes they are nicely shaped, for looks or to fit the shape of the hull, or both. Make the mast step as shown in your plans. Drill the hole in the mast step with a spade bit or hole saw, then chamfer the edge with a router or hand tools.

Take a minute to do the same thing to a scrap of the same thickness as the step. Put it away someplace safe; you'll need it to shape the heel of the mast, as the real mast step will be inconveniently attached to the boat by then.

Fitting the mast step

Mark the center of the mast heel across the keelson and onto the planking. Also mark the center of the mast heel across the top and down the sides of the step. Clamp a straightedge to the rails at the mast partner centerline. Attach a plywood "foot" to the square end of a second straightedge. Mark a square line from one edge of the straightedge down the edges and across the bottom of the foot. Attach the mast step to the foot with double-sided tape, lining up the line on the foot with the mast centerline on the step. Hold the top of the footed straightedge against the straightedge clamped at the sheer, then line up the mast heel centerline on the step with that on the keelson. Make sure that the upper end of the footed straightedge is centered between the gunwales on the first straightedge. Use a wooden hand-screw and a clamp to hold the straightedges together and keep the mast step level athwartships.

Scribe the bottom of the step to the keelson.

Trim the step on the bandsaw, and hand-plane until it fits well to the keelson. After shaping the bottom of the step, cut a shallow dado across the bottom for a drain.

Dealing with a Mast Step with Curved Sides

If your mast step has curved sides, nail a short plywood straightedge to the top, parallel to the fore-and-aft centerline, and flush with one side of the mast step, at the widest part. The straightedge will be on the table when you bandsaw the mast step's bottom for the angle of the keelson and also will run along the table saw fence when you cut the dado for a drain.

Installing the mast step

Unless your boat has a thick keelson, not a common situation in small boats, you'll want to drill for and drive the screws in through the bottom of the keelson.

Place the mast step in position and trace around it onto the keelson. Drill pilot holes through the keelson. Vacuum the step and its landing area, and wipe down both with alcohol to remove the last traces of dust. Attach the step in place with sailmaker's double-sided tape. You can employ a helper to help the step, but the double-sided tape works surprisingly well.

Drill for and drive the screws. Remove the screws and step. Apply a modest amount of bedding compound or epoxy putty and reattach. Ream out the squeeze out from the drainage slot(s).

AND NOW, THE KEEL

Now that the trunk and mast step are in, you may attach the keel (see Chapter 8, "Buildimg the Interior").

Measuring Heights Down from the Sheer

You'll need a plywood straightedge longer than the beam of the boat, and a framing square. Draw a square line about 8″ from the end of the straightedge. Lightly clamp the framing square to the straightedge at the line, then lower it to the height required.

Measuring heights down requires a little mental gymnastics for many of us, but this curved object we are building has precious few easy-to-measure-from, known points. The sheerline, the entire "sheerplane" in fact, contains the fixed points we need. So, measuring down it is. You can use this techniques for locating the riser blocks, risers, thwarts or seats, riser cleats, and the tops of partial bulkheads.

9.7 Marking the height of the riser using a plywood straightedge, a framing square, and a scrap of riser stock.

Seat and Thwart Attachment Systems

The seats and thwarts in your boat must be attached in some manner to the hull. There are three standard methods of doing this: 1) on fore-and-aft risers that attach to frames and blocks fastened to the hull, 2) on riser cleats fastened directly to the hull, and 3) as horizontal panels fastened to bulkheads and the hull. We'll talk about option No. 3 in a bit, in the section on bulkheads, so please scan through this section and take a look there if your boat is built this way. If your boat has risers and half-frames, or riser cleats, we'll deal with these now.

RISER SYSTEM: MAKING, FITTING, AND ATTACHING PARTS

As we mentioned at the beginning of this chapter, we favor a system of risers attached to half-frames and blocks for relatively small, open boats like the Ellen. If your boat has more (or fewer) frames, you should be able to use the following techniques, adapting to suit where necessary.

Before proceeding, you will need heights for the risers as measured down from the sheer, which you should have noted earlier during the first layout and marking phase (see page 172).

Riser blocks

These simple blocks, made of a hardwood such as oak or ash, support the bow and stern seats. Shape the blocks by cutting miters on both ends and bullnosing or chamfering the exposed edges. The blocks must be scribed to fit the hull and fastened with epoxy. It's a reasonably simple job, but first you have figure out where they go.

Locating the blocks. Set the blade of a try-square for a little longer than the riser height. Place the try-square on the "riser block" mark at the sheer, with the head toward the middle of the boat. Draw a line on the hull near the lower end of the blade. Make a "fitting block" by fastening a 4″ to 6″ scrap of riser stock to the middle of a riser block. Using the straightedge-and-framing square method of measuring down from the sheer (see Photo 9.7), clamp the framing square at the riser height, then line up the straightedge at the mark on the sheer. Hold the fitting block so its forward edge touches the line on the hull and the top of the riser scrap just touches the framing square. Trace along the top of the riser block onto the planking.

Mark the heights for the rest of the riser blocks on the same side of the hull. Measure and write down the heights of the top of the blocks, then measure and mark the other side of the boat.

Scribing and sawing out. Hold each riser block in position, then scribe the shape of the hull on the side of the block with a compass. Always mark the side facing the nearest end of the boat. (If you will be sawing these out with a handsaw, mark both sides.) If you have trouble marking the laps, use a small block held against the planking as a small square. Label each riser block for place in the boat and orientation.

Bandsaw or hand-saw along the scribed lines, cutting the angles out square.

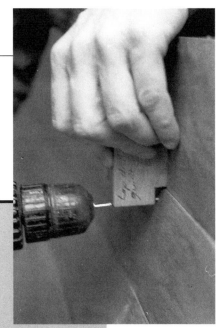

9.9 The Indispensable Perpendicular Drill Jig

9.8 Locating a riser block with a try-square.

The Indispensable Perpendicular Drilling Jig

This little jig is a simple, square piece of hardwood, cut with a notch to go over the lap on the bottom and a V-notch to align a drill bit on the front end. You will want one for drilling the holes through the laps, perpendicular to the plank above the lap. The jig is vital anywhere that perpendicular holes are required, including screws for the breasthook and quarter knees.

Dry-fastening. Check the blocks' fit. Unless they are really bad, they will do; the epoxy will fill the gaps and the blocks will look fine, even if varnished. Draw around each block and remove it. Mark the center of each lap with a compass, and drill a tapping hole at each mark using the indispensable perpendicular drilling jig (see box) to drill the holes perpendicular to the plank *above* the lap. Then, working from the outside of the hull, drill for and drive screws to fasten the riser block, countersinking for epoxy putty "bungs" (see box).

John likes to fasten the riser blocks with two screws through the laps in addition to gluing them in place with epoxy. This isn't strictly necessary—the screws can be drilled through any part of the planking—but it makes us feel better. If your block goes over only one lap, carefully drive the second screw through the single thickness of planking.

Mark the final riser heights on each riser blocks, using the straightedge and framing square. (If you prefer, you may leave the blocks in the hull, and mark the blocks and half-frames at the same time later on.)

Final fastening. We glue the riser blocks in after we've sanded the entire inside of the hull to the point where it's ready for finishing. Your pencil lines will be long gone, but the screw holes will serve to position the blocks. Label the blocks as you remove them. Glue the blocks in with epoxy putty, redrive the screws, and clean up the squeeze-out. Fill the bung holes on the outside of the hull.

Making Epoxy Putty "Bungs"

In many cases, the planking plywood used for glued-lapstrake boats is too thin to accept standard wooden bungs. Instead, countersink the screwheads slightly below the plank surface. Mask off the holes with the hole-filling tape and fill with epoxy putty (tinted slightly darker than the planking if you're planning to varnish). Scrape the putty flush after it has hardened sufficiently. If you place your holes with forethought and drill with care, these false "bungs" will look surprisingly like the real thing.

Half-frames

The half-frames should also be made of hardwood; we normally use white oak. When you plane the stock for these, make plenty of extra. Although you can nest the half-frames together on the board, it's usual to find that you can't fit as many in the width of a board as you would like. And it is wise to have extra wood available in case one or two don't fit and you need to make new ones.

Measuring the hull shape. The obvious way to obtain the shapes of the half-frames is by scribing, like the riser blocks, but the much longer half-frames would take a fair amount of wood and a good bit of time to scribe and cut each one properly.

For example, the middle of a rectangular block of wood long enough for a half-frame will necessarily rest several inches from the hull's inside curve. Scribing at this distance, say 2″ to 4″, will only approximate the shape of the hull, since it is nearly impossible to hold the points of a compass in a line that is perfectly perpendicular to the edge of the blank. So, you must scribe and cut out a rough shape first, then more accurately scribe the sawn blank once more, twice more in some cases. By the time you're done with several trips to the bandsaw and back to the hull, you'll find that most of the original blank has become kindling, and you may be growing a bit tetchy, especially when you think about repeating the process for all of the remaining half-frames.

To avoid this scenario, you can make a fingered jig to reproduce the hull shape accurately and quickly (see box). The jig cuts the time needed to lay out the half-frames shape enormously. Often, one setting of the jig can be used to mark the half-frames for both sides of the boat. (That is, if you built your boat carefully and both sides are identical.)

How it works:
- Line up one face of the jig's backbone on the punch marks for the half-frame on the sheerstrake.
- Firmly clamp the stop and clamping block in place on top of the rail (or sheerstrake), making sure that the stop block seats firmly on top edge of the sheerstrake.

Eager to Finish? Applying Clear Sealer and/or Primer, an Option at this Point

In many of our boats, including the Ellen, the riser blocks are the only parts glued to the interior of the hull with epoxy. Once the blocks are glued in, cleaned up, and sanded, we go ahead and start applying finishes: sealer, surfacing putty, and sometimes primer. Even if you have bulkheads and other parts that must be glued to the hull, you can go ahead with the finishing if you leave their attachment sites bare. Once these parts are in, sanding and sealing the areas around them goes quickly (see also Chapter 12, "Painting and Varnishing"). If you decide to prime, cut in the primer well shy of any area to be varnished.

If you'd rather wait to start finishing—a wise move if you're not completely sure about how the boat will go together—at least fill all holes, break and round the plank edges, and sand to readiness for sealing or priming before you begin installing parts. You'll be glad you did.

Making a Hull-Shape-Reproducing Jig

John's fingered jig, shown in the photographs, is rather fancy, with all sorts of dadoes and slots and captured nuts so that it can be fully adjusted with half-turns of a screwdriver. It's a bit much if you plan to build just one or two boats.

The drawing shows a simpler version that is screwed together. The stop block and clamping block should be held firmly together with two screws and a little glue. The backbone is fastened to the stop block with a single screw so that it can pivot to fit the curvature of the hull. Change the height of the backbone by moving where it is fastened to the stop block. In each finger, drill and countersink for screws in several likely positions. (The screw heads must be flush when tight.)

Fig 9.6 Simple fingered jig for measuring the shape of the hull to make the half-frames.

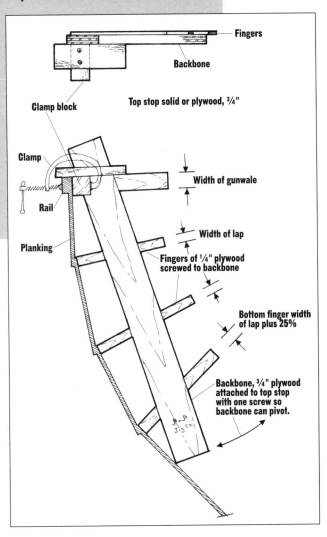

- Screw the jig's backbone in place at an angle that allows ample landing for all fingers. (Check your layout notes for the number of laps that the frame should contact.)
- Position the end of each finger firmly on a lap joint, lining up the top edge of the finger with the top edge of a plank. Drive a screw into one of the predrilled holes in each finger.
- Holding the fingers while fastening them will be a little awkward, but using short, say ¾", self-tapping screws will help. Be careful not to move anything. A small spring clamp or C-clamp also will make this job easier.
- Trace onto the hull along the fingers on the edge that lines up with the punch marks. This will help you position the finished half-frame. Check to make sure all screws are tight, then carefully remove the measuring jig and carry it to your waiting stock.

9.10 Measuring the shape of the hull with the hull-shape-reproducing jig.

9.11 Transferring the hull shape to the half-frame stock.

Laying out on the stock. Lay the jig on your half-frame stock, "fingers side" down. Line up the top and bottom fingers parallel with the edge of the half-frame stock. (The wood's grain should run roughly parallel to the stock edge.) Trace around the fingers. Draw straight lines be-

tween the U-shaped marks traced around the fingers.

Mark the widths with a compass or a ruler, then draw an attractive curve on the inboard face with a thin batten. Adjust the width in the middle up or down if the frame's taper looks funny. We prefer to round the lower ends of the frames to an attractive curve.

Lay out a twin to the first half-frame, unless the other side of your hull differs by ½″ or more. If so, you'd better measure a half-frame to fit it, and plan on doing

9.12 Fastening the half-frames in place.

9.13 Marking a half-frame for the final trim at the sheer and the rabbet to take the gunwale.

9.14 Cutting the rabbet in a half-frame using a shop-made tenon jig.

the same for all of the remaining frames. Swallow your pride, make 'em fit, and figure out how not to repeat the error on your next boat.

Measure and mark out the shapes for all of the half-frames on the stock.

Sawing out, trimming, and shaping. Saw the half-frames out on the bandsaw or jigsaw. Leave the line along the planking edge; split the line on the inside curve. Cut the tops slightly above the sheerline.

John uses the stationary sander to trim the edges of the half-frames to final shape (see Chapter 3, "Some Very Useful Techniques"). You also can use hand tools. Trim the frame at each of the laps first, nearly cutting off all the line traced from the fingers. Make sure that the edge stays square as you trim. This is easy to do on a frame that has been cut on the bandsaw: Quickly draw three pencil lines down the frame's edge, roughly parallel to the sides. As you trim, the pencil lines will disappear. If the lines' lengths remain equal as they shorten, you are trimming the frame edge square. If the lines are of different lengths, forming an angle across the edge's face, you're sanding or cutting at an angle. If you cut out the frames with a jigsaw or handsaw, you'll have to use a square to check as you trim. When all of the lap areas are trimmed, redraw the three lines on the edge face and trim the remaining areas between.

Installing, first-round. Back in the boat, hold each half-frame in place and trace around it. As you did with the riser blocks, mark the center of the laps and drill a tapping hole perpendicular to the plank above the lap, then drill for and drive screws to fasten the frame from the outside of the hull, countersinking for epoxy putty bungs. (You'll notice that the half-frames don't fully contact the planking between the laps. These small gaps allow water to drain away from behind the frames.)

Set a compass to the width of the gunwale. Rest a square on top of the sheerstrake, then use the compass to mark the half-frames with lines indicating the top of the sheerstrake, for final trimming, and the bottom of the gunwale, for a rabbet. (If your boat will not have gunwales, mark for just the top of the sheerstrake.)

Mark the height of the riser on the half-frames using the plywood straightedge-and-framing square method, as you did the riser blocks. Hold a scrap of riser under the framing square and tracing along it, top and bottom, onto the half-frame. Mark with pencil first, then a punch mark at the riser's top edge.

Once you've marked everything, and checked twice, you can remove the half-frames from the boat.

Cutting the rabbets. After trimming the top of the half-frames using the miter gauge on the table saw, John cuts the vertical portion of the rabbet on a shopmade tenon jig set for the thickness of the gunwale blocks for open gunwales or for the thickness of the gunwale for closed gunwales (see Photo 9.14). You also can make this cut on the bandsaw; mark the thickness of the gunwale blocks or gunwale with a marking gauge. Make the rabbet's horizontal cut on the bandsaw. It should be the second cut if you use the tenon jig for the vertical cut.

Shaping and sealing. Rout or hand-shape a chamfer or roundover along both edges of the half-frames' inside curves, except where the riser lands. Label the half-frames with a permanent marker on the faces that will be hidden against the planking. Sand the half-frames well, breaking any sharp chamfered edges. Seal the half-frames with clear sealer or varnish.

Installing the half-frames, final round. If your boat has open gunwales, the half-frames must be in before open gunwales can go on. Seal the half-frames' landing zones, then install sealed half-frames permanently in the hull by screwing them in place. Putty the bung holes.

If your boat has closed gunwales, the half-frames go in after the gunwales are fastened in place.

Note: We don't recommend gluing half-frames in the boat because the glue can prevent water from draining completely away from behind the frames. It is also much easier to replace a broken half-frame that is not epoxied in place, if your boat should have an accident . However, if your philosophy is to glue everything in place, follow suit with the half-frames.

If your boat has full frames and open gunwales

If your boat has open gunwales and one or several laminated full frames, mark the top of each for a rabbet just as you did the half-frames. Cut the rabbets with a hand saw, then clean up with a file using a wood scrap cut to the thickness of a gunwale block as a guide. Use a hacksaw if you hit a screw.

Those of you building with boats with closed gunwales should have cut the necessary rabbets when test-fitting the sheerstrake. If you didn't, swear now. Then mark out the rabbets, make a series of sawcuts in the waste, and cut the rabbets with a chisel.

Risers

The risers must be fairly thin, as they must bend to the curve of the hull, but wide enough to support the weight and activities of the occupants of the thwarts and seats. For example, the risers for the Ellen are about ½″ thick and 1¼″ to 1½″ wide. Make the risers of white oak, ash, or any similarly tough, flexible hardwood. (For a look at risers in place during the installation of a seat, see Photo 9.42, page 202; for a finished riser and seat, see Photo 9.1, page 170.)

You can make and install the risers now or wait

until they're needed, just before the thwarts and seats go in. For each riser length, measure from the forward face of the first riser block or half-frame to the aft face of the last riser block or half-frame. Add at least 3″. It's best to mark the final lengths of the risers after fastening them in the boat.

To install the risers, line up the top edge of the riser with the punch marks on the riser blocks and frames. Fasten the risers in place with roughly equal lengths protruding at the ends. Some risers, such as the Ellen's aft ones, require persuasion to make them settle into place. An extra pair of hands to either hold the drill or riser can be a help. When you're happy with the final lengths, remove the risers, and shape and round them with pleasing contours. Score identifying labels in the risers' backs as you remove them.

The risers can be painted or varnished along with the interior of the hull and installed after the interior is dry.

SEAT AND THWART RISER CLEAT SYSTEM
Making, fitting, and attaching riser cleats to the hull

In many designs, the thwarts and seats are fixed in the boat on cleats attached directly to the planking. Often rectangular in section, these riser cleats are scribed to fit the fore-and-aft curve of the planking and usually the top edge is beveled for the thwart or seat to sit on.

Riser cleats appear so simple to make, so easy to install—but they are deceptive. Fitting and installing them properly is a good workout for your skills and your patience.

Determining the top bevel. Cut the riser cleats out to the shape shown in your plans, except for the top bevel; this bevel will vary depending on the riser cleat's placement in the hull. There are a number of ways to determine the top bevel. For the thwarts near the middle of the boat, you can measure the angle from the sections on the full-sized patterns, the lofting, or even the molds. Draw a line parallel to the waterline at the thwart height, then measure the angle between this line and the hull. Yes, it is a good idea to draw a straight line between the laps to obtain an accurate angle of the planking.

The top bevels for riser cleats that support bow and stern seats must be measured in the boat. The angle for each must be measured square to the planking, which is quite divergent from the plane of the sections, especially in the bow.

Mark the fore-and-aft location of the riser cleat. Then mark the height of the top of the cleat (bottom of the seat) at the fore-and-aft location with the straightedge-and-framing square method (see page 179).

If the seats are level (and the boat is level) cut a section of the riser cleat stock that's a little longer than the finished riser cleat will be. Hold this on the mark on the hull. Use an 8″ or 10″ torpedo level set on the top edge of the riser cleat to position the cleat's other end, then mark a line on the planking along the top of the cleat. If your seats are angled, measure the height of the other end of the riser cleat, and mark it on the planking with the straightedge-and-framing square.

Scribing to the planking. Holding the length of cleat in position, scribe the curve of the planking onto the edges and ends, then trim to the lines, with a hand plane or on the stationary sander. First work to only the line you can clearly see, holding the cleat at an angle. After you have trimmed to the line on both edges and the ends, draw slash marks across the bevels and trim the back flat, edge to edge. Go carefully, and check your progress often.

Fasten the fitted cleat in place with two screws, then scribe, trim, and fasten its mate on the other side of the boat.

Make two lengths of straight cleat that are long enough to overlap when the end of each one is resting on the top of a riser cleat. These overlapping cleats mimic the plane of the bottom of the seat and are used at the ends of the riser cleats to scribe the angle of the top edge.

The top angle is a constant bevel so the riser cleats can be trimmed on the table saw, carefully. To trim by hand, mark the line of the bevel across the inboard face and parallel to the top edge, then us a block plane to trim the bevel to the line.

You can use this method of determining the bevel of all the riser cleats in the boat, if you prefer.

A suggestion: Trimming the top bevel of the riser cleats 3 to 5 degrees more than you marked will ensure that water drains off. When you fit the thwarts and seats you'll need to scribe and trim for this small over-bevel, but it is a quick job.

Installing the cleats, temporarily. *Do not permanently fasten the riser cleats to hull at this point.* You will mark the finished lengths after you measure and fit the thwarts and seats.

Breasthook, Quarter Knees, and Gunwales

The breasthook, quarter knees, and gunwales, along with optional related parts such as spacer blocks, mast partner, and partner reinforcing pieces, make up a unit that stiffens and strengthens the hull. Fitting these pieces accurately is important for your boat's stiffness and longevity—as well as looks. We often use white oak or ash, but also have used Honduras mahogany and domestic cherry to good effect. There are many other possibilities, including woods available only in your part of the world.

Before proceeding, replace the midship spreader in the hull, check the hull for twisting. Set up another

9.15 Spacer blocks for the breasthook fitted to the inner stem and fastened in the bow.

spreader made of 1″ by 3″ strapping roughly 2″ wider than the boat's beam at the first station, and place it near that station. This spreader will want to slide aft. Hold it in place with blocks clamped to the inside of the sheerstrake. Clamp the retaining blocks at the sheer inside the hull where the spreader goes in easily. Inch the retaining blocks, and spreader, toward the bow by tapping first one block, then the other. Clamp the blocks tight when the hull has spread to the proper width at the station. Keeping the spreader aft of the station make it possible to check width at the station with a tape measure or tick strip.

Double check for proper beams and no twist in the hull.

MAKING AND FITTING THE PARTS, FIRST ROUND
Breasthook and quarter-knee spacer blocks

Many of our boats have open gunwales that are installed with spacer blocks at the breasthook and quarter knees. If your boat has these, you'll need to make them now, of matching wood. If it does not, you may skip ahead and begin fitting your breasthook.

Scribe the ends of each of the two breasthook and two quarter-knee spacer blocks with a compass to fit the inner stem and transom. For the breasthook spacer blocks, trim the end to follow the chamfer on the aft side of the inner stem. This leaves small triangular holes on either side of the inner stem, which serve to drain water that would otherwise be trapped behind the breasthook when the boat is stored upside down. Trim with the band-saw or a handsaw, and finish up with a couple of swipes with a block plane.

Lay out for the screws that will hold the breasthook in place. Clamp the spacing block in place. Give the square end a tap with a hammer and softwood block to make sure the joint is tight. With a tapping bit, drill for the screws through the rails, planking, and spacer block. Be sure to drill perpendicular to the rail, vertically and horizontally. You may have to adjust the height of the screws to ensure that they will not come out through the top or bottom of the breasthook. (Adjust evenly, on both

9.16 A breasthook with the camber cut on the outboard edges.

9.17 Gluing the breasthook blank.

sides of the hull; the plugs for these screws will be on full display unless you install gunwale guard.) By drilling perpendicular holes, you have a much better chance of the part not crawling up or down as you drive the screws.

Scribe the quarter-knee spacer blocks to fit tight to the transom, and install them in the same way as the breasthook spacer blocks.

Drill with the clearance/countersink bit through the rail and planking the forward and aft screw holes of the spacer blocks, but not the middle ones; then hold the spacers in place with short screws that don't protrude into the hull.

Breasthook

Making the blank. On most boats, the breasthook is made of two pieces joined together by a spline joint at the centerline. The grain of the two pieces runs parallel to the adjacent planks and meets at the glue line, like a miter joint.

If you lofted your boat, you can lay out the shape of the breasthook on the half-breadths. If you didn't, most plans don't include a pattern for the breasthook. Determine the breasthook blank size by measuring the scale drawing.

Make a pattern of the breasthook and lay out the pieces on the blanks to find the best match of the grain pattern. Make the blanks larger than necessary, so there is plenty of wood and trim to fit in the boat.

We recommend that you make the breasthook as a flat blank and install it with the outboard edges above the edge of the sheerstrake, rising toward the stern, then camber it by cutting down this raised edge until it is flush with the planking and gunwales. (We'll talk about this in detail when installing the breasthook. To read ahead, see page 195, especially.) This method creates a good solid

glue joint through the thickest part of the breasthook, which is wise, as a small boat is often picked up by its breasthook (see Photo 9.16).

Bandsaw along the lines of the miter joint, then machine- or hand-plane the joint smooth and tight. This joint is the one that you, and everybody else, will look at on launching day and every day thereafter. Taking the time to make it look good will be worth it, especially when people stop, bend closer to look, trace their fingers over your lovely breasthook, look some more, then ask you, "How did you make that joint!?" Once you're happy, cut the dadoes for the spline.

To provide a solid landing zone for your clamp, make two triangular blocks (about 4″ to 6″ long) and screw them to breasthook's outboard edges with drywall screws. Glue and clamp well to make the glue line as thin and invisible as possible. Resin glue such as Weldwood makes a less visible joint than epoxy.

If you would like to include bands of contrasting woods at the breasthook's glue line, add them to the edges to be joined after sawing and cleaning up the miter joint, before you cut the dado for the spline. Once the glue has set, cut the dadoes for the spline as above.

Prepping the blank. With a small framing square positioned on the breasthook blank's glue line, mark a trim line for the forward end on the top of the breasthook blank where it is ¼″ to ½″ wider than the distance between the planks at the inner stem's aft face. Next, measure the angle between the top edge of the sheerstrake and the back of the inner stem. If your full-sized pattern or lofting is handy, use it, but John usually rests a scrap of plywood on the tops of the sheerstrakes and holds the bevel gauge up against it (underneath), making sure to hold the bevel gauge close to parallel to the centerline.

Trim the end of the breasthook blank a few degrees less than the angle you measured. This will accommodate the breasthook's camber.

To align the breasthook blank properly with its glue line right on the boat's centerline, the two legs of the blank must be of equal length (see box).

Trimming the Breasthook Legs to Equal Lengths

On the bottom of the blank, mark a point (A) and a point (B) on the glue line near the breasthook's forward and aft ends, as shown in the drawing. Draw two equal arcs (C1, C2) close to the sides of the blank. Draw a line tangent to each arc (D1, D2). You will have two lines that are equidistant from the centerline that are roughly parallel to the rough sides of the blank.

To make both legs the same length, use a tape to lay out the same distance from point (B) to points (F1) and (F2). Or, use a compass from point (E) to points (F1) and (F2.) Mark a square line (G1, G2) and trim each leg on the bandsaw. The trimmed breasthook blank must be longer than the finished breasthook.

With a square, carry the side lines down onto the newly trimmed ends.

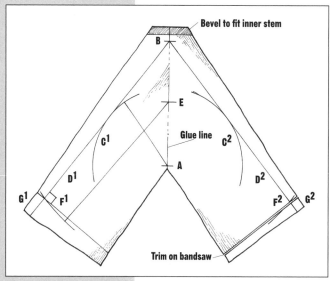

Fig 9.7: Centering layout.

Scribing and rough-fitting. Mark a centerline on the back of the inner stem with a compass. Rest the breasthook *upside down* in place on top of the edges of the sheerstrake. You will normally want the breasthook cambered. For a ¼″ of camber, rest the aft end on a strip of ¼″ plywood. If you want more camber, move the strip forward until the distance between the sheer and the breasthook is right, or use thicker spacers.

Center the breasthook on the forward end. At the aft ends, center the the pencil lines so they are at equal distances from the spacer blocks (or plank edges). Hold the breasthook firmly in place with weights.

By now, you should be a master at sharpening a pencil with a utility knife (or chisel). For this project, finish sharpening by planing flat a 2″-long strip down one side to the point of the lead.

Hold the breasthook firmly in place with your hand as well as the weights. Place the pencil's flat side against

9.18 Holding the breasthook upside down on the sheer to mark the curve of the planks. Shims at the aft end are required to mark the breasthook big enough for cutting the camber.

the spacer block (or planking) and trace the shape of the breasthook. This can be an awkward job. Darken your lines with several passes; don't try to engrave the wood in one authoritative effort. If the breasthook slips, swear, scrape off the line, reposition, and retrace.

Rest a straightedge against the spacer block (or the face of the plank) and mark the athwartships angle on the ends of the breasthook blank.

Remove the breasthook blank and turn it right-side up.

Trimming the edges to fit along the sheerstrake. Before you leave the hull for the bandsaw, set the breasthook blank roughly in position on top of the sheerstrakes and look at the angles you marked on the ends. Notice something wrong? Exactly. The angles face the wrong direction—because you marked them with the blank upside down. However, the *degree* of angle is correct. Quickly sketch lines that follow the planking and you'll see that these form the marked angles' mirror images. Don't worry about sketching accurately. The angles marked while the blank was upside down are all that's required to set up the bandsaw.

Place the blank on the bandsaw's table right-side up, behind the blade, with the aft end of the starboard side touching the back of the blade.

Adjust the table angle until it's close to the marked angle (*not* your sketched angle). Finely adjust the angle by lining up the blade edge with the cutting line on top of the blank. The blade edge should appear as a thin vertical line. The cutting line should extend into the distance alongside and exactly parallel to the blade. Adjust the table until the blade is parallel to the angle line on the end of the blank. At that point the cutting line and angle line should be hidden by the edge of the blade. Lock the table.

9.19 Hold the breasthook below the sheer for scribing if it needs to be marked again after the first cut.

Turn the piece around so that the aft end touches the teeth. Resight along the line to the blade from the back of the bandsaw to make sure you're sawing at the correct angle. The sketched angle will show you that the blade is going the right way.

Bandsaw along the cutting line. Leave the line on the breasthook itself so you'll have a little extra wood for fine-tuning the fit.

Turn your attention to the port side. With the breasthook in front of the blade and the aft end touching the blade, line up the marked angle with the blade, to make sure both sides of the boat are the same. (They should be.) Turn the piece around, then resight and bandsaw the port side.

You'll use this same technique when you cut the edges of the quarter knees.

Second scribing, if necessary. Try the breasthook in place. If it's pretty close, it's ready for final fitting. If the breasthook fit is not close, you'll have to scribe again.

Scrape off all lines. Hold the breasthook in the bow with the aft end just below the top of the spacer block (or sheerstrake) and the forward end below the top of the spacer block (or sheerstrake) by the amount of camber, plus little bit. Scribe the joints with a compass and bandsaw out. Make sure to trim both sides evenly so the glue joint will remain lined up on the centerline.

Set aside the breasthook for now, and attend to the quarter knees.

Quarter knees
Making the blanks. Using a pattern to make an identical pair of quarter knees is a sensible approach (see Chapter 3, "Some Very Useful Techniques"). Leave plenty of extra wood along the planking and transom edges.

Scribing and rough-fitting. First, you need to decide about the angle for the quarter knees on the transom. This is largely an aesthetic choice. We prefer to follow the top of the transom. If you agree, mark a line parallel to the top

of the transom using a compass set for the distance from the top of the transom to the top of the spacer block (or sheerstrake).

Before you commence scribing and trimming, lightly sketch the final shape you'd like to see in the boat on the blank.

Holding the knee in the position for the first scribing can be a little awkward, so set your compass for about ¼″ to ½″ shy of the final shape of the knee that you just sketched. Scribe along the spacer block (or sheerstrake) first, making sure to mark the front end of the knee, while holding the knee as close to the desired angle as you can. If it is easy to change your compass setting single-handed, you can also scribe along the transom. If not, then bandsaw along the scribed line for the planking, setting the angle of the table in the same way as you did the breasthook. Back in the hull, hold the knee in place and scribe along the transom on the top and the inboard end of the knee, then trim on the bandsaw.

Now it will be much easier to hold the quarter knee exactly where you want it. Scribe again and bandsaw the knee to the final shape, ready for fitting.

Again with the Pencil Slashes
Fitting a piece of wood in a boat, with its changing bevels and curves, is not easy. You will need all the helpful techniques you can muster to do it efficiently. We have often referred to using pencil slashes when cutting bevels. If you have insisted on not using them until now, you might want to reconsider their utility. Here's short refresher course: With a soft (No. 1) pencil, quickly draw slash marks across the face you need to trim. These penciled lines will tell you where your blade is cutting as you trim and fit the piece. There is nothing nearly so frustrating as holding a piece of wood in the boat, seeing where the gap is, working furiously with a plane to trim the maddeningly hard wood, working carefully not to trim too much, then trying the piece again—and discovering that it looks exactly as it did before. You look in the plane's throat; yup, you cut shavings. But where the @#! did you cut? The pencil slashes will tell you. Draw the marks closer together to see where you are cutting more clearly. As an added advantage, the pencil's graphite lubricates the plane, making cutting smoother, easier, and more controlled.

FITTING AND CUTTING PARTS, SECOND ROUND
The big secret of fitting one piece of wood against another is patience. But all the patience the in the world won't help you unless your tools are sharp. A little extra time spent at the grinder and stones with your block

planes and chisels will be well rewarded.

Fitting the breasthook is tricky because you have to work on three mating surfaces at once. The quarter knees are much simpler; not only is there one less mating surface, but you can work on each one independently of the other. So, let's tackle the quarter knees first.

Quarter knees

Hold a trimmed quarter knee in place to see how its joints look. Make sure to check if the knee is following the angle you marked on the transom to determine whether you need to adjust the angle along the spacer block (or sheerstrake).

Always fit the edge along the plank first. Mentally note where the high spots are and if you want to change the angle; then brace the knee on a sturdy, well-planted saw horse right next to you and start to trim the joint with a block plane set for a fairly fine cut and lubricated with a little wax. The plane should cut as smoothly as possible so you can maintain absolute control of where it cuts. Hold the plane at angle so it slices the shavings off, not chisels them.

Take three or four swipes with the plane. At this point, the bandsaw blade marks will help you see where you are cutting. Later on you will want pencil slashes.

Hold the knee in the boat again and check to see that you are headed in the right direction. Again, mentally note where and how you want to cut and then take a couple more swipes with the plane.

At this point, if you did a good job scribing and sawing, the joint should be getting pretty close to tight. Scrape off any pencil marks on top of the knee. Put a clamp lamp in the hull under the quarter knee so that it shines up through the joint, illuminating the high spots and gaps. The light will also show you whether the bottom edge is tight or open, and where to plane to improve the fit. Using a lamp takes much of the guesswork and blind luck out of fitting joints.

As the joint gets tighter, back off the blade of your plane so you can make finer, even more controlled cuts. A curved blade on your plane will help you trim exactly where you want to, and also will make the joint slightly concave, allowing the top and bottom to be so tight that the line between the two pieces of wood is nearly invisible yet leaving room for the epoxy (see Chapter 2, "Materials and Tools").

Often, the sheerstrake has a little twist in it where it runs along the quarter knee, which makes fitting the knee interesting. Once you've accomplished this, the rest of the job is almost a snap, because the joint with transom is a straight, angled cut.

Once you're happy with the first quarter knee, do the other.

On each quarter knee, mark the length along the plank side. Draw a square line across the top and cut along the line at 35 degrees on the bandsaw, then clean up the angle with a block plane. This surface will receive the aft end of the gunwale.

Breasthook

Your experience in fitting the quarter knees will serve you well in fitting the breasthook. Use the clamp lamp. Trim the sides evenly, to keep the glue line in the center. If the front is tight, the sides will never fit, so the front must be trimmed first.

Mark the height of camber on the aft ends. Position the breasthook at that height each time you test the fits.

One trick is to make the sides a little bit snug, so that you have to push the hull out a minute distance to make the front end tight. Also, you can relieve the bevel a tiny bit, so the bottom edge is not completely tight to the planking. This creates a tight joint on visible surface, but also leaves plenty of room for epoxy and, mainly, eases fitting. But be careful—it's easy to make that back bevel too big, very quickly. If the bevel is too big, a big fat ugly epoxy-filled joint will appear when you sand the breasthook to shape and will only grow worse the more you sand.

Pencil slashes are absolutely essential for seeing where you're cutting, particularly as the breasthook is so much thicker than the knees and therefore much harder to cut.

9.20 Scribing the transom angles onto a quarter knee.

9.21 Checking the fit of a joint with the aid of a small clamp lamp.

If the breasthook is not quite fitting back aft, reduce the amount of camber slightly. This will tighten up the joints along the spacer blocks (or planking).

When you're happy with the breasthook's fit, mark the desired length on both sides; trace the shape for the aft edge using your pattern; bandsaw out the shape; and clean it up. The end-grain of a thick hardwood breasthook is diabolical stuff to trim with hand tools. Cleaning up the shape on the belt sander clamped to the bench works well (see Chapter 3, "Some Very Useful Techniques"). It's nice to shape the bottom edge with a large bullnose or chamfer that will be comfortable for the hands that will one day carry the boat.

ATTACHING THE BREASTHOOK AND QUARTER KNEES, TEMPORARILY
Breasthook

While holding the breasthook in place, drill and drive a screw on each side. If the breasthook is not quite tight to the inner stem, you can tap it forward with a softwood block and hammer. Line up the breasthook exactly where you want it: flush forward; on the camber marks aft. then drill for and drive the remaining screws. Fasten one side so that it's perfect, then nudge the other side until it lines up just right. (See Photo 9.33, page 195.)

Quarter knees

Hold each quarter knee in place and draw around the end on the transom. Lay out positions for the screws inside the traced line, remembering that all and sundry will see the bungs if you plan to varnish the transom. If your transom has considerable rake to it, you'll want to drill near the lower line, otherwise your drill (and screws) will break out the top of the knee. Drill tapping holes on the marks in the transom, using the Indispensable Perpendicular Drilling Jig as a guide (see page 180).

Trying to hold the quarter knee in just the right place while drilling is difficult at best, and clamping is usually impossible. A piece of double-sided tape laid on the spacer block (or sheerstrake) edge of the knee works marvelously well at keeping the knee from sliding around as you drill. Put the tape on the knee. Tip the knee up so that just the top corner touches the spacer block (or sheerstrake). With the knee in position, it's easy to adjust the height as well as the fore-and-aft position. When it's just right, slowly roll the knee down into position. You'll still want to hold the knee as you drill for the first screw, but the tape keeps the knee in the right place, at least.

Drill and drive one screw along the planking, then drill and drive the screws in the transom. Finish up by drilling for and driving the rest of the screws along the planking.

Gently tunking with a softwood block and a hammer often will close up any persistent gaps.

9.22 Starting to clamp the gunwale to the sheer at the bow, letting the aft end run below the quarter knee at the stern.

9.23 Tapping on the gunwale adjustment tool moves an open gunwale forward to close up the joint with the breasthook.

GUNWALES AND MAST PARTNER

It is more efficient to leave the breasthook and quarter knees temporarily fastened in the boat, then work on fitting the gunwales dry. After that job is done, we'll explain how to permanently install the breasthook, quarter knees, gunwales, and related parts all at the same time.

Now that the breasthook and quarter knees are holding the boat in its proper shape at the ends, you can take out the spreaders. Stash the midship spreader someplace where you can find it; after the gunwales are in, you'll need to adjust the spreader for the thickness of the gunwales and put it back while you measure for and install the thwarts and seats.

Gunwales

If you decided to hold off on making the gunwales, spurred on by desire to see your boat off the jig, now is the time to make them (refer back to Chapter 8, "'Outbone' and Rails, Then Off the Jig").

Both open and solid gunwales should have their exposed lower corners routed (or otherwise shaped) and their bottoms and sides sanded to 100-grit. (The tops will be sanded after gunwales are installed.)

The tricky part of the job is fitting the gunwales' ends. If your boat has simple closed gunwales, the explanation below should cover your needs. If your boat has open gunwales with spacer blocks, see the box on page 193 for additional instructions.

Fitting the ends. First, mark the desired length of the gunwale by measuring from breasthook to quarter knee and adding several inches for insurance.

Fit the bow end first. Measure the vertical and horizontal angles of the breasthook and mark these on the end of the gunwale, just as you did the rails. Cut at the marks with a handsaw, then clean up with a very sharp block plane.

Clamp a 1½″ square block just aft of the breasthook for the gunwale end to rest upon. Hold the gunwale in place with a few clamps near the bow, letting the aft end of the gunwale run under the quarter knee. Tap the gunwale end under the quarter knee to close up the gap at the end of the breasthook. (See box, "Gunwale Adjustment Strategies," for other approaches to this vexing little job.) John is also not above giving the gunwale an extra tunk to encourage the joint tight. Tunk, don't wallop. Several tunks are better than one wallop. Inspect the joint. Where does it need trimming?

Fitting the joint is a tedious job, because you have to remove the whole gunwale for each trim. Pencil slashes are a big help, as usual. Usually after a couple of trims the joint will be looking pretty good. Resist the temptation to take off a lot of wood at once, thinking that this will make the job go faster; the joint will just open up somewhere else. Try scribing a line with a compass on the gunwale that is parallel to the end of the breasthook and about ⅛″ from the joint. Although you don't want to cut to this line, you'll find cutting parallel to it surprisingly helpful. You can also cut back (with a chisel) the invisible part of the joint a little bit so that the visible joint comes tight more easily. Don't cut a lot; this is a structural joint.

9.24 Laying out the length of the gunwale by marking the end of the spacer block on the gunwale. Measure and mark the distance to the end of the quarter knee at the sheer, add 1/4" or 1/2", then mark the angles and trim with a hand saw.

When the joint at the breasthook is tight, clamp the rest of the gunwale in place. Hold the end of the gunwale as close to the quarter knee as you can. Mark the gunwale where the joint ought to be, judging by eye or by measuring from where the gunwale is flush with the sheer to the joint and laying this distance out on the gunwale. Make another mark ¼″ to ½″ aft of the first. Measure the joint's horizontal and vertical angles on the quarter knee and lay out the joint at the second mark on the gunwale.

You don't have to take the gunwale out of the boat to cut and trim the joint. Put a small piece of plywood across the top of the sheerstrakes and lay the end of the gunwale on top to saw it. Trim with a small block plane. This is a little awkward, but it certainly beats taking the

9.25 Gunwale adjustment tool.

Gunwale Adjustment Strategies

If necessity is the mother of invention, frustration is the father of jigs. Using a block of wood and a hammer to move the gunwale forward to close up the joint just doesn't work well.

For open gunwales, make a gunwale adjustment tool. Grab a ¾″ hardwood scrap and bandsaw out the shape shown. Next, turn the blank on edge and resaw it for about half its length to a thickness 1/16″ less than the gunwale blocks. Leave the back end square, giving plenty of area for the hammer to hit.

For closed gunwales, you can tap the gunwale's square aft end before it is trimmed for the quarter

knee. After the joint for the quarter knee is cut, clamp a block to the top edge of the gunwale and tunk the block. You'll find that the block and clamp move, no matter how tight the clamp is. Just hope that the gunwale moves enough to close the joint. You might try sticking the block to the gunwale with double-sided tape or gluing a piece of sandpaper to the block. If you're painting the gunwales, you can screw a block to the gunwale face and address that.

9.26 Final trimming of the aft end of the gunwale in the boat.

9.27 Fasten the gunwale in place when the joint with the quarter knee is tight. The portion of the gunwale that is proud of the top of the knee will be trimmed when the top of the gunwales and rails are sanded.

gunwale out of the boat repeatedly. A sharp blade and a little wax helps.

If the gunwale is a little proud of the top of the quarter knee when the joint is tight, that's okay. Getting the joint tight is the main objective. Don't risk cutting the gunwale too short by trimming too much, trying to make it flush with the quarter knee. Leave it, and trim flush after the gunwale is permanently installed.

As the aft joint approaches tight, check the forward joint periodically. Once in a while, movement of the gunwale will make the forward joint crawl open. Tap it tight again.

Fastening in place, temporarily. Carefully drill for and gently drive two screws through the gunwale at each end. Drill the countersinks for shallow wood bungs and offset the screws to avoid splitting the wood. Drill for and drive every other screw. That's it for the first gunwale; on to the second.

Final attachment. Because you now have everything nicely screwed together, it's time to take everything apart, including the breasthook and quarter knees.

If you prefer to install the gunwales with bedding compound to allow their removal (someday), brush a coat

of clear sealer or thinned varnish on the mating surfaces of the breasthook, gunwales, sheerstrake, and quarter knees. Don't bother to seal entire parts—you'll just end up sanding a fair bit of it off later. Let the sealer or varnish dry.

If you prefer to glue the parts in with epoxy putty, all surfaces to be glued must be bare wood. Scrape away any errant sealer or varnish on the hull if you've already begun finishing.

Reinstall the parts with bedding compound or epoxy putty, beginning with the breasthook and quarter knees. If the parts don't quite come up tight, give them a tunk with a softwood block and a hammer. Install the goo-laden gunwales in much the same way you did when they were dry: clamp the forward end in place with the aft end under the quarter knee; tap forward until the joint at the breasthook is tight; *gently* drive the screws at the forward end, by hand; drive several screws into gunwale near the bow; position and clamp the after end of the gunwale on the quarter knee; drive the rest of the gunwale screws; and, finally, *gently* hand-drive the screws into the aft end. (See Appendix A, "Oh, @#!," if the gunwale splits at the ends.)

Drill for and drive the screws for the rest of the screws into the gunwales.

Clean up the worst of the squeeze-out with a putty knife, followed by a paper towel dampened with thinner, for bedding compound, or denatured alcohol, for epoxy (wear gloves). Expect the bedding compound to ooze for a day or so more. In a few days, the compound will be somewhat dry, and you can scrape or gently chisel off the later oozes. Just be careful when leaning over the gunwale in the meantime.

If your boat has half-frames, you may install them permanently now.

Oarlock socket blocks and filler pieces

Oarlock socket blocks range from straightforward pads with slightly rounded edges to ornate pedestals with

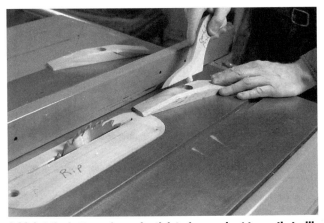

9.28 Cut the bottom of a push-stick to form a short tenon that will fit in the hole of an oarlock block to hold the block safely while you bevel the sides on the table saw.

If Your Boat Has Open Gunwales with or without Spacer Blocks

Fitting and installing open gunwales with spacer blocks involves a few extra steps. If your boat has open gunwales but no spacer blocks, follow the general instructions given above, but measure directly from the breasthook to the quarter knee. And, of course, you may skip past the bits involving installation the spacer blocks.

•If your boat has open gunwales and spacer blocks, measure the distance between the ends of the spacer blocks to get what we call the spacer length, then measure from the first gunwale block to the last for the gunwale block length. Subtract the gunwale block length from the spacer length and divide the result by two. Lay out this distance from the first and last gunwale blocks. On the forward end of the gunwale, mark off the distance from the end of the spacer block to the aft end of the breasthook, then layout the joint with the breasthook, just as you would for a closed gunwale. Cut and trim.

On the aft end of the gunwale, mark off the length from the forward end of the spacer block to the aft end of the joint on the quarter knee. Add a couple of inches and cut the end of the gunwale off square.

•During the trial fit you may find that some of the gunwale blocks fall on top of the half-frames (and full frame(s) if any). Mark these blocks with a dark X. Take the gunwale out, hold it next to its mate and mark Xs on the corresponding blocks. Cut the marked blocks on both gunwales off close to the glue line (John uses the bandsaw), then hand plane off the remaining slivers and glue.

•At some point when the gunwales are out of the boat, note which of the screws you put into the rail to pull the planking tight that fall under gunwale blocks, and back these out.

9.29 A strip of clear packing tape prevents a quarter knee from becoming stuck to the transom when gluing the knee to the spacer block.

•When you install the gunwales for the first time, drive screws in every other block. Drill for the rest of the blocks later, during final installation. Save drilling into the half-frame heads until after the gunwales are permanently in, as well.

•If you plan to use bedding compound for the final installation, the spacer blocks must be glued to the breasthook and quarter knees, but not to the hull. Remove the dry-fitted breasthook, quarter knees, and spacer blocks. Mask off the back of the inner stem and the inside of the transom with clear packing tape. If the tape overlaps the planking at the transom, trim it on the inside corner with a utility knife. (You don't have to worry about epoxy on the planking, because the spacer blocks sit between the glue joints and the planking.) Put a little paste wax on the screws you'll be using, to keep the epoxy from gluing them permanently in place.

Mix up a small batch of epoxy and wet out the surfaces to be glued: the mating surfaces between each spacer block and its quarter knee or breasthook side. Do not put epoxy between the spacer blocks and the hull. Mix some fine sawdust with the remaining epoxy to thicken and color it. Push screws through the rail/planking and just enough into the spacers to hold them in place. Put a little of the epoxy putty on the edges of each part, hold the part in place, and drive the middle screw.

If the breasthook is not quite tight at the inner stem, tap it into place with a hammer and block. This works for the quarter knees also, but try driving the screws into the transom first and only resort to persuasion if the joint doesn't pull up.

Drive the rest of the screws. Check the height of the quarter knees in relation to the spacer blocks. If they aren't flush, adjust them with a few taps. If this doesn't work, you'll have to wait for the glue to dry, then trim either the knee or spacer block.

Clean up the squeeze out and let the epoxy harden for at least 24 hours. As soon as the epoxy has kicked well (overnight), break the screws loose by backing each one out a few turns. Retighten the screws and leave in place until the epoxy fully cures.

•If you are gluing the breasthook, quarter knees, and gunwales in the boat, you don't have to fool around with the tape. Simply glue and screw the spacer blocks to the hull as well as to the appropriate breasthook or quarter knee.

•Permanently install open gunwales as you would closed gunwales. Try a paper towel wrapped around a stir stick or putty knife to remove the bedding compound or epoxy putty from the gunwale block slots.

scrolled, carved ends. We generally give our boats simple yet elegant tapered blocks with beveled sides and ends. We finish the socket blocks separately and install them, with their sockets, after the gunwales are varnished or painted (see Chapter 13, "Fitting Out").

For open gunwales, make filler pieces to fit in gunwale slots that will reside under the oarlock socket blocks. Coat these with bedding compound (or epoxy putty) and slip them into place. If you used bedding compound, fasten the filler pieces in place with screws driven from the inside of the hull, just as you did the half-frame heads. If you plan to install gunwale guard, you can drive the screws in through the rail, in the areas that will be covered by the gunwale guard.

Mast partner

Our boats have their mast partners installed under the gunwale, instead of on top; the boats just look better that way to us. A two-piece pattern makes the job go quicker and assures a tight fit.

Put the midship spreader in, remembering to adjust its blocks to compensate for the gunwales now in the boat.

Fitting the partner. Measure the width of and shape of the hull under the gunwales at the scored lines for the cen-

9.30 Scribing a mast partner reinforcing piece.

9.31 Fastening the mast partner reinforcing piece in place.

ter of the mast using two scraps of planking plywood for a pattern. Rip the scraps to the same width as the partner and cut them long enough to overlap each other in the boat. Mark a centerline on both patterns, then clamp them to each other and to the gunwales with small clamps. Make sure that the patterns' long edges are parallel to the mast's athwartships centerline. Scribe the curve of the hull onto the bottom of each pattern, remove the patterns, and trim to the lines. Reposition the patterns in the boat, lining them up and clamping as before. Likely as not, you'll have to rescribe and trim again to get a tight fit to the hull. When the patterns fit the hull, clamp them in the boat again, making sure the centerlines on the patterns line up with the score lines for the center of the mast.

Next, measure the angle between the top of the patterns and the face of the gunwale. Hold the bevel gauge *perpendicular* to the gunwale, not parallel to the edges of the pattern.

Without removing the clamps holding the patterns together, remove the pattern pair from the boat. Fasten the pair together with a couple of short screws, then remove the clamps.

Mark the mast partner blank using the pattern. Set the bandsaw or jigsaw to the gunwale angle, then trim the ends of the partner, making sure to leave a little extra wood for final fitting.

You can drill the hole for the mast and shape the partner's edges any time after the partner is fitted.

Hold the partner under the gunwales as far forward as it will go. Bevel the top of the partner ends a little to fit the angle of the gunwales. Trim the partner until its ends contact the hull nicely and the athwartships centerline on the partner lines up with the scored lines on the hull.

Making and installing mast partner reinforcing pieces. In many of our boats, the mast partner is bolted to reinforcing pieces attached to the gunwales.

Clamp the partner in place. Hold a blank for a reinforcing piece on top of the partner and scribe it with a compass to the gunwale's curve and angle. Trim on the bandsaw. Clean up the cut with a block plane, then hold the reinforcing piece on the partner. You'll note that the ends of the straight reinforcing piece dip below the lower edge of the curved gunwale. Mark the bottom of the gunwale on the reinforcing piece and also mark the width of the partner. Bandsaw and hand-plane the taper at the ends. Don't plane the area where the partner lands. This approach puts a lovely taper on the otherwise clunky reinforcing piece.

Mark the width of the partner on the exposed straight edge so you'll know where to stop your bullnose or chamfer on the bottom edge.

Do the other reinforcing piece. Draw pyramid half on each so you don't accidentally switch them. After

9.32 The mast partner in this Frances daysailer has two athwartship members bolted to the reinforcing pieces and a slot so the mast can be positioned for sailing with a jib (as shown here) or with main alone.

routing or otherwise shaping the reinforcing pieces' edges, dry-fasten them to the gunwales with screws. Remove the pieces, mix up some epoxy putty, and attach them, redriving the screws. Clean up as usual. Wait until the epoxy has hardened thoroughly before installing the mast partner.

Installing the mast partner (temporarily). On small boats with a partner over the bow seat, like the Ellen, we use carriage bolts and wing nuts so the partner can be removed easily without tools. In larger open boats where the partner doesn't interfere with the use of a seat or thwart, we recommend fastening the partner with screws but leaving the heads exposed, making it easier to remove the partner for refinishing.

Clamp the partner in place, lining up the partner's centerline with scored line on the hull. If you wish to install the mast partner with screws, drill for and drive them in the normal manner. If you are drilling for bolts, start with a drill no more than half the size of the bolt. A large twist drill is likely to breakout a chip or two as it starts. To prevent this: Drill with the smaller bit. Countersink a hole that is a little bigger than the bolt hole will be. Then drill with a bit that is $\frac{1}{64}$" or $\frac{1}{32}$" bigger than the bolt, giving enough room to allow removal of the bolt, even when the wood swells. Hold a scrap of wood under the hole as you drill so the bit doesn't rip out chips at the bottom of the hole. Lightly countersink rest of the edges of the drilled holes. This looks nice and makes it easier to put the bolts in.

To accommodate the square shank under the head of each carriage bolt: Install each bolt, alternately tapping down on the head with a hammer and tightening the wing nut, until the bottom of the head is tight against the reinforcing piece. Remove the bolt by tapping with the

hammer on the wing nut, not the end of the bolt. Using a sharp $\frac{1}{4}$" chisel, slightly enlarge the square hole in the reinforcing cleat until the bolt slips easily in and out of the hole, yet won't spin when the wing nut is tightened.

FINISHING UP THE BREASTHOOK, QUARTER KNEES, GUNWALES, AND RELATED PARTS
Installing bungs

Make up a batch of nicely matched bungs, and glue them in all screw holes in the gunwale and rail. If you're planning on gunwale guard, you can skip this step for the screws in the rail that the gunwale guard will cover. Trim the bungs flush after the glue dries.

Final shaping and sanding

Shaping the rails, gunwales, breasthook, and quarter knees offers a chance to indulge happily in artistic expression, after checking your plans for parts or hardware that might dictate some of your choices.

If you want a flush stem head, trim with a sharp hand saw, then shape and sand flush with the rest of the breasthook. If you'd like a decorative stem head like that possessed by our Ellen, *Iris* (see Photo 11.1, page 222)

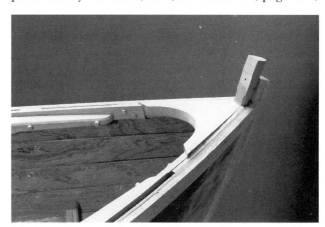

9.33 Bung the screw holes after all the gunwale parts are bedded and fastened in the boat.

9.34 Starting the camber of the breasthook by hand-planing a facet flush with the sheer.

trim the inner stem flush, the outer stem to the proper height, fit a piece on the aft side, and shape as desired.

Shape the camber (curve) of the top of the breasthook in a manner similar to making a spar round (see Chapter 11, "If Your Boat Has a Sail"). Cut large facets at the projecting square corners of the breasthook, then trim the corners of the facets to make a number of smaller facets and more corners. Trim these corners with a couple of swipes with a block plane, then knock off the corners the trimming creates. Keep trimming corners until the surface starts to feel curved. Your hand is the best judge. The top of the breasthook wants to blend into the rails and gunwales so the first facet is cut at the same angle as the top of rails and gunwales until it is flush with the spacer block and/or planking adjacent to the rails.

If you made a flexible sanding block for sanding the top of transom, you can sand cross-grain to help smooth the curve of the top of the breasthook, then finish with a belt sander cutting with the grain at the same time you sand the tops of the rails and gunwales.

A small rabbet plane is handy for blending the top of the gunwales into the quarter knees. Hand-plane the tops of gunwales and rails flush with the planking, then clearly mark where the oarlock blocks will land, if your boat has them. Chamfer or bullnose the top corners of the rails and gunwales, except where the oarlock blocks will reside. If you used a router for this shaping, finish the corner treatments at the gunwale and quarter knee meet with a chisel and sandpaper.

Sand, sand, sand. Prepare the gunwales, rails, etc. for finishing by sanding to 120-grit with a belt sander, random-orbit sander, and by hand. We sand and round the chamfered edges slightly, keeping the edges crisp enough

to satisfy aesthetics but soft enough to keep the varnish. Sand the mast partner to the same level, and set it aside for finishing separately. Sand all edges smooth, even those underneath. Well-sanded surfaces hold finish better, and poorly sanded areas lurking under breasthook, quarter knees, and such will be sorely obvious the moment you and your friends pick up the boat on launching day.

Stealth Varnishing

You can get ahead on varnishing the gunwales/rails and transom by finish-sanding now and sneaking in build coats as you work on the interior. Brush down onto the planking, feathering out with a dry brush—or do the whole sheerstrake. A 1" foam brush is absolutely the thing for the gunwale holes. Sand the varnished areas with 220-grit between coats; smooth the planking with 120.

Flotation

Before we continue on with the building of the hull's interior parts, we'd like to pause for a brief discussion of flotation. If your boat needs additional buoyancy in some form to keep her floating at the surface after she flips, your plans should specify exactly how and where to add extra flotation. If you have altered your boat's plans or intend to use the boat differently, you should carefully consider whether the boat now requires extra flotation in addition to that specified in the plans.

Your boat may not need extra flotation. For example, the wood in an Ellen is sufficiently buoyant to meet Coast Guard regulations if she is used without an outboard. The addition of a motor ups the buoyancy requirement significantly, largely due to adding its weight right on the stern.

ADDING EXTRA FLOTATION

Typically, flotation is added as air- and watertight tanks, closed-cell foam, or flotation bags. Any kind of flotation must be fastened securely in the boat. When the boat is flooded, the air trapped in your flotation compartments or bags will want to rise to the surface. Obviously, this is what helps float the boat, but it also puts a tremendous strain on the parts and fastenings holding the flotation in place. Water or air will find any imperfections in your work. Build carefully and well.

Underseat foam flotation boxes

Closed-cell foam is a convenient, easy-to-install, and effective material for flotation. It is ugly and deteriorates in sunlight, so you should build some sort of box for it. Our boats' foam boxes consist of panels that fasten to athwartship stiffening cleats under a seat or thwart. The

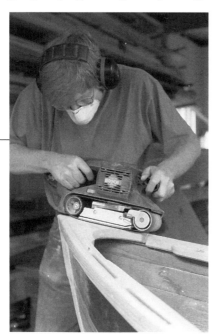

9.35 Finishing the curve of the camber with a belt sander when sanding the rail and gunwale top edges.

"motoring" Ellen has foam boxes under the bow and stern seats. The best time to fit the foam boxes' panels is while measuring and installing the thwarts and seats. You can complete the rest of the work on the boxes when it is convenient, at the bench.

Closed-cell foam billets intended for floating docks satisfy the U.S. Coast Guard's requirements. To install the foam, first rip it to the width. The bandsaw is the only stationary power tool that can handle cutting large blocks of foam. Because foam cuts easily with a handsaw, you can do all necessary cutting by hand.

Lay a block of foam in the bottom of the flotation box and trace its shape. Hold the foam on edge and cut along the lines with a hand saw. Trim the foam with a handheld piece of coarse sanding belt or grinding disc, 60-grit or coarser. Make as many pieces as needed to fill the box.

If your bow seat has a mast hole, cut a passage through the foam with a jigsaw. Clean up the hole, and line it with thin-walled sewer pipe. The interior of the pipe we use is black, and looks a whole lot better than bright blue foam.

Because cotton-candy-colored foam doesn't enhance varnished Douglas-fir seat panels, we make a plywood panel ($\frac{1}{8}$″ or $\frac{1}{4}$″) to fit underneath, and paint it like the rest of the foam box to match the hull interior.

Once the finish on the foam boxes, seats, and thwarts is good and dry, you can fasten the foam boxes in place.

Flotation tanks

Many small boats have seats and thwarts that are also flotation tanks. Each is essentially a bulkhead (or two) with a flat panel glued on top. The U.S. Coast Guard currently requires flotation tanks for most boats to be filled with foam or some sort of sealed flotation bags or bladders. (We have heard of people successfully using empty plastic, screwtop jugs.) The rationale behind this regulation is that if the boat hits a rock, the hull will have a hole and so will the tank. Sailboats are excepted from this requirement; they can have simple airtanks because they most frequently flood from capsizing. (If you have questions about how these requirements affect your boat's construction, contact the closest U.S. Coast Guard station. They can pass you along to person who handles small-boat construction matters for your district.)

The next section in this chapter explains how to measure for and install bulkheads and horizontal panels. The process of building these does not differ markedly for sealed flotation tanks. Just be sure to attach the panels very securely, with cleats and screws, and epoxy fillets. Thoroughly paint or epoxy-seal the inside of the tank and the bottom of top panel, leaving gluing areas bare, then attach the top panel. Ideally, for looks fillets should go on the inside of the tank, but this isn't always easy or possible. A small fillet (made with a $\frac{1}{2}$″ or $\frac{3}{4}$″ dowel) along the

outside edge of the panel will look fine. If you can, add some kind of air- and watertight access ports to your tanks for periodic inspection and refinishing.

Flotation bags

Our neighbors on the other side of the Atlantic often use flotation bags in small dinghies and daysailers, but you don't see them all that often in our part of the world, except in a few boats like the Optimist prams and, of course, kayaks and canoes. They are available from suppliers like Defender and Holt (see Appendix B, "Resources").

We haven't installed flotation bags in any of our boats, but we've been considering them for a small racing daysailer. Their great advantage is ease of construction: call up your supplier, melt a little plastic, and they're yours. No messing around with epoxy fillets and oddly shaped panels. They come right out of the boat for cleanups and refinishing. They'll also come right out of the boat when you dump her if you don't fasten them in very securely. Follow the manufacturer's recommendations, but several 2″-wide straps, tightly cinched around the bag and well-attached to the hull, is a starting place. Think about chafe from the straps and against the hull or framing when installing the bags. If the bag is headed for a location where it will see a lot of abuse, you might consider foam or a tank instead.

For small boats such as kayaks and canoes, dry bags filled with clothing and reasonably light gear provide significant flotation, if they stay in the boat.

Bulkheads and Horizontal Panels

Bulkheads may be small panels under the seats and thwarts for flotation tanks or fish wells, or full-hull panels that carry a deck. Glued-lapstrake boats typically have bulkheads made of plywood or a lighter panel material (see Chapter 2, "Materials and Tools"). Your boat may also have horizontal panels attached to the bulkheads for seats, thwarts, or side benches.

BULKHEADS
Measuring (spiling) the hull shape

You should have bulkhead positions laid out along the sheer and keelson (see page 171).

Clamp a straightedge on the bulkhead position. Line up the edge of the straightedge by sighting the mark on the keelson and mark the position of the bulkhead on the inside of the planking, drawing short lines every couple of inches.

You'll need a piece of pattern plywood that fits comfortably with a modest gap in the space you want to fit the bulkhead. For small boats $\frac{1}{4}$″ plywood will work fine; for

9.36 Spiling the shape of the hull with a yardstick on a piece of pattern plywood.

9.37 A little shaving with a block plane is all that is needed to make the bulkhead slide into place. The top will be marked for trimming after the bulkhead is fitted.

large bulkheads on bigger boats, stiffer ⅜″ plywood will make your measuring job easier.

Move the straightedge away from the bulkhead marks by the thickness of the pattern ply, and clamp the pattern to it. Hold the lower edge of the pattern ply on the marks on the hull with small blocks attached to the planking with double-sided tape or hot-melt glue. Once the pattern is positioned, screw it to the straightedge with drywall screws, countersinking the heads flush.

Put a yardstick (preferably a metal one) flat on the pattern ply and slide it until the end sits squarely against on the centerline on the keelson. Draw a line along one edge of the yardstick, then mark and label a standard distance on the pattern (for boats of the size we're primarily discussing in this book, we suggest using 10″ or 20″, but any number, English or metric, will do). Repeat this process, using the same standard distance, all along where the bulkhead will contact, and a little beyond for partial bulkheads. Measure the hull at each lap; any small gaps will be easily filled with epoxy when the bulkhead is installed and filleted.

If your standard distance won't work for some areas, pick a second standard distance that is clearly different from the first by a goodly amount, say 6″ to 10″.

Measuring the bulkhead shape this way is so delightfully accurate that you can measure for the cutouts for the keelson and, on a full bulkhead, gunwales or deck cleats.

With a square, transfer the line of the sheer from the bottom of the straightedge to the marked pattern face.

A builder's pyramid is always reassuring. Also mark which way the side of the marked pattern surface faces: A for aft and F for forward.

Working Ahead on Bulkheads

When making bulkheads, do as much work on them as you can before installing them. For example, structural cleats, hatches, and access ports are much easier to work on when the bulkhead is on the work bench.

Cutting out and installing

Pull the screws holding the pattern to the straightedge and lay the pattern on the bulkhead material. If the bulkhead is only a partial one, measure its height (usually from the sheer) and mark it on the pattern. Position the pattern with extra panel stock at the top, so you can fit and trim the bulkhead without having to worry about making it too short. Clamp the pattern in place. Lay out the shape of the bulkhead by reversing the process you used to measure it: line up the same yardstick with each line and the standard distance, and draw a short line at the end of the yardstick on the panel stock. A little trick is to use a small block with square sides and edges: butt the block squarely against the end of the yardstick and hold it in place; remove the yardstick; then draw along the edge of the block that touched the yardstick. This eliminates any inaccuracies from angling the pencil. If you use the block, save the line when you cut out the bulkhead, as the outer edge of the line represents the actual surface of the planking.

Repeat this process for all the lines on the pattern, then remove the pattern and connect the short lines with a ruler and pencil. Next, cut out the bulkhead. Unless the bulkhead is small and fits comfortably on the bandsaw, the jigsaw is the best tool for the job. Fit the bulkhead in the hull, trimming and beveling the panel with a block plane as necessary. Once the bulkhead fits nicely against of the hull, use the straightedge to lay out the top of a partial bulkhead or a deck beam to mark the curve of a bulkhead under a deck.

Trim the top of the bulkhead. Cut any holes for hatches, lightening holes, or access ports.

To secure the bulkhead to the boat, first drill through the planking for small screws or nails to hold the bulkhead firmly in place. Wet out with epoxy the edge of the bulkhead and the planking where the bulkhead will touch. Put the bulkhead in place and drive the screws or nails. Make putty out of the remaining epoxy and use a putty knife to fill any gaps between the planking and bulkhead. Clean up any excess epoxy and putty.

While the epoxy cures, decide the width of the fillet you want to use. For example, a ⅝″ fillet works well for the bulkheads in Ellen's nesting version. (Refer to suggestions given by the boat's designer or epoxy suppliers for definitive answers on the proper size fillet to use in your particular case.) Make a filleting tool: an 8″ piece of doweling of the appropriate diameter (twice the width of the fillet). Find a pair of gloves.

After the epoxy has hardened well (at least overnight) mark the width of the fillets on the planking and bulkhead with a compass, then run a strip of masking tape along the lines. Wet out the areas to be filleted, and mix a batch of putty that is about the consistency of smooth peanut butter. Use very fine sawdust and colloidal silica so the putty is smooth, not lumpy. The smoother you can form the fillets now, the easier the sanding job will be later.

First, use the fillet tool to distribute the putty in the corner for several feet. If you have made fillets in the past, you will find that the dowel works much better for this job than a plastic squeegee cut to the same radius as the dowel. Next, smooth out the blobs of putty into a clean fillet while holding the dowel at a low angle and tight in the corner. Excess putty will be pushed onto the tape and is easily cleaned up with a putty knife. If there are holes in the fillet, scoop up some putty on the end of the dowel and run it down the fillet again.

Form the fillets on the rest of the bulkhead. Let the putty kick to a rubbery consistency, then you can pull the tape. It does the heart good to see a nicely formed fillet and right next to it perfectly clean plywood that doesn't need any scraping or sanding. The tape does leave a very small ridge along the fillet; sanding the fillet with a piece of coarse-grit sanding belt will smooth up little bumps in the fillet and sand these ridges flush. Finish sanding the fillet with our favorite weapon for curves: a thin sanding sponge.

The sooner you sand the fillets after they pass the hopeless paper-clogging stage, the softer and easier to sand they will be. Sanding fillets is a pain in the posterior—at best. If the fillet will be clearly visible and looks like it will need plenty of sanding, try this: Sand off the major bumps. Mix a batch of epoxy putty with fairing compound, aiming for a putty that is smooth and as easy to sand as possible. Apply the putty over the bumpy fillet with the same-sized dowel, or one slightly larger.

HORIZONTAL PANELS

On some boats, you may need to make horizontal panels that fit against the side of the hull for seats, flotation

9.38 Fillets of epoxy putty strengthen the bond between the bulkhead and the hull. Keep the job neat and easy to clean up with masking tape. (This elaborate bulkhead is one side of a matched pair for the nesting version of Ellen.)

tanks, etc. You have a choice of two methods: scribing and spiling. Scribing is arguably simpler, and is the easiest technique for fitting side seats or benches that must follow the curve of the hull. For more complicated panels, such as the bow and stern seats, where several edges must fit tight, spiling is best.

Scribing

A common approach is to slide the horizontal panels into place and scribe the gentle fore-and-aft curve of the hull along the edge with a compass. This works fine as long as the point of the compass stays on the same plane as the panel, which takes practice. Using a yardstick, or the steel ruler from a try-square, either flat or on edge on the panel ensures that you stay on the same plane.

Important note: When scribing a horizontal panel, always hold the ruler or compass parallel to the direction the panel will be slid to fit tight against the hull. If you hold the ruler or compass perpendicular to the hull, the curve you draw will not match the hull at all.

To mark the hull shape, with a ruler, choose a standard distance for all measurements, usually the widest distance to the hull. Before you remove the panel, measure the angle of the hull at several points. A convenient place to record these is on the straight edge of the panel opposite the one where you marked the curve of the hull. Remove the panel. Draw the hull curve through the marks with a batten. Cut the curve on the bandsaw or with a jigsaw.

Determining the panel's bevel. To figure the amount of bevel necessary to fit the panel edge tight against the hull, set a try-square blade to the thickness of the panel and draw or score a line through the marked angles, parallel to the straight panel edge. Then use a square to draw a line at each angle from two points: where the angle crosses the straight edge of the panel, and where it crosses the parallel line. The distance between these two square lines is the width of the bevel you need to mark on the bottom of the panel along the cut-out curve. This is similar to the process for calculating the bevels for the transom, but you are looking for a different variable. For the transom, you were looking for the degree of angle to cut. On the horizontal panel, you measured the angle from the hull but you want to know the width of the bevel, which would be the distance between the lines on the transom pattern.

Transfer the measurements for the bevel to the bottom of the panel edge that will fit against the hull. Connect the points with the batten, then cut the bevel with a block plane or disc grinder.

Spiling

Spile the horizontal panel as you would a bulkhead: Tack a piece of pattern ply in place, then record the shape of the hull with a yardstick or shorter rule. Measure and record the angle between the panel top and the hull in several places, so you can bevel the panel edges (as above). Transfer the shape of the panel to the sheet material, cut out the shape, and bevel the edges. The panel should drop into place with a slight whoosh of air.

Floors and Floor Frames

Your plans may call for floors or floor frames to strengthen the bottom of the boat to support a lead keel or to stiffen the bottom of a powerboat. These structural members can be sawn. Floor frames are often laminated for modern hulls with few frames. It's not unusual for these parts to be attached to bulkheads.

Think about how water will drain through the bilge. John prefers to fit floor frames so that they contact only at the laps. You'll need to cut or drill limber holes in the bottom of floors.

Sawn. The shape of the hull can be marked on floors and floor frames by scribing. The shape of the bottom of most boats makes this a much easier job than scribing half-frames. On flatter-bottomed boats where the scribing distance is small, you can often get by with one scribe and trim. You'll probably need to scribe twice for boats with deeper bilges. If so, make the first scribe a quick one—all you want to do is cut off a majority of excess wood so you can make a smaller, more precise scribe. If the floors must be beveled to fit the planking, cut this bevel at least close on the first trim to make positioning and the second scribe easier and more precise.

Laminated. Laminated floor frames are best glued up on stout battens over the building jig before the hull is planked. (See Chapter 3, "Some Very Useful Techniques," for general instructions, and Chapter 6, "The Backbone, and Lining Off").

Thwarts and Seats

If you have not already done so, install the risers (see page 184). Put the midships spreader into place, making sure that it is adjusted for the gunwales.

MEASURING AND BUILDING THWARTS AND SEATS, FIRST ROUND

It is easier and more efficient to measure for all of the thwarts and seats at once, then fit and dry-fasten them in the boat—before gluing any of the parts together. Once you have assembled the thwarts and seats initially, you can remove them from the boat and take them to the bench for final shaping, corner treatments, sanding, and re-assembly with glue.

Laying out the thwart and seat positions

Lay out the horizontal distances for the edges of thwarts and seats from the nearest station. (Refer back to the box, "Laying Out from a Station Plane Inside the Hull, page 174). Mark the distances on the risers or riser cleats.

When you've located all of the thwarts and seats, check to see that each edge is the same distance from riser blocks, half-frames, or other structural members on both sides of the boat. Keeping the gap similar between a thwart or seat edge and its neighboring part is more important that aligning the thwart or seat perfectly with an invisible station line.

Measuring lengths of the thwarts and seats

To measure the length of the thwarts and the seats, you'll need a simple jig (see box). We strongly suggest that you use the jig. If you prefer to just go ahead and attempt cutting the thwarts and seats to fit without it, at least start with the longest one and make plenty of spare blanks.

9.39 Using a straight-edge clamped at a station and a tape measure to mark the positions of the thwarts and seats.

Making a Thwart- and Seat-Measuring Jig

The measuring jig is made of two 3"-wide strips of ½" plywood with blocks fastened to the ends. If you want to get fancy, you can make the short sleeves of cleats and ¼" plywood shown in the sketch. These should be a slip fit over the plywood strips. The sleeves only hold the strips together while you adjust the jig; you'll still want to clamp or screw them together.

The shape of blocks on the ends of the jig depends on the part you need to measure. For a thwart, the block needs to be as long as the thwart width. For narrow, athwartships support cleats used for paneled bow and stern seats, use a short piece of cleat. If you plan

to fasten the thwarts and seats directly to the risers, cutting simple square dadoes in the jig's end blocks will allow them to lock positively on top of the riser, and make measuring easier. If the thwarts and seats fasten to riser cleats attached to the hull, the dadoes are unnecessary, as the blocks merely need to touch the hull's surface. Attach the blocks to the ends of the plywood strips with one screw so they can pivot.

Adjust the jig by moving the strips over each other to the desired width, pivoting the blocks on the ends to the desired angle until the dado locks on the riser, or the block touches the hull, then clamping or screwing the strips together to hold them.

Fig 9.8 An essential jig for measuring for thwarts and seats.

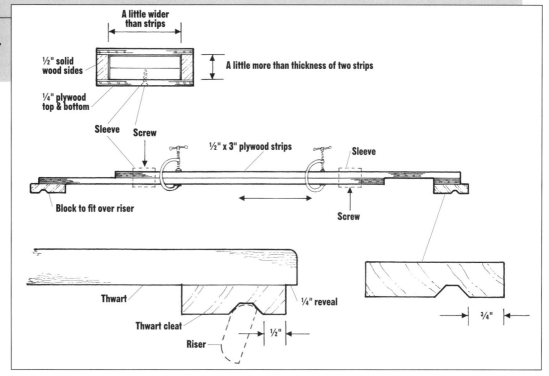

Measuring, fitting, and installing a simple thwart

In order to keep things clearer, we're first going to describe how to deal with one unadorned thwart.

Measuring with the thwart-measuring jig. Using the measuring jig is pretty straightforward. Put the blocks over the risers; adjust their position until one end is even with the edge of the thwart's mark. Clamp or screw the strips together. Driving another screw into each end block to hold its angle is a good idea, though not essential if you work carefully.

If you are attaching your thwart to riser cleats attached to the hull, you can use the thwart-measuring jig as a guide to measure the proper angle on the tops of each cleat. Adjust the jig until the lower corner of the jig's blocks push tight to the hull, then scribe along the bottom of each block to mark the angle on the end of each

cleat. Take the pair of riser cleats out of the boat and trim the tops to the scribed lines by ripping on the table saw

9.40 Measuring the length of a thwart with the thwart-measuring jig.

9.41 A thwart trimmed and ready for screws. (This simple thwart has extra support cleats under its ends.)

9.42 Clamp the thwart firmly in place before drilling for screws into the riser.

or bandsaw, then cleaning up with a few strokes of a block plane. Re-install the riser cleats, then measure the thwart's length. We recommend leaving the ends of the thwarts square; a joint fitted along the hull soon opens and collects dirt.

Lay the jig on the thwart stock, lining up the end of the blocks with the edge of the thwart. Trace along the end blocks with a pencil. If the blocks don't quite reach the opposite edge, extend the lines with a straightedge.

Sawing out and trimming. You can trim the thwart with the table saw's miter gauge. Place two spacers, at least ½″ thick, between the thwart and the miter gauge fence so you can see the table saw's miter gauge slot on both edges of the thwart. Set the fence at the proper angle by lining up the trim line on the thwart with the miter gauge slot. At the other end, mark the trim line on the edges of thwart and flip it over to check the trim angle. If the angle isn't the same, adjust the miter gauge to half the difference. Remove the spacer blocks and trim both ends of the thwart to the same angle. Clamp the thwart securely to the workbench and clean up with the belt sander, block plane, and/or sanding block.

You also can trim the ends with a bandsaw or jig-

saw, then clean up the cut with a belt sander. John likes to use a pattern to mark the ends of thwarts that rest on risers with a gentle curve. Make the pattern long enough to span the width of a thwart that will be trimmed to a steep angle.

Installing. Lay the thwart on the risers or cleats, lined up with the location marks. Clamp the thwart in place, then mark and drill for screws. Locate the screws just a little inboard of the center of the top of the riser or cleat (see box).

Tactics for Drilling Screws into the Risers or Riser Cleats

At first glance, you would think that you should drill the screws for the risers or riser cleats right through the middle of their tops. However, this is not so, as the risers or riser cleats follow the angle of the hull. Drill through the inside corner: on a riser, you will find more wood for the screws to address; on a riser cleat, your bit could bore through the outboard face of the planking if you try to drill in the middle.

Particular thwarts

Thwarts with stiffening cleats. Our boats' thwarts and seats often need one or two cleats fastened underneath, athwartships, to make them stiff enough to support hefty and energetic rowers and passengers. These cleats offer a good opportunity to indulge in a little shapely woodworking (see Photo 9.43). Use patterns to reproduce the desired form on each stiffening cleat (see Chapter 3, "Some Very Useful Techniques").

To attach the cleats, begin by trimming each one to length.

Mark the center on the top edge and one face of the stiffening cleat, and the center athwartships on the bottom of the thwart. Set the cleat back from the outer edge, and mark a line for screws.

9.43 Gluing and fastening a thwart's stiffening cleat on the bench.

If you need to install stiffening cleats with the thwart in the boat, position a small mirror under the thwart so that you can see the centerline. Hold the stiffening cleat in place, lining up its centerline with the centerline on the thwart. Clamp the stiffening cleat to the thwart in the middle with a wooden hand-screw. Use the try-square set to the setback distance to accurately position one end of the stiffening cleat, then clamp it. Remove the hand-screw in the middle, then position and clamp the other end of the stiffening cleat in the same manner, checking again to be certain that both centerlines are still lined up. Hold the stiffening cleat in place with two screws then drill for the rest, spacing them about 6″ to 8″ apart.

Under-thwart foam flotation. If your boat has foam flotation in a box under the thwarts, take a few minutes before you remove the thwarts to fit the panels that will hold and conceal the foam, if the panels must be scribed to fit the hull. We keep the foam boxes clear of the hull by about 1″, mostly so fingers or toes can't become jammed in the gap. (For more on foam flotation boxes and other types of flotation, refer back to page 196.)

Rowing thwart abutting the trunk. The Ellen and many other small sailboats have a rowing thwart that attaches to the trunk. The trunk and thwart support each other.

If you used a full-sized pattern to make the trunk, you should have been able to accurately shape the trunk to fit under the thwart. In an ideal world, a new thwart would always settle perfectly onto the trunk and its cleats. However, the top of the trunk sometimes needs to be trimmed. To measure the amount to be trimmed, place equal-sized spacers between the thwart and its hull supports. Use a third piece or a compass set to the same thickness to scribe a line on the trunk. Trim the trunk to the line with a block plane.

If your thwart should, but does not, rest on the trunk, make spacers (usually wedge-shaped) to fill the gap. Make the spacers a little thicker than needed and glue them to the trunk. Mark and trim the spacers to the right height as described above for trimming the trunk itself. The trunk cap normally will cover the ends of the spacers.

Movable rowing thwart. The Ellen and other boats of her size or larger often can be set up to be rowed from three positions: roughly amidships for a single rower; forward and aft for two rowers; and forward for a single rower with a passenger or gear. The riser system makes it easy to move the aftermost rowing thwart between two positions; the forward thwart remains fixed.

Use carriage bolts and wingnuts, with appropriate matching holes drilled through the riser, for a simple and effective movable rowing thwart.

9.44 Trimming the tops of the trunk cleats for a thwart. A beveled cut has been made to the scribed line on both trunk cleats. Next, the inboard edges will be trimmed until flat.

Thwarts with support posts. If your design calls for posts instead of stiffening cleats or you just like the looks of them, here's how to fit and install them.

Typically, the post is centered under the thwart. First, lay out the post's position on the bottom of the thwart, then measure the distance from the post to the thwart edge—a tick strip is the easiest and most accurate tool. Use the punch mark at the station lines to locate the same thwart edge on the keelson, then lay out the position of the post on the keelson, using the tick strip for the fore-and-aft position, and centered athwartships.

Cut two pieces of thin wood or plywood the width of the post but shorter than the length. Use these like the thwart measuring jig to measure the length of the post, from the underside of thwart to keelson with the help of a small mirror. Measure at the post's shortest point. Clamp the two pieces together. Scribe the post's fore-and-aft angles at the keelson and thwart with a compass. Remove the measuring rig, carefully.

Draw a pyramid so you know which angle belongs against the keelson. Record the length of the post-to-be on the tick strip, then layout the post on your stock. Cutting the post a little longer than your measurement will spring some curve into the thwart and firmly hold the post in place.

Thwart posts typically are held in place by tenons lodged in mortises. We don't recommend that you cut the mortises into the keelson or thwart because they make excellent water traps. Instead, make a base for each end of the post from two U-shaped pieces of wood or plywood. Position these around the end of the post to form a ⅛″ or ¼″ gap that will allow water to drain.

MEASURING, FITTING, AND INSTALLING SEATS
Plank seats

If your seats are glued up from a couple of planks, then sawed out to pleasing curves forward and aft, you can measure their length in much the same way as you measured the thwarts. When measuring and laying out for

9.45 A straightforward painted plank seat.

9.47 Measuring the length of the panel-carrying cleats for a paneled seat in the bow.

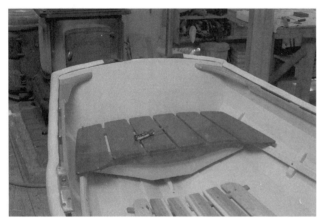

9.46 Seats made up of thin panels can be made of a lovely wood and varnished until they glow.

9.48 Cutting the dado for the riser in the panel-carrying cleat.

these seats, be sure to center the jig on the seat blank.

Trim the seat to length and clean up the ends. Put the seat on the risers or riser cleats, lining up with the marks for the edges. Center it athwartships on risers by feeling underneath the ends with your fingers. Clamp the seat in place and drill for the screws.

Multiple-panel seats

We like seats made of multiple panels and which have thin seat panels fastened to flat, athwartship, support cleats that rest on the risers or riser cleats. The seats' relatively thin panel-carrying cleats are prevented from bending by stiffening cleats.

Making the panel-carrying cleats. Measuring is the first job. Screw short pieces of panel-carrying cleat stock onto the ends of the thwart measuring jig. Measure for the various the panel-carrying cleats, marking the cleat stock the same way you did the thwarts. Compare the angles of the ends of the cleats for each seat, using a bevel gauge. Because you won't see the ends of the panel-carrying cleats, the angles on the ends don't have to be exactly the same, though they should be close. However, making the angles all the same will cut down on setting up for cutting the cleats to length. If you would like to cut dadoes in the

9.49 Fastening the dadoed panel-carrying cleats to the risers.

cleats to fit on the risers, do this after crosscutting the cleats to length.

Plan on using at least two screws in each end of the cleats. At this point you can drive one screw in each end, but drill for both.

9.50 Resawing a seat panel blank.

9.51 Holding the seat panels in place with weights and spacers while fastening them.

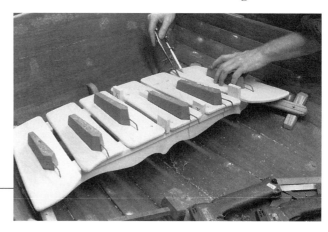

Figuring out the seats' panel size, shape, and spacing. Lay out the seat's fore and aft distance, and half the length (centerline to outboard end) of the panel-carrying cleats on a piece of pattern plywood. Draw the outline of the seat. Decide on the number of panels and the spacing between them.

For seats with four panels, draw circles with a circle template around the centerline for the middle space, then draw the line for one panel edge along the edges of the circles. Divide the remaining distance into two equal parts. Draw a line through these marks, lay out the space centered around the line, round the corners, and you have the shape of the panels.

For seats that have more than four panels, draw a line at half the space *beyond* the outboard edge of the seat panels, then divide the distance from the centerline. Draw lines connecting the dividing points, then mark out the spaces with circle template and ruler. If your seat has an odd number of panels, draw the middle panel's other half.

Making the seat panels. Seat panels for our boats are typically ½″ thick if they are of softwoods like pine, cedar, or Douglas-fir; ⅜″ thick if made of denser, more resilient woods like mahogany or ash. You will be resawing the panels to make pairs, so choose either 1¼″ (5⁄4) or 1½″ (6⁄4) lumber.

Saw apart and clean up your plywood patterns. Trace around them to mark the blanks onto the seat stock and bandsaw the shapes outside the line. Resaw and plane to final thickness. If you wish, attach the plywood patterns with double-sided tape or brads and pattern-rout (see Chapter 3, "Some Very Useful Techniques"). Or, use a different approach: Transfer the shapes to the stock; saw them out; clean up the edges with the stationary belt sander or hand tools; then resaw and plane to final thickness.

Installing the seat panels. Make little spacer blocks about 1″ by 2″ by the same thickness as your between-panel spaces, two per slot. Also make some blocks that are ¹⁄₁₆″ thicker and thinner than your spacing.

Draw centering circles on the cleats' centerlines. Lay the panels on the panel-carrying cleats with spacers blocks in the spaces. Hold the panels in place with weights. Center the edges of the middle panels on the circles you drew on the centerlines.

Is the whole seat not quite wide enough? Put in thicker spacers. Too wide? Get out the thinner spacers. If the front is just right but the back is too narrow, use thicker spacers in the back. You get the idea. Just choose a consistent pattern for the spaces, and the seat will look lovely. There's no need to make ten trips to the bandsaw and fiddle with the plane, trying to get the seat to fit just right. Just mix and match the spacers until the seat pleases you.

Mark for all of the screws, then drill and fasten each panel in place. On the outboard panels, drill now only for screws near the inboard edge; the screws through the outboard edge also go into the riser and will be drilled for later.

Particular seats

Seats with stiffening cleats. Many of our boats' seats benefit from the addition of a pair of stiffening cleats underneath. You can install these much as you would those for thwarts.

9.52 Attach stiffening cleats to the panel-carrying cleats before the seat panels.

9.53 Sighting along the forward and aft edges of the holes in the partner and mast step to mark for a mast hole in the bow seat.

9.54 Drilling a hole for the mast in the bow seat on a drill press.

Stiffening cleats offer an ideal place to attach foam flotation boxes—just make sure that you attach them well.

Bow seat with a hole for a mast. The Ellen, like many small sailboats, is a catboat with a mast that goes through her bow seat. Now is the time to lay out the hole, while the seats are fitted and temporarily fastened in place.

Locating the center of the mast on a paneled seat with a center space is simple, since you can see the step through the gap between the panels. Line up the forward and aft edges of the holes in the mast partner and step; mark each of the seat panels, then mark the mast's center halfway between the marks.

For plank seats, lay out the center of the mast from the nearest station, using the straightedge-and-tape measure method already employed for locating the thwarts and seats. Pick up the measurement by drawing the height of the seat on the lofting or full-sized pattern, or even scale it up from the construction drawing.

Take the seat out of the boat. If it's a panel seat, fit a block in the gap that runs through the hole and mark the mast center on it. Draw the hole to be cut with a compass if you plan use a jigsaw. If you prefer to use a hole saw, start the center drill in the block. Pre-drill the block with the center drill size (usually ¼″). This eliminates worry about the drill wandering off-center while cutting the hole. Clean up and sand the hole edges.

If your boat has a mast partner, the hole through the seat should be bigger than the mast. It is nice to have an even gap, but it is not essential. To check the size of the hole without a mast, or without hauling the boat out into the snow to put in the mast, sight down along the edge of the hole in the partner in the same way you located the center of the mast on a paneled seat. If the hole is off-center, trim with a rasp or jigsaw and sand smooth.

Bow seat is also a mast partner. If your seat or thwart doubles as a mast partner, see your plans for exactly how to build it. Much of the stress from the mast will be at work directly on your seat or thwart. The seats and thwarts we've just described are not designed for this, since we prefer to use a mast partner located at the gunwales.

Fancy seats. Go ahead. Have some fun building fancy passenger seats for your boat. We'll leave you to it at this point, as the creation of caned seats, contoured backrests, tufted cushions, and such is essentially furniture-building territory. Keep in mind that your seats will see a good bit more of Mother Nature than the typical household item, and build them accordingly.

Deciding about edge treatments

Now that you can see how the thwarts and seats look together in the boat, you can figure out how you want to finish the thwarts and seats; in particular, what about all those sharp edges?

Think bare feet, bare legs, thin bathing suits—and the occasional unintended hard landing or awkward movement. Whacking your toes or shins never feels good, but it shouldn't draw blood. And you really don't want permanent creases in your nether regions from sitting in your boat.

An additional consideration: Varnish and paint will not remain on sharp, newly cut corners. Round-over all edges, even those invisible underneath, at least enough to hold the finish.

Heavily rounded bullnosed corners give a soft, pillowy look. Small bullnoses impart a crisper, refined look. We personally like chamfers because they are elegant and emphasize the curves and straight lines of the parts. (A small disclaimer: Ruth loves the way chamfers look but

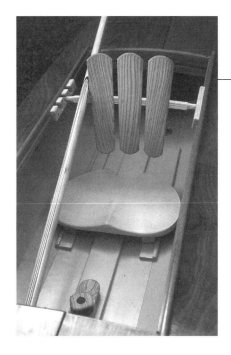

9.55 This Salicornia double-paddle canoe has a carved, contoured seat and tilting backrest.

9.56 If you can build a boat, you can cane. Caning adds class and comfort to bow and stern seats.

she does get a little tired of breaking and sanding all those extra edges. This is not as big a deal if there is only one boat in front of you at once, instead of a line-up of four or five.)

Of course, the easiest thing to do is chuck up one router bit and buzz off every corner with it. Of course, your boat will look like it came from Uncle Teddy's Discount Boat and Furniture Warehouse. Vary the corner treatments with the intended use of the part and the boat. Some suggestions:

Add interest. For example, the Ellen's trunk cap is ½″ thick and overhangs the trunk by ¼″. John puts a ⁵⁄₁₆″ bullnose on top and a ⅛″ bullnose on the bottom.

Lighten the part's appearance. Unless your boat is a heavy workboat, your thwarts and seats may look too heavy and thick as simple unadulterated planks. Beveling the lower edge makes the thwart or seat appear much thinner and lighter, while affecting the strength not at all. We usually rout a chamfer in the bottom, but you also can deploy your hand tools and shape a lovely taper perhaps a couple of inches wide.

Clearly mark where you would like the edge treatments to stop and start, especially if you will be using a router.

Marking riser and riser cleat lengths

Before you take the seats out of the boat, be sure that you've marked the final lengths of the risers or riser cleats.

ASSEMBLING AND INSTALLING THE THWARTS AND SEATS, FINAL ROUND

Once you're happy that the thwarts and seats are marked completely, remove them from the hull and set them on some horses nearby. Before you start unscrewing pieces, take a minute to mark a few more things.

Marking and labeling for easier reassembly

On the underside of the thwarts and seats, make score lines next to all of the various cleats. Draw pyramids on *everything* so you can tell quickly where each part goes. Label the parts underneath with light pencil if you think you might confuse similar pieces. Do a quick sketch of each seat and thwart and note crucial dimensions such as the diagonal distances and how far apart the horizontal cleats are. The sketches give you a quick way to double-check things as you reassemble thwarts and seats with glue that is setting rapidly.

Now you may take all of the seats and thwarts apart.

Shaping the edges

With the thwarts and seats disassembled, you can make short work of the edge treatments at the bench. Beware of router addiction. Don't be afraid to pull out your hand tools and "fix" routed edges that don't look just right. Routers are great, but they don't have eyes and hands. Use yours, as well as sharp tools and sandpaper, to create shapes that look and feel the way they should. Skip the router altogether if you can do it better by hand.

Sanding

When you're done with the edges, stack the pieces up near a comfortable sitting spot and sand them all well, with 80- and 100-grit paper. This way, you'll only have to do a quick touch up after the seats are back together. The tops of the thwarts and seats will have to be sanded smooth after you pare off the bungs, so don't worry about them too much at this point.

When you sand the parts, take off only the pencil marks that will show after the thwarts and seats are installed. Keep the rest for clarifying matters when you reassemble.

Gluing up

We recommend gluing the thwarts and seats together much as a furniture builder would: with enough glue to hold everything together, but not so much that there is a lot of squeeze-out. Waterproof, carpenter's yellow glue, works well for this job mainly because it is convenient, doesn't need to be mixed, dries in about an hour, and doesn't stain the wood. Any squeeze-out cleans up easily with a sharp chisel. This glue's only disadvantage is that it sets up fast. There isn't much time for adjustment once you've applied it and begun screwing or clamping a part in place.

If you would prefer to use epoxy, you certainly can. Epoxied joints will show more because of epoxy's tendency to stain the wood, but you can minimize the effect by at least matching your putty well. If you're planning to paint, of course you have no worries about stains in the wood.

Glue application tactics. Take care not to slather glue everywhere. With many parts, try putting a small bead of glue on, then spreading it out evenly with your finger. This cuts down on squeeze-out. After you put each seat or thwart together, glue wooden bungs in the countersunk holes.

Set each glued-up seat or thwart aside for five to ten minutes until the glue squeeze-out has cured to a leathery, rubbery consistency. Remove this with sharp chisels. After the glue has dried for an hour or more, you can trim the bungs.

Finishing and attaching riser cleats

Cut riser cleats to length, then shape and sand. Glue them in place with epoxy and redrive the screws. Clean

9.57 Fastening the edge of a paneled seat's outboard panel at the ends of the panel-carrying cleats with temporary screws through the holes for the screws that will hold the seat to the riser. Note the clamp at the end of the middle panel: A screw was driven a little too enthusiastically and split the end of the panel. To repair the split, waterproof carpenter's glue was forced in the crack with a putty knife, the screw that caused the crack was backed off to close the crack, and a clamp was applied to keep the crack tight until the glue dried.

up as usual, and fill the "bungs" over the screw holes with epoxy putty.

Final sanding and preparation for finish

Thwarts and plank seats. These are reasonably easy to smooth with a belt sander, but digging in at the edges can still be a problem. Keep the sander moving. Stop periodically—often at first—and run your hand quickly over the surface to feel for humps and bumps. If you find that you are sanding in dips that you cannot take out, lightly hand-plane the surface smooth and use another method of sanding such as the random-orbit sander. If this is happening on every thwart and seat, check the platen on your belt sander to see if it is worn and needs replacement.

Paneled seats. Clamp the seat to the bench using wooden hand-screws on the stiffening cleats. Sand the tops with a belt sander or random-orbit sander. If you use the belt sander, feel for high spots first and sand these down. This will help prevent the sander from becoming tipped and causing the edge of the belt to cut a groove in a panel.

Once you've sanded to your satisfaction, the thwarts and seats are ready for varnish or putty and paint, a project you can start now if it is possible to finish these separately and install them in the boat after the hull interior is painted or varnished.

FLOORBOARDS

We make removable floorboards for our lighter rowboats and sailboats from the clearest northern white cedar we can find (small tight knots are pretty much a given), with steambent white oak frames. An occasional light oiling is all that the floorboards need, or should have, to develop a sensible, foot-friendly patina in use.

Making floorboard frames

The most efficient way to make floorboard frames is to steam them, so they offer a short course in steambending (see Chapter 3, "Some Very Useful Techniques"). White oak is the best wood for the frames. Our frames are bent flat, so John cuts them out so that the annual rings of the grain run parallel to the wider upper surface. Think of the annual rings as strips in a laminated stack, and you'll see which way the strips should go for the stack to bend easily.

Measure and cut the floorboard frames longer than you need. In our smaller, open boats, the floorboard frames usually run up to the second lap. A small bullnose on the corners will help keep the frames from splitting when bent. Label each frame with its station number, using a dark, waterproof pen. Clearly label the stations on the keelson in pencil.

Steam the frames until they bend easily (typically

9.58 An extra pair of hands to help bending and clamping the quickly cooling frames is a big help.

9.59 Spiling the floorboard planks. The edges of the panels have been marked on the frames, so all of them are being spiled before they are cut out and resawn.

less than a half-hour for ⅜″-thick frames). Work from the middle of the boat toward the ends so the last frames to go in will be the ones requiring the most pronounced curves. Begin bending the frame as you stride to the boat, center it quickly, and push down to the hull. Hold the frame down at the first lap, then overbend it by pulling its upper end a couple of inches toward the middle of the boat. Hold it up for a few seconds, then let it relax onto the planking. Hold the frame in place by hand for a minute or so as it cools.

We hold the frames in place overnight with L-shaped brackets fastened firmly in place with a drywall screw through the laps. Aim the screws to miss the plank edge on the outside of the hull. Attach another bracket at the keelson if necessary. You will have to find your hole-filling syringe and attend to these holes later on. We've also used bricks to hold the frames in position, with marginal success. The L-brackets work better; the bricks don't make holes. Your choice.

The floorboard frames must carry fairly wide floorboard planks, so bend them in fairly gentle curves that will allow the planks to land fully on the frames. Use spacer blocks on the keelson if necessary to keep the curve sufficiently gentle. It's not unusual to need blocks for a couple of frames near the stern if you run the floorboards all the way aft and the boat's transom is narrow or has a wineglass shape (see Photo 9.59).

Let the frames cool and set themselves at least overnight. Mark the ends for trimming. As you remove the frames from the hull, mark each with a pyramid so you can put it back in the same orientation. Trim the frame ends on the bandsaw, then round their ends on the inverted belt sander. Screw the frames to the keelson.

Remember to fill the holes in the hull with epoxy putty if you used the L-brackets.

Laying out the floorboards

Mark the center of each frame from the centerline on the keelson. Mark the gap between floorboard planks using a circle template. Our typical gap is ⅝″.

Floorboards can be made as straight planks. Just don't rip them too wide, as you will need to edge-set them in the curved hull.

Floorboards are attractive when shaped to echo the lines of the planking. Use blocks sawn to the spacing width to mark a space on the frame on the inboard side of the garboard plank's upper edge. You will be needing four to six spacers blocks to assemble the floorboards, and more wouldn't hurt, so rip out the blocks now, label them, and save them in a box. Divide the space between this mark and the center edge-of-space mark in half or thirds—the aesthetic choice is yours. Lay out the remaining plank widths on the frames. You only need to do this layout on one side of the boat.

Making and attaching floorboard planks

Spile shaped floorboard planks just as you did the hull planks. Lay a segment or two of the spiling pattern in the bottom of the boat, positioning it close to the spaces along the centerline. Use weights to hold the pattern tight to all the frames. Up near the bow and stern you may have to hold the pattern with a few small nails.

Record the positions of the edge-of-space marks along the centerline and the first plank's outboard edge with compass arcs. For any outboard marks that are covered by the pattern, measure the floorboard plank width with the plank-width measuring jig (see page 134), ruler, or tape measure. The floorboards are nowhere near as fussy as the hull planks. So long as the curves of the floorboard planks are fair and spacings fairly consistent, the floorboards will look great.

9.60 Using spacer blocks to install the rest of the floorboard planks.

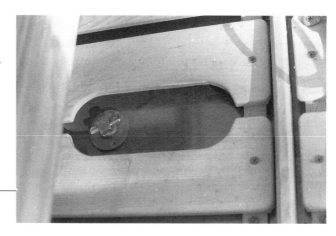

9.61 A hole in the floorboards large enough for a drainplug and a sponge.

Mark the locations of the frames and put a half-pyramid, pointing forward, on the inboard edge of the pattern.

Lay out the shape of the planks on stock thick enough to make two planks. For our small boats, we make the planks ⅜″ thick and get them out of 1¼″ (5/4) stock that has been planed down to 1″ or 1⅛″ thick. Nail battens around the marks and saw out the shapes on the table saw using the same jig used to cut out the keel, or on the bandsaw, following up with hand tools.

Remove the battens. Mark the lines of the frames on the floorboard edges and draw the pyramids on the inboard edges. Mark the middle of both edges of each floorboard blank with a compass and resaw into planks on the bandsaw. Plane the planks to the final thickness. Decide which faces look the best, remembering that the planks must be mirror images of each other in the boat. Rout or otherwise shape the upper edge to something bare-toe-friendly; we use an ⅛″ bullnose.

If the floorboards go around a trunk, hold the center panels in place with weights or temporarily screw them down, then scribe an even space around the trunk logs. Remove and trim the panels.

Position the first floorboard plank with its inboard edge just touching the edge of the spacing circles. Starting from the middle of the boat, fasten the floorboard with one screw into each frame, right in the middle of the plank. The weights are a big help for holding the planks in place while you drill and drive the screws. Use the spacer blocks to position and fasten the center plank's twin.

Spile, lay out, cut out, resaw, position (using the spacer blocks), and attach the other plank pairs.

Remove the assembled floorboards by unscrewing the frames from the keelson. Mark a pleasing curve across the ends of the floorboard planks and cut them out with a jigsaw or on the bandsaw. If you like, cut a hole for access

to a drainplug or for bailing and sponging the boat dry. Round and sand all edges smooth. Scrape off visible pencil marks and sand everything well. Oil the floorboards thoroughly with a penetrating marine oil (see also Chapter 12, "Painting and Varnishing"), and set aside until needed.

LAST DETAILS
Footrests

Footrests range from simple to complex. The simplest footrests are those used by not-too-fussy dinghy rowers: either the aft seat or a conveniently located pair of half-frames or frames. If you'd like more secure bracing and a classier approach, you'll want to make and install some sort of real footrests in your boat.

Fixed blocks. Simple beveled blocks are a good solution for one rower or for two rowers with legs of significantly different lengths. They can be attached directly to the keelson, to the bottom of a flat-bottomed boat, or to floorboards. We usually install fixed footrests after the rower(s) try the boat and settle on a desired position(s).

Notched blocks with stretcher bar. This setup can accommodate several rowers. The pair of notched blocks must be aligned for the stretcher bar to seat securely, so they must be scribed and beveled to fit the angle of the garboard planks or floorboards. Install these in the shop.

Fully adjustable footrest. A footrest with a sliding footplate must be attached to the keelson. If your boat has floorboards, you'll have to cut openings for the various footrest parts.

Trunk cap

Find the trunk cap and trim it to fit its thwart. We always make the trunk cap as a separate piece, as this is essential for installing a centerboard, but is also desirable for daggerboards. Finish the cap completely, top and bottom, then install with screws. The trunk cap is a nice place to use a beautiful piece of wood and many coats of varnish. It doesn't get much wear, is easy to finish (and refinish), and you'll be looking right at it much of the time.

Holes, bungs, dings, and things

Grab a roll of masking tape and mosey around your boat, flagging holes, splintered plank edges, and other major imperfections. Mask these off with the hole-filling tape, or strips of tape if appropriate. Mix up a batch of epoxy putty and fill. If you have missing bungs, glue these in. It's worth taking the time to do this last check for major imperfections carefully. Waiting for yet another epoxy patch to cure when you'd rather be varnishing or painting is annoying.

Finishing

We prefer to take the interior parts right out of the shop proper and finish them in a clean, warm, well-lit room, far away from the building zone. If you are able do this, you can work on additional projects such as spars, rudders, and daggerboards while the finishes on your seats, thwarts, risers, trunk cap, etc., dry in blissful, dust-free innocence.

See also Chapter 12, "Painting and Varnishing."

Putting everything back together

You may reinstall interior parts whenever it makes sense for your particular boat. If your boat has parts that must be glued in, these obviously must go in before you can start finishing in earnest. Because we finish interior parts separately, we usually wait until the hull is completely finished, then reinstall the risers, thwarts, seats, mast partner, etc., along with the boat's hardware (see Chapter 13, "Fitting Out").

Chapter 10

If Your Boat Has a Deck

Plywood makes it simple to build a deck that won't leak, and it also helps to make a tremendously strong boat. Even boats with laid (planked) decks frequently have plywood sub-decks to keep below-decks dry. A laid deck over plywood can be made quite thin for boats where weight is crucial.

A boat's deck plays much the same role as a lid on a shoe box. You can easily push, pull, and twist the box quite a bit when it is missing its lid. Add the lid, and it is much harder to distort the box. Tape the lid-to-box joint securely, and the bending and twisting is completely eliminated, unless you exert much greater force.

Nearly all decks have a double curve in them: fore-and-aft they curve with the sheer, and athwartships they curve over the deck beam camber. In theory, a panel of plywood does not readily accept bending in two directions. In practice this is often not a problem, especially on bigger boats. But it can be a definite challenge on some small boats with strong sheers and generous deck cambers.

A seam down the deck's centerline, with a cleat underneath to take the fastenings and a king plank cap on top to make her look nice, can really help because you're asking the plywood to cover only one side of the boat. Another strategy is to cover the deck with two thin layers of plywood that will bend into place much more easily than one thick layer.

Making the decks with a center seam also allows you to use the plywood more efficiently, as the two roughly triangular pieces can be nested to form a rectangle.

Marking the hull interior

Important: Do this before you do anything else to the inside of the hull.

Before you proceed with the decks, you must permanently mark the stations in the hull and clean up the excess epoxy, as you would for an open boat, though areas concealed by underdecks can receive a little less attention. (If you skipped ahead, see Chapter 9, "Building the Interior"). The only difference is in marking the stations at the sheer. The deck cleat will cover-up a scored line marked on the inside of the hull. Instead, score short station lines, small enough to be covered by the rail, on the outside.

DECK CLEATS

When the hull comes off the building jig it will be a little floppy, as it lacks rails. You'll find it much easier to work on the various interior parts if you install the deck cleats first.

Deck cleats (also known as deck or sheer clamps)

10.1 Deck framing in a canoe showing the deck cleats along the sheerstrake, centerline cleats, the carlins on either side of the cockpit, and the deck beams.

are usually installed along the upper edge of the sheerstrake to provide adequate surface area of solid wood for fastening and gluing the outer edge of the deck. Install a deck cleat with its top edge slightly above the edge of the plank so that the cleat can be beveled to match the deck beams' camber. You'll need to take a moment and make a camber pattern (see box).

Installing deck cleats

The deck cleats are fitted and installed much the same way that gunwales are, except their ends fit against the inner stem(s) and transom instead of to a breasthook and quarter knees. Blocking that does the same job as the breasthook and quarter knees is installed after the deck cleats.

Mark the angles between planking and inner stem and between the sheer and inner stem on one end of a deck cleat and trim with a handsaw. Push the end of the deck cleat tight to the inner stem, then clamp it to the sheerstrake as far along the length of the boat as you can.

Mark a reference line on the top edge of the cleat and the sheerstrake at the last clamp. Measure from this line to the inside face of the transom (or where the plank meets the aft inner stem) along the top edge of the plank. Lay out this distance on the deck cleat to mark where it will be trimmed. Mark the vertical and horizontal angles between the sheerstrake and transom (or inner stem on a double-ender) on the deck cleat and trim with a hand-saw.

Slide the aft end of the deck cleat into place. If it is too long, it can be trimmed with a block plane. If it is too short, slide in a little wedge to fill the gap. It will be under the deck, so no one will ever see.

Glue the deck cleats in place. Make sure to locate the screws holding the deck cleats so that the rails will cover the heads.

Making a Camber Pattern

A deckbeam camber pattern helps with clamping deck cleats at the proper height and is essential for trimming accurate bevels on the deck cleats. Your plans will specify the amount of camber in terms of so many inches of rise per measurement of beam.

Make the pattern long enough to go across the whole boat at the widest beam of the boat. To lay out the deck camber, you can use the same method as that used to lay out for spars (see Chapter 11, "If Your Boat has a Sail"), except that the curve will cross the baseline at the ends.

Beveling deck cleats

By now, you've done so much beveling that trimming the top of the deck cleats should be a snap. Starting amidships, set the camber pattern on the sheer to check which corner of the deck cleat is higher. Trim the high corner with several strokes of a block plane, then check the angle you are cutting with the camber pattern. Continue trimming the deck cleat and checking the angle until the cleat bevel just touches the top edge of the sheerstrake. Keep the camber pattern roughly centered over the centerline. This you can do by eye, as it's not super-crucial that the pattern be placed exactly. The curve should be uniform, but it is best to keep things consistent by approximately centering the pattern.

Move about a foot forward and trim the deck cleat again to the sheerstrake. Continue around the hull in this manner, then trim the remainder of the deck cleat in the places in between.

Even though the tops of the short deckbeams next to the cockpit and cabin are often cut straight because the curve is so shallow, you must bevel the deck cleats along the side decks, as the side decks angle upwards to follow the camber.

INTERIOR PARTS

Now that the deck cleats are in place and stiffening the hull appreciably, turn your attention to the interior. (Turn back to that chapter for the sections that apply to your boat.) Spare yourself considerable grief by laying out for and installing as many of the interior parts as you can before continuing on with the deck. It's very exciting to see the deckbeams, carlins, and various bits of blocking go into the boat—and a royal pain in the posterior to try and work around them when putting in seats, a trunk, bulkheads, floorboards, etc. This is true whether your boat is big or small. While you're being good to yourself, sand, putty, and seal every portion of the hull and attached interior parts that won't be involved in a glue joint. Depending on your boat design, you also may find that you can accomplish a good deal of priming and painting at this point. This is especially worthwhile in tanks and other soon-to-be-very-hard-to-reach areas.

Before you start fitting parts, brace the hull to its proper beam. Amidships, you can use the same type of spreader as that used for an open boat (see Chapter 9, "Building the Interior"). At the station nearest the bow, simply screw or nail a spreader to the deck cleats.

Deckbeams

Nearly every treatise on boatbuilding tells how to lay out for the curve—or camber—of the deckbeams. Less frequently do they talk about how to accurately locate and measure for the length of the deckbeams.

Use the same method used for locating the mast partner (see page 174) to locate the major deckbeams, the full beams situated at the ends of the openings in the deck for the cockpit and, on bigger boats, the cabin. Normally the other deckbeams are spaced at a consistent interval from the major beams. Clamp the straightedge to the major beam line, double-checking to see that it is square to the centerline by triangulating from the stem. Then lay out the beams from the straightedge, the same way you laid out the stations on the jig and keelson (see Chapter 5, "Building Jig and Molds"), making sure to keep the tape measure parallel to the centerline. Next to each measurement, including the one for the major beam, draw an X where the beam goes.

Fitting deckbeams

Here's a handy way to accurately fit the deckbeams:
- Lay the beam upside down in position and make a scored line along the top of the beam where it touches the deck cleat. To mark the vertical angle of the hull, hold a ruler against the side of the beam with its edge against the sheerstrake, on the outside of the hull. Pencil a line.
- Mark the other end of the beam with the scored line and penciled line.
- Find a straightedge that is at least as thick as the deckbeam (or stack several together). Fasten this flat on the bench (or floor).
- Clamp the curved deckbeam next to the straightedge so that the distance from the scored line at each end of the beam and the straightedge is the same.
- Use a bevel gauge on the straightedge to lay out the deckbeam ends. You'll notice that the vertical angle is going the wrong way. Line up the bevel gauge's blade with the angle, lock the blade, then flip the bevel gauge over to mark the angle the way it should go to match the hull.
- Use a tape measure to find the center of the beam (measuring the same distance from each scored line) then use a square on the straightedge to mark the centerline and the cutout for a centerline cleat, if there is one.

How you mark out the the ends of the beams will all depend on how the deck framing is designed.

If you need to mortise the deck cleat or clamp for the end of the beam, don't use a half-lap joint, because a heavy load on the deck is apt to cause the beam to split. You don't need to do fancy half-dovetail work. Though such joinerwork is challenging and fun, the plywood deck glued to the beams and deck cleats keeps the hull from pulling away from the ends of the beams.

On small boats with a deck cleat the same width as the beams (or wider), a shallow beveled mortise is used most often. Cut the mortise to a depth of about a third to half of the width of the cleat at the top, beveling the cut angle to flush with the cleat face at the bottom of the deckbeam.

For boats with a small deck cleat, such as our double-paddle canoe Salicornia, you can notch the ends of the beams around the cleat and flare the width like a trumpet bell to provide plenty of gluing area against the planking (see Photo 10.2). For extra insurance, add a small fillet around the ends of each beam.

Larger boats often have a deck shelf that attaches

10.2 The deckbeams on this Salicornia double-paddle canoe are notched around the deck cleats and flared like a trumpet bell for plenty of gluing area against the sheerstrake.

10.3 Marking out the joints for the deckbeams on the deck cleats and center cleat on a Somes Sound 12½. Note the straightedge clamped to the major beam to hold it straight for accurate layout.

to the deck cleat and runs under the beams. The shelf fully supports the beams without fancy joinery, provides a secure home for fastenings (often bolts), and helps stiffen the hull.

Swapping ends or moving angles. After marking and trimming the full deckbeams, you must install them with their ends swapped so the athwartships angles fit. The end that you marked on the port side of the boat should be fastened on the starboard side, for example. Because both sides of the boat are the same (right?), this is not a problem. You can use the same swapping method for short beams: mark a beam on one side of the boat and fasten it in place on the other.

If you don't want to do this, draw square lines from the ends of each athwartship angled line on the top of the beam, then draw a line to the ends of the squared lines to reverse the angle. Move the vertical angle to the ends of the new athwartship angle the same way you would if you hadn't reversed the athwartship angle.

Fitting and installing carlins and short deckbeams

Carlins typically are ripped out as straight pieces and bent into place. In frameless hulls, they are often attached to knees glued to the hull, then any short deckbeams required can be marked, trimmed, and fitted in place.

Carlins. To mark the length of a carlin, first consider its width, a vertical dimension in the boat. If the carlin is the same width as the deck beams, clamping it to the bottom of the deckbeams, with a spacer the size of the deckbeam between the camber pattern and the carlin, works well. If the carlin is narrower than the deckbeams, clamp it to the top of the deckbeams with deckbeam-sized spacers between the camber pattern and the top edge of the sheer on both sides of the boat.

Lay out the position of the deckbeam on the deckbeams and clamp it in place. Use the camber pattern to hold the middle of the carlin at the proper height, employing short lengths of the deckbeam for spacers.

For a carlin that follows the athwartships curve of the hull, use bar clamps or pipe clamps and temporary spacer blocks to bend it to the curve.

Mark the length of the carlin by tracing along the deckbeams on the top (or bottom) edge of the carlin. Mark the fore-and-aft rake of the deckbeams by laying a straightedge on the side of the carlin with its edge touching the side of the deckbeam and drawing a line on the carlin along the straightedge.

Draw a builder's pyramid on the top edge to mark the orientation of the carlin, then unclamp and set the carlin on a couple of horses.

The length you marked on one edge of the carlin is actually the length for the opposite edge. (For example, if you clamped the carlin to the bottom of the deckbeams,

the length you marked is for the bottom of the carlin— but to keep angles going the right way, you marked it on the top edge.) Draw square lines on the side of the carlin from each end of a length line, then connect the ends of the squared lines on the opposite edge. Use a bevel gauge to move the deckbeam rake lines to the ends of the new length lines. Repeat this layout work on the other end of the carlin.

The same type of shallow mortises that work well in the deck cleats for holding the ends of deckbeams also can be cut in the sides of the deck beams for the ends of the carlins. If you decide to use these mortises, make sure to add to the length of the carlin when you are doing the layout work.

You may find that the end of your carlin is soon covered with pencil lines. To keep from cutting the wrong ones, mark the actual cut lines with a utility knife or pocket knife instead of a pencil. Mark the score lines all the way around the carlin.

You will find this method of measuring and marking parts to accurately fit between two other pieces useful in other places in the boat.

Use a handsaw to trim the ends of the carlins, and a block plane if the saw cut missed the line.

Carlins are usually fastened with screws through the deckbeams. You'll want to hold the middle of the carlin in place with the camber pattern until all the short deckbeams (or blocking for very narrow side decks) are fitted and fastened in place.

Short deckbeams. To fit and install short deckbeams, position the carlin at the proper distance from the hull, then use the camber pattern to establish the correct height. Clamp the carlin in place. Mark the positions of the short beams, which are typically parallel to the full beams and spaced at similar intervals. Mark the length of each short beam just as you did the full beams: held upside down and scored with a knife along the top of the beam, against the deck cleat and the carlin.

To mark the vertical angles at the carlin and deck cleat, turn the deckbeam topside up, and place a straightedge flat on the side of the beam with its edge against the deck cleat or carlin, then mark the line on the beam. Usually, these vertical angle lines will not touch the scored lines on top of the beams; you must use a bevel gauge to move them so they contact their respective scored lines.

To reposition vertical angles on curved short beams, use the same method you used with full-length beams. Lay each beam against a straightedge, then measure the vertical angles with a bevel gauge. Move the bevel gauge along the straightedge to draw the same angle at the scored line located on top of the beam. As with full deck beams, mark from these lines for any joints to be cut in the deck cleat and carlins.

DECK PANELS
Making patterns and laying out the panels

Patterns will help you use your decking plywood most efficiently. Here's a choice of two methods for making the patterns:

Plywood method. Lay pattern plywood over the deck, then trace along the outside of the hull and the deckbeams, carlins, and cleats that border the panel. The pattern plywood must be thin enough to bend easily over the deckbeams. Hold it tight to the deck framing primarily with weights, employing a few clamps at the carlins and center cleat, if possible. Cutting the pattern roughly to shape can be a big help.

To mark the center cleat's centerline (the deck panel's inboard edge), trace along both sides of the cleat onto the pattern ply while it is in place. Remove the pattern, and lay out for the centerline between the traced lines.

Trim each pattern to its outlines, then trace around each onto the deck plywood.

Plastic sheeting method. Cut a piece of 6-mil clear plastic sheeting roughly to size. Hold the piece in place on deck with tape and weights. Trim the plastic to within a couple of inches of the desired deck panel borders. Carefully reposition the plastic and its weights to eliminate all wrinkles. Mark the edges of the panel with a fine-tipped permanent marker. Mark the center cleat's centerline as well as any other lines and points likely to prove helpful.

Lay the plastic pattern on the deck plywood, then mark the pattern's outlines and relevant points by pricking through the plastic into the plywood.

10.4 Holding down thin pattern plywood on the deck framing with lead ducks to make a pattern of the deck panel.

A Couple of Hints on Panel Layout

On many small boats, the deckbeams are too narrow to land two pieces of plywood for a joint. Make the joint between the deckbeams and reinforce with a butt block.

The corners of deck openings are high-stress areas; it is wise not to put the joints in the deck panels next to them.

Cutting out and fitting deck panels

When you saw out the panels (a jigsaw works well), cut about ½″ outside the line along the edges of the hull and deck openings. Plan to trim the edges flush after you fasten the deck in place. For those edges that butt against another deck panel, cut close to the line, then final-trim right to the line with a sharp block plane.

Important note: The panels should be installed from the ends of the boat toward the middle, and the last joint should be marked, trimmed, and fitted right on the boat. Leave one panel long enough to overlap its neighbor; don't cut to the line.

Test-fit the panels by tacking them in place with brads. Neatly fit the joints between the panels, especially if you plan to varnish. For the final joint, tack the overlong panel in place first, then fit and tack down the mating panel. On both panels, avoid driving any nails near the joint so you can lift the ends. Mark the edge of the shorter panel on the face of the longer panel with a sharp pencil or knife. Hold the end of the short panel clear by wedging a block underneath. Slide a piece of scrap plywood under the marked line on the longer panel. Trim close to the line with a handsaw. Lift the freshly trimmed end, and remove the scrap and block. Drop the end of the short panel onto the deck framing. Fit the joint right on the boat, trimming with a sharp block plane and undercutting the edge of the plywood a little. Given the benefit of a little patience, this joint will fit perfectly.

Before you remove the fitted deck panels, trace underneath along the beams, carlins, and cleats. Remove the panels and mask off these areas and any other places that will be glued, then seal and paint or varnish the remaining surface on the underside of the deck.

INSTALLING THE DECK
Covered deck

If your deck is to be painted or covered with cloth or a laid deck, putting it on is pretty straightforward. Apply epoxy in the prescribed manner: Wet out the tops of the beams and cleats, and the glue zones on the bottom of the panels. Apply a small amount of epoxy putty to the beams and cleats. Fasten the panels along the centerline first, then fasten along the beams, working out to the edges. Start in the middle of each panel and work toward the ends. We recommend using screws to locate and secure the panel; if there is a problem it's easy to fix it by removing a few.

Until you are sure that the panel is properly located, drive widely spaced screws, just enough to hold the plywood in place. When you're happy, screw the remainder of the panel down securely, or drive bronze ring nails

10.5 Trimming the overhanging cloth on the deck of a Somes Sound 12 ½ covered with Dynel and epoxy. The coamings and rails will cover the exposed edges of cloth.

if you prefer. Note that these nails are almost impossible to remove once driven home.

We have used Dynel cloth with success on a Somes Sound 12½ (see Appendix B, "Resources"). Follow the general instructions given in Chapter 7, "Planking."

Bright-finished deck

The siren call of varnish will sound for many as you consider your lovely sapele deck panels. We have built a couple of double-paddle canoes with varnished decks. Because there's nothing to clamp a deck to while the epoxy cures, John reached back into his past for a lovely technique he used when building a harpsichord.

A harpsichord's sound board also must be held in place while its glue dries. The temporary fastenings of choice are small, headed nails ½" to ¾" long that have been pushed through cardboard squares about 1" across. These padded nails can be driven tight without the heads

10.6 Gluing down a deck that will be varnished. Small, headed nails and squares of cardboard hold the deck panel tight to the framing while the epoxy hardens, then will be removed and the tiny holes filled.

marring the wood. After the glue is dry, grasping and pulling on the cardboard with a pair of pliers cleanly pulls most of the nails. If the cardboard should tear away, the claw of a small hammer, padded to protect the wood, will fit in the gap under the nailhead.

Once all the nails are pulled, you are left with tiny holes that can be filled quickly, and nearly invisibly, with epoxy putty tinted a shade darker than the deck panels.

To use this method on your deck:
- Figure out a neat nailing pattern for your deck, spacing the nails about 4" apart for a relatively small, light boat like a double-paddle canoe.
- Count the number of nails needed, and make up a full batch of padded nails. We use ¾" brass nails left over from weatherstripping our house windows, padded with squares of fairly thick corrugated cardboard.
- Epoxy, position, and fasten the deck panels, working as you would for a covered deck, but use the padded nails.
- When the epoxy has cured well, pull the nails and cleanly fill the holes. Scrape away the excess epoxy thoroughly when it has hardened.

Catching a Few Rays on Your Deck

We inadvertently discovered a method for deepening and darkening the color of a bright-finished sapele deck. We built one of our Salicornia double-paddle canoes, varnished her decks with three coats, and then were interrupted. The boat had to go outside into the summer sunshine with her thin varnish for a couple of weeks. We were surprised and pleased to watch her decks deepen to a very rich mahogany with pleasing reddish-purple undertones. The grain pattern settled down as the wood darkened, a plus in our view. This boat had black walnut king plank caps and Honduras mahogany rails and coaming. Nice things happened to these woods as well.

If you try this, make sure that you have scraped and sanded every bit of epoxy off the wood, and inspect the varnishwork carefully for runs, sags, and built-up places. Places with lingering epoxy or protected from the sun's UV rays by extra varnish will remain light-colored or, at the very least, will not change color at the same rate as the rest of the wood, resulting in noticeable patchiness.

Trimming the decks

To trim the deck overhangs around the sides of the hull and the openings in the deck:

Mark the perimeter of the hull and openings on top of the decking with the transom-marking gauge set for flush, just as you did for trimming the planking at the transom.

Trim the deck ⅛″ to ¼″ outside the line. Use a hand saw to make quick work of the job on thinner decks. The handsaw bends around the curves of the outside of the hull and won't chip-out the top surface of the deck. The thin blade of a Japanese saw bends easily around the sharp curves of smaller boats, but hold it at a low angle because it cuts on the pull stroke.

If you use a jigsaw for this job, set it at an angle or break off a portion of the blade if there is a chance the tip of the full-length blade, sticking several inches below the deck, will accidentally gouge the sheerstrake. Watch for chip-out, especially if the deck is to be varnished. Direct the saw so that most of the chip-out is on the piece being trimmed off. Pad the base of the jigsaw with several layers of masking tape.

The jigsaw usually works well in the deck openings where angles between and the deck and the structural members are 90 degrees or less and where it is more difficult to use a handsaw.

You can trim the last bit of projecting deck with a router fitted with a flush-trimming bit if the angle between the deck and the surface below it are 90 degrees or if the corner of the deck is complete covered. In general, John trims the edges around the deck openings with the router and the edges at the hull with hand tools.

Trim the decking by hand with a block plane, letting the sole of the plane ride against the sheerstrake, carlin, or deckbeam. In the deck openings you'll need to switch to a spokeshave and finally a chisel in the corners.

There is almost nothing more disappointing than trimming the deck too much, particularly at the sheer when the deck or the rail are to be varnished. Check progress frequently with your finger and stop when the deck edge is still just a touch proud of the sheerstrake.

10.7 Trimming the deck: leave the deck edge just a touch proud of the sheer so the joint between the deck and the rail is tight.

10.8 Rails on a decked boat aren't structural members as they are on open boats so they can be smaller and easier to install without the aid of clamps.

Rails

Clamping a rail in place on a decked boat is difficult, at best, and usually impossible at the bow and stern. However, on a decked boat the rail is not a structural member as it is on an open boat, but is there to cover the deck edge or hold the edge of a deck covering, and to protect the hull from bumps and scrapes with docks and pilings. It is often smaller and easier to install than its open-boat counterpart.

Trim, fit, and fasten the rail at the bow just as you would on an open boat (see Chapter 8, "'Outbone' and Rails, Then Off the Jig"). Angling the first screw to help pull the end of the rail tight to the outer stem is even more helpful here where you can only use hand pressure to hold the rail in place. Lay out the distance of the screw spacing from the first screw and drill for a second screw.

Remove the rail and set it in on saw horses. Lay out the screw spacing, then butter the rail with the goo of your choice. Reattach the rail to the boat.

Raise the aft end of the rail (adjust the line from the ceiling, move the stepladder, or point "up" to your helper) until the top edge is flush with the top of the deck at the next screw position. Push the rail to the hull and deck edge, rub a finger across the joint between the deck and the rail to check that they are flush (or nearly so—it is better to have the rail a little proud of the deck and trim it later than to have it below the deck), then drill and drive a screw. Repeat this process for each successive screw to the stern.

Once you are comfortable with this process, you can speed things up by bending and attaching the rail at every other or every third screw position. The rail should be very nearly flush with the deck between the screws. Then you won't have to fiddle with raising and lowering the aft end of the rail to drill and drive the remaining screws.

On a transomed boat you can fasten the rail all the way to the stern, then trim the end flush with the transom.

On a double-ender with an outer sternpost, you'll have to stop a few feet forward of the stern to measure and trim the rail to fit against the outer sternpost. Run the blade of a tape measure along the sheer on the sheerstrake, starting from the joint between the hull and the outer sternpost at the sheer (for accuracy line up the 1″ mark with the joint, not the bulky hook on the end of the tape). Near the last screw into the rail mark a whole inch increment on the top of the deck. Push the rail to the deck edge and transfer the mark on the deck to the rail. Measure off the distance to the outer sternpost joint on the top edge of the rail, then measure and mark the vertical and horizontal angles between the hull and the outer sternpost.

Saw the end of the rail a little fat of the lines to give yourself some wood to trim.

Fit the end of the rail to the outer sternpost. John considers the joint perfect when the rail is tight to the outer sternpost and there is a slim gap along the hull. The last screw should close the gap, and this method ensures that the joint along the outer sternpost never opens up.

Rail trimmed too short? Fear not, we've been there. See Chapter 8, "'Outbone' and Rails, Then Off the Jig," for a cure.

COAMINGS AND CABIN SIDES: A FEW THOUGHTS

Generally, coamings are fastened against the face of carlins and cabin sides are installed with their lower edges resting on the deck. But no matter how the designer of your boat shows them, mark out their shape with patterns rather than trying to armwrestle thick, long, heavy, and unwieldy pieces of wood in the boat.

Make the patterns from ¼″ plywood or ⅛″ "doorskin" plywood from a lumberyard. There are two ways to make the patterns. Both have their advantages

10.9 The coamings in the Salicornia canoe are installed on top of the deck, and trim pieces in the cockpit cover the deck edge, in much the same way that cabin sides are commonly installed.

10.10 Clamping a laminated coaming against the carlins in a Somes Sound 12½.

and disadvantages, their advocates and detractors. And both methods can be used for other parts of the boat.

You can make the pattern as a single panel that roughly fits where the cabin side or coaming is to go. Roughly trim the panel to fit in the hole with a jigsaw. Nail or clamp it in place, then spile the actual shape with a ruler the same way you measure the shape of the hull for a bulkhead (see Chapter 9, "Building the Interior"). Trace the curve of the deck or carlin on the pattern.

For the other method, rip the plywood into strips 2″ or 3″ wide. Position the strips around the perimeter of the coaming or cabin side, trimming their length by scoring the plywood with a utility knife, then snapping the strip in two. Tack the strips to the boat with small finish nails. Glue the strips together with hot-melt glue. Where the finished piece needs to fit tight against another part of the boat, scribe and trim a strip to fit tight, then glue it to the neighboring strips of the pattern. A large pattern will be very floppy and might break, so glue on extra strips to brace and strengthen it. If you want all the strips to be flush with each other, cut short lengths of the strip to make pads to glue over where two strips butt.

With the strip method, you can record any bevels right on the pattern. For the panel method, you often have to record the bevels on a separate scrap of wood or plywood.

There is nothing worse than a cabin that leaks. Take pains to make the joints tight and thoroughly watertight with epoxy, bedding compound, or caulking.

Detailed discussion of the installation of cabins and coamings is outside the scope of this book. Please see Appendix C, "References," for suggested reading on the subject.

Chapter 11

If Your Boat
Has a Sail

Raising sail on IRIS.

Sails and Rigging

RIGGING

Unless you're planning to plop a sailboard rig in your boat, rigging the boat will go along much better if you take a few minutes to plan and organize the process. Lists help, but it is more helpful to sketch each assembly, showing the splices required as well as the fittings, such as strap-eyes or blocks, that go with it. Label the sketches with the size and length of rope or wire required and the size of the fittings.

If the rigging attaches to a piece of hardware that must be shop-made, note the measurements and any other information needed on a separate piece of paper, as these will be your working sketches for that process also. (See Chapter 13, "Fitting Out.") If you're not completely sure about the commercial sizes available for certain hardware items, label their key dimensions and any other useful information, such as the distance to interfering objects on the boat. It's especially nice to have a measured sketch in front of you when confronted with two pieces of hardware—one a little smaller than you wanted,

the other a little bigger—so you can choose the one that will work with the rest of the rigging and fittings.

Once you've completed your sketches, you can sit down with a pile of catalogs or head off to your local chandlery. If you have a long list of things to mail-order, send a fax, e-mail, or letter, then confirm by phone.

If you picked out the hardware, line, etc., yourself, you can shelve it until you're ready to work with it. If you ordered from catalogs, sit down with your sketches and go through the boxes when they arrive. We deal with some of the best marine suppliers around, but mistakes and confusion happen. Did you get the proper fittings? Are they the right size? Are your lines the right material, construction, and length? Is everything you ordered in the box?

Carefully check your hardware for flaws. Cosmetic imperfections can be filed away or lived with, but functional faults, such as sharp edges on sheaves, and pintles and gudgeons that cannot be made to fit each other, are fatal. Shop carefully. Good-quality bronze or stainless

11.1 Mast in place and rigged for sail.

11.2 The hardware on the masthead and the end of the yard for a gunter rig (Ellen). Note also leather chafing collar.

hardware is not inexpensive, but it will last the life of this boat and probably longer.

Sort your rigging gear into small boxes or zippered clear plastic bags according to their final relationships.

If your plans don't have a complete rigging list, you'll have to make some decisions. This is best done in a marine supply store so you can compare different items. If this is impossible for you, ordering samples of the items of interest can be worthwhile.

A few suggestions:
- The size of wire rope should be specified in your plans. If the turnbuckles are not, the diameter of the turnbuckle's threaded rod should be twice the diameter of the wire.
- The comfortable minimum size for a sheet is about ⅜″. For very small sails, especially jibs, ⁵⁄₁₆″ is fine.
- Low-friction blocks really make a difference. Light-weight ones are best above deck level, to reduce weight aloft and lessen the chance of a painful whack in the head (especially important on smaller boats)
- Friction and stretch will be your two main enemies in the pursuit of an efficient, functional rig. Anything you can do to reduce these will make sailing your boat more fun. For example, try high-tech low-stretch rope for standing rigging on smallish boats, especially those that must be rigged and unrigged often.
- Install the block, sheave, or fairlead that relates to a particular cleat first, then run the line to the cleat location. Install the cleat at about a 15-degree angle to the line, not parallel to it. This will help keep the line from jamming under tension.
- Fishermen's "tarred" nylon twine is useful for all sorts of small-boat rigging jobs, from seizings to keeper lines for the oarlocks. It can be a little hard to find outside of fishermen's supply stores. Buy extra; you'll use this stuff

for the boat and will have to hunt down the spools carried off to garden and house.
- When splicing, use twine to make a constrictor knot at the point where the strands should stop unraveling.
- Mark where an eyesplice is to start with a permanent marker.
- A piece of ½″ copper pipe, cut and smoothed appropriately, makes a nice, inexpensive fid for small lines.
- Plastic electrician's tape (not the very gummy kind) makes useful quick servings, but will eventually unwind itself in sun, water, and wind. Put on a real serving or melt the ends of the line.
- Some official "rigger's tape" looks suspiciously like white electrician's tape and doesn't hold as well. Test a roll before doing the whole boat.
- Think chafe. Wrap sharp points and apply chafing gear wherever needed.

SAILS
Sailcloth

Until fairly recently, the sailcloth options for small-boat sails were not particularly ideal: "standard" Dacron, a stiff, hard, slippery material that dries quickly and is not prone to rot; traditional cotton, a cloth lovely to handle and look at that stretches when wet and must be dried carefully to avoid rot; and nylon, a superlight material that dries fast and is rot-resistant but that stretches under strain, limiting its use to very small or downwind sails.

In the mid-1990s, sailmaker Nathaniel Wilson and cloth manufacturer North Sails developed Oceanus, a Dacron cloth with a soft, cottonlike hand. It handles and looks a great deal like cotton, but it doesn't stretch when wet or rot if not dried perfectly. It doesn't hold its shape as well as standard Dacrons with a higher resin content, but this is of negligible concern with sails made for small

11.3 Talking to a sail-maker early in the building season—late fall to early winter—will dramatically increase your chances of having a sail for your boat in the spring.

daysailers and other non-racing craft. If you can't find Oceanus, ask your sailmaker; similar cloths may be available.

The softer Dacron cloths are perfect for the Ellen and most of our other small sailboats. It is, unfortunately, not the least expensive option. If cost is of concern, you probably will choose regular Dacron, which will work just fine.

Working with a sailmaker

The sail plan included in your boat's set of plans will tell the sailmaker most, but not all, of what he or she needs to know in order to give you a quote, then make the sail(s). In addition to the shape and area of each sail, the sailmaker will want to know how the sail will be used and how it attaches to the spars and/or stays, plus how many battens (if any), how much hardware (such as headboards), and how many reefs (if any). You will probably receive a separate price for reefs, as you may have a choice of no reef, one, or two. Racers hate reefs, as they wreck the perfect shape of a sail; cruisers love 'em, as they make sailing the boat saner or, in some situations, possible. Sailmakers in general tend toward the racier end of things.

Which reminds us of an important point: Look for a sailmaker who understands small-boat sails and wants to make yours. The sailmaker beloved by the local racing crowd may not be the best choice for a spritsail for a 12′ dinghy. And shop around. Sailmakers vary widely in their prices. Once you've found someone you trust to make the sail for a reasonable amount, you're set.

However, do both of you a favor and shop for a sail early, preferably before you start building. (Especially if you're planning on a spring launching.) Sailmakers who are familiar with the type of sail you need often can give you a working quote over the telephone. Others will want to see the sail plan to be sure of all details before offering

an estimate. Most sailmakers request a deposit of fifty percent up front before they begin work on your sail.

Making your own sail

If you're reasonably accomplished with sewing machine and needles, making your own sail is not an unreasonable option. We can't offer direct experience here, but there are several good books on sailmaking available. A sail kit is another interesting option that some of our plans customers have chosen.

SPARS

We build solid spars for our small boats, so that's what we'll focus on here. However, many of the same techniques can be applied to the building of hollow spars.

Wood Selection

The lumberyard can be a fine place to find appropriate stock for small-boat spars. If that fails you, a local sawmill may have what you need, or you can order stock from boat wood suppliers that will ship.

Eastern spruce

Here in Maine, we have several local spruce species that make decent spars, especially black spruce. Much of the dimensional lumber available is also made of the same woods. Most of the trees that are cut for this purpose are relatively small (especially compared with trees on the West Coast), and of course the beautiful clear stock does not normally wind up as framing lumber. (Lately, much of it has been going to Europe for cabinet moldings.) However, it is possible to sort carefully through the stacks (restack as carefully) of larger dimensional lumber and find pieces with good, reasonably straight grain and small tight knots. Unfortunately, balsam fir also is sawn into dimensional lumber, and it is nowhere near as resilient and rot-resistant as the spruces. Telling spruce wood from fir isn't always easy.

You may be able to find someone who regularly saws clear spruce, but the wood they offer will probably be green and require at least six months' drying time before you can turn it into spars.

The Eastern spruces make a light, tough, springy spar, but one that can be prone to warping and unwinding grain. Plan to seal your spars well the instant they are done, and consider gluing up the blanks to limit these tendencies.

Douglas-fir

In recent years we have made most of our spars from Douglas-fir. It is heavier than spruce, but it is also stronger, allowing us to make the Douglas-fir spars thinner and therefore about the same weight as spruce ones. Douglas-fir is used extensively in the building industry. High-quality wood winds up as moldings and trim,

Determining the Taper of a Spar

Draw a horizontal baseline on a scrap of smooth plywood or a piece of paper, then use a square to draw a vertical line. Set a compass to the largest diameter of the spar, and draw an arc with the pointer of the compass stuck where the two lines cross.

If the spar is the same diameter at both ends, such as a boom, you only need to draw a quarter of a circle as the figure shows. If the ends of the spar are of different diameters, such as a mast, draw a half circle to do this layout twice.

Set the compass for the smallest diameter of the taper of the spar (This is not always the end of the spar. At the heel of the mast, for example, you'll want to use the diameter above the tenon that goes into the maststep.) Put the pointer where the largest-diameter arc crosses the baseline at B, and draw a short arc that crosses the larger-diameter arc at C. Now put the pointer on C and draw an arc that crosses the horizontal line twice, at B (of course) and at D.

Divide the distance between A and D into equal segments. Dividing any distance in half with a compass is the easiest way to do this (see Chapter 3, "Some Very Useful Techniques"). Set the compass for roughly half the distance between A and D, then mark short arcs across the baseline from both points. Marking a point halfway between these closely spaced short arcs by eye is easy and surprisingly accurate. Repeat the process between A and this midpoint, then D and the midpoint, to divide the total distance into four, which usually is plenty for small spars. Divide the distance into eight for large spars.

Now divide the arc between E and C into the the same number of equal parts. Here is where the compass method of splitting distances in half makes quick work of the job.

11.4 Mark the taper of a spar using an index card as a tick strip. Pick up the dimensions from a taper layout.

Connect the points with lines as shown. The distance from the baseline to the arc is the diameter of the spar at a point between the largest and smallest diameter.

To find those points on the spar, divide the distance between the largest diameter and the smallest into the same number of equal spaces. Let us say your boom is 10' long with the largest diameter in the middle. Divide the distance between the middle and each end into four equal segments (5' divided by four is 1'-3"). On a mast 10' long the largest diameter will be at the partner which, we will say, is 2' from the heel. Divide the remaining 8' of the mast into four equal segments 2' long.

Transfer the diameters from the layout to the spar using a piece of card stock as a tick strip.

In general, the side of a simple tapered spar along the edge of the sail is straight. When you make a mast the aft edge will be straight and on a boom, the top edge is straight. To draw the shape of the forward edge of the mast and the bottom edge of the boom you use the full diameters from the layout. On the other hand, both sides of a spar taper and are marked from a centerline. In that case you will want to divide all the layout distances in half (love that compass) and record the half diameters on your tick strip when you mark out the spar's width.

This layout method also works for making a deckbeam camber pattern. The only difference is that the small diameter is zero, so you divide the baseline between point A and B into equal segments and the arc (the height of the camber at the widest beam) from point B to point F into the same number of segments.

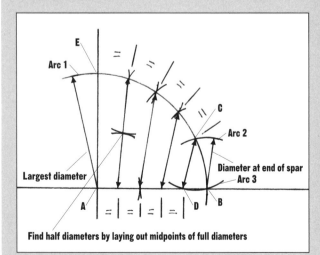

Fig 11.1 Spar taper layout.

among other things. We glue-up our spar blanks from simple straight molding (basically flat planed boards) ordered from the local lumberyard.

Douglas-fir spars are stunning when varnished, especially if set off by complementary varnish and paint work.

Sitka spruce

Good Sitka spruce has a very high strength-to-weight ratio and therefore makes the lightest spars. It is also scarce, in demand, and expensive. We normally reserve it for high-performance boats where every ounce counts.

You will probably have to order Sitka from a specialty supplier, unless you live in the Pacific Northwest (see Appendix B, "Resources").

SPAR CONSTRUCTION
Flat, tapered spars

Spars with flat sides and a straightforward taper are the simplest option. These usually are tapered in profile (the upper and lower edges of a boom), but little or not at all on the plan view (athwartships on the boom). The edges may be rounded with a routed bullnose or by hand. Generally, this sort of spar is suitable for lower spars where excess weight is not a problem: booms, clubs, sprit booms, and bowsprits. The vertical yard on on our sliding gunter-rigged boats is also made this way.

With a planed blank in hand, you can trim the spar's tapered width. On most flat, tapered spars, one edge is straight. This can be marked with a string and a straightedge.

To lay out the tapered side, find the spar's widest point, which may well not be the middle. Some plans give you widths at intervals all along the spar. If so, you should have little trouble laying out the taper. If your plans offer only a few key dimensions, like the widest point and the ends, you have a bit more work to do (see box).

There are two approaches to cutting out the shape of the spar. The straightforward and safer way is to mark the curve with a batten. Bend a batten around nails driven at each width mark and check for fair. Run a pencil along the batten, then remove the batten and nails. Cut along the lines with the bandsaw, jigsaw, or circular saw (if you're good). Clean up the cuts with a hand plane.

The really slick way is to use a nailed-on batten as a guide with the long-curve table saw jig, just like you did for the keel (see page 146). You can do this on both curved and straight edges of the spar. Just mind the offcuts! It is a very good idea, and easier on the saw blade, to trim the spar about ⅛" from the batten on the bandsaw, then finish the job on the table saw. You will need either an outfeed table or a truly able assistant to support the end of the spar.

It might seem like a good idea to achieve the spar's final shape by routing with a large flush-trimming bit, but grain direction is a big problem, especially with Douglas-fir, which splits easily.

If the spar is to have holes running athwartships, now is a good time to drill them so they will be square to the center of the finished spar. If there is a slot, drill the holes at the ends now and trim the rest after the spar is tapered on all sides. Mark and drill the holes running up or down (for a boom) after tapering the sides of the spar.

Small rectangular spars usually taper very little in thickness. With these, you can mark the thickness at each end, then hand-plane down to the marks, gauging the taper by eye.

If there is a fair amount of taper in thickness, as is likely to be the case on spars for bigger boats, use the same taper layout method you used for the fore-and-aft taper to determine the thickness at one or two places between the thickest point and the ends. This time, you need half the thickest dimension of the spar because you are measuring from a centerline. Lay out for the end of the spar using only half of the smallest dimension, as well.

Mark a centerline down the middle of the edge of the spar using a compass. Then lay out the thicknesses. Cut down to the marks with a hand plane. Look along the corners of the spar to be sure that the taper is nice and even.

If your spar has warped a little, you can correct this by removing the taper largely or completely from one side. In this case, lay out for the taper using the full thickness of the spar, instead of half. If there is a lot of wood to remove, you can mark with a batten, rough cut on the bandsaw and finish up with a hand plane. Again, your eye is the most important measuring tool for the taper.

Once the spar is tapered, trim and shape the ends, drill any remaining holes, and cut any slots. Rout all the edges with the biggest bullnose you can (usually a little less than half the thickness at the ends), then sand the spar thoroughly.

Thoroughly coat the spar with clear sealer or thinned varnish as soon as you're done with it, and store it well supported in a rack.

11.5 Shape the ends and drill holes for hardware before shaping the edges of a tapered spar.

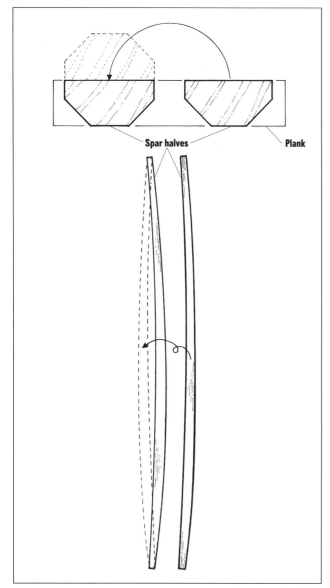

Fig 11.2 Making the halves of a laminated spar from the same piece of wood and flipping one half when they are glued together will counteract any warping to a surprising degree.

Making and Using the Eight-Siding Marking Gauge

To lay out for the eight-siding gauge, draw a circle of a little larger (say, ¼″) than the spar's largest diameter near a true edge of a piece of plywood. Draw a line parallel to the edge that just touches the circle, using a try-square. Next, use the try-square to draw lines at 45 degrees to the edge that are tangent to the circle. Set the gauge's two sharp scoring pins at points A and B. Locate the inside edges (not the centers) of the two outer guide pins at points C and D, the outside diameter of the circle. Use 6d or 8d smooth finish nails for the pins, and drill the holes for them slightly smaller than the nails' diameter.

Laminated round spars

A two-piece laminated spar is much less likely to warp than one made of a single piece of wood, so it is worth the trouble. We laminate all of our masts, even (especially) the smallest ones.

It's best to make the halves from the same piece of wood. Not only does this make the spar look better, the pieces will have almost identical warping characteristics. Before you cut out the pieces, mark the blank with a big dark pyramid so that later on you'll know which faces to glue together. If the pieces warp in any direction as you shape them, gluing the same original face together should cancel out the warp. It is truly amazing how warped the pieces can be and still end up as a straight spar (see Figure 11.2).

Plane the halves down to half the diameter of the thickest part of the spar (usually at the partner) for a mast. Mark the gluing face with a pyramid. Rip the halves apart on the table saw if you haven't done so already.

Mark the fore-and-aft taper on the inside face of one half spar. Nail a batten along the marks and cut out the shape on the table saw with the curved ripping jig.

Using drywall screws, fasten the first side to the second, just as they will eventually be glued up. Make sure that the pyramid portions are on the same edge and pointing the same way.

Trim the second half as you did the first, preferably with the curved ripping jig setup. If you bandsaw out the taper, do the final trim with a hand plane while the halves are fastened together so they will be exactly the same.

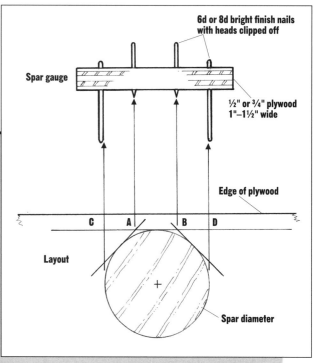

Fig 11.3 A gauge for marking the eight-siding on a spar.

With the spar halves still together, mark the athwartships taper using the joint as the centerline. Separate the halves, bandsaw most of the waste off and finish with a hand plane.

If you are making a mast, you can rough cut its heel at this point, measuring from the maststep template you made earlier (see Chapter 9, "Building the Interior").

Prefer a Hollow Mast?

If you want a hollow mast, scoop out the insides with gouges and hollowing planes before you glue the mast halves together. The diameter of the mast must be larger than for a solid mast, so this cannot be a last-minute decision. The mast must be redesigned.

It is much easier to eight-side the spar before gluing the halves together. Score the eight-siding lines on both faces of each piece using the eight-siding jig (see box). Nail a batten along the score line on the inside face just like you did for the shape. With the curved ripping

11.6 Hold the eight-siding marking gauge at an angle so both pins touch the sides of the spar.

11.7 A batten nailed along the scored line made by the eight-siding marking gauge rides against the curved ripping jig to cut a perfect tapered chamfer with the table saw blade set at 45 degrees.

11.8 Sighting along a taut string to check the alignment of the glue line on a laminated mast.

jig still in place, set the table saw at 45 degrees and cut the large chamfer. This method is so accurate that when you finish the cut and turn the spar over to inspect the visible side, you'll likely find that the saw cut has split the score line.

If this technique makes you a little too nervous, screw the halves back together and mark the eight-siding on all four sides, separate the halves, set the bandsaw for 45 degrees, and cut close to the score line. Finish the beveling with a hand plane on the separate pieces or after gluing the halves together.

Gluing-up and rounding the spar

Glue the spar together with epoxy. If one side of the mast is straight, you can put it directly down on plastic or waxed paper on a series of horses or a long bench. (The planking table works great.) If the mast tapers on all sides, support its ends with spacers. If you are gluing-up the mast on horses or the planking table, be sure that the largest part of the spar is well supported. If the spar is long, you may want additional spacers between the mast's ends and its largest diameter.

To make sure the glue line (the spar's centerline) is straight, tilt the end clamps as close to the spar as you dare, then run a string from these clamps. Sight the string. Hold the spar in alignment while it cures with small blocks screwed to the horses or bench.

Once the epoxy has kicked well (for at least twenty-four hours), clean up the excess and true up any slight discrepancies between halves. Mark for holes or slots then drill or cut as appropriate. Shape the heel of the mast, also.

Sixteen-side the spar. You can do this by eye, with liberal use of pencil slashes so you can clearly see how much you've cut. The facets should all be the same

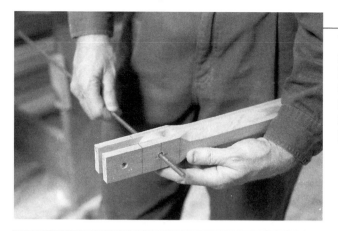

11.9 Fitting a halyard sheave and pin in a slot and hole cut in the glued-up mast before the top is trimmed to length and shaped.

11.11 Use the now familiar pencil slashes to help accurately cut the facets with a hand plane as the spar is trimmed for the final round shape.

11.10 Shape the heel of the mast before rounding. Cut the shoulder for a mast that fits in a chamfered mast step with a handsaw held against the 45-degree portion of the head of a combination square.

11.12 Hold one end of spars (and oars) for shaping and sanding on a braced post with a V-block on top. The other end of the spar is held in a wooden hand-screw fastened to the top of the workbench.

width. Now, go around again to cut the spar into thirty-two even facets. One stroke of the plane on each corner often will do it.

Sand the spar smooth and finish the shaping of the mast head and heel.

Sanding spars

It is possible to sand spars with a shop-made rig featuring a 3″ or 4″ spindle drum set up to hold an inside-out sanding belt and chucked into a drill. The spindle has to be made just right or it won't work. Small spars tend to vibrate annoyingly when attacked in this manner. The belt will cut plenty of cross-grain scratches. On big spars requiring lots of wood removal, the drum rig works better and the scratches are much less noticeable.

We recommend sanding small spars by hand. Take a whole sanding belt and flatten it. Wrap the belt around the spar in a semi-complete lengthwise spiral. The grit on the top actually helps you hang on, and of course the belt can be flipped over when necessary. Start with 36- or 50-grit, turning the spar four times with each grit, and work your way up to 120-grit. This goes pretty quickly (honest), and the final result is stunningly smooth with no cross-grain scratches. The stand shown in Photo 11.12 is a big help.

Daggerboards and Centerboards
DAGGERBOARDS

Daggerboards have one distinct advantage over centerboards. The whole rig is lighter: since the trunk is much smaller and the daggerboard comes out of the boat. This is a much coveted asset for dinghies and other small boats that need to be lifted often. You also never have to worry about sand or rocks jamming the slot.

The disadvantages can be considerable, however. When the daggerboard strikes bottom, the boat comes to an abrupt halt. Build your trunk well (see Chapter 9,

Making Your Spar Straight and Keeping It That Way

There is hardly anything more depressing than watching the lovely, fully shaped spar that you've slaved over for days gently but irreversibly adopt the shape of a long, skinny banana.

Keeping your spar wood straight as you work is a constant battle. When it arrives in the shop, let it sit for a few days or a week to acclimate to ambient humidity. Set the wood up on edge so the air can flow around it, out of direct sunlight, and well away from the woodstove. If you are getting a couple of spars out of single piece, rough rip the blanks (leaving plenty of wood for later trimming) to allow the pieces adjust themselves separately.

Once the wood has settled down and become fairly stable, trim each blank a few inches longer than the finished spar. Straighten along the thinner dimension of the blank by trimming the concave side at the ends with

a hand plane. You can check your progress by eye, or use a string stretched taut from the ends. With small spars, be careful not to let the taut string bend the spar stock.

If the blank is thick enough to require several trips through the planer, run it through first to cut the full length of the unstraightened side, then flip the piece over after each pass to keep the moisture content the same on each face.

Flattening the concave side with a hand plane is important. It is likely that the thickness planer will take the spar down to the final thickness without cutting any wood at the ends. That's okay; you can deal with that. However, if you had trimmed the middle of the convex side of the blank to straighten it, the planer will trim only the ends of the blank and the middle will wind up too thin.

"Building the Interior") and the only damage, besides a ding in the board, will be a few bruises to the arms, legs, and ego.

Choosing your wood

We often use good-quality but aesthetically unappealing Honduras mahogany for daggerboards (as well as centerboards and rudder blades), as these should be painted. You can use marine ply of sufficient thickness, though it will be harder to shape. Glue-up a blank with epoxy if necessary.

Shaping the daggerboard

Plans typically give an outline showing the daggerboard's shape, plus a cross section through the middle. That's fine, but how do you get from a flat board to that fine underwater foil shape?

The technique used to shape an underwater foil is similar to that used to round a spar. The first bevels cut

from the piece remove the lion's share of wood and rough out the blunt nose and long tapering tail of the foil. After that the bevels you cut are small, for the aim is to refine and round off the rough angular shape. (see Figure 11.4). A good sanding with a flexible block knocks off the corners and fairs out the board's final shape.

Bandsaw out the basic shape of the daggerboard if you have not done so already. Clean up the edges with hand tools, a belt sander, or by pattern-routing.

Figure out the widths of the leading and trailing edges of the daggerboard by using the formulas shown in the sketch. Mark them with a marking gauge.

Set a compass to the width of the forward bevel and mark this width on both sides of the front of the blank, to the very bottom of the daggerboard. Now set the compass to the width of the aft first bevel and mark both sides of the blank. At the bottom, the forward bevel will taper into the aft bevel. Fair out this area when you cut and sand the bevel.

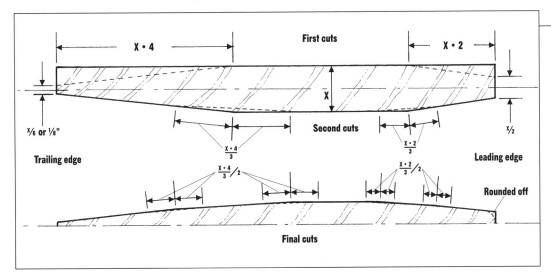

Fig 11.4 Shaping a foil is similar to rounding a mast: On the first cut, large amounts of wood are removed to make a rough, angular version of the shape; then the corners are trimmed in smaller and smaller facets until the curve is smooth enough to be sanded.

You need only shape the portion of the daggerboard that interacts with water, so check your plans to see how much of the board rests in the trunk and mark this distance.

Clamp the daggerboard on edge on the bench or in a vise, and trim down to the score lines with a spokeshave. As with beveling the stem and transom, when roughing out work to the line you can clearly see and leave the angle blunt enough that you don't cut past the pencil lines.

After trimming both sides of each edge, clamp the daggerboard flat on the bench and roughcut the bevel to the pencil line, using pencil slashes. Don't cut to the score line on the edge. There should now be a double cut with a ridge running near the middle between the scored line and pencil line.

Mark the ridge with pencil slashes, then trim off the ridge and pencil slashes until the cut almost touches the pencil line and the edge of the daggerboard.

Now mark out the widths of the second bevels and draw the lines with a compass. These bevels remove a small amount of wood, so you should start right out with the pencil slash marks and trim to both lines. Repeat this procedure for the third bevel.

Chamfer and round the leading edge of the daggerboard with the spokeshave.

To sand the daggerboard fair, try a flexible sanding block (see Chapter 6, "The Backbone, and Lining Off"). Start with 50- or 60-grit paper. Work in various directions across the curve of the foil and finish up by sanding with the grain. Hand-sand the leading edge. Finish up with progressively finer grits (to 100 or 120), sanding with a random-orbit sander and by hand.

Shape and sand the board's handles separately. Glue and screw them on, then bung the screwholes.

Daggerboard trunk plug

A daggerboard trunk *sans* daggerboard becomes a marvelous conduit for water any time the dinghy has any forward motion. A trunk plug is required, especially if you plan to tow the boat. But you'll want one regardless, unless you want a wet posterior every time you row seated behind the trunk.

The trunk plug for the Ellen and similar boats is a twin of the top of the daggerboard, with the same handles, but 1/8" thinner. Trim the plug off about 1/2" up from the bottom of the keel. Cut a piece of 1/16"-thick rubber the same size as the slot in the trunk and fasten it to the bottom of the plug with a length of brass half-oval (usually 1/2") drilled for screws every 4". Punch holes in the rubber for the screws with a leather-punching tool. The friction of the rubber against the trunk sides keeps the water out and keeps the plug firmly in place, even when the boat travels upside down on our Jeep.

CENTERBOARDS
Making and shaping the board

Centerboards commonly are wider than daggerboards and spend more time immersed in water, so they must be made of very stable woods that won't warp much. Mahogany is a good choice. Most modern centerboards are made of marine plywood and sheathed with epoxy and a cloth such as Xynole or Dynel (see Appendix B, "Resources").

Many centerboards are shaped in section for efficient water flow. Use the same general approach as that outlined for a daggerboard, adapting it for the shape of your boat's centerboard. This sort of shaping is less important for centerboards that are more traditionally shaped (usually looking like a triangle below the keel), but it is still worth thinning and rounding the edges to reduce turbulence and drag.

Installation and lifting arrangements

Centerboard designs are many and varied. For the most part, you'll need to follow your plans and put the board and trunk together in the manner specified by your boat's designer. However, the following suggestions may prove useful. It's a good idea to make the centerboard and test its fit before attaching the centerboard trunk permanently to the boat.

The most common and simplest approach to raising and lowering a centerboard is a lifting line connected to a weighted wooden centerboard. Many designs are rather vague on how the line should be attached, so we'll spend a moment explaining some excellent ways to accomplish the job.

On small boards, drill two holes: a small one down into the upper edge of the board, half again as big as the lifting line; and a large one through the side of the board, big enough for a knot tied in the end of the lifting line (see Figure 11.5). Drill the larger hole about 1" from the edge and through the end of the smaller hole.

For boards at least 3/4" thick, the lifting line can be fed into the small hole and out the big hole, an overhand or figure-eight knot tied in the end, and then the line pulled back until the knot fits neatly and snugly in the large hole.

For thinner boards, particularly ones made of 1/2" plywood, chisel out a V-groove on the inside perimeter of the large hole. Feed the lifting line down through the small hole and around the groove in the large hole. Take a piece of appropriately sized doweling and shave the end to make a short length of tapered dowel. Push this into the middle of the large hole, and mark the dowel when it is snug. Remove the dowel and make a groove 1/4" or 3/8" farther up toward the fatter end of the dowel. With a hammer, drive the dowel back in the large hole until the lifting line is in the groove. (The fit should be snug enough to hold the line securely, but the dowel will hold

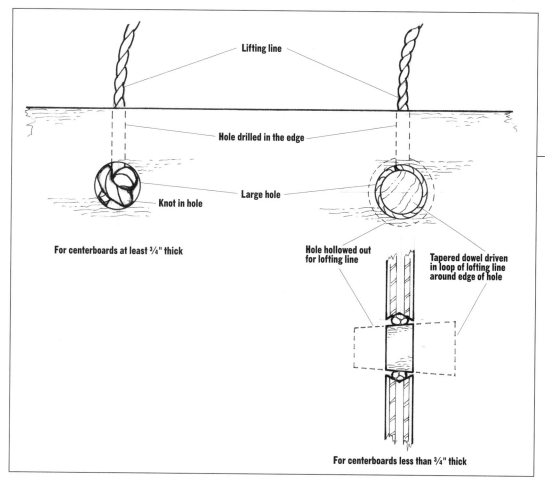

Lifting line

Hole drilled in the edge

Large hole

Knot in hole

For centerboards at least ¾" thick

Hole hollowed out for lofting line

Tapered dowel driven in loop of lofting line around edge of hole

For centerboards less than ¾" thick

Fig 11.5 Bore a large hole on the face and a small hole on the edge of small centerboards for the lifting line. A simple knot is tied in the end of the line for ¾"-thick centerboards, a tapered dowel holds the end of the line in thinner ones.

even better after it swells up in the water.) Trim the dowel flush with the sides of the board and put a coat of sealer on the ends of the dowel. To change the lifting line with this arrangement, just drive the dowel out with a short piece of smaller dowel or rod, install the new line, and refasten with a new tapered dowel.

For heavy boards in bigger boats, it is a good idea to attach the lifting line to bronze plates fastened to the sides of the board. Your plans should show the details for your particular boat, but often the top of the plates have a pin which goes through a thimble spliced on the end of the lifting line. Chisel out recesses in the board for the plates so they won't chew up the inside of the trunk.

Fig 11.6 The handle of an unweighted British-style centerboard projects forward of the pivot pin through a slot in the trunk cap. A short length of rubber hose screwed to leading edge of the board presses against the sides of the trunk to hold the board in position.

For an alternate lifting arrangement, consider this. The British are fond of unweighted boards that don't use a lifting line. Instead, the front end of the board projects well forward of the pivot pin and sticks up above the top

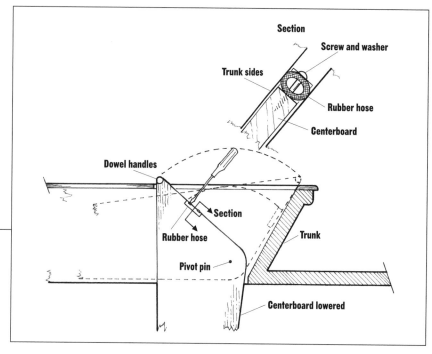

Section

Screw and washer

Trunk sides

Rubber hose

Centerboard

Dowel handles

Section

Rubber hose

Trunk

Pivot pin

Centerboard lowered

of the trunk. Two short pieces of large doweling (about 1″ or 1¼″) fastened to the very forward end of the board act as stops when the board is all the way up and as a handle, to pull and push the board up and down. These boards don't need any weight to make them stay down. The secret is a short piece of rubber hose or tubing fastened with screws to the front edge of the board, positioned so that it will be just below the top of the trunk when the board is all the way down (see Figure 11.6). This piece of hose, when partially squashed by the screws, rubs against the sides of the trunk and holds the board in whatever position you shift it to. You adjust how hard the board is to raise and lower by tightening or loosening the screws, so make sure you can get at the hose with a screwdriver when the board is in the trunk (usually all the way down)!

This type of board has many advantages: you can always clear a jam in the slot; if you hit bottom hard, the handle goes down instead of popping up like some oth-

WEIGHTING CENTERBOARDS AND RUDDERS

You can cut lead flashing into discs or rectangles and epoxy them in place, pour molten lead directly into the board, or cast weights in a separate mold. John used to pour or cast all of the weights for our boards but now prefers sheet lead for the modest weights required by small boat daggerboards and rudders. It's less work, considerably less toxic, and much less exciting. Cast weights are denser, however, and a better choice when more weight is required.

For all methods, chamfer the edges of the hole on both sides of the board unless noted otherwise.

Obligatory stern warnings: Lead is not good for you. Wear a mask whenever you cut lead; don't eat or drink while handling lead; and wash your hands thoroughly immediately after finishing with the lead (gloves are a good idea). Thoroughly vacuum up chips and dust.

If you elect to cast your lead weight, do it outdoors where there is abundant air exchange. Also, be advised that when lead contacts water, a spectacular "explosion" results, sending droplets of molten lead flying—which will burn you badly if they hit you. Make sure that everything that will come in contact with the heating or hot lead is thoroughly dry. John likes to gently warm the containers, tools, mold, etc., that will be used to heat and pour the lead to make sure that there is no moisture remaining on them.

How much lead?

To calculate the amount of lead required to submerse the board or blade, first weigh the whole thing. (For small boat boards and blades, it is best and certainly easier to ignore the portion that remains out of the water, since it is typically a small percentage of the total. Figuring it this way adds a little extra lead, which is good.)

Divide the weight of the board by 35 pounds per cubic foot for mahogany (or the applicable wood density) to arrive at the measurement of the board in cubic feet.

Multiply this by 64 pounds per cubic foot, the den-sity of water, for the board's displacement.

Subtract the weight of the board from its displace-ment; this gives amount of weight for neutral buoyancy.

Because you want the board to sink, add several pounds, at least ten percent of the weight required for neutral buoyancy.

Divide the resulting total by 700 pounds per cubic foot, the density of lead, arriving at the volume of lead required in cubic feet.

Multiply by 1,728 to get the volume of lead required in cubic inches.

Divide cubic inches by the thickness of the board to arrive at square inches or to calculate the size of the hole needed.

A sample calculation. *Here's how to figure the weight for a sample centerboard, in this case a board for a Somes Sound 12½.*

Weights: Water, 64 pounds per cubic foot; center-board, 16 lbs.; mahogany, 35 pounds per cubic foot; lead, 700 pounds per cubic foot.

Cubic inches per cubic foot: 1,728.

Volume of the centerboard: 16 divided by 35 equals .46 cubic feet.

Displacement of the centerboard: .46 times 64 equals 29.44 lbs.

Ballast needed for neutral buoyancy: 29.44 minus 16 equals 13.44 lbs.

Extra ballast: 29.44 times .10 equals 3 lbs.

Volume of lead needed: 16.44 divided by 700 equals .0235 cubic feet, or 40.6 cubic inches.

Size of weight, given centerboard thickness: 1″ x 4½″ x 9″ equals 40.5 cubic inches; 1″ x 5″ x 8¼″ equals 41.25 cubic inches.

Or, try this shortcut. 700 divided by 1,728 equals .405 pounds per cubic inch; 16.44 divided by .405 equals 40.6 cubic inches of lead needed.

Using sheet lead and epoxy

Lead flashing from your local building-supply emporium works just fine. To cut round discs, fold the lead several times and securely clamp the "pile" to the table of the

ers; and you always know how deep the board is by the position of the handle. The only disadvantage John has found is that when you sail slowly over soft bottom, the board won't gently lift like a board that can pivot freely; the board sticks in the mud or sand. Beating up a narrow, shallow channel in a light breeze requires hypersensitivity to the board's touching bottom and a quick tack to stay in water deep enough to keep the board down (and the boat's speed up) so you don't slip back down the channel.

11.13 Fair the irregularities in the lead weight in a centerboard with epoxy putty.

drill press. Remove the center bit from the hole saw you used to drill the hole in the board. Working at the drill press's slowest speed, gently cut through the lead, clearing chips often by raising the hole saw. (Keep a hand on the on/off switch in case the lead jams the hole saw.) When you are done, turn the drill press off, remove all the lead discs, reposition your folded pile, clamp it firmly, and cut out another stack of discs. Cut enough discs to fit flush in the hole in the board.

If you happen to have a rectilinear hole in your board, sheet lead cuts easily with a utility knife.

Pound the stack of lead flat.

Tape one side of the hole in the board with good clear packing tape and make sure it is well stuck. Mix a two-squirt batch of epoxy and thicken it a little with wood dust, aiming for a mix that still pours easily. Pour a puddle about ¼" deep in the hole, then place the lead stack in the hole, pushing down gently to encourage the epoxy into the interstices, but not out through the tape. Pour enough epoxy on top to fill any remaining voids and just a little more, then tape off the top of the hole. Clamp or weight a board over the hole and leave it overnight.

Bright and early the next morning, strip the tape off and plane the slightly rubbery excess epoxy fair. There will be bubble craters in the epoxy. If they are bigger than ¹⁄₁₆", fill with thickened epoxy. Fill small holes with surfacing putty. Sand everything fair.

Casting lead

Remember: Do this outside and stay upwind! A respirator and face shield are good precautions. Are your containers, tools, molds, etc., completely dry?

One weight at a time. *Cast-off wheel weights are an inexpensive source of lead. (Ask at the local tire store.) You also may be able to find lead shot.*

Cut two scraps of ½" plywood larger than the weight hole in your board, and drill a 1" hole in one. Put the intact piece on the bottom of the board, the one with the hole on top, and clamp the sandwich firmly together. (If you are making a larger weight than the Ellen or a similar boat requires, drill a bigger hole.)

Pinch a spout in the top of a coffee can. Muckle onto the opposite side of the rim with a pair of Vise-Grips and bend it out about 90 degrees so your "handle" (and hand) won't be over the top of the molten lead. Fill the can about three-quarters full with lead pieces. We melt lead with our backpacking stove, which has a steady, strong burner. Make sure the stove is firmly supported and set up a windscreen if necessary. Make or buy a wooden ladle to scoop off the slag and metal clips that float to the surface.

Gently and carefully pour the lead into the board cavity until the hole in the plywood scrap is full. The lead will shrink as it cools. Go have a long lunch.

When the lead is cool, remove the plywood covers and saw off the protrusion with a coarse hacksaw blade. Fill large voids with epoxy putty, small ones with surfacing putty, then sand fair.

Multiple weights. To make identical lead weights, make a mold by cutting a proper-sized hole in a scrap board the same thickness as your blade or board. Chamfer only one side of the hole. Clamp plywood covers over the hole as above. Melt and pour the lead. Start a second batch melting. By the time it's ready, the poured weight will be solidified enough to tip out from the mold—but still hot. Reassemble the mold and pour again. The wood burns a little with each new pour, so the mold won't last forever, but it will make a number of weights.

Installing cast weights. Wet out the edges of the wood with epoxy and epoxy putty. Set the weight so that it rests on its flange, allowing the gravity to hold it in place while the epoxy cures. Once the epoxy is hard, flip the board over and fill with epoxy putty spread with a wide, flexible putty knife.

This system makes a nice, dense poured-lead insert without any voids between it and the wood; without any nice little hidden nurseries for rot.

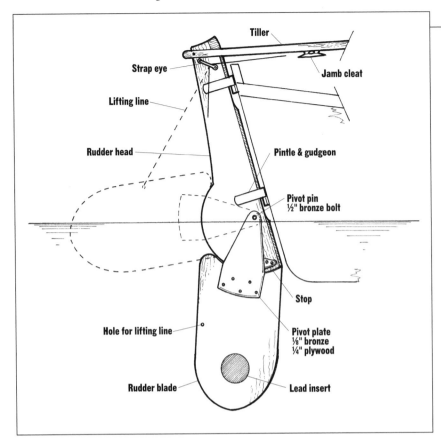

Tiller

Strap eye

Jamb cleat

Lifting line

Rudder head

Pintle & gudgeon

Pivot pin
½" bronze bolt

Stop

Hole for lifting line

Pivot plate
⅛" bronze
¼" plywood

Rudder blade

Lead insert

Fig 11.7 This pivoting rudder is adapted from an L. Francis Herreshoff rudder on his Meadow Lark, 33' sharpie design. It relies on simple weight, which never wears out or breaks, to hold the blade down.

Rudders and Tillers

RUDDERS
Pivoting rudder

Many small boats have rudders that protrude well beneath of the hull. This can be a real problem, particularly when you launch and beach the boat—or run into the bottom in an unscheduled manner.

We've never built a small boat without a pivoting (or kick-up) rudder. Here's how to build one using Ellen's version as an example. It is wise to work out the details for your rudder on paper first, check to see that it works using inexpensive pattern plywood, and only then build the real thing.

First, locate the rudder's pivot point. Figuring this out has to be done by trial and error on tracing paper. The pivot point usually will be located a couple of inches back from the rudder's leading edge and often just above the waterline. Start there and follow the steps below, adjusting the location of the pivot point until the blade pivots enough to at least be in line with the bottom of the boat.

Draw an arc across the rudder blade from the pivot point. Trace and cut out the shape of the rudder-blade-to-be, with the arc as its upper edge. Swing the blade along the arc until the edge of the arc hits the aft edge of the rudderhead. Using a straightedge, check to see whether the lower edge of the blade will clear the bottom when the boat goes aground. Trimming the portion of the

blade that touches the head will raise the blade about 1". If you need to raise the board more, move the pivot point and try again.

When you're happy, make final patterns for the blade and head.

See Figure 11.7 for the proportions of the pivot cheek plates, and make a pattern. Our boats have pivot cheek plates made from ⅛" bronze plate (see Chapter 13, "Fitting Out"). They can also be made of scrap sapele plywood: 6mm for boats up to 16'; 9mm for bigger boats.

Make the rudder blade a touch thicker than the head so it will swing freely without the pivot cheek plates rubbing on the head. If that isn't possible (if, for example, you're converting an existing single-piece rudder), shim the pivot cheek plates with several pieces of plastic sheeting.

Our boats have special pivot pins made from ½" rod, but a ½" hex-head bolt and nut will work just fine. When using the bolt-nut combination, round over the head and the nut by chucking them in drill press and shaping with a file. At the pivot point, drill the rudder-head for a piece of ½" copper pipe. Glue the pipe piece in place with five-minute epoxy.

Shape the rudder blade as you would a daggerboard or centerboard. Treat the rudderhead just like that for a fixed-blade rudder. The rudder blade must be weighted with lead (see box, page 233). Drill a ⅜" hole near the aft edge of the blade for a lanyard to raise and lower it.

Sand and paint the rudder blade; sand and paint or varnish the rudderhead.

Assemble the pivoting rudder. Attach the pivot cheek plates on the rudder head with the pivot pin. Lay the head on the bench and slide the blade between the cheek plates, maintaining a gap of at least ¹⁄₁₆" between the blade and head with shims. Drill for and drive two screws in one plate. Flip the rudder over. Drill for and drive two screws to secure the other plate.

Test the assembled rudder. It should move very easily. If the blade touches the head, reposition it with a wider gap and drill fresh holes. If the cheeks bind on the head, shim them out with strips of plastic. Make sure that the pivot pin isn't holding the plates tight against the

11.14 Attach the pivoting rudder hardware to the rudderhead with the pivot pin and to the rudder blade with a few screws, then test to see that the blade moves freely.

head. When everything moves well, drill for and drive the rest of the screws into the cheek plates.

Trim the extra length of the bolt portion of the pivot pin, then secure the nut from backing off with a punch or two between the nut and bolt or a drop of Lock-Tite.

For most small boats, $\frac{3}{16}$″ line will be fine for the lanyard. Tie an overhand knot in one end and feed the line through the hole in the blade. Attach a strap-eye as a fairlead on the rudderhead just under the tiller, then lead the line to a jam cleat on the tiller's underside. This arrangement minimizes chafe on the rudderhead and keeps the sheet from snagging itself on the jam cleat.

You'll also want a small stop made of the same material as the cheek plates. Fasten the stop with two screws. If your boat and rudder are large, you may want two stops, one on each side of the rudder.

Pintles and Gudgeons

Most of our boats have a transom, so we can use commercial small-boat pintles and gudgeons. If your boat is a double-ender, you'll have to bend flat-based, stainless steel gudgeons to fit the stem; find some appropriate ones for sale; or fabricate your own. We also have used screw-eyes on a small boat with surprising success. Although the boat's sternpost is likely to be curved, the pintles and gudgeons must be lined up in a straight line. Interesting geometric complexities encountered here can lead to interesting little problems with basic matters such as installing and removing the rudder: For example, often-times the rudder must be held at angle off the centerline so the pintles can be slid into the gudgeons. It is well worth testing the pintle-and-gudgeon arrangement before painting or varnishing the boat and rudder, just in case strategic trimming is required on either (or both) for the rudder to work.

Attaching pintles. John prefers to cut out recesses for the pintles on the front edge of the rudder to close the gap between the rudder and transom.

Most pintles have holes for fastenings that are directly opposite each other, so that the pintles must be fastened with rivets or machine screws. Rivets are a bother to take off and redo when refinishing, so we suggest machine screws. With the bronze pintles we use, it is possible to countersink the holes on one side of the pintles and use flat-head machine screws. Stainless pintles are too thin for this approach, so you'll have to use hex-head or round-head machine screws.

To make the pintles look a little more elegant, round-over the nuts. (See page 255.)

Slip the pintle on the rudder, square it up with the front edge, drill for one machine screw, and fasten. Check for square again and install the other screw.

Hold the nuts on with a drop of Lock-Tite or a couple of punches around the inside of the nut. Snap off the extra length of the machine screws with Vise-Grips and clean up with a file.

Check the gudgeons for fit. If they are bronze, you can drill them out to fit the pintles. Clamp or fasten the gudgeon to a piece of wood large enough to hang onto when (not if) the large (usually $\frac{1}{2}$″) drill bit catches. Stainless steel gudgeons for small boats are made of bent flat stock. The fit can be adjusted by prying with a length of close-fitting metal rod after the gudgeons are fastened to the boat.

Attaching gudgeons. Mark the centerline on the transom on painter's masking tape.

Using the rudder with its pintles attached, lay out where they go, based on where the pintles are. Make sure the tiller clears the transom properly.

With a small framing square, mark a horizontal line from centerline at the top of each gudgeon landing site

11.15 Attach the rudder to the boat with pintles (on the rudder) and gudgeons (on the transom). The Ellen has a tiller that fits around the rudderhead. This Ellen (IRIS) is also rigged with a hiking stick on the tiller

(the bottom of the pintle strap on the rudder).

Hold the first gudgeon level on the transom and mark one screw hole. Drill it and drive the lone screw to hold the gudgeon in place. Attach the second gudgeon with a single screw.

Try the rudder in the gudgeons to make sure everything works. Adjust the pintles and/or gudgeons if it doesn't. (A wallop with a hammer on the pin usually does the trick.)

When you're happy with alignment, drill for the other holes. Remove them, remove the tape, and fasten the gudgeons on for good.

TILLERS

There are three basic types of tillers: ones that fit between wood or metal cheeks on the rudder, ones that have wood or metal cheeks formed or attached to the tiller that fit around the rudder, and ones that have a metal fitting attached to the end of the tiller that can be fastened to hardware on the end of a metal rudderpost.

A rudder affixed to a rudderpost is impractical for smaller boats that will be hauled up on a beach or boat ramp, since you'll want to be able to easily take the rudder off. The strength of a rudder post isn't really needed until the boat is big enough to warrant a rudder under the hull.

Tiller that fits in a slot in the rudderhead

This is the simplest tiller to make. This can be made out of the same thickness of stock as the rudder. Consult your plans for the basic shape, add your own ideas for a pleasing contours, and make a pattern. Although most tillers of this type are held in place with a pin or bolt through the cheeks, an Iain Oughtred design we built a few years ago cleverly was held from slipping too far into the rudder by a small shoulder formed on the lower edge of the tiller.

Cut out the tiller blank, by pattern-routing if you prefer. If the handle tapers, mark its thickness at the handle and hand-plane down to the marks. On most small boats this will require just a few strokes. On bigger boats you likely will want to remove the bulk of the taper with a bandsaw, then finish up with a hand plane. If the tiller is warped at all you can help to straighten it by cutting all or most of the taper just on one side. If your tiller has a ball formed on the end, carve out the sides of the ball, then taper the rest of the tiller to match the diameter just aft of the ball. It's a time-consuming job but a very elegant touch.

Test the tiller in the rudder slot, shaving off the sides of the tenon until it is a loose slip fit. Keep in mind that coats of varnish and paint will make the fit tighter. Rout the edges, except at the tenon, to finish up the tiller.

Tiller shaped to fit over the rudderhead

A tiller with integral cheeks that fit over the rudderhead isn't terribly hard to make, and it looks good and works

well. Many of our boats, including the Ellen, have this kind of tiller. In profile it is straight. Seen from above, it tapers from a comfortable handle at the forward end to swell out to form the "cheeks," with a slot for the rudderhead at the aft end. A pin near the aft end of the tiller fits in a shallow notch on the aft side of the rudderhead to hold the tiller in place. A small lip on the rudder's forward edge holds the tiller at the proper angle.

This type of tiller can also be held securely with a removable bolt through a hole located near the aft edge of the rudder. This is simpler to build, and the tiller can still pivot but can't come loose in case of a capsize. Racing dinghies often have the tiller fitted this way.

Lay out the widths and the slot of the tiller on a piece of ¼" plywood to make a pattern. Mark the shape of the tiller with a batten, then saw out and clean up the pattern. Check to see that the shape of both edges are identical. Shave the edge of the pattern with a spokeshave, a rasp, a piece of sanding belt, or a small sanding block. When you first make the tiller pattern, clean up the slot only enough to take out most of the bandsaw marks. Use the tracing to check that the slot is centered, then test the width of the slot on the rudder blank. Remember not to make the fit too tight. The tiller must slip easily over the rudderhead, allowing room for paint and varnish.

Make the tiller and rudder blanks, then drill both for the pin or bolt. The hole in the tiller for a pin should be the same size as the pin (usually ¼"); the hole in the rudder, slightly bigger (¹⁷⁄₆₄" or ⁹⁄₃₂"). On the tiller, a small spacer block near the forward end will help you drill the pin hole perpendicular to the centerline on the drill press. Locate the spacer block where the width of the tiller tapers down by double the thickness of the spacer, from the tiller's widest point.

Check the fit of the tiller to the rudder, with a pin or dowel in the hole. If the slot is too tight it is easier to trim the rudderhead rather than trying to shave the inside of the slot on the tiller.

John likes to taper the tiller to about ⅝" thick at the handle. Check to see if the tiller has developed any curve. It will look best with the "hump" up, so trim the taper off the other side. Rough-trim the taper on the bandsaw, then clean it up with a hand plane or a belt sander. Rout and shape the edges to your liking.

More fun with tillers

If you like, you can steam your tiller and clamp it to a curved form. (See Chapter 3, "Some Very Useful Techniques"). The tiller will spring back a little after it cools, so it is a good idea to wait on trimming the small shoulder on the rudder until you can check the angle of the tiller on the hull, on the full-sized patterns or lofting.

On the Shellback and Nutshell dinghies, the tillers are shaped like socket tillers with a curve cut into the pro-

11.16 Bronze plates are fastened at the end of a nicely curved tiller to hold the pin that slips into a notch in the rudder on this Doug Hylan Beach Pea peapod.

large) back from the universal joint. Flatten the tubing in a vise, then fasten it securely to the bottom of your lovely wooden stick with screws. To further hide the mashed aluminum tube, cut a shallow dado in the bottom of your hiking stick.

file at the after end. They have plywood cheeks attached to the sides to fit around the rudder and are drilled for a pin that fits into the notch on the aft side of the rudder. The Beach Pea peapod, designed by Doug Hylan, also has this type of tiller. John built one of cherry, with bronze cheeks, for a customer's Beach Pea (see Photo 11.16).

Another clever and elegant way to make a cheeked tiller is to cut out the profile in roughly 1″ stock, drill for the pin near the aft end, then make a vertical cut on the table saw to split the tiller down the middle for half to two-thirds its length (the shorter the tiller, the longer the cut, proportionally speaking). The "fingers" are then formed into the cheeks around the rudder and held in place with several blocks shaped and glued in place between the fingers. This makes a very lightweight tiller that would look good on a racing dinghy. This tiller also would be interesting if the shaped block between the fingers was a single piece from the end of the saw cut to the forward face of the rudder and made of a contrasting wood.

Tillers with profile shape are often laminated; the curves are gentle, so the veneers can be fairly thick. You may even be seized with the desire to glue the tiller up out of veneers of contrasting wood. We'd resist this temptation, since we think this type of tiller has been way overdone—they seem to be on nearly every cheap production boat that doesn't have a wheel.

Hiking stick. If your boat is an athletic sailer, you may want a hiking stick for your tiller. You can make one of wood, but the making functional hardware offers some interesting complications. The easiest and most efficient approach is to buy one. Most major marine suppliers offer a selection of moderately priced, simple black "tiller extensions" with spiffy universal joints (see Appendix B, "Resources"). If you have your heart set on a beautiful wooden hiking stick, it should be possible to meld your handmade handle with the universal joint hardware from a commercial hiking stick. Try cutting the commercial stick's aluminum tubing about 6″ (more if your boat is

Pulling tape and masking foil.

Chapter 12

Painting and Varnishing

We spend a lot of time at boat shows talking about finishing.

"What paint did you use? Is this two-part? What's the varnish? Have you used no-sand varnishes?" "What about oils?" "How did you paint the waterline?" "How do you keep the varnish looking like that?" "How do you paint neatly next to varnished rails?" "How did you get the paint work so smooth?"

And, our favorite: "This is fiberglass, right? It's too nice to be wood."

A wooden boat doesn't have to look as if it was taken out behind the shed, beaten with sticks, and painted with a mop. We aren't any more enamored of the finishing process than most people, but we want our boats to look good. As an added incentive to keep sanding, a finishing job that is done right the first time holds up better and requires less work in the long run. Many of our boats go several years between paint jobs—and still look good.

We haven't found any magical shortcuts to apply to the finishing process. We have learned a lot over the years, and we learn more every time we open a can—sometimes more than we'd like.

Getting Ready to Finish

CHOOSING THE RIGHT EQUIPMENT
Painter protection

Dust mask, respirator, gloves…you'll need them. Please see Chapter 2, "Materials and Tools" for a detailed discussion.

Brushes

Decent brushes. Buy good brushes. You may need to shop around to find some, but about twenty bucks ought to get you an acceptable 2½″ brush from a marine supplier. We prefer natural bristle brushes. Get a brush for paint (or better yet, two: one for light colors and another for dark) and one for varnish. We tend to spend a little more on varnish brushes—for the positive psychological effect if nothing else. Look for a nice, full brush with well-flagged bristles.

New brushes shed bristle parts for a short introductory period. You can minimize this by dipping each brush in thinner, then gently massaging it and spinning dry. Try not to use a brand-new brush for a final coat.

We find ourselves using 2½″ brushes for nearly everything, with the addition of a couple of good small artist's brushes, particularly a flat one about ¾″ wide, and a fine one for the niggly bits.

As the brushes age, they can be demoted in this order: varnish, final painting, early coats and priming, antifouling paint.

Cheap brushes. The classic cheap brush is the throwaway (tab) brush; those thin, flat-bristled brushes with wooden handles. We apply epoxy putty and bedding compound with them, but they are useless for painting and varnishing. Tab brushes shed their bristles continuously. It is impossible to load one of these brushes with a reasonable amount of paint and brush it out smoothly. Tab brushes seem like a good deal, especially if you don't want to clean brushes, but they cost plenty in time, flying paint, and a lousy finish.

Foam brushes. We hated foam brushes when we first tried them. We either squished on too much paint or swiped too much off. We still don't like them for most painting, but there are times when we feel downright fond of them.

Foam brushes are ideal for applying clear sealer, oils, and build coats of varnish; getting paint and varnish into awkward places like open gunwales and around the inner stem; painting inside daggerboard and centerboard trunks (tape the handle to a stick); painting small parts; and touching up small flaws in paint and varnish work. We know people who swear by them for final coats, but we prefer traditional bristle brushes.

These brushes hold up reasonably well when used with most marine finishes. They get floppy fairly quickly when used with sealer and antifouling paints. If in doubt, test the brush with your finish first.

Painting containers

You can buy official plastic or paper containers, but we usually eat enough yogurt and sour cream during the year to keep us in clean containers throughout the finishing season. A fresh container for each coat is cheap insurance.

Paint strainers

Buy good paper-and-mesh cone strainers for straining paint, and use them every time you pour paint or varnish from the can to your working container. This is especially important if you're using a glossy finish, but it is better to use them every time, if possible. If the brand of paint you are using is too thick to go through a strainer (in this lifetime) and is also too thick to paint with, add thinner and stir well (but gently) before you strain. If the paint handles best without thinner, try to use a fresh can for a last coat.

Tack rags

We use commercial tack rags to remove the last specks of dust before finishing. Unfold and scrunch these to use up every bit of surface area. Store partially used ones in tight plastic bags with the air squished out. Be extremely careful of the plank edges when tacking off bare or sealed wood; even though you've rounded and sanded well, it's easy to start a splinter with the tag rag's tacky cheesecloth. At best, you'll have a little piece of wood to reattach with five-minute epoxy. At worst, you'll have a painful repair requiring the attentions of the local emergency room. Wear a latex or similar glove when you tack to eliminate gummy fingers.

Tape

You'll need good marine painter's tape wherever you want a sharp line of demarcation between finishes—varnish and paint, topside and boottop, topside or boottop and bottom paint—and you don't want to cut the line by hand. Brown crepe "painter's masking tape" leaves a messy leaky edge. Instead, buy a marine finishing tape such as the light green slightly stretchy tape called Fine Line from 3M. This tape is not designed to be exposed to the elements or left on the boat for long periods. Ask your supplier for special tapes made for these conditions.

Cleaning Brushes

Cleaning varnish and paint brushes need not be a horrible job, unless you are like Ruth and have a habit of dunking them in thinner and forgetting about them.

Wearing protective gloves, work the thinner gently but firmly into the brush with your fingers. Tip the brush upside down to run thinner under the ferrule. Spin the brush with a brush spinner (in an empty garbage can) as you progress. When the brush is clean, hand-mold the bristles into the proper shape, wrap the brush in clean paper or tin foil, and hang it by the hole.

To conserve thinner, assemble three or four empty gallon containers and label them from best to worst. Pour the used thinner back into the jugs in order. The paint sediments will settle to the bottom of the jugs, allowing you to reuse the clarified thinner. It takes us years to fill a jug with sediments.

You can sometimes salvage brushes left in thinner by soaking them in acetone or lacquer thinner. Wear protective gloves! These solvents are hard on the bristles, so you might want to soak the cleaned brushes in linseed oil for a few days afterward. Remember to take them out and clean them with thinner before they get gummy.

Light

You can't do good paint and varnish work if you can't see. Sunlight is ideal, but the weather doesn't always cooperate. Most shops, ours included, are not lighted ideally for decent finishing.

Overhead lights provide good overall illumination, but leave the sides of the boat in shadow, especially if the boat is sitting upright. We've affixed clamp lamps to various objects in the shop, with varied success. White plastic shades are less glaring than shiny metal ones.

When we started taking pictures for this book, we dug out an old lightweight camera tripod and stuck a clamp lamp on it. This has turned out to be useful little rig for highlighting dark areas and creating a raking light to illuminate holidays (missed areas) and thin spots. You can put it just about anywhere, including in or on the boat, and aim it where needed, raising and lowering the height of the light to suit.

The ultimate finishing light is a photographer's portable spotlight with a silver reflective umbrella. If you shop for one of these lights, be sure to emphasize that you require a rig with a bulb that can withstand jostling and bumps, even when lit. We bought an inexpensive (i.e., heavy) telescoping 11' stand for ours. If you do lots of finishing work (or decide to take up indoor photography) and can justify the expense, having your own portable sun is grand.

If you are having trouble getting ample indirect light, try using reflective material. We covered the ceiling of a small area used for painting and varnishing parts with a plastic foil-faced bubble-wrap-type insulation. The slightly irregular silvery surface bounces indirect light all over the place, greatly multiplying the available light from windows and lamps. Portable panels made of the same stuff can reflect extra light where you need it.

DEALING WITH IMPEDIMENTA
Dust and its relatives

Oh, expletive. Building—and sanding—boats creates flying particles, from chips to motes. Finish work requires no free-ranging particles of any size. There's no way around it, if you're going to finish in the shop, the dust's gotta go. The best weapons are an air filtration unit along with an efficient dust collection system and, after that, an efficient shop vacuum.

If you seem to have an excessive problem with dust, it may be that the shop is exceptionally dry. Bringing the air back to normal humidity should help.

Don't forgot to rinse the sanding dust off your person and change to clean, non-lint-dispensing clothes. Also, be advised that it's easy to get chilly and absentmindedly pull on a sweater and look down, much later, to find dozens of little wooly tendrils protruding from your fresh varnish.

Fluorescent light advisory. Hanging fluorescent shop lights collect dust. They also shed dust as they vibrate, especially when turned on and off—even if you vacuum them very, very well. We can attest, to our sorrow, that this formerly hidden dust is quite noticeable in fresh glossy paint and varnish. If you can't use other lights or move the boat, you're a candidate for the last resort: suspend clear plastic sheeting under the lights (loads of fun, but it works).

Natural hazards

Insects wish to kill themselves in your varnish- and paintwork. Use a knife point or brush to flick away the big ones (deerflies, moths, monster blackflies) that land in fresh finish that you can still brush out, but leave the rest to their fate and rub the corpses away when the finish dries. Six (or eight) tiny footprints show up less than the field of battle with a bug stuck in tacky finish.

Trees shed body parts throughout the warmer months. If you live with pines, check for pollen loading up in the flowers in spring or early summer so you don't end up with a yellow boat.

MARKING A WATERLINE

The easiest way to mark the waterline of a small boat is with a pencil on a spacer block. The floor doesn't necessarily need to be level but it is does need to be flat, without hills and valleys.

The closer you can get the boat to the floor, the smaller the marking block has to be and the more accurate your waterline will be. A smooth floor is a big help. The planks of our shop floor are slightly cupped, requiring a big marking block to average out the differences. It would be quicker if we invested in several sheets of ½" plywood for a temporary floor.

Figure 12.1 shows an adjustable waterline marking block.

12.1 Scribing the waterline using the floor as a guide. This jig is rather tall, cumbersome, prone to inaccuracies, and the cradles holding the boat are always in the way. Using the shorter jig shown in the figure on page 242, with the boat sitting on the floor, is much better and easier.

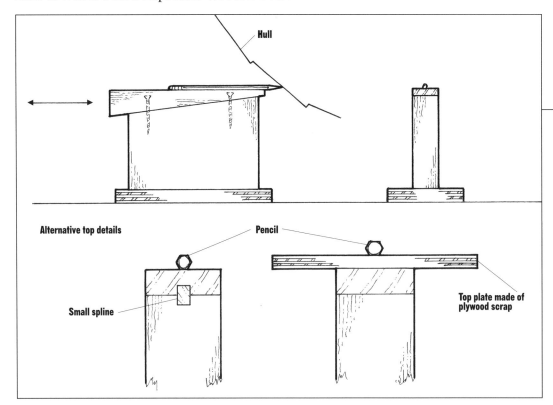

Fig 12.1 An adjustable jig for marking the waterline from the floor. Add dadoes and a spline to hold the top wedge in place while adjusting the height of the pencil. Slide the pencil along a top plate to mark the hull while holding the block firmly in place on a rough floor such as concrete.

Positioning the boat

The first job is make the boat's waterline parallel to the floor, which may or not be level with the rest of the universe. Start at the bow and stern, with the keel resting on the floor.

If you marked the waterline on the transom, skeg or sternpost, and on the stem, your job is easy. Measure from these marks to the floor, adjusting the height with blocks under the keel until both measurements are the same.

If, on the other hand, there are no marks, go back to the full-sized patterns or lofting to find the distance from the sheer to the waterline at the stem and transom. Armed with these numbers, measure the distance from the sheer to the floor at both ends of the boat and write these down. Subtract the sheer-to-waterline distances from their respective sheer-to-floor measurements to get the waterline-to-floor distances.

Ideally, the waterline-to-floor distances will be the same on both ends of the boat, but usually are not at this point. To rectify this situation: Find the difference between the two distances. Divide this number in half, then add the halved amount to the smaller distance and subtract it from the larger. When the two waterline-to-floor distances are the same, write the number down and circle it. You will be adding this distance back to the two sheer-to-waterline measurements to level the boat. The waterline-to-floor distance is also the height of the marking pencil.

You don't have to be overly fussy at this point; just get it close.

Next, measure from the sheer to the floor near the middle of the boat, where the sheer is parallel to the floor. Do this on both sides of the boat. Adjust the boat athwartships until the measurements are equal.

To hold the boat's position athwartships, clamp posts (¾" x 2", for example) to the rails on each side of the boat, resting the ends firmly on the floor. If the boat's sides have a lot of flare, insert a wedge between the rail and post to hold the post nearly vertical. Hold the wedges in place with double-sided tape. An identical wedge inside the hull will protect the gunwale and make clamping the post much more secure. Or, you can place large wedges under the boat. Make sure that the wedges won't interfere with marking the waterline.

Because any adjustment in one direction affects everything else, first get the boat reasonably parallel to the floor in both directions, then go around the boat, fine-tuning in increments until you're satisfied.

Using the marking block, and fine-tuning the waterline

Set the waterline marking block, complete with pencil, to the proper height. Mark the hull by sliding the block along the floor. If a rough floor makes this difficult, fasten a scrap of plywood on top of the wedge as a plate, then hold the block in place and slide the pencil along the plywood plate to mark the hull. Be sure to mark on the edges of the planks as far as you can.

If you would like a boottop, set the marking block for the desired height and make another trip around the hull.

Obviously, the pencil lines will disappear the moment you start sanding. Turn the hull over. Compare the two sides of the boat, especially at the bow and stern, to see if the lap jogs fall in the same places and look about the same. Tweak those that don't. When you're pleased with how things look, tap small, rounded depressions into the wood every 1″ or 2″ along the penciled waterline with a centerpunch. These will survive sanding, normally will not fill with paint, and are nearly invisible on the finished boat. Make enough of them that you will be able to follow them easily when it's time to tape off for the bottom paint. You can also score the waterline into the wood if you prefer.

Other methods

If this approach to marking the waterline doesn't suit you or your boat, we recommend the method described on page 219 of Greg Rössel's fine book, *Building Small Boats* (see Appendix C, "References").

The Finishing Procedures

FILLING DINGS AND OTHER IMPERFECTIONS

By now, your boat should have only superficial flaws that need filling only for cosmetic reasons. (See Chapter 8, "'Outbone' and Rail, Then Off the Jig," and Chapter 9, "Building the Interior.")

In varnished areas, you can try healing small imperfections by putting on a couple of coats of varnish, filling the flaws with clear epoxy and continuing to varnish after the epoxy cures. Scrape and sand the epoxy well before varnishing. In painted areas, catch imperfections lingering after the sealer and prime coats with trowel cement. Trowel cement is harder than many primers. Sand carefully or you'll take the primer right off.

If you dropped a tool and now have a ding in an all-to-obvious place, see Appendix A, "Oh, @#!," "Sweating Out a Ding," for a little magic that will make it disappear.

FINISH SANDING…AND RELATED TECHNIQUES

When people ask us what magic potions we use to create smooth and glossy finishes, we're tempted to show them our fingertips—the ones that don't have a lot of fingerprints left on them. Using decent marine paints and varnishes, and a little surfacing putty and trowel cement, is vital, but mostly what it takes is sanding, lots of sanding.

One of us (John) rather likes to sand, the other (Ruth) rather hates it. If you love it, wonderful. If you hate it, you're just going to have to grit your teeth and do it. We have some suggestions that will make finish-sanding go as easily and efficiently as possible, but there is procession of sandpaper in your future.

Scrapers

We've talked about using scrapers during the building process. Don't put them away. Keep them razor sharp and nearby, for zipping off hardened epoxy; shaving down ex-

cess surfacing putty and trowel cement; and paring off drips, runs, and sags. For offending globs higher than the surface, reach for a scraper first, then sand.

Sandpaper and related materials

Buy good-quality sandpaper that is designed to resist clogging, an attribute you'll instantly appreciate if you've been sanding paint with inexpensive papers from the hardware store. These cheap, "brown" papers can be fine for bare wood, but they quickly clog with paint and varnish. Religiously toss worn or clogged paper. Certain operations, sanding epoxy and sealer for example, are just plain hard on sandpaper—so plan on using more.

Our stack of finishing paper includes: 80, 100, 120, 150, and 220 grits. We occasionally use finer grits, but not often. Anything coarser than 80-grit belongs to the stages before finishing, unless you've had a disaster and need to remove a lot of finish.

Other abrasive materials. We like the thin sanding sponges that are about ¼″ thick, in medium and fine grits. These work well for curved and rounded surfaces, and for really awkward places. Try folding one around a small flat stick to do the slots in open gunwales. We also use thin, flat abrasive pads—the green kitchen pot scrubbie's finer marine cousins—for lightly scuffing edges on final coats, when you don't want to take off any more finish than absolutely necessary (see Appendix B, "Resources").

Sanding blocks. Use blocks wherever possible for finish sanding. This way, you'll be fairing out the surface as you sand. Our current favorites are made of hardwood and padded with worn abrasive pads or thin sanding sponges cut to fit.

Power tools for sanding

Admit it: When we said "easily and efficiently," you had visions of sleek tools with cords attached, dancing their way to a perfect finish. We've had those dreams, too. In our

12.2 It's best to fill all the little imperfections in the hull on the bare wood, then sand in preparation for sealer and primer.

12.3 It's a very good idea to wear a respirator when putting on sealer, even outside.

12.4 Varnishing a set of spars suspended from strings tied to the tall sawhorses.

dreams, the sanding machines are utterly silent, collect all their own dust, never leave swirl marks, fit easily in any tight corner, and hardly ever need the paper changed. Oh, and our dream machines are affordable and run forever.

These are dreams. We haven't found power sanders to be particularly useful for finish-sanding our smaller boats. Given the multitude of edges, tight spots, and curves, it isn't possible to fit a sander in many places. By the time you subtract all that area, there's not much left. You can use a palm sander or small orbital on the keelson and flatter runs of planking, but it's often not worth the hassle of loading the machine with paper. However, if your boat has a flat bottom or is large enough, go for it.

Use care when wielding sanding machines. It's extremely easy to take too much paint or varnish off, especially along the planking edges. Avoid knocking the sander along the planking edges, gunwales, or rails.

FINISHING ORDER OF OPERATIONS

Once the holes are filled and the surfaces sanded smooth, you may begin applying finishes. Our standard order of operations goes like this:

1. apply sealer on all surfaces to be varnished or painted,
2. varnish until done, at least four or five coats,
3. prime all surfaces to be painted, cutting in 1/4″ shy of varnish lines (along with the varnish coats),
4. when the varnish is good and hard, tape and mask off for interior and topside paint,
5. paint the interior,
6. paint the topsides (right after the interior),
7. tape and mask off for bottom paint (if any),
8. apply bottom paint,
9. remove masking and tape,
10. when finishes are well-cured, apply penetrating oil to parts receiving this finish.

WORKING WITH SEALER

Finish paints and varnishes are not meant to be used on bare wood. You must start with sealer and/or primer first. If you're varnishing, you may use sealer or thinned varnish for a first coat (see below). If you're painting, you may use sealer alone, sealer and primer, or primer alone, depending on the manufacturer's recommendations and your own preferences.

We like using clear sealer as a first coat, especially on the plywood. It isn't difficult to apply and dries very quickly. It does contain plenty of volatile ingredients, so spare yourself a spectacular headache (and worse) by wearing a respirator. Foam brushes work fine. Aim for a good continuous coating, but don't slather the stuff on. It will run and sag, and it's not all that easy to sand. You don't have to worry much about keeping a wet edge, just do a neat and thorough job. You'll be sanding this coat well to smooth the surface.

WORKING WITH VARNISH

Varnishing is the focus of more heated discussion than any other finish. Rarely is anyone ambivalent about varnish. A large segment of the marine coatings industry is devoted to supplying products that purport to look just like varnish, but are much less work, or better yet, "no work," to apply.

We might as well confess right here that we like regular, unadulterated marine varnish. While other coatings may look decent, nothing matches the warm glow of real varnish. This is not to say that we always have a relaxing happy time varnishing; we have our share of runs, sags, thin spots, and holidays (missed places) that somehow escape our devoted attentions. Nevertheless, like anything else, the more you varnish the more skilled you become. So long as it is adhering

Taping Off the Waterline

Taping off the waterline on a lapstrake boat requires a little extra fiddling. Here's how to do it.

12.5 Apply the tape for a waterline from amidships toward the ends of the boat. Cut the tape off past the plank edge and carefully work the end of the tape over the edge and onto the second plank so there are no wrinkles or gaps.

12.6 Lay tape along the waterline on the second plank and trim it several inches past the lap. Work the tape into the corner, over the edge, and overlap it onto the first piece of tape. A putty knife with soft edges (either from age or broken with a file) is ideal for getting the tape tight.

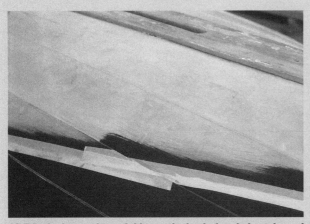

12.7 Both pieces of tape laid over the lap before being trimmed.

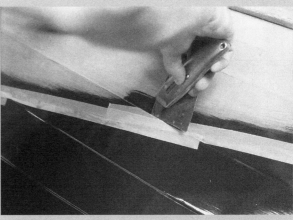

12.8 Trim the tape on the plank edge using a putty knife as a straightedge guide for the utility knife blade. Trim the tape on the first plank along the edge of the first piece of tape.

12.9 The finished taping of a lap.

12.10 The Finished Waterline.

properly, an imperfect coat of varnish is not a total waste of time. Just think of it as another build coat and try to fix the things that went wrong when you do the next, perhaps final, coat.

It isn't necessary to take up holy orders and surrender your life to the rituals of maintaining varnish work if you simply want a little boat that looks grand and has well-protected wood. We leave the 600-grit to the possessed and aim for a decent finish that suits a boat that is likely to find herself occasionally rubbing elbows with evil aluminum skiffs and barnacle-encrusted pilings.

First coat

Delving into the literature reveals that opinions are quite thoroughly divided as whether sealer or thinned varnish makes the best first coat for varnishwork. We've done both with equal success. The clear sealer is rather dark, so you might want to go with thinned varnish if main-

taining the lightest color possible is a concern. The purpose of this first coat is to lock the varnish and the wood together. To do this, the varnish or sealer needs to flow and soak into well-sanded bare wood. We do our first coat over wood that has been sanded with 120-grit paper.

Whatever you do, don't put on full-strength varnish for this first coat, thinking that you can cheat a couple of coats. It is bound to lift, and then you will be stuck scraping and sanding everything down to bare wood. Thin the varnish according to the manufacturer's instructions.

12.11 Masking a varnished transom with aluminum foil is the best insurance against any accidental drips and splatters. On this boat the bottom and the sheerstrake were painted one right after the other and the varnished rails have been masked off to keep them from becoming speckled, or worse.

Techniques for Taping and Masking Off

Crisp, neat, boundary lines where varnish meets paint or paint meets paint make a good finishing job great. Here's a few tactics that will help you achieve a sharp-looking finish:

- *Varnish down onto areas to be painted and feather the edge. Sand well between coats to keep the area to be painted smooth. Tape or cut in when painting for a crisp juncture between varnish and paint. Do the same thing with paint junctions, say between topsides and bottom paint.*
- *To prevent an ugly white primer line on taped edges: Cut in the primer by hand, just shy (⅛″ or so) of the final paint line. Tape for the finish coats only.*
- *Avoid retaping for successive coats if at all possible. (And it usually is, given a little forethought.)*
- *Burnish the tape with fingers or a putty knife, then sand the tape edge lightly with 220-grit to seal the edge.*
- *If you're having problems with adhesion, too little or too much, the tape may have been around for awhile. Try a fresh roll. We also have had problems getting tape to adhere to hard but still youthful (several days old) paint. Try wiping the areas to be taped with denatured alcohol and letting dry thoroughly before taping.*
- *Tape sometimes leaves a haze of adhesive behind. Remove this with denatured alcohol or an adhesive remover (read the label; aggressive stuff). Tape also can imprint noticeably into fresh glossy finishes. Minimize this by burnishing just the business edges. If your tape does imprint, you may find that the marks disappear magically after a few days. Paint*

and varnish continue to cure—and flow—for quite a while after they appear to be "dry." If the marks don't go away on their own, you could buff them out with a finishing compound. Or you can launch her and forget it.

- *It is worth the effort to mask off areas that will not be improved with the addition of errant droplets of flying paint (or worse). Mask off your nicely varnished transom with aluminum foil. (If your boat is large, marine suppliers carry special masking materials and related equipment.) We do it when we tape off for the topside and interior coats, but definitely do it before you paint her bottom. If you're painting the entire outside with topside paint, seriously consider the great benefits of completely masking off your newly varnished rails. Before we bottom paint an upside-down boat, we mask off the topsides (or at least along the waterline on a larger boat) with sheets of newspaper.*
- *Pull the tape when the finish is hard, not brittle. Paint that has leaked under the tape will be less cured than the exposed finish and tiny spots often can be wiped away with clean finger. Barely moisten a small bit of paper towel with thinner if necessary, but don't overdo it, as the solvent will flatten a fresh finish.*

Build and final coats

Unveil your good varnish brush. Reread your varnish can carefully. Some varnishes must be thinned to some degree for each coat.

Warm and sunny breezy dry days are perfect for varnishing. Your job will be more aerobic and more frustrating than it needs to be if you try varnishing out in that bright hot sunshine. One of the advantages of little boats is that they can be moved, so set up in the shade if at all possible. (But beware of trees.) If you must work in the open, see if you can work in morning shade, then let the boat cure in the afternoon sun. If you must work in the sun, try to keep the varnish nearby but shaded.

If you find that your varnish is going off—becoming sticky and hard to brush—too quickly, you can slow things down by adding a little retarding oil. Adding too much retarding oil will kill the gloss, but a few strategically applied drops can make the difference between a horrid varnish job and one that's manageable. If the varnish is still hard to work—drying too quickly, pulling hard, not leveling, and producing lap marks—add a little thinner. Don't be afraid to dribble in oil or thinner as you work. If your varnish is seizing up quickly on a breezy warm day, you have a lot more to worry about than a few microscopic specks of dust. Better to doctor the varnish quickly and keep going, maintaining a good wet edge.

If the weather is cold and clammy, try to get some drying heat to the boat, even if it's just for the few crucial hours after application to get the surface tack-free. Watch your heat sources to make sure that they aren't too close to the boat or anything else.

Let the varnish dry thoroughly before recoating. Remove runs and sags with a sharp scraper. A light preliminary sanding will highlight these. We sand the first coat with 150-grit, then go to 220 for the remaining coats. The first couple of coats typically need thorough but not aggressive sanding to smooth the surface. After that the goal is to build varnish, not take it off, so sand lightly, especially on edges.

Figure on four coats minimum to achieve a basic finish that may survive the boat's first season. A couple more coats will last longer and look better.

Picky finishers wouldn't dream of pouring used varnish back in the can. Whether to pour 100 percent pure varnish back in the can is up to you, but don't ever pour thinned varnish back. Some thinners cause varnish to gel in very unpleasant ways. Clean your varnish brushes immediately after use for the same reason. We've had the varnish set up in horrid little plasticky bits when the brushes were stored overnight in thinner. Cheaper thinners seem to be more of a problem.

"No-sand" varnishes

Quite a few of these "easy-to-use" products have appeared on the market in recent years, with new ones appearing seemingly every week. We have used one typical offering, for build coats followed by regular marine varnish, as recommended by the manufacturer. The no-sand varnish was certainly faster to apply, but it was also thin and raised the grain, making sanding necessary after a few coats.

If you give one of these varnishes a try, follow the manufacturer's instructions, but also use your own judgement. If the surface is becoming rougher than you'd like your varnishwork to be, sand it smooth.

Varnish/oil finishes

There is a whole class of finishes that fall somewhere between varnish and oil. We've never used them, mostly because we like varnish, but also because we don't like the strong orange-yellow tones that many possess. Many people have had good luck with these finishes, especially on solid wood.

WORKING WITH PAINT
Primer

We prime with traditional marine enamel flat white undercoater, one or two coats depending on the level of finish desired. We have used high-build primers, but find them to be generally more trouble than they are worth. If you have filled your holes and dings well, the surface of your boat should be pretty smooth by the time it is ready for primer. Sanding off all the excess high-build primer is largely extra work, especially at the laps. High-build primer can be helpful if your design calls for sheathing the bottom or other areas in epoxy-saturated cloth.

Don't leave your primed boat exposed to the weather. Standard primers absorb rather than repel moisture. If you must paint outside, pick a good day so that you can prime in the morning and get the first finish coat on in time for it to dry sufficiently before the evening dew appears. The primer we use dries for sanding and recoating in four hours, less if it's dry and warm.

12.12 Freehand cutting-in a line with a paintbrush is the neatest way to paint along the bottom edge of open gunwales.

Finish coats: Topside paints

We use quality marine enamels with ample, but not excessive, gloss. Traditional, lower gloss, marine enamels are probably the easiest, most forgiving finish to apply and are also appropriate (see Appendix B, "Resources").

If you lust after the high-gloss two-part finish that looks great on your neighbor's 40′ fiberglass yacht, consider that the yacht keeps its shine with a bevy of fleece-covered fenders and regular trips to the yard. The typical small boat doesn't live the life of a cosseted yacht. It will look awful and suffer lasting harm when it begins to acquire the inevitable dings and scratches unless you can touch up the finish easily. To us, "easily" means grabbing a foam brush and opening a can, not conducting chemistry experiments while wearing a respirator, then trying to make a patch disappear on an unforgivingly shiny surface with buffing compound and a polisher. Many of the high-tech finishes are still the province of the professional with a sprayer, clean room, and full-face, positive-flow respirator—and the boat owner who has the wherewithal to pay such a person on a regular basis. Paint companies keep striving to give the amateur boat painter a maximum-gloss "gelcoat-in-a-can" that can be applied with a brush on a Saturday morning, but these finishes can be tricky to apply and chemically noxious. Their hard, glossy surface will highlight every imperfection in your building and prep work, and thereafter show every encounter with unfriendly surfaces. We don't recommend these finishes.

The same techniques used for varnishing apply to painting. Keep going to maintain a wet edge, and resist the temptation to overwork areas, especially as the paint begins to seize up. The judicious application of retarding oil or thinner can make the difference between a decent job and a mess. Don't be afraid to doctor the paint a little if temperature or temperament warrant.

12.13 Mask off the freshly finished topsides to keep tiny droplets of thick antifouling paint that like to leap off the ends of brush bristles as you paint the bottom. The respirator is a good idea, too.

Finish coats: Bottom paint

If you don't plan to leave your boat in the water for more than a few days at a time, topside enamel or even varnish will be fine on her bottom. If you will be leaving the boat in the water for the season, you might find that an old-fashioned sloughing antifouling paint will do. Because we are constantly putting our own boats in and taking them out of the water, and carrying them to and from vehicles and trailers, we prefer a hard antifouling paint that doesn't rub off on everything that touches it.

Read the can. Most bottom paints come with specific instructions regarding the timing of launching after the application of the paint.

OIL

Many people turn to a marine penetrating oil for a no-maintenance, easy-to-apply finish. These oils are often sold as "teak" oil, and each manufacturer has its own special formula. Oil is certainly simple to apply, but it's not

---

Gloss vs. Semi-gloss vs. Flat

Glossy paints and varnishes reflect the sun's damaging rays better than semi-gloss and therefore last little longer and offer better protection to the wood underneath. Those same reflected solar rays are hard on the eyes, so we prefer to compromise and use paint that is semi-gloss or a bit flatter on the interior of our boats. Glossy seats are slippery and can make rowing and sailing the boat difficult, so you might consider using a less shiny finish for them (or for at least the part where you sit). As an added benefit, flatter finishes tend to hide small imperfections—in the workmanship and the finishing.

Most marine paint manufacturers offer only a few colors in semi-gloss or flat. You may be able to dull the standard glossy marine paints by mixing in a compatible flatter paint. More likely, you will need to add an appropriate amount of the manufacturer's flattener or "satin additive," following the instructions on the can. Make sure you mix enough for the whole job. Keep the flattening agent evenly distributed throughout the paint by stirring it every now and then as you paint. Newly applied flattened paint tends to look awful as it begins to set up, with irregular flattened and shiny patches, but there's usually no reason to panic. It will come together as the paint finishes drying.

You also can flatten varnish and paint with a judicious rub-down with very fine bronze wool. (Don't use steel wool on a boat, ever. It will leave countless microscopic, rusting bits of itself behind in your finish.)

low-maintenance, unless you don't mind gray or black-ened unbrightwork. We recommend oiling cedar floor-boards, which weather to a practical gray patina. Our *Iris* has oiled northern white cedar seats and thwarts. Keeping these a gorgeous honey color requires storing her with plenty of air circulation, and wet-sanding the seats with oil several times a year. The result is a beautiful soft finish, not slippery and ideal for sitting on. Nevertheless, we'll probably paint the seats in another year or two.

We don't recommend oiling mahogany, especially transoms. It develops ugly black streaks and looks awful within days, quicker if it's raining.

"OH, @!#," FINISHING DIVISION

The following hints come under the category of "Things We Learned the Hard Way." We pass them along with our compliments.

Patience will be rewarded

When working with one-part polyurethane modified marine enamels, obey the words of our local paint rep: "Apply the product thinly." If your first brush strokes cover well, you're putting it on too thick. If your arm is getting tired, you are probably brushing it out enough. The paint is meant to go on in a thin layer; don't try to speed things up by laying it on thick. You will pay with sags, runs, drips, and s-l-o-w drying. You will also have to sand off most of what you put on to make her look halfway decent. Three good thin coats are less work than two awful thick coats.

What do you mean it's not dry?

It is possible to buy a can of paint that will not dry—at least not for a very, very long time—from one of the major manufacturers of marine paint. Bad batches rarely but occasionally happen and, trust us, finding out that you've just painted your boat with one wrecks your day (week). Prevention is the cure; paint some scrap wood with all newly opened paint and make sure it dries and otherwise behaves as it should before applying it to the boat.

In fact, it's a good idea to test all your finishes. A passenger schooner crew of our acquaintance spent much quality time wooding their varnish work because the company decided to save money by using up some old, partially used varnish that had been stored over the winter in a unheated garage. The varnish set up as a viscous goo. Store your finishes in a room in which you'd be reasonably comfortable: no freezing sheds or superheated attics.

Why there was only one Yellow Submarine

The behavior of paint varies markedly amongst different colors in a given line of paint from a single company. Some colors are a joy to apply, others are a royal pain in the nether regions. Take reds, for example. We and our fellow boatbuilders have plenty of horror stories about

12.14 A little planning makes sure IRIS is neatly varnished and painted just in time for a road trip to a boat show.

painting boats red. "Four coats!" "No way!" "Mine took six!" Yellow is also on our list of despised colors. (Seven coats.) On the other hand, dark greens and dark blues are often docile, well-behaved paints that look perfect after two coats.

So, if you're having difficulties painting, it might be you, but it could be the paint. Collect war stories from other boat people. Call the company's local rep—the person who deals with boatyards. If there's a problem with a color or a batch, it probably won't be news to him or her.

Chapter 13

Fitting Out

An Ellen fitted out as a tender.

At this point, the end is in sight. Much of work remaining requires a few simple tools and very little production of saw- or sanding dust.

Collect all of the freshly painted and varnished interior parts. Assemble parts that require it, such as foam-filled boxes and their seats.

Before you reinstall all of those lovely parts in the boat, save yourself the grief of vacuuming little wood chips from all sorts of nooks and crannies by installing as much hardware as possible before putting the boat back together.

Hardware and Fittings

FINDING GOOD HARDWARE

Nothing causes us more consternation and frustration each season than the arduous process of finding and actually acquiring decent bronze hardware for our small boats. It is possible to find some items in stainless steel or die-cast (often chromed) zinc, but these aren't usually appropriate in terms of looks, and many are decidedly inferior in quality. We prefer bronze, but it's a challenge to find well-made bronze hardware for smaller boats.

Small-boat hardware experiences hard wear, especially in the marine environment. Looks aren't enough; the gear must work well and keep working. We've heard tales of snapped oarlocks (including some made of bronze), and we've received orders of bronze hardware with roughly machined sheaves that would instantly shred a line, pintles and gudgeons that fit so sloppily as to never work, oarlocks that had to be pared down to fit in their sockets, and assorted other pieces that were just plain unattractive, clunky, or poorly designed. Then, of course, there are the items that never appear at all, lost in the timeless zone known as "back order."

There seems to be a good deal of flux in the bronze hardware business. Major manufacturers can suddenly begin producing junk instead of reasonably decent stuff, or simply disappear. Good little companies come and go. We have listed companies with which we have had positive experiences in Appendix B, "Resources." They are just a beginning. When you start thinking about building a boat, commence the search for hardware. Collect catalogs from marine supply houses. Contact the little shops and foundries that advertise in the classifieds of boating magazines. Let them know what you're looking for. Even if they don't have it and can't help you, you'll be generating half of the economic equation that may someday improve the situation: demand.

The other solution to the hardware problem is to fabricate the pieces. You can do the work yourself or employ a machine shop. A surprising amount can be done with plate, rod, bar, and tube stock to create hardware that is often better than what you can buy.

John is not a machinist, though he's enjoyed hours of watching machinists work their magic. This chapter reflects what he managed to soak up while idling about watching others work, and plenty that he learned the hard way, making hardware for our own boats.

FABRICATING YOUR OWN BRONZE HARDWARE AND FITTINGS
Working with bronze

Bronze is a reasonably easy metal to work with the tools found in most wood shops. This is a good thing, as it's often best to make your own hardware, especially for small boats with traditional or uncommon rigs. You can make bronze hardware by fabricating it from rod and plate or by making patterns for casting it.

Bronze rod and all-thread are readily available through marine suppliers that deal in materials and equipment for wooden and traditional boats. You'll probably have to order bronze plate through the mail (see Appendix B, "Resources"). If you live near a boatyard that is using something other than stainless, try them. They might be willing to sell you a small square. Machine shops and metal fabricators are another possibility, though a dim one, if they actually build and rebuild parts.

Most of the fittings for smaller boats can be made by cutting out shapes from plate and rod. Though simple, these shop-made fittings often look better than manufactured fittings made for boats bigger than yours.

Bronze? brass? naval bronze? naval brass?!

The terminology for the range of bronze to brass alloys is confusing. Generally speaking, both contain copper, tin, and zinc. Brass contains copper and zinc, with small amounts of tin sometimes added for strength and color. Bronze is a combination of copper and tin, with small amounts of zinc occasionally added to aid fusing and machining.

For boat hardware, you need a metal on the bronze end of the continuum. Brass, especially the cheaper alloys typically used for inexpensive household hardware, rapidly disappears in the marine environment. The best way to be sure that you're getting the right stuff is to talk with a reputable supplier who understands marine applications. Tell him or her exactly what you need to do with the metal. As you read plans and specifications, you will discover references to different bronzes. Some of these, such

as silicon, phosphor, or manganese, name elements added to improve certain characteristics. Others, such as Tobin or naval bronze, are proprietary "name-brand" alloys, with their own particular proportions and added elements.

We have worked with two forms of plate bronze: silicon bronze and naval bronze. Silicon bronze is a very strong and long-lived bronze. It is also hard to cut and drill. Just to drive everyone a little crazy, naval bronze sometimes is called naval brass. This alloy has a high percentage of zinc, which makes it easier to work with woodshop tools. Though this metal is more than strong enough for small-boat fittings, we have had reservations about using it below the waterline on boats that are kept in the water for any significant amount of time. However, we also have heard high praise for naval bronze from a manufacturer of high-quality marine hardware.

Recently, we asked a metal supplier to recommend a bronze alloy that was strong and long-lasting but easier to work than silicon bronze. He suggested 90/10 copper-nickel (see Appendix B, "Resources").

Laying out for the fittings

Your plans may show the needed hardware, or you may have to measure your boat parts and figure things out for yourself. Wait to make hardware until you have the rele-

13.1 An awl scores accurate lines on bronze plate.

13.2 A fine, permanent marker marks bronze rod for holes and cuts.

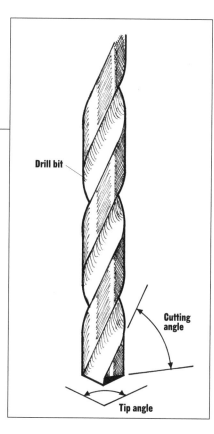

Fig 13.1 Drill bits ground with a blunt tip angle and blunt cutting angle drill holes in bronze smoothly and safely. Running the drill at slow speed helps reduce heat buildup, the enemy of working with most metals, including bronze.

Drill bit

Cutting angle

Tip angle

vant pieces of boat ready for measuring. Make freehand sketches showing the necessary dimensions: length, width, radius of ends, hole centers, etc. Then you can accurately draft the pieces right on the bronze plate. If you want accurate drawings beforehand, make them full-size on graph paper. If you'd like to see how the pieces will fit on the boat, make a simple mock-up of card stock.

On bronze plate, use an awl to draw thin, accurate score lines ideal for centerlines and other precise markings. (Because the awl cuts a fine groove in the surface, the tip of a centerpunch will stick right on the line.) However, the score line can be hard to see, especially when bandsawing. A strong light helps. One trick is to mark a broad line with a medium-width permanent marker, then score an accurate line with an awl through it. The bright awl mark shows up very crisply on the black ink. For most other marking jobs, a fine-tipped, permanent marker's clean but somewhat fat black line will do. It is certainly easier to see and use. If you make a mistake with the marker, clean it off with a little denatured alcohol. If you make a mistake with the awl, ah well, see if you can flip the piece over....

For the most part, a fine-tipped permanent marker is the best tool for marking the rod. To clearly mark a line to help locate the tip of a centerpunch for a hole, score the marker line a couple of times with the corner of a file.

Draw all of your fittings on the plate and rod. Leave a healthy 1/16" between them for the width of the metal-cutting bandsaw or hacksaw blade. Add 1/16" to the length of any rod piece that will have the head peened over.

Punch the centers of all holes-to-be. To punch for holes in the rod, clamp the rod to the bench with softwood blocks and punch on the file-scored line.

Drilling

It is much safer and easier to drill the plate and rod before sawing the pieces apart. A drill press really is the tool for this job. If you don't have one, it is best to borrow one to use or find someone willing to do the job for you.

One important exception: Drill the holes located in or near curved areas of pieces to be bent after you bend them. The plate has a nasty habit of kinking at holes.

Set the drill press on its slowest speed. Make sure your drills are sharp. Shape a blunt tip angle and blunt cutting angle on a grinder (see Figure 13.1). The drill must cut efficiently without requiring you to apply a lot of pressure or increase the drill's feed rate too much.

If the feed rate is too high, life gets exciting: The tip of the bit emerges through the bottom of the plate but doesn't cut all the way around the hole, so two little tips of leftover metal become caught in the bit's flutes. The plate ascends the spinning bit. When it reaches the top of the flutes, either the little metal bits break off or the plate starts spinning (while you try to hang onto it)—not good. This scenario is worse with big drill bits, so clamp the plate firmly to the table. If you can't do that, position the plate so it will spin a quarter-turn and hit the drill press post instead of making nearly a complete round, taking a swipe at you on the way by.

Heat is your enemy when cutting bronze. If the metal overheats, it will suddenly become work-hardened and very reluctant to yield to cutting implements. To cool the metal and bit, and aid the drilling process, drop a little light oil or machinist's oil in the centerpunch dimple be-

13.3 A shop-made V-block holds rod for drilling and countersinking.

13.4 Countersinking holes in bronze plate with a machinist's one-flute countersink.

fore drilling, then apply a little more as the bit progresses.

For drilling rod, you will need a V-block at least 12″ long. (You can buy one or make one of hardwood.) Holding the rod at the very bottom of the V ensures that the drill bit, lined up with the V, goes through the middle of the rod (see Photo 13.3).

Countersinking

Circle the holes requiring countersinking with a fine-tipped permanent marker. Determine the countersink required by testing with the appropriate screws. If the holes will receive pins, just touch them with the countersink to break the sharp edge. A single-flute machinist's countersink works best.

Cutting plate

You'll need a bimetal-cutting blade for the bandsaw. Tell your blade supplier what you're cutting so they can steer you to the best type. Buy at least two.

Wear safety goggles. Bandsawing bronze plate

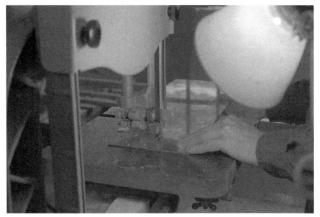

13.5 Good light is a big help in cutting plate stock accurately.

sends little shards flying everywhere. Keep pets and barefoot people out of the shop until you're done and have vacuumed the floor well, or you'll be picking out bronze splinters.

Cutting plate is pretty straightforward. Let the blade do the cutting. Forcing the issue only dulls the blade and builds up unwanted heat. You can usually get through one small sailboat's hardware on a single blade, depending on the bronze alloy. It's time to change blades when the cutting slows and the metal gets hot if you push hard.

Cutting rod

A nifty trick: Start the cut, then rotate the rod against the direction of the blade. This makes a very square cut and never puts too much pressure against the blade or creates too much heat.

Final trimming, shaping, and cleanup

Load a good-quality, 50- or 60-grit belt into the belt sander and set it up for stationary sanding (See Chapter 3, "Some Very Useful Techniques"). Inexpensive belts simply will not work for shaping metal. Set a bucket of water close to hand. If the sander has a speed control, set it for moderately low. Trim each part's edges to final size by sanding until just a hint of the black marker line remains. Remove rough saw marks and smooth the curves. Regularly quench the parts in water to keep them cool, but don't let the water drip on the belt sander—you'll wreck the belt, or short out the sander (or yourself).

Hold each part in your hands as you grind it, so you can tell when the metal begins to warm significantly. Cool the piece long before it overheats. Different types of bronze react differently to heat. Some become pliable, while others get brittle. Keep them cool, and you won't have to worry about a fitting snapping apart in your hands while you're bending it, or later on when under load in the boat.

Break sharp edges on the sander if you're feeling brave. If not, you can do this, and all of the final shaping, with a file.

Shaping the ends of rod fittings. Chuck the rod fittings in the drill press and shape the ends with a file. If you need a perfectly square end, clamp the rod in the chuck very firmly, then lower the spinning rod until its end meets a file lying flat on the table. Hold the file firmly. Touch the rod to the file for few seconds, lift the rod, move the file a little, and lower the rod again.

To peen over a rod end, drill a hole the same size as the rod in a scrap of mahogany or similar wood that is thin enough to allow both ends of the rod to protrude. Place the end not to be peened on a hard metal surface such as a vise, *not* your table saw or bandsaw table. Dig out that ball-peen hammer and peen away, working around the edges and thence into the middle. Many mod-

13.6 Shaping the end of a rod fitting on a "vertical lathe," better known as a drill press.

13.7 A scrap of wood holds a rod fitting for peening the end.

erate blows are better than a few heavy ones.

Clean up the peened head by chucking the rod into the drill press and dressing the rough edges with a file.

Polishing and other refinements

Buff the pieces to an even satin sheen with a fine abrasive pad (see Appendix B, "Resources"). If you prefer a brilliant shine, treat the pieces to some time at a buffing wheel. Rod fittings requiring attentions to their ends can be polished in the drill press after the shaping is done.

Improving the appearance of nuts and bolts. Exposed nuts and hex-head bolts are sharp-edged and pretty ugly. To improve the nuts: Cut the head off a proper-sized bolt and jam two nuts together at one end, leaving just enough room for a third nut, your patient. Wind on your nut, chuck the collection in the drill press, and shape your nut's exposed end to a more pleasing rounded contour with a file. We often use these shaped nuts on rudder pintles.

To shape hex-head bolts, chuck them upside down in the drill press and file to suit.

Bending plate fittings

Most bronzes are best bent cold. Some bronzes become very brittle when heated and will snap when bent. Most of the time you will need to bend thin plate, which is easy. If you require bends in heavier material, we recommend that you seek out the professionals in a machine shop, who will have the expertise and proper equipment.

Sharp bend. To bend plate into a sharp angled bend, stick the plate in a vise at the point of the bend, then hammer the plate to the desired angle, directing your blows at the metal right next to the vise.

Gently curved bend. You'll need a rod, pipe, or curved form (technically known as a mandrill) to bend bronze plate into a curve. It would be nice if you could bend the metal around the exact curve needed, but the bronze springs back like steamed or laminated wood does. If you try to hammer the curve tighter, the metal just springs and bounces, not yielding a bit. To solve this problem, bend the metal around a smaller curve and farther than you want. It will spring back to approximately the desired shape. If you need an exact fit, bend the metal around the desired curve and transfix it with clamps or in the vise, then hammer around the outside of the fittings to stretch the metal, making it retain its shape better.

Firmly clamp fittings with holes located near the portion to be bent in the vise so that the metal cannot kink at the holes.

To bend properly, the fitting must be held firmly and positively to the form. Clamp the form and fitting in the vise. Apply pressure to bend the fitting as close to the form as you can. Tapping the fitting just where it touches the form is helpful. If you just grab the end of the fitting

13.8 To bend plate stock, first clamp a length of rod mandrill onto the unbent fitting at the point in the center of the bend. Bend one end of the fitting around the mandrill until it is vertical.

13.9 A wooden hand-screw helps press the fitting (for the forward end of a sliding gunter rig yard) tight to the mandrill after the second end is bent.

and bend it as you would a laminated part, the fitting can bend anywhere between the form and your hand—most often exactly where you don't want it to.

Many U-shaped bends must be located precisely. To do this, mark the middle of the curve and lay the fitting flat on the bench. Clamp the bending form to the mark on the fitting. Placing a scrap of plate under the other end of the form to makes clamping much easier. Bend each leg of the fitting until vertical (or a little past the angle desired). Unclamp, then reclamp the fitting and form in the vise and hammer around it as above.

Bending in situ. Some fittings are best bent right on the boat or spar. The masthead straps on many of our boats' rigs are in this category. A simple masthead strap, like the Ellen's, has two screw holes and one hole for a sheave pin. The second hole for the pin must be drilled after the strap is bent into shape.

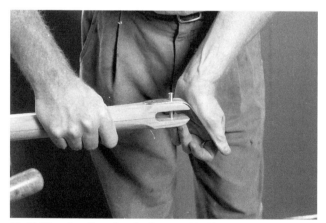

13.10 When bending plate in situ, as with this masthead strap, locate the strap with the sheave pin and fasten the end with a screw, then bend the strap and clamp it in place.

Position the strap on the mast with the sheave pin. Drill for the screw just below the hole for the sheave pin and fasten the strap to the spar. Place a piece of tape crossways (as opposed to lengthwise) across the sheave pin hole on the other side of the mast from the strap. Mark its horizontal center on the tape, out to the edges of the mast past the strap landing zone. Bend the strap over the top into place onto the tape and clamp it in place. Tap it tight to the top of the mast with a hammer if necessary. Drill for and drive the second screw. It would be nice if you could remove the pin and drill through the hole in the mast for the second sheave pin hole, but the mast's wood is soft, the bronze hard, and the bit will wander before cutting the metal. It's better to mark the hole's center by using the marks on the tape and measuring to the center of the strap's width. Small holes ($\frac{1}{4}$″ or less) can be drilled with the fitting in place. For bigger holes remove the strap, and drill the hole with the drill press. Fasten the fitting to a scrap of wood long enough to hang onto as you drill.

ASSEMBLED FITTINGS

Bronze fittings made up of plate and rod can be brazed or welded together. This is best done by a machine shop unless you have the equipment and experience. Make clear drawings with all relevant dimensions (including holes and slots) on graph paper and give them photocopies. Clearly labeled wooden mock-ups can save everyone the experience of standing around looking at a piece of hardware that couldn't possibly be built backwards, but was.

CASTING PARTS

You can make wooden patterns for the hardware you need and have them cast by a foundry. The nuances of this

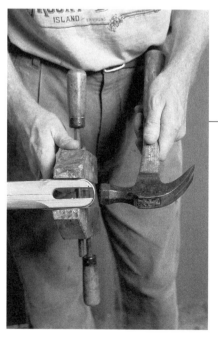

13.11 Hammering helps form the curved portion of the masthead strap tight to the mast.

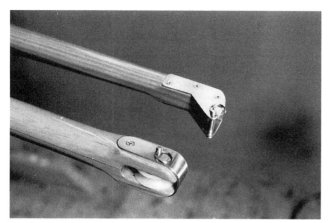

13.12 The finished hardware on the masthead, and the aft end of the yard for a sliding gunter rig (Ellen).

process are outside the scope of this book, but you should know that you can't just whip up a nice little fitting just the way you want it in wood and hope to have the casting come out right. Molten bronze shrinks when it cools, on the order of ³/₁₆″ in 12″, so your pattern must be made oversized, especially for portions that must be machined to fit other parts. And, for an added challenge, the pattern must be shaped so that it can be used to form the shape in the mold, then removed without disturbing the casting sand. Many times, this means making a split pattern in half. Holes in the casting require special treatment, and so on.

Once your pieces are cast, you will need to clean up the pebbly pattern left by the casting sand where it is not wanted, and you may have to machine shafts or mating surfaces.

Having your own hardware cast is serious fun, though. If you can, find a good foundry with someone willing to explain how to make your patterns to their specifications. It is definitely worth the effort.

INSTALLING SPECIFIC HARDWARE AND FITTINGS

Here are some useful techniques for installing the hardware and fittings common to most small boats. Please see the box for general hints that will help you deal with the assortment of other hardware and fittings your boat may possess.

Oarlock sockets

Top-mounted sockets. Top-mounted sockets usually are installed in blocks that raise the oarlocks above the sheer for a more comfortable rowing position and better oar clearance over waves. We prefer to finish oarlock socket blocks

---

Some General Hints for Installing Hardware and Fittings

- *Paint or varnish before drilling the holes for hardware. This way, you don't have to deal with drips from the holes and holes filled with finish.*
- *A little concerned about marking and drilling the holes on your brandy-new glossy boat? Tape the fittings' landing zones with painter's masking tape. Don't be shy with the tape—it's much easier to remove than an errant line from a fine-tipped, permanent marker. (Should you be swearing already, marker ink can often be removed by rubbing gently with denatured alcohol.) Measure and mark for the hardware with ruler, tape, and square, or simply position the piece until it looks right and mark.*
- *Mark the holes to be drilled by tracing the inside of the hardware holes with a fine-tipped, permanent marker. Remove the hardware and dimple the center of the circle with a centerpunch.*
- *Leave the tape on while drilling. It seems to help prevent chip-out, and you can see whether your drill has wandered away from the designated hole circle.*
- *Drill the holes, using the perpendicular drilling jig (see Chapter 9, "Builing the Interior"). If the hole is large, drill it in several steps, starting with a drill bit about half the size desired.*
- *Unless you're absolutely sure, test-fasten the fittings. Correct if necessary. Then remove the tape.*
- *Put a little varnish, bedding compound, or 3M 101 sealant in all newly drilled bolt holes.*

- *Don't overtighten the bolts. Once the nut is snug, any further tightening will only crush the wood, providing a happy home for rot. If the fastenings should be tighter, you need bigger washers or backing plates.*
- *It is a good idea to install any nut with lock washers or a drop of Lock-Tite to keep vibration from working things loose. On hardware that you don't want to remove and reinstall often, an effective trick is to make dimples in the threads of the nuts and its bolt with a centerpunch. Try this on bolts that have been cut or broken off flush with the nut.*
- *To break off the end of a bolt, grab ahold of it with Vise-Grips near the nut. Wiggle it back and forth, gently at first, until the metal fatigues and breaks. File smooth.*
- *Bed large fittings in plenty of goo so you get good squeeze-out all around.*
- *For less work cleaning up the goo, mask the perimeter of the fitting. Tape around it, if that's possible. If not, mask the area where the fitting will land (including under the edges), then put the fitting in place, using a couple of fastenings to accurately locate it. Trace around the hardware, remove it, and cut out the hardware landing site carefully with with a sharp artist's knife. Your aim is to cut only along the line, and only the tape. Install the fitting and clean up the goo with putty knife and thinner, then pull the tape. Be cautious with the thinner—it will kill the gloss in fresh finishes.*

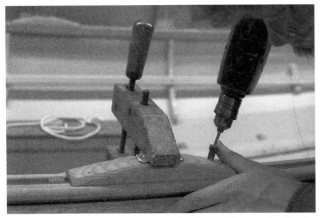

13.13 Clamping the oarlock block to the sheer with a wooden hand-screw while it is fastened to the top edges of the rail and gunwale.

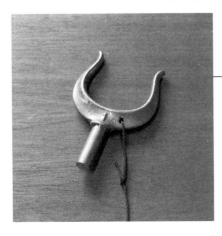

13.14 An oarlock with its tip sawn off, and one horn drilled for a lanyard.

Side-mounted and edge-mounted sockets. These are the simplest to install, as they normally are attached to the inside of the gunwale, with four screws.

Oarlocks

After trimming the bottom of each oarlock—relieving it of the manufactured lanyard eye at its tip—drill and lightly countersink a hole for a lanyard in the flange near the bottom on one side of the horn. Gently round the cut shaft edge with a file. We tie our boats' oarlocks to the risers with fisherman's nylon twine.

Brass half-oval molding

For a boat that will experience normal use, we like to install protective brass half-oval on the outer stem and skeg. If your boat will be beached regularly on hard or rough surfaces, you may want additional half-oval along the keel and garboard edges.

Brass half-oval comes undrilled, so you must centerpunch, drill, and countersink it yourself. The simple jig shown in Figure 13.2 markedly improves the speed and accuracy of the centerpunching operation. Drilling the half-oval is easiest with a drill press, but you can certainly do it with a handheld drill, as the brass is soft enough. Avoid drilling holes where the half-oval must be bent sharply, for it will crimp over at the holes.

Round-over the ends neatly on the stationary belt sander and finish up with a file, or do the whole job with a file.

Name plate

It is worth spending some time searching for a person who can cut letters for your name plate with a router and template, as opposed to the prevalent computer-driven

separately, then attach them when installing the hardware (see Chapter 8, "'Outbone' and Rails, Then Off the Jig"). Before you attach the oarlock sockets to their blocks and thence to the boat, try all of your oarlocks in all of the sockets. If they don't fit, the sockets can be drilled out and filed or the oarlocks chucked in the drill press (before cutting off the tip; see below) and filed down. Use a slow speed and watch out for the whirling horns.

At the bench, rest the oarlock socket blocks on two cleats. Drop a socket in each block, and drill for and drive the screws, centering each socket as best you can.

On many boats, the socket tube will project past the block base and so will the oarlock shaft. To make the oarlocks fit better, we recommend that you bandsaw off the irritating little lanyard eye at the end of the oarlock shaft. This is a start, but you still must drill a tiered hole in the gunwale/rail for the socket tube as well as the remaining oarlock shaft. The upper portion should be $^{13}/_{16}''$ and drilled a little deeper than the projecting $^{3}/_{4}''$ socket tube. The middle portion should be a $^{5}/_{8}''$ or $^{9}/_{16}''$ hole, a little deeper than the remaining $^{1}/_{2}''$ oarlock shaft. At the bottom, drill a $^{1}/_{4}''$ drainage hole. Dab varnish on the newly exposed surfaces.

Clamp each oarlock socket block in place on the rail/gunwale with a wooden hand-screw and fasten with four screws. (Two has proven insufficient.)

13.15 Installing brass half-oval over the outer stem of a Peregrine rowboat.

Painter rigs

Holes drilled through the bow

surface-scratching technique

Painter rigs

surface-scratching technique

Fitting Out

surface-scratching technique

Painter rigs

Holes drilled through the bow

surface-scratching technique

surface-scratching technique

surface-scratching technique

Fitting Out

surface-scratching technique

surface-scratching technique

surface-scratching technique

surface-scratching technique

Painter rigs

surface-scratching technique

surface-scratching technique

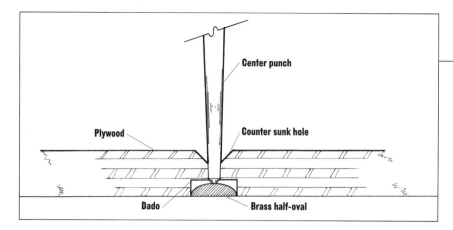

Fig 13.2 To locate the holes for screws in brass half-oval molding, cut a dado the same size as the brass half-oval in a piece of plywood, then drill a hole just big enough for the tip of a centerpunch in the center of the dado. A shallow countersink helps keep the centerpunch from becoming stuck in the hole.

surface-scratching technique. Deeply engraved plates withstand years of exposure and buffing; the scratched plates remain legible for a year or two, at best.

Painter rigs

A painter is nothing more than a rope with a boat attached, but it bears thinking about, as it will be handled every time you use the boat. If you plan to tow your boat in addition to the usual painter tasks of attaching to docks, moorings, other boats, vehicles, and shoreline trees, you will need a towing eye as well (see below).

Strap-eye on the stem. For boats the size of the Ellen, we use $7/16''$ twisted spun-Dacron rope, spliced to a thimble over a bronze ring. The ring is attached to a $2\frac{1}{2}''$ strap eye bolted through both stems with #10 bronze flathead machine screws. To protect the stem, make a $1/16''$ bronze plate to go under the strap-eye, if you like. Make your painter plenty long; $20'$ is about right.

The bronze-ring setup can be replaced with a shackle or fireman's snaphook or snapshackle.

13.16 A painter with an eyesplice around a thimble that has had a ring inserted in it. The ring is held by a strap-eye bolted through the outer and inner stems.

Holes drilled through the bow. For a simple painter rig for a small boat, drill holes through the planking at the appropriate altitude, just aft of the inner stem. Round the edges of the planking well. Sew leather around the painter to protect it and the planking from excessive chafe. Run the well-dressed painter through the holes and around the inner stem, then splice.

Retractable. We used this rig on a small (10′) decked sailboat where we didn't want the painter snaking across the deck and possibly going over the side. Drill a hole oversized for the painter straight through the stems. Run the painter line through and tie a stopper knot at each end. Tie a thin messenger line to the inner knot and lead it aft. Pull the painter inboard when you're sailing, and pull it out when you need to tie up. To avoid weakening the stem, use a relatively small-diameter painter run through a modest hole. A $5/16''$ painter with a $1/2''$ hole worked well for this sailboat.

Towing eye (bow eye)

If you plan to tow your boat behind a larger boat, don't plan on using the painter. The painter is generally too lightweight and located too high on the bow. You need a good, beefy towing eye, situated correctly.

We use a bronze towing eye (sometimes called a bow eye) on our Ellens and other tenders. The towing eye should be located roughly 6″ above the waterline for the proper towing angle. The eye's $3/8''$ threaded rod is exciting to install. Drill successively larger holes until you reach final size. If you haven't marked the location of the outer-stem screws, you are guaranteed to hit at least one while engaging in this enterprise. Once you've finished the hole, and the bluish tinge has cleared from the air, coat the base of the eye and a portion of the threaded rod with 3M 101 (or similar) sealant or bedding compound and insert. If the base of the eye doesn't quite line up with the stem, a couple of tunks with a hammer as the nut is tightened will close the gap.

Lock the eye well with two nuts, a lock washer, or a drop of Lock-Tite.

13.17 Fastening gunwale guard along the top of the rails.

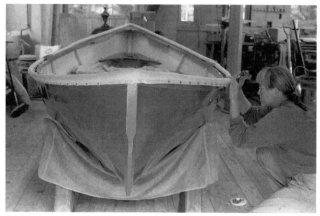

13.18 Fastening the lower edge of the gunwale guard to the face of the rail. An awl helps open the weave for the screws while it is fastened to the top edges of the rail and gunwale.

Cleats and strap-eyes, for extra lines

Even a very small boat can use a stern line. For example, you can snap or tie a bridle setup onto the two sheet-traveler strap eyes on the Ellen's quarter knees, allowing you to tow a light dinghy back to the dock, keep the beer cold, or carry an anchor out for setting. If you don't have strap-eyes in the stern, you may want a strategically located cleat or two.

You may or may not want breast or spring lines, especially if your boat is small, but consider installing cleats amidships that will allow you to use the painter or another line to spring the boat alongside a dock or another boat.

Drain plugs

For drain plugs, we normally use simple screw-in bronze "garboard drains." Install these by drilling through the garboard at the hull's lowest point and bed the through-hull fastening with 3M 101 (or similar) sealant. Greasing the plug threads with petroleum jelly (lip balm works in a pinch) makes it easier to remove.

"Software," Oars, and the Last Few Things

INSTALLING GUNWALE GUARD

We like the 1¼″ cotton canvas–covered rubber, three-quarter–round gunwale guard. It's not the cheapest, but it is soft and resilient. It lasts reasonably well, if you take decent care of it. Because the gunwale guard is made of moisture-trapping rubber, it is important to install it over well-varnished or well-painted rails; store the boat so that moving air can thoroughly dry the gunwale guard; and periodically remove it and refinish underneath.

Affixing gunwale guard is one of those jobs that goes better with two people, but can be done by one.

To install:

- Mark a line for the screws on the edge of the rail ¼″ from the face. Lay out and drill for #6 x ½″ panhead stainless-steel screws (bronze is also fine) every 4″ along

the top of the rail. If you have oarlock socket blocks on top of the rails/gunwales, drill the screw holes in their sides, about ¼″ up from the bottom.

- Make up a trayful of panhead stainless (or bronze) screws inserted through matching washers.
- Fasten the top edge of the gunwale guard in place, starting at the stern end of the rail. Leave enough extra on the end of the gunwale guard to turn the corner and fasten along the top of the transom as far you wish, but don't attach this yet. Use an awl to punch holes for the screws through the canvas. Don't stretch the gunwale guard too tightly, but do pull it smooth. Work it around the oarlock socket blocks. Stop just short of the bow.
- Note: If your boat is a double-ender, start at one oarlock block and do the forward end of the boat in one piece, the aft section in another. Cover the joints with leather.
- Use a compass to mark a line below the top of the rail for the lower #6 x ½″ round-head bronze wood screws into the rail face. Drill for these screws directly below the upper screws.
- Make up a trayful of bronze screws and washers.
- Fasten the gunwale's lower edge to the rail, using the awl to open the canvas. The person working ahead with

13.19 Gently but firmly fitting gunwale guard around the stem results in a neat appearance.

the awl can insert screws in the holes to speed things up. Work up to the place where you stopped at the bow.

- At the bow, gently encourage the gunwale guard around the outer stem. Don't pull hard, or the canvas may eventually tear. The top edge should be pleated around the corner. Only one or two screws should be necessary to hold it in place. The bottom edge should be stretched smooth, not tight.
- Finish installing the rest of the gunwale guard along the rail.
- At the stern, cut the gunwale guard to length. Carefully work the gunwale guard around the corner and up over the transom. Attach the upper edges, then the lowers.
- Design an attractive leather end cover using a paper pattern. Cut out a leather for each end, mark for screws, and punch out the holes. Fasten with screws and washers.

BOAT COVERS

A protective canvas cover can be a very worthwhile investment, especially if your boat has a significant amount of varnishwork. A local sailmaker builds the covers for our boats. Note: If you live where it is hot, especially hot and humid, devise some means of effectively ventilating the cover, or your lovely varnishwork will have mold growing on it.

Marine suppliers offer simple bow holders in metal and tough plastic. You can buy ready-made fiberglass bows from marine suppliers or from the person who makes the cover. We sometimes make our own thin oak or ash bows. If you do make your own wooden bows, varnish or paint them well. Use enough bows to prevent rainwater from pooling in the cover and to support the cover tautly, especially if you plan to tow the boat at highway speeds. Generally speaking, a bow roughly every 3' is about right.

OARS

Decently shaped, good-quality, reasonably light spruce oars suitable for normal use are available from several reputable suppliers (see Appendix B, "Resources"). Flat-blade oars are the most versatile, especially if you expect you will have to row backwards now and again; spoon-blade oars are arguably more efficient for pure rowing. If your boat is a high-performance rowing craft, you probably will want to investigate finer oars made of wood or composites. You also can make your own oars, a pleasant and satisfying project. Most commercial oars come with an adequate varnish finish. A few more coats isn't a bad idea.

What size oars does your boat need? In general, long oars work better for rowing downwind and short oars are more efficient when going to windward. Unless you're racing, you're probably not planning to carry two sets of oars and swap them as conditions change. Here are our oar-length rules of thumb: For pure rowboats

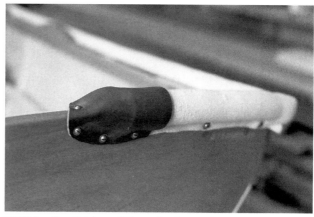

13.20 Leather finishes off the ends of gunwale guard nicely.

with oarlocks on the gunwale (as opposed to on outriggers), select oars that measure twice the boat's beam amidships. For multi-purpose boats like the Ellen that must be maneuvered in tight places and backed down, we pick oars one size smaller than twice the beam amidships. Ellen has a 4' beam, so we use 7½' oars most of the time. We also own a pair of 7' oars for rowing in short, nasty chop and in confined areas like tight harbors and narrow creeks. The 7' oars also work well for the person in the aft position when the boat is rowed double.

Don't buy oars that are too short. If the oars must fit in a short dinghy, acquire a set of break-apart oars.

Leathering oars

Protect your nicely varnished oars with sewn-on leathers. We buy leathers from a local leather craftsman and shoe repairman, who obligingly cuts the rectangles for us, and sew them on with fisherman's tarred nylon twine. Leathering kits are also available. The leathers should be at least 12" long and wide enough to wrap completely around the oar loom with a little overlap—about 6" for most commercially available oars 6' to 8' long. Wait until the varnish on the oars is well-cured before installing the leathers. Keep the leathers supple and quiet with a little petroleum jelly.

Do not tack the leathers on. The leathers will need to be replaced at least several times over the life of the oars, and each time you replace them you'll create a new batch of little tack holes, every one of which is a rot pocket. Someday one of your oars will break when you least expect it.

Sliding seat oars and rigs

Removable sliding seat rigs can be installed to good effect in light, fast glued-lapstrake rowboats. We've done a couple, one in an 18' Peregrine. You will have to shop for a rig and oars that will work for your boat, then do a little thinking about how to adapt the boat to suit. We installed a commercial rig on shopmade stringers. The rig could be removed by pulling a couple of pins. Thwarts could then be installed, and the boat rowed fixed seats.

NOW, PUT HER BACK TOGETHER

Once the hardware (or nearly all of it) is fastened in place, you can get on with the fun of re-installing the risers, floorboards, seats, thwarts, trunk cap, etc. If your boat has a sailing rig (see Chapter 11, "If Your Boat Has a Sail"), pull her outside and put up the mast(s). Run the rigging so that you can decide exactly where the cleats and other related rigging hardware should go, and test the sails for fit.

In fact, even if your boat doesn't have a rig, bring her out of the shop if it's a nice day. One of life's little pleasures is putting the finishing touches on a new boat while the paint glows and the varnish sparkles in the sunshine.

Chapter 14

All Done

There. You can put away the sandpaper (Yesss!), paint, and tools. There's only one big decision left: how and where to launch her. Congratulations. (And please forget about that little sag in the varnish on the aft seat; no one else will notice, and neither will you once you get your boat on the water where she belongs.)

ALL DONE?

In the excitement, it can be very easy to overlook small crucial details, like the drain plug. Before everyone arrives for the launching, take a few minutes to check everything over: Are all knots securely tied? Shackles tight? Painter firmly attached? Oarlocks and oars at hand? Fuel in the tank? Sails rigged properly and ready to go? Will the motor/engine start? Anchor ready, just in case? And it's never too late to make sure that all holes are filled, with their proper hardware...or five-minute epoxy.

Small canning jars made for jelly are perfect for decanting a collection of finish paints and varnishes for last-minute touch-ups. Put them back in their convenient little divided box, along with foam brushes, tiny cotton rags, thinner, and disposable gloves.

And don't forget the chamois for spiffing up the varnishwork.

LAUNCHING

We believe in doing a launching right. The future fortunes of your boat depend on it. We've gone so far as to tell our customers that they will void the warranty on the boats we build if they don't conduct a launching ceremony—and we are only half joking.

How you define "proper launching ceremony" is entirely up to you. Presumably you will not want to go back to the old Norse practice of ensuring good luck and a long life for your boat with human sacrifices, but you may

14.1 A 14' daysailer Frances all rigged up, ready for launching.

14.2 & 14.3 A proper libation, and she's on her way.

not realize that breaking a bottle of bubbly over the bow is a remnant of those ancient practices. Actually, the champagne is a relatively recent innovation; once those in charge deemed blood to be politically incorrect, the liquid of choice became red wine and this remained popular for centuries.

We tend to favor the traditional speech(es), with Neptune's offering poured over the bow, as whacking a full-grown champagne bottle on the stem is rather hard on small boats. Of course, if you have a pre-scored bottle (and a towing eye or a hand-held monkey wrench), go for it. We're not fussy about the libation, as we imagine Neptune tolerates diversity. We've sent boats on their way with the finest champagne, wine of various colors, good local beer, so-so commercial beer, homemade root beer, and a variety of other non-alcoholic brews including a little ginger ale. As far as the speechifying goes, you can't go far wrong with the following:

"I christen thee (your boat's name here), may the gods of the sea protect all who voyage upon her."

Or, "I christen thee (your boat's name here), may she always have fair winds and following seas."

The cheering and grins tend to arise spontaneously.

ON THE ROAD
Trailers

Quite a few of the boats we have built spend much of their time on small trailers. This is a trouble-free existence, provided you keep one important point in mind:

Make sure that your boat rests on her keel, well supported by rollers. Buy extra rollers if necessary. If her weight bears on the beds at the turn of the bilge, she'll be subjected to the bane of all hulls, point-loading. Hard jouncing up and down at highway speeds can crack the planking at the lap joints. This is especially likely if you've

packed a load of gear in the boat, but it can happen with an empty boat.

If you read this too late, locate the leak and scrape the area clean. Usually the break is at the lap joint. Insert a little epoxy putty, then clamp with batten, blocks, and screws. Remove these once the epoxy cures, and fill the holes. Clean up and refinish.

A few trailering hints:

- Ratcheting tie-down straps made of wide, reasonably soft webbing work well. Pad at the gunwales with scrap fleece tucked inside short lengths of pipe insulation.
- Pull the drain plug, and stash it someplace safe. Make sure the painter will stay in the boat. Lash everything else down very securely.
- As mentioned above, a boat isn't meant to be a cargo carrier. Pack heavy gear in or on the vehicle.
- If your boat will be trailered with a cover on, be sure to mention this to the person who makes the cover (see also Chapter 13, "Fitting Out").
- Always use the trailer's safety chains. Cross these and hook them to the holes on your hitch.
- Bigger tires are better for long-distance trailering. Most of our boats go home on 12″ wheels. A spare is an excellent idea.
- Small galvanized steel trailers work fine, but you might want to investigate lighter, springier aluminum trailers meant for smaller, lighter boats if you will be doing a lot of trailering (see Appendix B, "Resources"). There are also very lightweight trailers that can be towed short distances with a bicycle or a car.

Racks

We carry our Ellen, *Iris*, and other boats we can flip and hoist up over our heads on our Jeep Cherokee. Any of the major manufacturers of "roof rack systems" can provide you with a simple bar rack or fancier rigs designed for carrying small boats (usually canoes and kayaks) that may work for your boat. When selecting a rack setup, make sure that the boat's gunwales won't rest directly on the rack's support posts. Check the rack's loading limit, but keep in mind that this number is aimed primarily at preventing weekend warriors from overloading the middle of the rack with lumber. A boat that rests on its gunwales near the rack's posts poses less of a concern, and you may be able to squeak on a little more weight. (This applies only to racks fitted to vehicles with roof gutters, where the weight is transferred directly to the vehicle's framework.) If you have a truck, you can make or buy an even stronger rack.

More hints:
- Pipe insulation is a cheap, somewhat satisfactory solution to the padding problem. It compresses, so the addition of pads made of scrap fleece is a good idea. Fleece alone tends to slide.
- Tubular nylon 1″ climbing webbing makes great tie-downs but is the very devil to untie when it's wet. It also stretches when wet and shrinks back when dry, so check often during and after rain or fog. Melt the ends of cut webbing, or it will unravel rapidly.
- Always tie down the bow to the vehicle's underbody framework. Tie down the stern also if your boat is long.
- Learn the trucker's hitch. It is an invaluable knot for tying your boat down. (See *The Ashley Book of Knots* or any other good knot-tying book.)

Pickup-truck beds

Many smaller boats can ride happily in the back of a pickup. Keep the point-loading problem in mind, and support the boat so her sides won't rest or bounce up and down on the wheel wells.

Unaccompanied travel

You may never need to move your boat someplace far away without taking her there yourself, but if you do, find a reputable yacht transporter who understands boats. During the years, we have heard plenty of horror stories of what can happen to boats packed in crates and shipped by common carrier. We finally met someone who had indeed had one of his boats skewered in its crate by a forklift.

Pad and wrap the boat well. Fleece, pipe insulation, thin plywood, foam sheets, bubble wrap, "housewrap," and miles of clear packing tape are all part of our boat-shipping arsenal. Unless your boat will be traveling inside a truck box, use housewrap or plastic and plenty of tape to create a package that the wind cannot undo. If the picture of your boat traveling down the highway at 80 miles per hour, with plastic and tape and what-all flapping madly against the hull, bothers you, cinch the whole parcel down with nylon webbing, just as you would a sail. If at all possible, be present when your boat is loaded.

Plan on being patient. Unless you're willing to pay a premium, little boats travel when big boats do. Missed production deadlines, storms, breakdowns, and other unforeseen events keep a boat shipper's schedule in constant flux. It is not unusual for a boat to arrive a week or two after the original delivery date. Better a little late and in one piece.

Unintentional Product Testing

We have not set out to destroy one of our boats, but a few years ago the owners of a rowing 12′ Ellen gave us a chance to see what might happen if we did. The boat lives on an outhaul off a retaining wall on a large open bay. She grounds out for a fair bit of every tide, on mud, gravel, and rocks. This is fine during decent weather, but the boat was caught out in a late summer storm that was one small step short of a hurricane (it didn't have a name). At first she began to fill with rainwater. As the tide went out, she began to pound on bottom in the surf, then fill with bay water as well when seas started breaking over her rails. The tide receded, leaving the boat aground and filled with just over a ton of water. Her owners left her there. When the tide came in, they pulled the full boat to the shore, bailed her, and sent her back out. Come morning, they called to say that the boat was filling with water, from below now, not above. The tide was going out, so the boat again grounded out while full of water. Despite our pleas, the owners went off for several hours without bailing out the boat. When they returned home and the tide came in, they hauled the boat in, bailed, and beached her.

It is fair to say that we approached the boat with some concern. From a distance, she looked surprisingly whole. Up close, she still looked pretty good—a little battered but otherwise unharmed. It took us several minutes to find her injury. She had a foot-long split in the plywood veneer at the garboard lap near the middle of her bottom, probably caused by bouncing on a rock. A small pebble had been sucked into the crack, wedging it open. We removed the pebble, stuffed a little cotton into her new "seam" (traditional materials have their uses), taped over it neatly with duct tape, and rowed her about a half-mile down the shore to the boat landing. Back in the shop, a little cleaning, epoxy, and paint fixed her. The insurance adjuster expected kindling and was amazed. We are still amazed and are glad to know that glued-lapstrake hulls are indeed as strong as we thought they were.

Please don't do this to your boat. Boats are not designed to hold water, but to keep water out. An unsupported hull full of water (or anything else) is a very unhappy hull indeed. A swamped boat in the water will be in much less distress, but she would really appreciate it if you bailed her out.

14.4 IRIS, waiting for the tide.

MOORING THE BOAT

The stresses on a small boat at a mooring are pretty light unless the boat becomes flooded or the wind comes up. For short stays on a big-boat mooring, a snaphook on the end of the painter can be handy. For more robust mooring, attaching to a towing eye is prudent. A short line attached to the towing eye and brought aboard allows you to tie or clip to the mooring without having to fumble around under the bow in search of the towing eye while the boat tips precariously from your shifting weight.

STORING THE BOAT

Glued-lapstrake boats are pretty tough, and they don't ask for much. But they do appreciate what might be called good storage for any wooden boat: a spot with average humidity and good air circulation that is protected from direct hot sun and wide temperature swings. If you store your boat outside, please keep her well up off the ground and rig some form of tarp-tent that allows air to circulate underneath.

TAKING CARE OF HER

"She's so beautiful! If she were mine, I couldn't bear to use her. She should be in a museum!"

Oh, please don't say that about a boat. We build boats to use, and they aren't truly alive until they are in the water. Of course, part of being alive is a skinned knee (so to speak) every now and then.

If you scrape or scratch the boat down to the bare wood, dry her out and cover the naked spots with slightly thinned paint or varnish as soon as you can. Covered quickly now is better than picky-perfect later. We paint many of our boats' bottoms with hard antifouling paint partly for ease of maintenance. Drag her over the rocks in a bit of surf? Flip her over to dry, paint the bad spots, let the paint dry overnight, and you're back on the water.

Your boat won't rot beyond recall if you let the minor scratches go for the season (and we are definitely not ones to criticize harshly here), but it really is better to get in the habit of touching her up regularly, especially the varnishwork. If water gets in the under the varnish, it will lift the varnish and/or blacken the wood. The only cure for this is a good scraping down to bare wood. Avoiding this is highly desirable.

So please get out there and enjoy your new boat. Accept the compliments about her suitability for museum status, and keep right on going out to that rocky island for your picnic. And have a wonderful time.

14.5 IRIS in a nice fall breeze.

Appendix A

"Oh, @#!"

A SAMPLING OF OUR FAVORITE NEAR-DISASTERS AND FIXES

Q: How do you tell the difference between an "Oh, [bad word]!" and an "Oh, [incredibly bad word]!"?
A: You can fix an "Oh, [bad word]!"

Here are 15 bad-word situations culled from our current collection. Creative license and invention were not needed here; these "Oh, @#!"'s all happened in our shop or in John's classes or both. You may notice that there aren't many photographs documenting these events. We, ah, tended to have other things on our minds at the time….

Inner stem or transom won't reach the end beam or transom blocks

Encouraging the inner stem and transom down to their respective attachment points on the jig almost always takes some firm persuasion, fine words, and sometimes a couple of pipe clamps. But if you really have to force the issue, consider that something else may be wrong. One of John's classes had this problem, and they managed to crack the boat's transom trying to force it to its marks on the transom blocks.

The fix: After double-checking everything—station spacing, location of the end beams, etc.—the class discovered that the keelson had been laid out and cut ½″ short. So they moved the transom blocks forward by the amount of the mismeasurement. The repaired transom went right down into place perfectly. Their Peregrine ended up about ½″ shorter, but the fix saved the situation and no one will ever know the difference.

Plank layout missing a point

When you lay out the points for a plank on the planking stock, you discover a little omission: You missed a mold when spiling. Oops.

The fix: Lay out all of the points you do have, then bend a batten in a fair curve around them. It is usually possible to determine where the batten should go in the area of the missed point. If the missed point is at the end of the plank, bend the batten around the known points as above, but this time you really will be guessing about exactly where the plank edge should be. Leave plenty of extra wood for trimming when you fit the plank.

If this operation makes you nervous, scrape the spiling pattern and planking stock clean of all marks, and re-spile the plank.

Plank breaks in two

Stepping, sitting, or leaning on a plank with sufficient force or mass can indeed snap a 4mm or 6mm plywood plank rather neatly in two.

The fix: Pick up the pieces and the person. With any luck, you will not have installed the plank's twin, as you will need it for a template. Make a dutchman (a wooden patch) the full width of the plank and cut scarfs (at opposite angles) to fit. Lay plastic or waxed paper on the intact plank. Line up the broken pieces and dutchman on top of the covered plank. Drive a couple of small nails to hold the broken plank pieces in place, then remove the dutchman. Glue the dutchman in place with epoxy as usual, and drive a couple small nails through it to hold the joints in alignment while the epoxy cures. Place plastic and a caul (see Photo 4.10, page 61) over the joints, and clamp.

After the epoxy hardens, trim the edges of the dutchman fair with the plank edges.

Misplaced gain

You, or your helpers, cut a gain on the wrong side or the wrong end of a plank.

The fix: Glue in a strip of mahogany a little thicker than the deepest part of the gain with five-minute epoxy, and let cure. Trim the filler piece, and recut the gain in the right place. Swear to mark planks more clearly from now on.

Clamping batten breaks

You've gotten the plank on, and you've just bent the clamping batten into place at the bow and screwed it in place—CRACKKK!

The fix: Peel yourself off the ceiling. Replacing the batten is usually not the desirable option, as the steadily hardening epoxy isn't likely to give you time. Cut a short section of batten, place it over the crack, and drill for two screws either side of the crack. Gently drive and tighten the screws, drawing everything fair again. Add more screws if necessary.

"I thought we put in enough hardener!"

You pull off the clamping batten, and the plank goes *boink* and pops open from bow to stern.

The fix: Gently open the joint with wedges, clean out the epoxy with sticks, paper towel, and acetone or alcohol (wear gloves). Remove most of the wedges. Reglue the joint with epoxy (both parts) and reclamp with the batten.
Prevention: Methodically dispense one pump resin, one pump hardener; then repeat. Be careful not to let the epoxy resin or hardener drop to the bottom of a pump's inlets, as the pumped amount may be shy of the proper measure.

After nearly all the planks have been made, the remaining plywood has been rescarfed at an angle to cut out a curvy sheerstrake.

Last planks don't fit on the remaining plywood

You sketched and planned, but the spiling pattern for the sheerstrake curves out into free space.

The fix: Re-cut and re-scarf the planking stock with a kink to fit the pattern. Here's how:
- Figure out where the kink ought to occur and crosscut the planking stock at half the angle ultimately wanted. (If you can cut at the original scarf, it is better because it eliminates an extra scarf, a concern if you plan to varnish the sheerstrake.)
- Mark the length of the scarf-to-be on one of the longer pieces of planking stock.
- Flip the top short piece over edge-for-edge on the bench and line it up at the proper angle in the "scarfed" position on the long piece. Try the spiling pattern. If it fits, you're ready to cut the new scarfs. If not, trim to adjust the plank stock angle until it does. When you're happy, cut the second sheets to the correct angle.
- Line up the planking stock edges and cut the new scarfs just as you did the original ones. (See Chapter 4, "Milling Solid Lumber and Scarfing the Planking Plywood.")

Sheer looks kinda funny

You are temporarily attaching the sheerstrake and notice that there is something distinctly odd about the sweep of that plank. It doesn't follow the curve of the previous plank in one area—not even close.

What happened: It is easiest to spile the sheerstrake from the sheer marks on the molds, then lay out the widths. If you did it this way, the odds are good that the plank's shape was derived from at least one mark that looked like a plank's edge-of-plank mark at the sheer, but was not.

One good clue to this heart-stopping condition is that the cutting batten missed a mark by a lot, say ¾″.

The fix: Pull the plank off and be thankful that you saw this during the period B.E. (Before Epoxy.) Your choice: Make a new pair of planks (ouch), or salvage the situation by cutting the old planks a little narrower, if the error is not too bad. In either case, put the pattern back on the boat and figure out what went wrong. If you're making a new plank, remove all old marks and re-mark clearly. Make the new plank as usual.

If you don't mind a little less freeboard, tack the sheerstrake back into place and trace the edge of the second-to-last plank. Remove the plank to the planking table. Tack a batten along the line you just drew. Now lay out the widths of the plank using a spacer block between the batten and the edge of the notch in the plank-width marking jig.

The shortened sheer may require modifications from the plans and different measurements when fitting the interior parts.

Prevention: Scrape off *all* extraneous marks. Clearly mark the edge-of-plank marks on the molds. Confusion is more likely if several people are involved, particularly if the marking and cutting crews are different. It's easy to get swept up in the excitement of the last plank. Slow down and carefully double-check all of your measurements—then tear into making that plank.

Driving a screw splits the end of the rail or gunwale

Oak is particularly prone to this problem. Drive screws gently and firmly home, but no farther.

The fix: Mix some properly colored sawdust with five-minute epoxy to make a proper putty. With the screw tight and the crack open, force the putty into the crack, making sure that it goes all the way in. Loosen the screw so that the crack closes. Quickly clean up the squeeze-out. If you can, put a wooden hand-screw on the top and bottom edges to squeeze the joint tighter.

Rail snaps off

You pull the rail to the sheerstrake near the transom, twisting it so that the rail's inner face will contact the plank fully, and the rail snaps off right through a screw hole.

The fix: Take a moment to put your shattered world back together. Gaze thoughtfully at the 2′-long piece in your hand and be thankful that you cut the rail longer than necessary.

Remove the rail from the hull, then cut a scarf at the break. Glue the scarf together and let the epoxy cure for a couple of days. When you reinstall the rail, be sure to place a clamp as close to the transom as possible to help pull the rail in tight.

Transom breaks

This ought to happen only once in a lifetime: In an attempt to free the boat from the jig, you lift up hard to free the transom and it breaks along weak grain.

The fix: Yes, well, go have a quiet cup of tea. Do not pitch the broken-off piece across the room. Trim the excess off the piece on the bandsaw. Clamp the piece to the rest of the transom with the help of a couple of 1½″-square cleats. Drill and drive screws down through the top of the piece into the transom. Remove the screws and reattach the piece with clear epoxy, covering the joint with clear packing tape where you need clamps to line things up. Redrive the screws, remove the clamps and tape, and clean up the excess epoxy (of which there should be plenty). Plug the screw holes. Scrape off the excess epoxy inside and out after it hardens. Trim the top curve to the marks with a hand plane and a flexible sanding block.

Extra or irregularly placed holes in the rails

To make quarter knees fit tightly to the sheerstrake you had to drill another set of screw holes, and now you realize that the rails are going to look the very devil when varnished.

The fix: Well, you could paint the rails. If you'd rather not, remove the quarter knee, and plane the aft section of the rail nearly down to the screws into the transom. (You'll have to do exactly the same thing to the other side of the boat make this fix look even remotely intentional.) Fill the screw holes with epoxy putty. Finish the tapers, trimming down the putty and making the newly trimmed surfaces as flat as possible. Glue on strips with matching color and grain that are a little thicker and wider than the rail. Use waterproof carpenter's glue for a less visible joint, and clamp tightly. Trim the edges flush. Mark the finished thickness top and bottom with a ruler and a sharp-pointed compass. Trim the sides to the scored line, then trim the middle using slash marks (see Chapter 9, "Building the Interior"). Mark for screws in the right places, redrill, drive and plug.

If the breasthook zone of your boat has a similar problem, you've pretty much got an "Oh, [very bad word indeed]," as the outer stem is in the way of a plane. A tasteful, creamy white looks good with most any topside color.

"@#!" — "!#@"

One thing to keep in mind as you repair little, and big, slip-ups: Most boat parts have (or should have) two identical ends or sides. If you fix a ding or chip-out by paring down an area until it looks good again, do the same to the perfectly good wood on the other side or end. That way, the repairs will look intentional, and no one need ever know that they were not.

Gunwale a little too short

You trimmed a little too much off the gunwale while fitting it.

The fix: Using the gunwale offcut, make a cross-grain wedge to fit between the end of the gunwale and the knee. (The grain must run the same way as the grain of the gunwale.) This isn't especially easy, but it is doable. For the first edge of the wedge, mark and cut the angle of the end of the gunwale on the offcut and clean up with a block plane. Mark the second edge of the wedge and carefully cut it with a sharp, fine-toothed handsaw or on the bandsaw. Trim and clean up the wedge on the stationary sander.

Up and down, make the joint a little more open at the bottom to allow insertion of the wedge. Use waterproof yellow glue (not epoxy) to make a nearly invisible repair.

This works for small gaps.

Wild boatbuilder with router

You're zooming along, chamfering or bullnosing those edges in fine style, then you notice that you've zoomed right into an edge that was supposed to remain untouched.

The fix: If it's bullnosed edge, cut a chamfer. Saw out a triangular strip bigger than the chamfer from a piece with similar color and grain. Glue the piece in place with five-minute epoxy and tape in place to hold. After the epoxy hardens well, trim off the excess. This repair will be nearly invisible.

"Ackk! A ding!"

You drop a corner of your plane on the face of a thwart destined for varnish. Before you try making it look intentional as part of a design comprised of little indented triangles, try the following fix, known as sweating out a ding.

The fix: Set a household iron on the hottest setting. (We call it "setting the iron on mahogany.") When the iron is hot, fold a wet paper towel and place it over the ding. Touch the iron to the wet paper. A cloud of steam will billow up for a few seconds. Lift the paper and inspect the injury. Small dings typically require several repetitions of this procedure to bring the crushed wood fibers back to nearly flush with the surface.

If the ding is relatively big, do a half-dozen sweats, let the wood dry for an hour, and then sweat it several more times.

Been honing your own finer expletives?

Given time and sufficient hard work, we all should be able to add to this important section in the next edition of this book. If you would like to share your best efforts with your fellow boatbuilders, we welcome stories of your near-disasters and the fixes, through our Web site www.brooksboats.net.

Resources

PLANS
Brooks Boats designs

Plans for the Ellen, Peregrine, Compass Harbor Pram, and others are available directly from us:

John Brooks
Brooks Boats Plans
HC64, Box 491, Reach Road
West Brooklin, ME 04616
207-359-2491
www.brooksboats.net

As we are always designing boats and adding new plans, please contact us to inquire about our current offerings.

Other designs

The following designers also offer plans for boats designed to be built with glued-lapstrake construction:

Phil Bolger and Friends
Post Office Box 1209
Gloucester, MA 01930
978-282-1349 (fax)

Antonio Dias
171 Cedar Island Road
Narragansett, RI 02882
401-783-4959
www.diasdesign.com

Arch Davis Design
RR4 Box 39
Belfast, ME 04915
800-357-8091; fax 207-338-1103
www.by-the-sea.com/archdavisdesign/

Doug Hylan
Post Office Box 58
Brooklin, ME 04616
www.dhylanboats.com

Iain Oughtred
Struan Cottage
Isle of Skye
Scotland IV519NS
U.K.
011 44 1470 532 732

Steve Redmond
30 Oak Ridge Drive
North Easton, MA 02356
www.sredmond.com
orders@sredmond.com

Selway Fisher Design
15 King Street
Melksham, Wilts SN12 6HB
U.K.
011 44 122 570 5074

The WoodenBoat Store
Naskeag Road
Brooklin, ME 04616
800-273-7447; fax 207-359-2058
email: wbstore@woodenboat.com
www.woodenboatstore.com

The following periodicals may feature glued-lapstrake designs:

Boat Design Quarterly
Available from
The WoodenBoat Store
Post Office Box 78
Brooklin, ME 04616
800-273-7447

The Complete Guide to Boat Kits and Plans
Post Office Box 420235
Palm Coast, FL 32142-0235
800-786-3459

Messing About in Boats
29 Burley Street
Wenham, MA 01984-1943
978-774-0906
www.messingaboutinboats.com

Watercraft
Bridge Shop
Cornwall TR12 6UD
U.K.

WoodenBoat
Post Office Box 78
Brooklin, ME 04616
207-359-4651
www.woodenboat.com

SUPPLIES

Atlas Metal Sales
1401 Umatilla Street
Denver, CO 80204
800-662-0143; fax 303-623-3034
   Silicon-bronze sheet, plate, rod, tube, and bar, also naval brass.

Barkley Sound Oar and Paddle
3073 Van Horne Road
Qualicum Beach, BC, V9K 1X3
250-752-5115
www.barkleysoundoar.com

Davey & Co., London Ltd.
1 Chelmford Road, Ind Est.
Great Dunmow
UK, CM6 1HD
011 44137 187 6361
   Traditional marine hardware, paints, etc.

Defender
42 Great Neck Road
Waterford, CT 06385
800-628-8225; fax 800-654-1616
www.defenderus.com
   Xynole, Dynel, and other cloths for sheathing. All manner of boat supplies and equipage: paints, putties, WEST System epoxy and supplies, some useful hardware, etc.

Epifanes North America, Inc.
70 Water Street
Thomaston, ME 04861
800-269-0961
www.epifanes.com
   Marine varnishes and paints. Great colors.

Flounder Bay Boat Lumber
1019 Third Street
Anacortes, WA 98221
800-228-4691; fax 360-293-4749
email: boatkit@flounderbay.com
www.flounderbay.com
   Shelmarine sapele marine plywood; also okoume, meranti marine ply, Rigid Plus panel material; Sitka spruce, etc.

Gougeon Brothers, Inc.
Post Office Box 908
Bay City, MI 48707
517-684-7286
   WEST System epoxy and supplies.

Hamilton Marine
Route One
Searsport, ME 04974
800-639-2715; fax 800-548-6352
email: mail@hamilton.com
www.hamiltonmarine.com
   Fastenings, hardware, WEST System and MAS epoxies, Dolfinite bedding compound, paints and varnishes (including Epifanes, Pettit, and Interlux), clear sealer, putties, oil finishes, sandpaper, decent brushes, cotton canvas gunwale guard, all manner of good and often hard-to-find marine supplies.

Harbor Sales
1000 Harbor Court
Sudlersville, MD 21668-1818
800-345-1712; fax 800-868-9257
   Shelmarine sapele marine plywood; also okoume, meranti marine ply, Rigid Plus panel material, etc. Call the main office for regional distributors.

H. M. Hillman Brass & Copper, Inc.
2345 Maryland Road
Post Office Box "R"
Willow Grove, PA 19090
800-441-5992; fax 215-659-0807
   Silicon bronze, 90/10 copper nickel, and naval brass sheet, plate, rod, pipe, and tube.

Jack Holt Ltd.
Post Office Box 89
177 Lynden Road
Lynden, ON, L0R 1T0
Canada
888-390-3242; fax 519-647-3226
   Buoyancy bags; high-tech hardware for smaller performance sailboats.

Jamestown Distributors
Post Office Box 348
Jamestown, RI 02835
800-423-0030; fax 800-423-0542
   Fastenings, Reed & Prince (Frearson) driver bits, hardware, bits and other tools, paints, sandpaper.

George Kirby, Jr., Paint Co.
163 Mount Vernon Street
New Bedford, MA 02740
508-997-9008
   Traditional topsides paints in traditional colors.

Maine Coast Lumber
35 Birch Hill Road
York, ME 03909
800-899-1664
   Shelmarine sapele marine plywood; also okoume, meranti marine ply, Rigid Plus panel material; foreign and domestic hardwood and softwood lumber.

MAS Epoxies
2615 River Road #3A
Cinnaminson, NJ 08077
888-MASEPOXY
www.masepoxies.com
   Epoxies and related materials.

J. M. Reineck & Son
9 Willow Street
Hull, MA 02045-1121
781-925-3312; fax 781-925-8984
email: sales@bronzeblocks.com
www.bronzeblocks.com
   Bronze Herreshoff-pattern blocks with Delrin ball bearings. Beautifully made; will probably last the life of this boat and into the next. Assorted other small and larger boat hardware.

Robbins Timber
Merrywood Road
Bedminster, Bristol BS3 1DX
U.K.
(0)117 963 3136; fax (0)117 963 7927
   WEST System epoxy, lumber, more.

Rostand R.I., Inc.
Box 737, 335 Long Entry Road
Chepachet, RI 02814
401-949-4268
carrollharrington@compuserve.com
   Traditional bronze castings, to be finished by you. Mostly big-boat hardware, but some items possibly of use.

Shaw & Tenney
Post Office Box 213W
Orono, ME 04473
207-866-4867
   Fine oars and paddles, since 1858.

Standard Fastenings
800 Mount Pleasant Street
New Bedford, MA 02745
800-678-8811; fax 508-995-3886
   Wholesale only. Bronze and stainless fastenings; Reed & Prince driver bits.

System Three Resins
Post Office Box 70436
Seattle, WA 98107
800-333-5514; fax 206-782-4426
www.systemthree.com
   Epoxies and related supplies.

Trailex
Post Office Box 553
1 Industrial Park Drive
Canfield, OH 44406
800-282-5042
trailex1@aol.com
www.trailex.com
   Lightweight trailers, some with shock-absorbing suspensions.

Wessex Resins and Adhesives Ltd.
Cupernham House
Cupernham Lane
Romsey, Hants SO51 7LF
U.K.
(0)179 452 111; fax (0)179 451 7779
   WEST System epoxy and supplies.

West Marine
Post Office Box 50050
Watsonville, CA 95077-5050
800-262-8464; fax 831-761-4421
www.westmarine.com
   Almost complete emphasis on hardware, supplies, etc., for production boats made of That Other Stuff, but occasionally they'll have what you need, including varnishes, paints, oils, and hiking sticks.

Nathaniel S. Wilson, Sailmaker
Post Office Box 71
Lincoln Street
East Boothbay, ME 04544
207-633-5071
   Finely hand-built sails for dinghies to ships. Oceanus sailcloth, a polyester cloth with the feel, look, and handling characteristics of cotton, and others.

TOOLS

B&H Photo-Video
420 Ninth Avenue
New York, NY 10001
800-947-9954
www.bhphotovideo.com
　　Lowel Tota lights and stands for finishing illumination; professional films and other necessities to record your boat's progress for posterity.

Garrett Wade
161 Avenue of the Americas
New York, NY 10013
800-221-2942; fax 800-566-9525
　　Quality hand tools.

Highland Hardware
1045 N. Highland Avenue
Atlanta, GA 30306
800-241-6748; fax 404-876-1941
www.highlandhardware.com
　　Good selection of hand tools and shop essentials.

The Japan Woodworker
1731 Clement Avenue
Alameda, CA 94501
800-537-7820; fax 510-521-1864
　　Japanese hand tools, including a good assortment of saws.

Lee Valley Tools
Post Office Box 1780
Ogdensburg, NY 13669-6780
800-871-8158; fax 800-513-7885
www.leevalley.com
　　Quality hand tools, other shop essentials.

Lie-Nielsen Toolworks, Inc.
Post Office Box 9
Route One
Warren, ME 04864
800-327-2520; fax 207-273-2657
email: toolworks@lie-nielson.com
www.lie-neilson.com/
　　Low-angle adjustable mouth block plane, low-angle and standard block planes, more. High-quality bronze and ductile-iron planes.

Sommerfield's Tools for Wood
Post Office Box 416
Remsen, IA 51050
888-228-9268; fax 712-786-2770
　　CMT-brand router bits.

Tool Crib of the North
P.O. Box 14930
Grand Forks, ND 58208-4930
800-635-5140
www.toolcrib.amazon.com
　　No, you really can't get by without that right-angle battery drill for one more day.

Woodcraft
560 Airport Industrial Park
Post Office Box 1686
Parkersburg, WV 26102-1686
800-225-1153; fax 304-428-8271
　　A wide assortment of woodworking tools and supplies, including carving tools.

The WoodenBoat Store
Post Office Box 78
Brooklin, ME 04616
800-273-7447; 207-359-8920
email: wbstore@woodenboat.com
www.woodenboatstore.com
　　A selection of tools, aprons, and other useful items for boatbuilders; official WoodenBoat attire.

BOOKS

Cambium Books
57 Stony Hill Road
Bethel, CT 06801
800-238-7724; fax 203-778-2785
www.cambiumbooks.com
　　Books for woodworkers, including hard-to-find texts on rather obscure, but useful, topics.

The Taunton Press
63 S. Main Street
P.O. Box 5506
Newtown, CT 06470-5506
203-426-8171
www.taunton.com
　　Books for woodworkers.

The WoodenBoat Store
Post Office Box 78
Brooklin, ME 04616
800-273-7447; 207-359-8920
email: wbstore@woodenboat.com
www.woodenboatstore.com
　　Books for boatbuilders and boat lovers.

Appendix C

References

General Woodworking and Related Matters

The Encyclopedia of Wood. Rev. ed. (Reprint of 1987 rev. ed. of *Wood Handbook: Wood as an Engineering Material*, U.S. Government Printing Office.) New York: Sterling Publishing Co., 1989. ISBN 0-8069-6994-6.

Though this book is aimed primarily at folks who won't be floating their work, it is a good source of basic information on the characteristics of various domestic and foreign woods as well as much technical detail on how wood performs under different conditions.

Hampton, C. W., and E. Clifford. *Planecraft: Hand Planing by Modern Methods.* 1934. Reprint. Parkersburg, WV: Woodcraft Supply Corp., 1994. ISBN 0-918036-00-3.

Originally published as a complete guide to the use of Record planes, this small volume offers a plenty of hints to help you get the most out of your planes.

Landis, Scott. *The Workshop Book.* Newtown, CT: The Taunton Press, Inc., 1991. ISBN 0-942391-37-3.

A sensible and thorough discussion of how to set up a comfortable, efficient, and safe shop, with plenty of examples of different approaches used by woodworkers with varied needs and budgets.

Wearing, Robert. *Making Woodwork Aids & Devices.* New York: Sterling Publishing Co., Inc., 1985. ISBN 0-8069-6264-X.

Very useful shopmade tools and a host of helpful techniques. Well illustrated.

Wearing, Robert. *Woodworker's Essential Shop Aids & Jigs: Original Devices You Can Make.* New York: Sterling Publishing Co., Inc., 1992. ISBN 0-8069-8564-4.

Do you love jigs and shop-made tools—and working efficiently at everything from marking to routing? Another clearly illustrated and written book from this English author.

Boatbuilding and Design

Ashley, Clifford W. *The Ashley Book of Knots.* New York: Doubleday, Inc., 1993. Reissue. ISBN 0-3850-4025-3.

The book of knots. A classic.

Butler, Paul and Marya. *Fine Boat Finishes.* Camden, ME: International Marine, 1987. ISBN 0-87742-311-3. (Currrently out of print.)

A practical manual for varnishing, painting, and oiling.

Chapelle, Howard I. *Boatbuilding*. New York: W. W. Norton & Co., 1941, 1994. ISBN 0-393-03554-9.

This boatbuilding "bible" is an essential inhabitant of any boatbuilder's bookshelf.

Creagh-Osbourne, Richard. *Dinghy Building*. 1963. Revised, 1977; reprint, Adlard Coles, 1978. ISBN 0-8286-0073-2. (Currently out of print.)

Covers a wide range of types of "dinghy" (i.e., small racing sailboat) construction, including a short section on glued, lapstrake. Useful techniques and methods from an English perspective; especially helpful if your boat is a decked sailing dinghy.

The Epoxy Book. Seattle, WA: System Three Resin, Inc., 1992.

Pithy, clear, amusing, and very useful guide to using System Three epoxies.

Gardner, John. *Classic Small Craft You Can Build*. Mystic, CT: Mystic Seaport Museum, 1993. ISBN 0-913372-66-8.

Although this book deals primarily with small boats built in the traditional manner, John Gardner offers an abundance of good advice, inspiration, and instruction of interest to the glued-lapstrake boatbuilder, including a section on balancing the rigs for small sailboats. The book includes the designs for several traditional lapstrake boats that could be built in glued-lapstrake, if you've a mind to try.

Gougeon Brothers. *The Gougeon Brothers on Boat Construction*. 1979. 4th ed., rev. Bay City: MI: Gougeon Brothers, Inc., 1985. ISBN 0-87812-166-8.

A complete manual for the handling of WEST System epoxies, and an excellent general reference.

Hanna, Jay S. *Shipcarver's Handbook*. Brooklin, ME: WoodenBoat Books, 1987. ISBN 0-937822-14-0.

This classic little book will inspire you to add some lovely flourishes to your boat.

Hill, Thomas J. *Ultralight Boatbuilding*. Camden, ME: McGraw-Hill Professional Publications, 1987. ISBN 0-071567-03-8.

A guide to building Hill's lightweight glued-lapstrake boats.

Leather, John. *Clinker Boatbuilding*. 1973. Reprint. London: Adlard Coles Nautical, 1996. ISBN 0-7136-3643-2.

A classic English reference for the builder of traditional lapstrake (clinker) boats; a useful reference for the glued-lapstrake boatbuilder, particularly on matters other than hull construction.

Oughtred, Iain. *Clinker Plywood Boatbuilding Manual*. Brooklin, ME: WoodenBoat Publications, Inc., ISBN 0-937822-61-2.

A well-illustrated guide to building Iain Oughtred's glued-lapstrake designs, including his popular Whilly Boat.

Rose, Joshua. *The Patternmaker's Assistant*. 1889. Reprint. Mendham, NJ: The Astragal Press, 1995. ISBN 1-879335-59-X.

If you are taken with the idea of casting your own bronze hardware, this 19th-century work offers much vital information on the casting process and making patterns.

Rössel, Greg. *Building Small Boats*. Brooklin, ME: WoodenBoat Publications, Inc., 1998. ISBN 0-937822-50-7.

A thorough, understandable, and essential manual for the builder of small boats. Rössel covers traditional building techniques, many of which are of use to the glued-lapstrake builder as well, including a delightfully clear section entitled "Lofting Demystified."

Spectre, Peter H., ed. *Painting & Varnishing*. Brooklin, ME: WoodenBoat Publications, Inc., 1995. ISBN 0-937822-33-7.

Succinct advice on the art of fine painting and varnishing, gleaned from the pages of *WoodenBoat* magazine.

Steward, Robert M. *Boatbuilding Manual*. 4th ed. Camden, ME: International Marine, 1994. ISBN 0-87742-379-2.

One of the must-have basic boatbuilding books that will repay its space on the bookshelf many times over. You won't find much on the glued-lapstrake method in here, but you will find answers to many other questions.

Toss, Brion. *The Complete Rigger's Apprentice: Tools and Techniques for Modern and Traditional Rigging*. Camden, ME: International Marine (McGraw-Hill), 1998. ISBN 0-07-064840-9.

If it must be rigged, the odds are exceptionally good that you'll find the expert advice you need in this book, a compilation of Toss's *The Rigger's Apprentice* and *The Rigger's Locker*.

Vaitses, Allan H. *Lofting*. 1980. Reprint. Brooklin, ME: WoodenBoat Publications, Inc., ISBN 0-957822-55-8.

If your boat's plans don't have full-sized patterns, you need to learn how to loft, and Vaitses is an excellent teacher.

Index